RAFFAELE MATTIOLI LECTURES

In honour of the memory of Raffaele Mattioli, who was for many years its manager and chairman, Banca Commerciale Italiana has established the Mattioli Fund as a testimony to the continuing survival and influence of his deep interest in economics, the humanities and sciences.

As its first enterprise the Fund has established a series of annual lectures on the history of economic thought, to be called the Raffaele Mattioli Lectures.

In view of the long association between the Università Commerciale Luigi Bocconi and Raffaele Mattioli, who was an active scholar, adviser and member of the governing body of the University, it was decided that the lectures in honour of his memory should be delivered at the University, which together with Banca Commerciale Italiana, has undertaken the task of organizing them.

Distinguished academics of all nationalities, researchers and others concerned with economic problems will be invited to take part in this enterprise, in the hope of linking pure historical research with a debate on economic theory and practical policy.

In creating a memorial to the cultural legacy left by Raffaele Mattioli, it is hoped above all that these lectures and the debates to which they give rise will prove a fruitful inspiration and starting point for the development of a tradition of research and academic studies like that already long established in other countries, and that this tradition will flourish thanks to the new partnership between the Università Commerciale Luigi Bocconi and Banca Commerciale Italiana.

MONEY AND THE ECONOMY
ISSUES IN MONETARY ANALYSIS

RAFFAELE MATTIOLI FOUNDATION

Money and the Economy
Issues in Monetary Analysis

KARL BRUNNER
AND
ALLAN H. MELTZER

CAMBRIDGE
UNIVERSITY PRESS

Published by the Press Syndicate of the University of Cambridge
The Pitt Building, Trumpington Street, Cambridge CB2 IRP
40 West 20th Street, New York, NY 10011-4211, USA
10 Stamford Road, Oakleigh, Melbourne 3166, Australia

Edited by Giovanna Nicodano

First published 1993
First paperback edition 1997

Library of Congress Cataloging in Publication Data
Main entry under title:
Money and the Economy Issues in Monetary Analysis
(Raffaele Mattioli Lectures)
At head of title: Raffaele Mattioli Foundation.
Bibliography.

1. Monetary Policy

2. Fiscal Policy

I. Brunner, Karl and Meltzer, Allan H.   II. Raffaele Mattioli
Foundation.   III. Title.   IV. Series.

HG 230.3.B78   1993   332.4   dc20

A catalogue record for this book is available from the British Library

Brunner, Karl and Meltzer, Allan H.
Money and the Economy Issues in Monetary Analysis
(Raffaele Mattioli Lectures)
1. Economics
I. Title   II. Series
339 HB 172.5
ISBN 0 521 59974 1

93-17996 CIP

Transferred to digital printing 2004

CONTENTS

List of Figures in the Lectures

List of Tables in the Lectures

PREFACE

For the past thirty years, we have worked – alone and together – on various problems in monetary theory. Although we often discussed bringing our ideas together, we had not done so. The 1987 Raffaele Mattioli Lectures provided an opportunity to present many of these ideas in a single volume, to review them in the light of new information and developments in the intervening years and to extend some aspects to new problems or in new directions.

Our lectures give particular attention to uncertainty, the role of information and particularly to costs of acquiring information. Costs of acquiring information have been a missing element in the development of macroeconomic theories, in discussions of sticky prices and wages and in discussion of policy rules. While the lectures are not the place to develop the role of these costs formally, we suggest some of the ways in which formal work might proceed.

We are indebted to the organizers for providing the opportunity to present and extend our ideas. We are grateful particularly to Bernardo Crippa of the Raffaele Mattioli Foundation and the Banca Commerciale Italiana for the excellent arrangements and many kindnesses he showed before, during and after the lectures. The faculty and students of Università Commerciale Luigi Bocconi provided an attentive audience, and our discussants – Professors Mario Arcelli, Eduard Bomhoff and Mario Monti, Dr. Rainer S. Masera, Prof. Gianluigi Mengarelli and Prof. Riccardo Rovelli provided stimulating discussion and helpful comments.

Many colleagues offered suggestions and comments. We are indebted particularly to Michael Bordo, Phillip Cagan, Alex Cukierman, Robert King, Alvin Marty, Johan Myrhman, Charles Plosser, Scott Richard and Guido Tabellini.

Giovanna Nicodano provided gracious and helpful assistance from preparation to final publication. We are in her debt.

KARL BRUNNER   ALLAN H. MELTZER

KARL BRUNNER

These lectures were the last project on which Karl Brunner worked. Our last conversation about the volume took place about a month before he died.

In early April, 1989 I sent Karl a draft of our reply to the discussants, based on conversations we had in February or March. He was not entirely in agreement with the draft. Although his voice was weak, his mind was clear, and his comments were sharp and to the point. As we had done on scores of previous occasions, we discussed the issues and the wording or formulation where one or the other of us wanted changes. When we agreed we turned to other matters.

So it was on that April day. There was one major difference. We both knew it was the last time we would work together. Karl was pleased to see the volume finished. I am sure he did not expect to see the printed version. He knew his remaining time was short.

I would like to remember him by describing how we worked together. Our work on this volume was typical of our collaboration. We discussed the general framework, the topics to be covered and the main ideas that we would address. These discussions never went into details and rarely went beyond broad agreement about what we would try to bring out. For example, the importance of information and costs of acquiring information had been a theme in some of our previous work. We could easily agree that it would be one of the themes in these lectures. We left to each other decisions about how it would be incorporated, but each always expected to make whatever changes he believed useful.

We put a bit more flesh on this loose framework at Interlaken in the spring of 1987, divided the work of writing first drafts, and agreed on a date, in early August, when we would exchange drafts. Karl was much better at taking criticism of what he planned to do than at giving criticism of what I planned to do, so much of our time was spent on his plans. Karl remained in Switzerland, but we talked on the telephone at least weekly throughout the summer. He was often in pain, and he could not use his right hand. He summoned all of the courage, personal strength, and that unbending will that I knew so well from the past. He learned to write with his left hand. He was much too proud, too determined, too committed to the task to consider shirking or not completing what he had agreed to do. In late August or early September we exchanged second drafts and discussed some remaining issues on the telephone. Of course, the lectures were completed and sent to the discussants in ample time for them to prepare their presentations.

Karl was a penetrating critic of parts of the material I had written. Although his eyesight was poor, very little escaped him. He would often call during the week, on the weekend, in the evening, anytime, about a paper he was reading. Whether it was mine, or someone else's, we would go through the argument step by step until we were both satisfied. I work very differently, often preferring to think through as much of the issue as I can before beginning a discussion. Sometimes this takes me in a wrong direction. We used the telephone to discuss these differences. On occasion, we supplemented the discussion by exchanging written notes. Usually, we worked out differences in a series of phone calls, at times interrupted to complete analytic work which we communicated by phone.

Despite his illness, Karl was determined to present half of the lectures in Milan. Since he could not see to read notes, he memorized four hours of material and presented it without a mistake at two of the sessions. It was a remarkable performance, and I am sure that many of those who were present share my admiration of his outstanding presentation.

Although we collaborated for many years, we also worked with others and alone. Usually we talked about the topic and the substance of these papers in our telephone conversations. Karl often made a contribution to what I was doing, and vice versa. I cannot recall that we ever discussed whether something was part of our collaboration, and I know that we did not have a formal rule for making such decisions. Yet, we never disputed each other's judgment about whether the work was collaborative. Perhaps that was why we were able to work together so long and, I believe, so fruitfully.

Karl Brunner was a remarkable man of great intellectual ability, courage and iron determination, capable of giving and receiving a deep and lasting friendship. Many will miss him, none more than I.

ALLAN H. MELTZER

KARL BRUNNER   ALLAN H. MELTZER

MONEY AND THE ECONOMY
ISSUES IN MONETARY ANALYSIS

To Rosmarie and Marilyn

The *Raffaele Mattioli Lectures* were delivered by
Karl Brunner and Allan H. Meltzer at the Università Commerciale
Luigi Bocconi, in Milano, from 2nd to 4th November 1987.

FIRST LECTURE*
A Review of the Issues

1. *Before the General Theory.* – 2. *Classical Policy Discussion.* – 3. *The Keynesian Era.* – 4. *Critique and Counter-Revolution*: i) *The First Stage*; ii) *The Second Stage*; iii) *The Third Stage.* – 5. *The Grand Traverse.* – 6. *Conclusion.*

Beginning with the earliest systematic work on economic theory, men have observed a relation between the stock of money and the price level.[1] Two remarkable features of this early literature are (1) the relation was observed and noted independently in many different places and times, and (2) a common observation was of an inverse relation between the stock called money and the value of a unit of that stock.[2] Often, early writers suggested, or explicitly stated, that the relation was one of proportionality; an increase in money had no effect on the real value of the stock of money. No later than the middle of the eighteenth century, writers went beyond these early statements, distinguishing the initial effect on output from the final effect on prices.[3]

By the mid-eighteenth century, we have two propositions about the relation of money to income that remain through most of the history of systematic economic thinking. Modern versions of these propositions are summarized in statements that have been made in different ways. Money is neutral in the long-run but not in the short-run. Changes in money affect output first, but this effect vanishes once prices adjust fully. The long-run effect of money is on prices, but money changes output and other real variables during the adjustment from one long-run equilibrium to the next.

---

* September 1987; revised July 1988.

1. Hugo Hegeland, in *The Quantity Theory of Money*, Goteborg: Elanders, 1951, traces the origins of these observations to Confucius, Xenophon and Copernicus among others. Hegeland does not attempt to find the earliest statement.

2. *Id., op. cit.*, chap. 1.

3. Jacob Viner, *Studies in the Theory of International Trade*, 1937, reprinted, New York: Kelley, 1965, pp. 84-85.

As Viner,[1] Laidler[2] and others have noted, disputes about these propositions and about their empirical relevance were not far behind the initial statements. Issues arose about the proper definition of money, the effect of credit and intermediation, and reverse causation from prices and output to money. These, and other issues, have remained. Professional opinion has shifted to and fro. At times, the prevalent belief has been that money can be defined with sufficient precision to be useful for observation and empirical research. At other times, the prevalent view has held either that the objects used as money shift too often for the concept to be useful empirically, or that the demand for money shifts erratically − that monetary velocity is unstable. Parallel to these shifts there are changes in the interpretation of the relation of money to income − from the belief that money has a causal role in fluctuations to the belief that money is a residual at the end of the causal chain.

1. *Ibid.*
2. DAVID E. W. LAIDLER, 'English Classical Monetary Economics in the 1870s', unpublished, London, Ontario: University of Western Ontario, 1986.

1. Before the General Theory

By the 1930s, money or the financial system had a central role in most explanations of the "credit" or business cycle. Haberler[1] classifies a number of different explanations as monetary theories. Several explanations have as a common feature that a change in money is the impulse starting the cycle. Wicksell's lecture,[2] though concerned with secular not cyclical change, was an influential example of a monetary impulse that starts by lowering the market rate below the natural rate of interest. Some explanations, that Haberler calls non-monetary, begin with real shocks but are propagated by loans from the financial system at rates below the borrower's expected return to capital. Schumpeter's entrepreneur, Marshall's and Keynes's waves of optimism and pessimism, and numerous other explanations start with a change in the expected return to capital that raises expected profitability above the market rate. The differences that much of this literature emphasized concerned the source of the initial impulse. It could be monetary – a gold inflow (or outflow) or a decision by the central banks to change the market rate relative to the natural rate. It could be real – new invention or innovation, sunspots affecting weather and agricultural production or, as in Cambridge, a change in anticipations. Whatever the source of the initial impulse, the relation between the market rate and the expected return to investment often had a critical role in propagation, although writers did not always use these terms to express the central relationship.

One reason for hesitation in accepting money as a dominant impulse may have come from the gold standard itself. The classical gold standard admits an entirely monetary explanation of the relation of money to income for the world as a whole only if there are new discoveries of gold, changes in costs of gold production or changes in the demand for gold to be used as currency or as reserves. The reason is that autonomous central

1. GOTTFRIED HABERLER, *Prosperity and Depression*, 3rd ed., New York: United Nations, 1952.
2. KNUT WICKSELL, 'The Influence of the Rate of Interest on Prices', *Economic Journal*, June 1907, pp. 213-219.

7

bank action is precluded, so monetary changes can only serve as an impulse if there are changes in gold demand or supply. This restriction holds at the world level. For an individual country, gold flows can initiate an expansion or contraction if there are changes, whether nominal or real, abroad. Equally important, gold standard countries did not uniformly follow the rules. Wicksell's hypothesis[1] assumes autonomous central bank behavior.

Irving Fisher,[2] a leading proponent of a monetary explanation of fluctuations in the level of income and output, treats changes in money (gold) as the most common cause of cyclical disturbances, although he recognizes that crop failures, inventions and other real events can be causal factors also.[3] Prices and market interest rates adjust slowly in Fisher's account.[4] The slow adjustment of the price level allows real expenditure to increase in expansions and decline in contractions; the slow adjustment of market interest rates encourages businesses to borrow and invest during expansions but reduces investment and spending during contractions. Fisher assumed that businessmen are debtors, hence the gradual adjustment of interest rates affected profits. He did not explain the gradual adjustment of prices and interest rates in micro-theoretic terms. In this respect, Fisher is representative of many others before and after who rely on the sluggish adjustment of prices or wages but do not provide a micro foundation for the observation.

Gradual adjustment of prices or wages or interest rates typically was treated as a fact, based on observation. Attempts at careful empirical studies of wages, prices or interest rates seemed to confirm the fact. While no single statement can summarize the different positions taken by classical economists, the best of the classical and neo-classical economists understood that lagged adjustment of interest rates, real wages or differences between expected and actual values was essential for a relation

---

1. *Ibid.*
2. IRVING FISHER, *The Purchasing Power of Money*, rev. ed., New York: Macmillan, 1920.
3. *Id., op. cit.*, p. 70.
4. *Id., op. cit.*, pp. 62-68.

between money and real variables. Hence, they accepted gradual adjustment as a working hypothesis.[1] For these writers, money is neutral in long-run adjustment. Equilibrium typically means a position on the (dynamic) production frontier, and business cycles (or fluctuations) are departures from equilibrium. The departures that concerned these economists could persist for years. Fisher speaks of a ten-year period for the full credit or business cycle;[2] Keynes speaks of a downward movement lasting three to five years.[3] It is during periods of adjustment that money affects real variables including real output.

The propagation of a monetary business cycle, as described by Fisher,[4] is broadly similar to the propagation of the real business cycle discussed in Keynes' *Treatise*.[5] Keynes, like Fisher, recognizes that both real and nominal disturbances can start a cumulative expansion or contraction, but he emphasized changes in investment[6] while Fisher emphasizes monetary disturbances. Keynes recognized, however, that differences between real and monetary "disequilibrium" (sic) "are not always separated by a sharp line . . . and, after the initial stage has passed, they shade off into one another".[7]

Three of the principal analytic shortcomings found in many of the business cycle theories developed prior to the *General Theory* are (1) an absence of any explanation of the demand for money, or monetary velocity, as part of the theory, (2) a failure to explain changes in output and prices or to separate changes in nominal output into price and output changes and (3) a failure

1. ALFRED MARSHALL is representative of those who believed that wages adjust more slowly than prices, so real wages fall in expansion and rise in contractions. JOHN MAYNARD KEYNES, in 'Relative Movements of Real Wages and Output', *Economic Journal*, 1939, reprinted in *The Collected Writings of John Maynard Keynes*, vol. 7, London: Macmillan, 1973, pp. 394-412, reports that Marshall based his conclusion on a statistical study by Bowley.

2. IRVING FISHER, *op. cit.*, p. 70.

3. JOHN MAYNARD KEYNES, *The General Theory of Employment Interest and Money*, London: Macmillan, 1936, p. 317.

4. IRVING FISHER, *op. cit.*

5. JOHN MAYNARD KEYNES, *A Treatise on Money*, 1930, reprinted in *The Collected Writings of John Maynard Keynes*, vols. 5 and 6, London: Macmillan, 1971.

6. *Ibid.*, pp. 232-233 and 248-262.

7. *Ibid.*, p. 248.

to distinguish between real and nominal rates of interest. The last is particularly surprising given the substantial development of the theory of real and nominal interest rates by Wicksell, Fisher, Keynes, Robertson and other economists during this period.

Most classical writers recognized that velocity is not constant. In their discussions, velocity changes cyclically with confidence − anticipations − and secularly with payments, technology and other variables. Typically, these links are not developed as part of the explanation of cycles. Similarly, real expenditure change depended on a lag of prices or wages, or a slow and gradual adjustment of actual values, but the reasons for slow adjustment are missing or obscure. As we know from recent discussions, dynamic theories relating actual and anticipated values within a general equilibrium system did not become part of mainstream economics until the development of rational expectations models in the 1970s.

Business cycle theorists in the 1920s and before devoted considerable attention to the causes or impulses initiating business cycles. Nineteenth century experience, not surprisingly, focused attention on harvests, innovations such as railroads and the development of new industries and new productive techniques, and on gold discoveries and gold movements. A variety of real and monetary impulses were offered as causes, or principal causes. The modern analogue of these earlier studies is the recent attempt to show that all business cycles are started either by real or by monetary shocks. The earlier work did not successfully isolate a single cause or set of causes and was not conclusive. Recent work, using new tools and techniques, has been no more successful.

2. Classical Policy Discussion

In the years after World War II, economic policy discussion relied increasingly on forecasts of short-term changes obtained with the aid of a multi-equation, econometric model of the economy. Much policy discussion concentrated on actions to be taken. Often these actions were a mix of fiscal, monetary and other policies to increase output and employment, reduce inflation or achieve other short-term objectives.

In contrast, classical policy discussion was mainly about rules. Discretionary action, if admissible, took the form of adjustments within the framework of a rule. The most common rule was some form of gold standard, so discussion by economists was most often about the gold standard. Experience with a paper standard during the Napoleonic wars did much to convince economists of that period about the disadvantages of a paper standard and the advantages of some type of gold standard.[1] Many neo-classical economists, including Jevons, Marshall, Fisher, Graham and Wicksell commented on the variability of economic activity and prices under the gold standard and proposed alternatives. None favored a paper standard or a system of freely fluctuating exchange rates. None favored discretionary policy action unrestrained by a monetary rule. Typically, the aim of the neo-classicals' proposals for reform was to reduce the variability arising under a commodity standard based on a single commodity – gold. There were two problems. First, gold discoveries, changes in costs of production and changes in the demand for gold changed the relative price of gold. Under a gold standard adjustment to these events introduced changes in prices and output. Second, gold flows required countries to expand and contract. Productive opportunities that gave rise to expansion

1. The discussion in this section is based on JACOB VINER, *Studies in the Theory of International Trade*, 1937, reprinted New York: Kelley, 1956, and the extensive, very useful summary of the arguments and alternatives to the gold standard in MICHAEL DAVID BORDO, 'The Gold Standard: The Traditional Approach', in MICHAEL DAVID BORDO and ANNA JACOBSON SCHWARTZ, eds., *A Retrospective on the Classical Gold Standard*, 1821-1931, Chicago: University of Chicago Press for the National Bureau of Economic Research, 1984, pp. 23-113.

attracted gold flows that added to the expansion, magnifying the initial impulse.

The alternatives proposed during the neo-classical period – bimetallism, symmetalism, a tabular standard, Fisher's compensated dollar – sought to reduce price variability by reducing reliance on a single commodity. Each of these proposals advanced a rule limiting the quantity of money or its rate of change. The proposed rules restricted actions by governments or monetary authorities but, like the various gold standards, they did not prescribe the quantity of money precisely. Instead, they relied on individual incentives to protect personal wealth or to gain from exchange by taking advantage of actual or expected differences between the market and mint prices of gold or other commodities.[1]

Critics of the gold standard did not limit their objections to price variability. The resource cost of the gold standard was recognized early, and it is a main reason that Ricardo proposed a bullion standard with limits on the circulation of gold coins. Later proposals for reform included the use of paper, redeemable into gold, to reduce the resource cost of holding gold as a reserve. Other criticisms by neo-classical writers included the effect of gold movements on output, particularly the necessity of accepting recessions as part of the adjustment to an unanticipated reduction in gold and money.

---

1. In this respect, the proposals may be said to provide a private 'punishment' mechanism to sustain the monetary rule. The older mechanism is superior to the 'punishment' emphasized in recent research based on the so-called trigger strategy. See ROBERT J. BARRO and DAVID M. GORDON, 'Rules, Discretion and Reputation in a Model of Monetary Policy', *Journal of Monetary Economics*, 12, June 1983, pp. 101-122. The trigger strategy, unlike earlier work, does not provide an incentive for any individual member of society to enforce the monetary rule, and it does not provide a mechanism by which an individual can enforce the rule. The problem of incentives for enforcement is neglected by assuming that society consists of a single, representative individual. Earlier work was less formal but did not rely on such heroic assumptions.

3. *The Keynesian Era*[1]

The emphasis on institutional arrangements and the design of policy rules was one of the casualties of the Keynesian revolution. Emphasis shifted from concern for the variability imposed by a particular rule to the idea that central banks and governments should act to offset specific events based on their judgment about the event and their forecast of the future. Policy came to mean action – usually discretionary action – rather than a rule.

The shift was subtle but significant. Neo-classical discussion saw business cycles or fluctuations as departures from equilibrium. Different rules implied different frequency or amplitude of these departures, so policy could, in principle, affect the severity or frequency of cyclical changes. Neo-classical analysis, at its best, was based on a model of an individual whose income or wealth varied over time, as the harvests or the fish catch varied in practice from one period to another. Variability could arise in nature, or by chance, or as a result of changes in opportunities, in anticipations, or in gold stocks and money. Institutional arrangements could enhance or dampen these fluctuations.

Keynesian analysis shifted the focus from the general to the specific problem. Income took on the meaning of current receipts or current spending, not the longer-term notion related to wealth or the present value of lifetime receipts. When classical economists accepted that money could not affect income, they generally meant that money was neutral in the long-run – that real wealth or expected real income was independent of the quantity of money. When Keynesian economists talked about

1. The term Keynesian, as used here, does not refer to Keynes. There is, at best, a loose relation between the *General Theory* and much of the analytic apparatus and many of the policy views called Keynesian. Our use of the term Keynesian refers to the changing analytic and policy views of a group that have in common their support for activist, discretionary policy. This characteristic distinguishes Keynesians from earlier and later writers who favored some type of rule. Usually, Keynesians are distinguished from others based on a shared belief that wages adjust more slowly than prices. This view was held by many classical writers – Hume, Thornton, Marshall to name three – and by many, recent non-Keynesian writers who drew different policy conclusions, for example preferring rules to discretion.

money affecting income and employment, most often they meant that in the short-run money was non-neutral.[1] This was particularly true of Keynesian analyses based on Hicks' influential interpretation,[2] where the entire emphasis is on short-term effects, and adjustments of prices, asset stocks and expectations are neglected.

In the *General Theory*, as in the *Treatise*, Keynes conjectured about the possibility that there was a portion of the demand curve for money in which increases in the stock of money did not lower the rate of interest. Interest rates reached a floor set by habits or customs; the interest elasticity of the demand for money approached (minus) infinity. This section of the demand curve was later called the liquidity trap. With money wages rigid and interest rates at their floor, monetary policy became incapable of changing any relative price or the absolute price level.

Although Keynes dismissed this possibility as of no practical relevance,[3] later writers developed the Keynesian special case. Tobin[4] presented some empirical evidence suggesting that there had been a liquidity trap in the United States during the thirties.[5] This suggested that changes in money, if not totally powerless,

1. An example of this difference, which developed later, is the use of income (permanent income) as in MILTON FRIEDMAN, *A Theory of the Consumption Function*, Princeton: Princeton University Press for the National Bureau of Economic Research, 1957. In the Keynesian consumption function, income became identified as current receipts.

2. JOHN RICHARD HICKS, 'Mr. Keynes and the "Classics": A Suggested Interpretation', *Econometrica*, 5, April 1937, pp. 147-159.

3. JOHN MAYNARD KEYNES, *The General Theory of Employment Interest and Money*, London: Macmillan, 1936, p. 207.

4. JAMES TOBIN, 'Liquidity Preference and Monetary Policy', *Review of Economics and Statistics*, 29, May 1947, pp. 124-131.

5. JAMES TOBIN's evidence was shown subsequently to result from an arbitrary method of measuring asset balances. MARTIN BRONFENBRENNER and THOMAS MAYER, in 'Liquidity Functions in the American Economy', *Econometrica*, 28, 1960, pp. 810-834, and ALLAN H. MELTZER, in 'The Demand for Money: The Evidence from the Time Series', *Journal of Political Economy*, 71, June 1963, pp. 219-246, rejected the empirical case for a liquidity trap, and KARL BRUNNER and ALLAN H. MELTZER, in 'Liquidity Traps for Money, Bank Credit and Interest Rates', *Journal of Political Economy*, 76, January-February 1968, pp. 1-38, demonstrated that a liquidity trap cannot arise, in the sense that money has no effect on asset prices, if money, bonds and capital are distinct assets.

were of limited use for changing nominal income or stimulating economic activity during recessions. Reinforcing this view, surveys of business investment reported that businessmen took little notice of the rate of interest when making investment decisions.[1] The central bank might be able to reduce the rate of interest, but the reduction would have little effect on output, employment or prices.

The relation of money to income, at the time, was typically described as weak, and monetary policy action was written off as "broadly ineffective".[2] The problem, as seen in the Keynesian era, was to affect aggregate demand, increasing demand in recessions and reducing demand during booms. Given the weak effects of monetary policy, the more reliable response was to act directly by changing spending and taxes. Credit controls, down payment requirements and other direct restrictions on lending and borrowing supplemented fiscal action.

Looking back after forty years, the view that money has little influence on prices and employment seems extreme.[3] That this was the dominant view in the profession is suggested by any thorough examination of the journals of the period, by the 1948 survey of monetary theory written for the American Economic Association's sponsored *Survey of Contemporary Economics*,[4] or by the 1959 report of the Radcliffe Committee in Britain.[5] Econometric models of this period often had no role for money, reflecting the, then, widely held view.[6] The view survives today in the writings

1. HUMBERT D. HENDERSON, 'The Significance of the Rate of Interest', *Oxford Economic Papers*, 1, October 1938.

2. HENRY H. VILLARD, 'Monetary Theory', in H. S. ELLIS, ed., *A Survey of Contemporary Economics*, Blakiston for the American Economic Association, 1948, pp. 314-351.

3. An exception was often made for inflation. Monetary policy was believed to affect nominal income in periods of inflation, but even this view was challenged by NICHOLAS KALDOR, in *The Scourge of Monetarism*, Oxford: Oxford University Press, 1982, JOAN ROBINSON and FRANK WILKINSON, 'Ideology and Logic', in FAUSTO VICARELLI, ed., *Keynes's Relevance Today*, Philadelphia: University of Pennsylvania Press, 1985, pp. 73-98. A sample from JOAN ROBINSON, *Ibid.*, p. 90, suffices: "The notion that inflation is a monetary phenomenon and that it can be prevented by refusing to allow the quantity of money to increase is to mistake a symptom for a cause".

4. HENRY H. VILLARD, *op. cit.*

5. Committee on the Working of the Monetary System, *Report*, London: Her Majesty's Stationery Office, 1959.

6. HARRY GORDON JOHNSON's review, in 'Monetary Theory and Policy', *American*

of Kaldor,[1] Robinson[2] and their followers who deny any causal influence of money on inflation or economic activity.

In the Keynesian heyday, fluctuations in economic activity were assumed to result mainly from changes in investment, the latter driven by changes in anticipations. Businessmen's anticipations – waves of optimism and pessimism – had been used by Marshall and later Cambridge economists, including Keynes, as the principal force driving the cycle. In this view, business cycles are, mainly, real events in which money has a minor role or no role at all. The private sector is unstable and must be tamed by appropriately timed government action. In the simplest versions, represented by the Keynesian cross model, aggregate supply responds passively to shifts in the aggregate demand curve. Interest rates, prices and money have no role. In more sophisticated expositions, the multiplier and accelerator interact to produce changes in output and employment without affecting interest rates or the demand for money. Since recessions were caused by insufficient aggregate demand, they could be eliminated, or reduced in severity, by policies to control aggregate demand. Lerner's[3] *Economics of Control* is an early influential statement of this position.

Economic Review, 52, June 1962, pp. 335-384, discusses the change in professional views and also the changing reasons given for the denial of any reliable influence of money on income during the period up to early 1960s.

1. NICHOLAS KALDOR, *The Scourge of Monetarism*, Oxford: Oxford University Press, 1982.

2. JOAN ROBINSON and FRANK WILKINSON, 'Ideology and Logic', *cit.* in FAUSTO VICARELLI, ed., see footnote 3, p. 15.

3. ABBA PTACHYA LERNER, *The Economics of Control*, New York: Macmillan, 1944.

4. *Critique and Counter-Revolution*

Criticisms of the Keynesian position started mildly but gained in intensity. There are three distinct stages. At first, the critics centered attention on the minor role of money in Keynesian analysis and in policy discussions. The critics insisted on the relevance of money and produced evidence to support their position. In the second stage, the center of the discussion shifted to the role of fiscal policy, the alleged tradeoff between inflation and unemployment and the problem of inflation in the open economy. By the 1970s, the critique had become a counter-revolution. A result of the revolution was that leading proponents of the Keynesian view sought to demonstrate that fiscal policy affected aggregate spending. In the third and most recent stage, the center of the discussion has shifted again to the role of rational expectations and, most importantly, to the relevance of new classical economics where, in some versions, money has no influence on economic activity, and the business cycle is, once again, a real phenomenon.

i) *The First Stage*

Clark Warburton was an active, early critic of the neglect of money in Keynesian economics.[1] Warburton started with a real business cycle hypothesis in which money typically had a minor role but was capable of converting a relatively mild recession into a severe contraction. Since Warburton was a careful scientist, he set out to test this hypothesis using the data and tools available to him. His results convinced him that an erratic money supply is the chief originating factor, or impulse, causing recessions. The initial effect of a change in money is on output, so short-run changes in money are non-neutral. With a lag, prices adjust to fully reflect the effect of money. In the long-run, money is neutral. Warburton recognized that real factors have

[1]. Our discussion of Warburton is based mainly on the review of his work in MICHAEL DAVID BORDO and ANNA JACOBSON SCHWARTZ, 'Clark Warburton Pioneer Monetarist', *Journal of Monetary Economics*, 5, January 1979, pp. 43-66; and JAMES A. DORN, 'The Search for Stable Money: A Historical Perspective', in JAMES A. DORN and ANNA JACOBSON SCHWARTZ, eds., *The Search for Stable Money*, Chicago: University of Chicago Press, 1987, pp. 1-28.

a role, but he concluded that theirs was a secondary role. Business cycles, for Warburton, were periods of monetary disequilibrium, a view that he traced back to earlier writers in the pre-Keynesian period.

Warburton's work was far removed from the main views of the day and was largely neglected. His criticisms of business cycle theory, fiscal policy, and Federal Reserve procedures are carefully documented. His work on the relation of money to income is supported by extensive empirical work, particularly for the pre-computer age. Warburton anticipated many of the discussions that filled the macroeconomics literature of the 1960s, but his criticisms were not answered, and his evidence was ignored.

Milton Friedman was more difficult to ignore. Some of his early criticisms of work done in the Keynesian era by Lange, Lerner, Salant and others are reprinted in his *Essays in Positive Economics*.[1] His positive analysis and accumulation of evidence, including the work of his students and collaborators, appeared in a series of books and articles beginning in the mid-1950s. Three contributions had particular impact: *Studies in the Quantity Theory of Money*,[2] *A Monetary History of the United States, 1867-1960*,[3] and 'The Relative Stability of Monetary Velocity and the Investment Multiplier in the United States 1897-1958.[4]

These books and papers resurrected the role of money in several ways that challenged the Keynesian view. In his introduction to *Studies in the Quantity Theory*, Friedman emphasized that money is a substitute for real and nominal assets, not solely a substitute for bonds. Much of the early Keynesian discussion emphasized that the interest rate as a measure of bond prices

1. MILTON FRIEDMAN, *Essays in Positive Economics*, Chicago: University of Chicago Press, 1953.

2. MILTON FRIEDMAN, ed., *Studies in the Quantity Theory of Money*, Chicago: University of Chicago Press, 1956.

3. MILTON FRIEDMAN and ANNA JACOBSON SCHWARTZ, *A Monetary History of the United States, 1867-1960*, Princeton: Princeton University Press for the National Bureau of Economic Research, 1963 a.

4. MILTON FRIEDMAN and DAVID J. MEISELMAN, 'The Relative Stability of Monetary Velocity and the Investment Multiplier in the United States, 1897-1958', in *Stabilization Policies*, Englewood Cliffs: Prentice Hall for the Commission on Money and Credit, 1963, pp. 167-268.

ignored intertemporal substitution and left open and puzzling how money could affect output in a country without a bond market. Friedman argued that changes in money affected the relative prices on a wide variety of assets, so the potency or impotency of money could not be judged by such devices as surveys showing that businessmen ignored interest rates. To deny that money affects nominal income, economists must deny either that relative prices affect real demands or that money affects relative prices (including anticipated future prices relative to current prices). Further, Friedman introduced the expected rate of inflation as an argument in the demand function, opening the way for analysis of the effects of inflation on the demand for money – the inflation tax on real money balances.[1] Other studies in the book, particularly Cagan's,[2] had a lasting influence on subsequent work on the theory of inflation and the relation of money to nominal income or prices in periods of high or hyper-inflation.

In the *Monetary History*, Friedman and Schwartz examined the historical data relating money to income for almost a century. They concluded that changes in money are closely associated with changes in economic activity, prices and money income, and that changes in money often have an independent origin.[3] In subsequent work,[4] they investigated leads and lags at business cycle turning points for a century, with results that an independent observer described as follows:

The Friedman and Schwartz paper, together with Friedman's other published works, provide the strongest empirical foundation for the proposition that the supply of money is a – probably the – dominant variable in determining the level of total spending on current output...

1. An early analysis of the inflation tax is in JOHN MAYNARD KEYNES, *A Tract on Monetary Reform*, 1923, reprinted in *The Collected Writings of John Maynard Keynes*, vol. 4, London: Macmillan, 1971.

2. PHILIP D. CAGAN, 'The Monetary Dynamics of Hyper-inflation', in MILTON FRIEDMAN, *Studies in the Quantity Theory of Money*, Chicago: University of Chicago Press, 1956.

3. MILTON FRIEDMAN and ANNA JACOBSON SCHWARTZ, 1963a, *op. cit.*, p. 676.

4. MILTON FRIEDMAN and ANNA JACOBSON SCHWARTZ, 'Money and Business Cycles', in *The State of Monetary Economics*, *Review of Economics and Statistics*, 45, suppl., February 1963 b, pp. 32-64.

[T]here was a general willingness to admit that the supply of money does now appear to be an important variable in explaining the level of aggregate spending.[1]

Related work on the demand for money and velocity by Brunner and Meltzer,[2] Meltzer,[3] Laidler[4] and others showed that the demand for real balances could be estimated from time series data as a function of an interest rate, some measure of wealth or permanent income and perhaps a small number of other variables. Related work for other countries generally produced qualitatively similar results.

On the basis of these studies, and other studies by a number of researchers, the consensus view shifted away from the Keynesian consensus. By the 1970s we believe the following four propositions were widely accepted about the relation of money to income, although differences of opinion about precise phrasing remained.

(1) money growth rises and falls pro-cyclically;

(2) accelerations and decelerations of money are frequently followed, after a lag, by cyclical expansions and contractions of real output;[5]

(3) sustained money growth relative to the growth of output is a sufficient condition for inflation;

(4) velocity growth is pro-cyclical.

A fifth proposition was less widely accepted:

(5) discretionary monetary action increases variability by inducing (or augmenting) cyclical expansions and contractions.

Evidence of the extent of the consensus, and the change from the consensus achieved in the Keynesian era, is a statement by

1. GEORGE LELAND BACH, Introduction, *The State of Monetary Economics, Review of Economics and Statistics*, 45, suppl., February 1963, p. 3.

2. KARL BRUNNER and ALLAN H. MELTZER, 'Predicting Velocity: Implications for Theory and Policy', *Journal of Finance*, 18, May 1963, pp. 319-354.

3. ALLAN H. MELTZER, 'The Demand for Money: the Evidence from the Time Series', *Journal of Political Economy*, 71, June 1963, pp. 219-246.

4. DAVID E. W. LAIDLER, 'The Rate of Interest and the Demand for Money: Some Empirical Evidence', *Journal of Political Economy*, 74, December 1966, pp. 545-555.

5. Many would now substitute unanticipated changes in money for accelerations and decelerations.

Walter Heller,[1] a leading proponent of Keynesian policies. Heller described the issue as *"not* whether money matters [for output] – we all grant that – but whether *only* money matters . . ."[2] Further, Heller felt the need to defend the Keynesian proposition that changes in taxes and spending have predictable effects on aggregate output, holding money constant.

The first stage of the critique of the earlier Keynesian consensus was marked also by a critique of the method of conducting monetary policy actions. The critics complained that the Federal Reserve's use of market interest rates, member bank borrowing and other measures of credit market conditions is a principal reason for the pro-cyclical movements of the money stock thereby reviving, in a different form, the criticism of the classical gold standard. When business activity increases, the public sells securities and increases borrowing from the banking system. The Federal Reserve supplies additional reserves to keep interest rates from rising, so the reserve component of the monetary base rises and the money stock rises.[3] The expansion of private spending and the increase in demand deposits also increase the demand for currency. In a fractional reserve system, a shift from demand deposits to currency raises interest rates. Under the chosen operating procedure, the Federal Reserve prevents the rise by supplying additional base money, further increasing the stocks of money and bank credit.

The result of the chosen operating procedure is that the stock of money rises during periods of expansion, encouraging expansion and inducing a rise in prices, and declines in recessions, thereby increasing the length or severity of recessions. The two main implications of the critique are (1) that the economy can achieve greater stability if the operating procedures are changed to eliminate pro-cyclicality of money and (2) that the observed relation between money and income is, at least in part, the consequence of operating procedures and, therefore, avoidable.

1. WALTER W. HELLER, 'Is Monetary Policy Being Oversold?', in MILTON FRIEDMAN and WALTER W. HELLER, eds., *Monetary vs. Fiscal Policy*, New York: Norton, 1969.

2. *Id.*, p. 16 emphasis in the original.

3. The monetary base is the monetary liability of the consolidated government sector and is equal to bank reserves plus currency held by the public.

I – A REVIEW OF THE ISSUES

In the *Monetary History*, Friedman and Schwartz[1] presented evidence showing that the Federal Reserve had either caused or magnified the major downturns of 1920-1921, 1929-1933 and 1937-1938 by permitting the money stock to decline. Brunner and Meltzer[2] traced the reason for the Federal Reserve's actions and their concern with credit conditions to the analytic framework developed by the Federal Reserve staff in the 1920s. This framework led the Federal Reserve to identify "low" interest rates with monetary "ease" and "high" interest rates with "tight" money. Hence, when interest rates declined, for example following a decline in the public's demand for loans, the Federal Reserve allowed the monetary base and the money stock to fall (or fall relative to trend) and conversely in periods of expansion. Brunner and Meltzer developed a scale to measure Federal Reserve judgments about the "degree of ease and restraint" and showed that the scale accurately predicted Federal Reserve decisions to adjust credit market conditions.[3]

The critics of operating procedures did not always distinguish carefully between the impulse and its amplification – whether the Federal Reserve's operating procedures initiated the downturn or expansion or amplified the effects of other impulses or shocks. At times, the emphasis was on monetary forces as the dominant impulse, as in Brunner and Meltzer.[4] There, monetary impulses are shown to have a leading, but not exclusive, role in starting recessions, expansions and inflations in several countries.

1. MILTON FRIEDMAN and ANNA JACOBSON SCHWARTZ, 1963a, *op. cit.*
2. KARL BRUNNER and ALLAN H. MELTZER, *The Federal Reserve's Attachment to the Free Reserve Concept*, Washington: House Committee on Banking and Currency, May 1964, reprinted as chapter 1 of KARL BRUNNER and ALLAN H. MELTZER, eds., *Monetary Economics*, London: Basil Blackwell, 1990.
3. Mention should also be made of two additional studies: PHILIP D. CAGAN, in *Determinants and Effects of Changes in the Stock of Money*, New York: Columbia University Press for the National Bureau of Economic Research, 1965, used National Bureau dating to study cyclical changes in the factors affecting the money stock. JAMES A. MEIGS, *Free Reserves and the Money Supply*, Chicago: University of Chicago Press, 1962, developed and tested hypotheses about credit market conditions (free reserves) and their relation to Federal Reserve behavior.
4. KARL BRUNNER and ALLAN H. MELTZER, eds., 'The Problem of Inflation', *Carnegie-Rochester Conference Series on Public Policy*, 8, Amsterdam: North-Holland, 1978.

The issue about whether shocks are dominantly nominal or real, fiscal or monetary, real shocks to productivity or to expectations, or shocks of some other kind has remained contentious. The first step was to reverse the Keynesian claim that money is irrelevant. Researchers observed the relevance of changes in money for output and prices. This was followed by efforts to characterize the distribution of shocks by type of shock. Such efforts are not likely to be successful. There are three reasons.

First, there is no reason to expect that the distributions of shocks are constant from one decade or period to the next. If product or technical innovations are bunched, as has often been suggested, productivity shocks may be bunched also. These shocks may be relatively important during periods of rapid technical change. Studies of the 1970s often show that real shocks are relatively important, but the oil price increases contribute to the result. It is difficult to think of a series of shocks in earlier decades of this century comparable to the oil shocks of the 1970s and 1980s, so the relevance of the result is limited. Gold discoveries were, at one time, important monetary impulses. If studies of early periods should reveal that monetary impulses were relatively important, the finding would be relevant to that arrangement and would not survive in a regime of constant money. The relative importance of individual shocks changes, and there is ample reason to believe that this will continue to be true in the future. There is, therefore, no reason to believe that the analysis of the past distribution of shocks will have useful, predictive content for the present or the future.

Second, the relative importance of shocks is not independent of the type of monetary system and other institutional arrangements. Under a classical gold standard, with no central bank and gold serving as the medium of exchange, monetary shocks would be restricted to discoveries of gold, improvements in gold production, processing and other technical changes in the demand for gold. Although shocks of this kind might be relatively small, and infrequent, the gold standard could be a source of instability by amplifying real shocks such as good or poor harvests or productivity shocks. Under a gold standard, a positive shock to productivity increases output but also induces a capital flow that increases domestic demand, output and the price level. The gold standard does not buffer the economy against a shock of this kind; the standard augments the shock to output by combining the shock to aggregate supply with an increase in aggregate demand. Nineteenth century critics of the gold standard often had this characteristic in mind when they commented on excessive variability, as noted earlier.[1]

Third, suppose – contrary to what we believe the evidence shows – that 80% or more of the initial shocks, or impulses, are random real disturbances while only 20% or fewer are monetary. The choice of monetary regime can increase stability in two ways, first, by reducing the size and frequency of monetary shocks and, second, by eliminating (or reducing) the induced monetary responses that augment real shocks. Reform of the monetary regime to reduce variability would remain as a topic for monetary analysis.

The first stage of the critique of Keynesian policy did not exactly draw to a close. It seems more accurate to say that discussion moved to other issues. An increase in the maintained rate of inflation in all countries under the Bretton Woods system, combined with an increase in the average rate of money growth in the United States (relative to the growth of output) after the middle of the 1960s made it difficult for most economists to claim that money is irrelevant for prices and nominal output.

At about this time, Brunner summarized the issues and the critics' position in three propositions.

First, monetary impulses are a major factor accounting for variations in output, employment and prices. Second, movements of the money

1. A considerable amount of work on the relative importance of real and monetary shocks in recent years using vector autoregression has produced mixed results. JAMES H. STOCK and MARK W. WATSON, 'Interpreting the Evidence on Money-Income Causality', Working Paper n. 2228, National Bureau of Economic Research, April 1987, note that small differences in specification produce substantial differences in result. In part, the differences reflect differences in sample period, but results are also sensitive to the method of detrending data. The treatment of trend is an important issue to which we return in the discussion of normal output. STOCK and WATSON conclude that innovations in money have significant effects on industrial production, holding prices and interest rates constant, in postwar monthly U.S. data. They are able to reconcile contrary findings in earlier studies as the result of different procedures for removing the time trend.

stock are the most reliable measures of the thrust of monetary impulses. Third, the behavior of the monetary authorites dominates movements in the money stock over business cycles.[1]

Neither events nor the first stage of the critique changed some well entrenched Keynesian views. In the mid-1960s, it was still common to find discussions of fluctuations in which money had a minor role or no role at all. The American Economic Association's *Readings in Business Cycle Theory*[2] is but one example. By the late 1970s, or thereabouts, the importance of money as a factor – possibly the dominant factor – in business cycles was more firmly re-established. Franco Modigliani accepted that "the stock of money has a major role in determining output and prices".[3] James Tobin pointed out that three recessions in the 1970s "were deliberate acts of policy, especially monetary policy".[4]

One sign of the change in professional opinion about money is shown by the changing discussion of monetary policy and the resulting changes in government policy in the mid-1960s. The argument that monetary policy is weak and ineffective was replaced by the argument that the effects of money are uneven. Housing and construction were said to bear the major effect; the social cost of using monetary policy to prevent or reduce inflation was said to be too high. Money was no longer impotent; it was now too powerful and too selective. In the belief that social cost could be reduced, controls of deposit rates under regulation Q were extended from banks to thrift institutions, a policy error that proved to be costly and disruptive for the financial system.

A by-product of the change in professional opinion about money reveals that a major policy issue lay behind the discussion of the role of money and its relevance for income. Friedman,

1. KARL BRUNNER, 'The Role of Money and Monetary Policy', *Federal Reserve Bank of St. Louis Review*, 50, July 1968, pp. 8-24.

2. ROBERT J. GORDON and L. KLEIN, eds., *Readings in Business Cycles*, Homewood, Ill.: Irwin, 1965.

3. FRANCO MODIGLIANI, 'The Monetarist Controversy or, Should We Forsake Stabilization Policies?', *American Economic Review*, 67, March 1977, pp. 1-19, p.1.

4. JAMES TOBIN, 'The Monetarist Counter-Revolution Today - An Appraisal', *Economic Journal*, 91, March 1980, pp. 29-42, p. 32.

Schwartz, Brunner, Meltzer and other critics drew the inference from their own work, and the work of many others, that economic stability would be increased – and welfare enhanced – if monetary actions were more stable and predictable. Hence, they interpreted the empirical evidence showing a stable relation between the demand for money and its determinants, under a variety of different monetary arrangements for this century or longer, as evidence that economic instability could be reduced by some type of monetary rule. Proponents of discretionary policy increasingly interpreted the same research findings as evidence that activist, discretionary monetary policy could be used to stabilize the economy. Their focus shifted from fiscal actions, requiring lengthy delays to obtain legislative approval, to discretionary monetary changes that did not require such approval. By estimating the demand for money as a function of interest rates and other variables, the Federal Reserve staff expected to set an interest rate-money combination consistent with the level of income they forecast or desired to reach. To this end, quarterly, and later monthly, econometric models were developed to direct monetary policy or advise policymakers about the interest rate presumed to be consistent with policy objectives for income, prices and employment.

Estimates of the demand for money were not sufficiently accurate to bear the weight placed on them.[1] Our comparison, at the time, of the predictions made using more than fifteen different specifications of velocity equations showed that the mean absolute prediction error for any decade in this century was never less than 2% per year. Generally, the error was larger. The smallest average error for the 39 annual predictions was above 4%.[2] Even if the forecast error could be held to 2% in practice, forecasts could not distinguish one year ahead between booms and recessions, or periods of slow growth, on average.[3]

1. By the mid-1970s, skepticism about the stability of the demand for money had returned. We consider forecast accuracy in Lecture 4 where we present errors of forecast from official and private forecasts.

2. KARL BRUNNER and ALLAN H. MELTZER, 'Predicting Velocity: Implications for Theory and Policy', *Journal of Finance*, 18, May 1963, pp. 319-354.

3. If money is closely controlled (and the error in money demand is unaffected by the change in policy) the 2% error in predicting velocity becomes a 2% error in

ii) *The Second Stage*

Discussion shifted in the mid-1960s to three different issues. First, papers by Friedman and Meiselman[1] and by Andersen and Jordan[2] suggested that, except during the years of the 1930s depression, fiscal action has small and often insignificant effect on aggregate economic activity. Second, an empirical study of the relation between unemployment and the rate of change of money wages by A. W. Phillips[3] seemed to show evidence of a reliable trade-off between unemployment and the rate of inflation. Although Phillips did not draw a policy conclusion, others did. They interpreted Phillips' result as implying a stable relation between inflation and real output or unemployment that could be used to set economic policy variables. Third, the spread of the United States' inflation to the rest of the world, under the monetary arrangements based on the Bretton Woods agreement, raised issues about the source of the inflation. Harry Johnson,[4] Robert Mundell[5] and others extended analysis of the relation of money to income to the world economy. These authors explained world inflation as principally a consequence of inflationary policies in the United States under a fixed exchange rate system. The second stage of the critique of Keynesian policy centered on these three issues.

Andersen and Jordan[6] presented their results as a test of the

predicting nominal GNP. A 2% error is large relative to the average growth of the economy. As discussed below, forecasters generally cannot distinguish booms and recessions on average.

1. MILTON FRIEDMAN and DAVID J. MEISELMAN, 'The Relative Stability of Monetary Velocity and the Investment Multiplier in the United States, 1897-1958', in *Stabilization Policies*, Englewood Cliffs: Prentice-Hall for the Commission on Money and Credit, 1963, pp. 167-268.

2. LEINALL ANDERSEN and JERRY L. JORDAN, 'Monetary and Fiscal Action: A Test of Their Relative Importance in Economic Stabilization', *Federal Reserve Bank of St. Louis Review*, 50, 1968, pp. 11-24.

3. ALBAN W. H. PHILLIPS, 'The Relation Between Unemployment and the Rate of Change of Money Wage Rates in the United Kingdom, 1861-1957', *Economica*, N.S. 25, November 1958, pp. 283-299.

4. HARRY GORDON JOHNSON, *Inflation and the Monetarist Controversy*, Amsterdam: North-Holland, 1972.

5. ROBERT MUNDELL, *Monetary Theory: Inflation, Interest and Growth in the World Economy*, Pacific Palisades: Goodyear, 1971.

6. LEINALL ANDERSEN and JERRY L. JORDAN, *op. cit.*

relative effectiveness of monetary and fiscal actions. Regressing changes in GNP on current and lagged values of quarterly changes in money, high employment expenditure and revenue or the high employment budget surplus, Andersen and Jordan found that the fiscal variables had very little effect on nominal GNP while the sum of the responses to the monetary variables was typically close to unity. These and other results of their tests suggested that the effect of fiscal changes on aggregate income was small and unreliable while the effect of monetary changes was larger per dollar and more reliable.

Although a large literature challenged the result and criticized the procedures used by Andersen and Jordan, the basic result seems robust, and the procedure has long since become one of the commonly used, or standard, procedures for checking results of empirical research. Recent surveys of the literature that followed publication of the Andersen-Jordan results, concentrate mainly on the criticisms of econometric procedures, but they accept the broad conclusion that bond financed changes in high employment government spending or taxes have much smaller – or negligible – effects on GNP relative to a maintained, equal dollar, change in money.[1]

The Andersen-Jordan paper found much less than an additional dollar of GNP per dollar of additional government spending. Further, much of the initial effect was quickly reversed. The response to changes in high employment revenues was smaller and less reliable. These findings challenged the practical relevance of the Keynesian multiplier and the usefulness of fiscal policy for stabilization of output. If Congress and an administration could be persuaded to change high employment spending permanently by $ 100 billion, the test implied that the effect on GNP would be at most $ 20 billion at the end of

1. LAWRENCE H. MEYER and ROBERT H. RASCHE, 'Empirical Evidence on the Effect of Stabilization Policy', in *Stabilization Policies: Lessons from the 70s and Implications for the 80s*, St. Louis: Center for the American Business, 1980; KARL BRUNNER, 'Fiscal Policy in Macro Theory: A Survey and Evaluation', in R. W. HAFER, ed., *The Monetary Versus Fiscal Policy Debate*, Totowa, N.J.: Rowman and Allanheld, January 1986, pp. 33-116; and BENNETT T. McCALLUM, 'Monetary Versus Fiscal Policy Effects: A Review of the Debate', in R. W. HAFER, ed., *The Monetary Versus Fiscal Policy Debate*, Totowa, N.J.: Rowman and Allanheld, 1986, pp. 33-116.

four quarters holding money constant. The multiplier of bond financed government spending appeared to be not only less than unity; it was in the range that can be described as politically unimportant.[1]

The results appeared in the midst of a major policy discussion. To finance rising expenditures for the Vietnam war and social welfare, Congress had been persuaded after much hesitation to impose a 10% surtax on personal incomes. Many economists, both in and outside government, were concerned that the timing and magnitude of the surtax would cause a recession. To soften the effect, they urged the Federal Reserve to increase money growth. The compound annual rate of money (M_1) growth rose above 8.5% in the summer of 1968, despite the rise in the consumer price index at a 5% annual rate, considered a high rate in the United States at the time.

The reason for increasing money growth, in Keynesian analysis, was to get a proper mix of monetary and fiscal policy. The tax surcharge was a tightening of fiscal policy – a move to more restrictive policy – that was often described at the time as "fiscal overkill." To offset the effects on income and employment, while moving toward budget balance, monetary growth was increased. The presumption behind these maneuvers was that economists have knowledge of the way in which the economy operates that can be used to maintain the desired degree of employment, output and inflation.

The Andersen-Jordan equation attacked this presumption and suggested that there was no danger of a recession induced by "fiscal overkill." The greater risk was higher inflation resulting from the increased money growth. The measured rate of inflation increased subsequently. The Federal Reserve sharply reversed direction in the following year, and the economy experienced a recession beginning in late 1969. To the outside observer, and to many non-economists who had followed the public discussion, these events seemed to support the critics of Keynesian policy.

1. To put the numbers into the context of the time, total Federal government spending for fiscal year 1968 was $153 billion and nominal GNP for calendar 1968 was $893 billion. A 60% increase in government spending would achieve only a 2% increase in GNP after four quarters.

There is little doubt that the discussion of fiscal policy changed. The consensus of Keynesian economists had been a high degree of certitude about the magnitude of the multiplier of government spending or taxes and a strong conviction that fiscal policy was a both potent and reliable means of controlling income. They now responded by defending the proposition that fiscal policy has a demonstrable effect on aggregate demand and employment. At a conference, held at Brown University in 1972, Franco Modigliani and Albert Ando described the magnitude of the short- and medium-run response of aggregate money income to fiscal actions as "the main significant area of remaining disagreement".[1] James Tobin and Willem Buiter[2] used the occasion to show that, in their model, with the stock of money constant, fiscal policy has a permanent effect on real output provided the interest elasticity of the demand for money is not zero. Their result depends on the wealth effect of government debt. As Phillip Cagan[3] pointed out in his comment, the demonstration was marred by the assumption that the price level remained fixed throughout.[4] A rise in the price level during a fiscal expansion would alter Tobin and Buiter's result as shown in Brunner and Meltzer's paper in the same volume.[5] Contrary to Tobin and Buiter, Brunner and Meltzer show that the role of fiscal policy cannot be analyzed adequately within the *IS-LM* framework when bonds and capital are not perfect substitutes.[6]

1. See FRANCO MODIGLIANI and ALBERT ANDO, 'Impact of Fiscal Action on Aggregative Income and the Monetarist Controversy: Theory and Evidence', in JEROME STEIN, ed., *Monetarism*, Amsterdam: North-Holland, 1976, pp. 17-42, p. 17.

2. JAMES TOBIN and WILLEM H. BUITER, 'Long-Run Effects of Fiscal and Monetary Policy on Aggregate Demand', in JEROME STEIN, *op. cit.*

3. PHILLIP CAGAN, 'Comments on Tobin and Buiter', in JEROME STEIN, *op. cit.*, pp. 318-321.

4. PHILLIP CAGAN comments that if future tax liabilities are fully discounted there would be no effect of debt financed fiscal policy on interest rates or output, but "no one wants to press that possibility", *ibid.*, p. 319. Later, Ricardian equivalence pressed that possibility.

5. KARL BRUNNER and ALLAN H. MELTZER, 'An Aggregative Theory for a Closed Economy', in JEROME STEIN, ed., *op. cit.* pp. 69-103.

5. KARL BRUNNER and ALLAN H. MELTZER, 'An Aggregative Theory for a Closed Economy', in JEROME STEIN, ed., *op. cit.*

6. Some of the papers in the Jerome Stein volume make clear that much of the discussion by Keynesians was a response to Milton Friedman's claim that the effects

A remarkable feature of the discussion of fiscal policy following publication of the Andersen-Jordan paper is the effort made to discredit the results on econometric or other grounds. The proponents of activist fiscal policy, with a few exceptions, challenged the results by criticizing the method used to obtain them. Very little effort was made to show that changes in taxes and spending had quantitatively large, statistically reliable and economically meaningful effects on aggregate spending or output.[1]

The effect of debt financed fiscal policy on aggregate output and prices continues to stir lively controversy. However, the discussion shifted, following Barro's paper on Ricardian equivalence.[2] Barro shows that in the presence of operative bequests, private savers neutralize the wealth effect on current and future generations of debt issued or withdrawn to finance tax changes. Barro's paper and the failure to find significant effects of debt issues or deficits on interest rates or wealth following the 1981 tax reduction in the United States has again altered professional opinions about the size of the response to tax changes. Unlike earlier work, however, Barro's paper and subsequent literature challenge the belief in both an aggregate effect and an effect on relative prices and resource allocation. We return to these issues in the third lecture.

The second stage of the critique included the response by non-Keynesians to early versions of the Phillips curve which presented the curve as an empirical regularity – a stable relation between unemployment or output on one side and the rate of change

of fiscal policy were certain to be temporary and likely to be minor. This claim was made with respect to the proposed 1968 tax surcharge to reduce inflation, though repeated elsewhere. The discussion was marred by a failure to distinguish between one-time effects of the tax surcharge prices (and output) and effects on the rate of price change (inflation). FRIEDMAN's claim concerned inflation – a maintained rate of increase of prices. A one-time increase in the price level leaves the price level higher and the rate of inflation unchanged.

1. KARL BRUNNER, 'Fiscal Policy in Macro Theory: A Survey and Evaluation', in R. W. HAFER, ed., *The Monetary Versus Fiscal Policy Debate*, Totowa, N.J.: Rowman and Allanheld, 1986, pp. 33-116.

2. ROBERT J. BARRO, 'Are Government Bonds Net Wealth?', *Journal of Political Economy*, 82, 1974, pp. 1015-1117.

of prices or wages on the other. The idea of a relation between the price *level* and output, or between wages (costs of production) and output can be found as far back as Hume and Thornton. The appeal of Phillips' paper arose not from the novelty of the idea, but from the contribution to the Keynesian analysis of that time.[1] The assumption of wage rigidity left the Keynesian model incomplete and incapable of explaining how nominal GNP was divided between prices and real output. Moreover, the assumption of fixed money wages became less tenable as inflation rose. Phillips' paper filled the gap. With the assumption of constant productivity growth, the Phillips curve became an aggregate supply curve relating not the price level (as in traditional analysis) but the rate of price change to the level of excess supply, the latter measured by unemployment. The apparent stability of the curve suggested that, by shifting demand along the aggregate supply curve, policymakers could, in principle, choose the combination of unemployment and inflation that maximized social welfare or, more likely, that achieved their political aims.

The stability and reliability of the Phillips curve tradeoff arose as an issue early in the discussion. The amount of additional inflation required to get a given reduction in unemployment varied markedly from one study to the next, but many estimates suggested that the adjustment of inflation was both relatively slow and small; the reduction in unemployment appeared to be not only permanent, but the response of inflation was delayed. Delay reduced the present value of the social cost of inflation required by the tradeoff. Other studies showed – or concluded – that desirable combinations of inflation and unemployment did not lie in the feasible range. Guideposts, guidelines, wage and price controls and measures such as retraining were proposed as means of shifting the Phillips curve to a more favorable position – one involving less inflation for the same level of steady state unemployment.[2]

1. ALBAN W. H. PHILLIPS, *op. cit.*
2. JAMES TOBIN, 'Inflation and Unemployment', *American Economic Review*, 62, March 1972, pp. 1-18.

Friedman[1] and Phelps[2] made a major advance in the discussion by introducing what has become known as the natural rate hypothesis. The main implication of these papers for the relation of money to income is to reaffirm the neutrality of money and to deny that there is any long-run relation between the average rate of inflation and the average rate of unemployment. The permanent reduction in unemployment, implied by early Phillips curves, vanished once these authors extended the analysis to include expectations of inflation. The adjusted relation relates excess supply or unemployment to unanticipated inflation (or unanticipated changes in real wages). Expected inflation shifts the position of the Phillips curve. An increase in inflation, if unanticipated, increases output and employment in an economy operating below capacity. Once the inflation is anticipated, prices and wages rise, and unemployment returns to the "natural" rate. Adjustment of expectations does not occur instantly, so there is a short-term but not a long-term change in employment following a change in money growth.

An implication of the revised Phillips curve is that monetary policy cannot change the average unemployment rate in the economy or the natural rate, although it can change the timing of unemployment between present and future. To change the natural rate, policy must change some real factor including social arrangements and tax rates that affect incentives and productivity.[3] A related implication is that the short-run effects of changes in money growth are on output, while the long-run effects of money growth are on inflation.

The natural rate hypothesis completely altered the implications of the original Phillips curve. Instead of a relation between the

1. MILTON FRIEDMAN, 'The Role of Monetary Policy', *American Economic Review*, 58, March 1968, pp. 1-17.

2. EDMUND S. PHELPS, 'Phillips Curves, Expectation of Inflation and Optimal Unemployment Over Time', *Economica*, N.S. 34, August 1967, pp. 254-281.

3. DAVID E. W. LAIDLER 'Monetarism: An Interpretation and An Assessment', *Economic Journal*, 91, March 1980, pp. 1-28, has a more complete discussion of the development of the Phillips curve literature. The natural rate hypothesis was not accepted by some Keynesians as late as 1980. See GEORGE L. PERRY, 'Inflation in Theory and Practice', *Brookings Papers on Economic Activity*, 1, 1980, pp. 207-241, who denies the natural rate hypothesis and denies any relevant effect of slower money growth on inflation.

rate of inflation and excess supply of labor, the Phillips curve became a supply curve of output relating deviations of output (or employment) from the natural rate to the unanticipated rate of price change. Instead of policymakers choosing a permanent tradeoff between higher inflation and lower unemployment, the choice was now between permanently lower unemployment and an ever rising rate of inflation. To reduce unemployment by monetary means, inflation had to increase without bound.

Friedman's[1] paper re-established the monetarist position that there was short-term non-neutrality of money but not long-term. The critique did not end at this point however. Within a few years, Robert Lucas[2] joined the natural rate hypothesis to John Muth's[3] rational expectations hypothesis, further reducing the scope for monetary policy to affect real output. We consider these developments presently.

A parallel, but largely separate, development criticized the Keynesian analysis of the open economy. Although Keynes was concerned with international aspects of monetary economics throughout his professional career, his major work, the *General Theory*, analyzes a closed economy. Extensions of Keynesian analysis to the open economy developed the theory of the multiplier for an economy with exports and imports. Much of this work took a partial equilibrium approach and analyzed such issues as devaluation in terms of the effects on relative prices and the elasticities of the flows of exports and imports. Monetary changes were neglected on the assumption, not always explicitly made, that monetary effects are neutralized by central banks. The spread of inflation during the late 1960s from the United States to other member countries in the Bretton Woods system made the neglect of monetary influences difficult to sustain. And the rising rate of inflation in the 1970s could be blamed on recalcitrant labor unions (as in the prototypical Keynesian model)

---

1. MILTON FRIEDMAN, *op. cit.*, 1968.
2. ROBERT E. LUCAS JR., 'Expectations and the Neutrality of Money', *Journal of Economic Theory*, 4, April 1972, pp. 103-124.
3. JOHN F. MUTH, 'Rational Expectations and the Theory of Price Movements', *Econometrica*, 29, July 1961, pp. 315-335.

only by claiming that unions had become increasingly recalcitrant.

Mundell, Johnson and several of their students shifted the emphasis from real trade flows to the adjustment of the balance of payments.[1] The monetary approach to the balance of payments revived the classical tradition of open economy macroeconomics according to which a small open economy was a price taker in world markets, just as a competitive firm is a price taker in the markets in which it buys and sells. The strong form of the monetary approach invoked interest parity and the so-called law of one price. The latter is a special form of purchasing power parity under which commodity prices are the same everywhere when valued at the market exchange rate. Differences in the movement of price levels across countries, evaluated at the exchange rate, are a consequence of the difference in the mix of tradeable and non-tradeable goods, differences in tax rates and transport costs, and differences in rates of inflation as reflected in the adjustment of nominal exchange rates. Real interest rates depend on world productivity and time preference and are assumed to be the same and constant everywhere. Nominal interest rates differ across countries by differences in the fully anticipated rates of inflation.

In the simplest version of the model with fixed exchange rates, as in Johnson,[2] the rate of inflation is the same everywhere, so the nominal rate of interest is the same everywhere. With fixed exchange rates and integrated capital markets, the long-run effect of monetary policy is on the distribution of the sources of the monetary base between domestic and foreign components. Expansion of money relative to the demand for money raises prices, induces a loss of foreign exchange reserves and reduces the monetary base. The outflow of reserves raises the monetary base and the price levels abroad.

Johnson used the simplified model to show that world inflation would be equalized at the United States rate, since the United States was the major producer of world monetary reserves under

1. Jacob A. Frenkel and Harry Gordon Johnson, eds., *The Monetary Approach to Balance of Payments Theory*, London: George Allen and Unwin, 1976.
2. Harry Gordon Johnson, *op. cit.*, 1972.

the Bretton Woods system. Given the inflationary policy of the United States, other countries could choose either inflation or currency revaluation.

To relax the assumption that purchasing power parity always holds and that income (or its growth rate) is constant, a Phillips curve was brought into the open economy model.[1] With the addition of the Phillips curve, faster money growth in the United States increases aggregate demand at home and abroad. Initially output expands followed later by increases in wages, prices and interest rates throughout the world.[2] Other changes brought the model closer to observations without changing the main implications for long-run adjustment. Thus, the principal implications for the relation of money to income in a closed economy were extended to the open economy. In the short-run, acceleration of money (or unanticipated changes in money growth) increase real income, but the lasting effect is on the rate of inflation.

One feature of the literature on the monetary approach to the balance of payments is the modest or negligible role assigned to fiscal policy. Either fiscal variables do not appear in the models, or their effect is subsumed by the change in the domestic component of the monetary base. The latter assumption assigns the entire effect of fiscal change to the monetary impulse. This suggests the degree to which the critique of early Keynesian models had been accepted.[3]

1. DAVID E. W. LAIDLER, *Essays on Money and Inflation*, Manchester: Manchester University Press, 1975, and NIGEL W. DUCK, *et al.*, 'The Determination of the Rate of Change of Wages and Prices in the Fixed Exchange Rate World Economy: 1956-70', in MICHAEL PARKIN and GEORGE ZIS, eds., *Inflation in the World Economy*, Manchester: Manchester University Press, 1979.

2. Discussion of the effects of expected inflation on nominal interest rates ran parallel to the discussion of expected inflation on wages. Many Keynesians at first denied the relevance of the so-called Fisher effect and attributed the rise in interest rates to other factors. Gradually, the Fisher effect became a standard feature of Keynesian and non-Keynesian models.

3. There are a few exceptions. DAVID E. W. LAIDLER and P. O'SHEA 'An Empirical Macro-model of an Open Economy under Fixed Exchange Rates', *Economica*, 47, May 1980, pp. 141-58, found small, but statistically significant effects of government spending in an open economy model of the U.K. BRUNNER and MELTZER, in 'Monetary and Fiscal Policy in Open, Interdependent Economies with Fixed Exchange Rates' in EMIL CLAASSEN and PASCAL SALIN, eds., *Recent Issues in International*

The monetary approach also raised an issue about the endogeneity of money under fixed exchange rates. The model imposes conditions under which the money stock is endogenous in the long-run. During the adjustment to long-run equilibrium, the money stock is predetermined; the change in the money stock is endogenous. Endogeneity does not affect the causal relation between money and prices or nominal output, however. For example, in a classical gold standard country without a central bank, the money stock is determined by demand. Yet, it remains true that changes in money cause changes in prices in the important sense that a higher money stock implies a higher level of prices and nominal income, and a lower money stock implies a lower level of prices and nominal income. In general, endogeneity and causality are separate issues.

iii) *The Third Stage*

The third stage of the critique starts with Lucas'[1] paper that joined rational expectations and the natural rate hypothesis in a general equilibrium framework. Analysis in this tradition is called new classical economics. The literature on new classical economics has been the subject of several surveys and a summary of the main developments by two leading contributors.[2] For our purposes the important novel proposition arises from the extension of rational behavior to the use of information and the

Monetary Economics, Amsterdam: North Holland, 1976, pp. 327-361, extended to an open economy earlier work by CARL FINLEY CHRIST, 'A Simple Macro-Economic Model with a Government Budget Restraint', *Journal of Political Economy*, 76, January-February 1968 pp. 53-67, and others incorporating a government budget equation into a macro model. The home country and rest of the world issue debt and money to finance fiscal policy and engage in open market operations. Debt, money and capital are not perfect substitutes. The paper shows that if countries pursue independent fiscal or monetary policies, exchange rates cannot remain fixed. The reason is that fiscal policy changes the mix of money, bonds and capital and affects real interest rates and exchange rates.

1. ROBERT E. LUCAS JR., 'Econometric Policy Evaluation: A Critique', in *The Phillips Curve and Labor Markets, Carnegie-Rochester Conference Series on Public Policy*, 1 1976, pp. 19-46.

2. ROBERT E. LUCAS JR. and THOMAS J. SARGENT, eds., *Rational Expectations and Econometric Practice*, Minneapolis: University of Minnesota Press, 1981. ALEX CUKIERMAN, *Inflation, Stagflation, Relative Prices and Imperfect Information*, Cambridge: Cambridge University Press, 1984, is another useful source. He develops and extends several rational expectations models using different assumptions about information.

formation of expectations. According to the rational expectations hypothesis, individuals use information efficiently and learn from past experience. In this form, the proposition is accepted by many economists including such leading Keynesians as Modigliani[1] and Tobin[2] who do not accept many of the implications of new classical economics. Many of the implications depend on a much stronger proposition – that expectations are formed in a way that makes the subjective probabilities used to form expectations the same as the true probability distribution of the events to be forecast.

An attractive feature of rational expectations models is that expectations are formed by forward looking decision makers. Earlier work allowed expectations to be determined by extrapolating past behavior and ignoring currently available information about future events. However, rational expectations models go to the opposite extreme. They assume that policy operates according to a relatively precise rule. People are assumed to know the policy rule used by the monetary (and fiscal) authorities and to have detailed knowledge about the structure of the economy including the size and timing of responses to shocks of various kinds. These assumptions make the models analytically tractable but, taken literally (as they often are), they distort the economist's view of the policy problem by ignoring uncertainty, incomplete knowledge about the structure of the economy and costs of acquiring information and reducing uncertainty.

Introduction of rational expectations into economic models is a major advance in the treatment of information. The problem is that analysis in this tradition treats the benefits of information and the costs of acquiring information asymmetrically. Costs are assumed to be zero or negligible, and they are neglected. In our work,[3] costly information gives rise to institutions such as money as a medium of exchange. Explanations of the role of money, "sticky" prices and other arrangements that are difficult to un-

1. FRANCO MODIGLIANI, op. cit., 1977.
2. JAMES TOBIN, op. cit., 1980.
3. KARL BRUNNER and ALLAN H. MELTZER, 'The Uses of Money: Money in the Theory of an Exchange Economy', American Economic Review, 61, 5, 1971, pp. 784-805.

derstand in a new classical analysis become clearer once acquisition of information is recognized as costly.[1]

The principal policy implication derived from the analysis is the policy ineffectiveness proposition.[2] The proposition states that systematic monetary policy does not affect aggregate real demand. The public forms rational expectations about policy action to be taken by the authorities and adjusts nominal values. The only effective action is unanticipated action, i.e., policy surprises. McCallum[3] summarizes the literature up to 1980.

Statements about the ineffectiveness of fully anticipated monetary policy antedate rational expectations. Even Keynes believed that fully anticipated monetary changes have no real effects.[4] Differences arise over the issue of how fast the adjustment to new information occurs – about what the public knows and how quickly it learns. Costly information delays the adjustment of prices. Assuming that prices instantly clear markets, that the public knows the complete structure of the economy, knows the policy rule and knows policy action up to the current realization delivers the ineffectiveness proposition. If the public is less informed and more uncertain, the real effects of monetary action may endure longer.

1. This theme has been developed also in a series of papers by Laidler and forms the basis for his development of the 'buffer stock' theory of money. See for example DAVID E. LAIDLER, *Monetarist Perspectives*, Oxford: Philip Allan, 1982, and 'The "Buffer Stock" Notion in Monetary Economics', *Economic Journal*, 1984, pp. 17-34. See also ALEX CUKIERMAN, 'Rational Expectations and the Role of Monetary Policy: A Generalization', *Journal of Monetary Economics*, 5, April 1979, pp. 213-229, where information is costly and the level of information is determined endogenously.

2. THOMAS J. SARGENT and NEIL WALLACE, 'Rational Expectations, the Optimal Monetary Instrument and the Optimal Money Supply Rule', *Journal of Political Economy*, 83, April 1975, pp. 241-254.

3. BENNETT T. McCALLUM, 'Rational Expectations and Macroeconomic Stabilization Policy', *Journal of Money, Credit and Banking*, 12, November 1980, part 2, pp. 716-746.

4. Keynes wrote to Hicks, commenting on JOHN RICHARD HICKS, 'Mr. Keynes and the Classics: A Suggested Interpretation', *Econometrica*, 5, April 1937, pp. 147-159, about an inconsistency in economics: "The inconsistency creeps in, I suggest, as soon as it comes to be generally agreed the increase in the quantity of money is capable of increasing employment. . . . We used to admit it without realizing how inconsistent it was with our other premises . . ." (JOHN MAYNARD KEYNES, *Collected Writings*, vol. 14, London: 1973, p. 79).

Nothing in the idea of rational expectations requires the strong assumptions about information used in rational expectations models. There are reasons to doubt that the strong assumptions are satisfied.

The standard approach proceeds on the implicit assumption that people expect the current state expressed by the prevailing deterministic and stochastic structure to persist forever, or at least for a sufficiently indefinite future. This presumption is difficult to reconcile with reality. If the trend growth of output, prices and other relevant variables is stochastic, rather than deterministic, individuals may be unable to form subjective probabilities that exactly match the objective probabilities of events they forecast. The reason is that the parameters of the probability distributions may not be constants. In particular, the variance of the level and growth rate of output and prices need not be constant. Further, people have experienced changes in policy regimes in the past, so they know that changes in policy regimes can affect the structure of the economy.

Analytic tractability requires an assumption of constant variances, but some data suggest that the variance depends on the monetary regime.[1] The experience of shifting stochastic structures representing policy regimes and other shocks contradicts the assumption of rational expectation combined with the expectation of an unchanging structure.

It could be argued that one of the following arguments may save this class of rational expectations models. First, the models are not supposed to be descriptive of reality. They do not provide explanation of observations. They simply determine the long-run implication of the currently prevailing structure, once people have absorbed the relevant information. On this interpretation, rational expectations offers an analysis, in the Ricardian tradi-

1. ALLAN H. MELTZER. 'Some Evidence on the Comparative Uncertainty Experienced under Different Monetary Regimes', in C. D. CAMPBELL and W. R. DOUGAN, eds., *Alternative Monetary Regimes*, Baltimore: Johns Hopkins, 1986 a, pp. 122-153; *id.*, 'Size, Persistence and Interrelation of Nominal and Real Shocks: Some Evidence from Four Countries', *Journal of Monetary Economics*, 17, January 1986 b, pp. 161-194; RENÉ M. STULTZ and WALTER WASSERFALLEN, 'Macroeconomic Time Series, Business Cycles and Macroeconomic Policies', *Carnegie-Rochester Conference Series on Public Policy*, 22, 1985, pp. 9-53.

tion, of the long-term consequences of the current state under the assumption of indefinite persistence.

A second course may seem to maintain the descriptive sense of the models. Similar to Arrow-Debreu, there is a class of contingent states that may be realized in the future. Each state is associated with a different stochastic structure of shocks and policy regimes. The information available to people includes knowledge of this exhaustive class and an (objective) probability distribution over the class. Current decisions are formed in response to this extended information that has been impounded into a rational expectation.

The second solution to the problem fails, however. It introduces an essentially impossible and extreme information requirement – the existence of a meta distribution.[1] We see no way to identify a meaningful meta distribution over the class of possible states. Moreover, the solution clashes with the sense of realism occasionally expressed by the new classical macroeconomists. They understand that knowledge about stochastic structures is not immediately acquired. It involves a lengthy learning process. As time unfolds and the system moves to another state within the class of possible states, people do not immediately know their location within the class of possible states. Uncertainty prevails, even if the system persists for some time in the same state. The knowledge of a variety of possible future states with non-vanishing probability generates heterogeneous beliefs among people about the actual situation. Actual objective probabilities and subjective probabilities tend to diverge under the circumstances.

Once we admit a range of possible states potentially realized as the system moves over time, we must admit uncertainty beyond the level recognized by the standard analysis. The strong version of the rational expectations analysis is either forced to retreat to unrealism, i.e., knowledge of a meta distribution and immediate knowledge of the actual state, or it must abandon its position and admit incomplete information about the actual state.

1. BENJAMIN M. FRIEDMAN, 'Optimal Expectations and the Extreme Information Assumptions of "Rational Expectations" Macromodels', *Journal of Monetary Economics*, 5, January 1979, pp. 23-42, was one of the first to point out the "extreme information" assumptions of new classical economics.

This result is reinforced by the fact that people can never know an exhaustive and stable class of possible states. We conclude that the strong rational expectations view cannot be accepted as a serious empirical hypothesis.[1]

Our aim is *not* to reject rational expectations or to propose non-rational expectations. We accept that people use available information and form expectations by looking forward as well as back. The strong form of rational expectations is useful and necessary for some analytic results.

The problem is that these analytic results obscure, rather than clarify, the policy problem by endowing everyone with information that they cannot have at zero cost. This obscures the problem of choosing institutions or designing institutions and policy rules that minimize the cost of uncertainty. To us, the difference between strong and weak forms of rational expectations is a measure of uncertainty. Part of the problem is recognized even in the rational expectations literature. In a widely cited paper, Lucas[2] argues that people *cannot* know the distributions from which outcomes are drawn if there are large changes in policy actions that take them outside the range of past experience or if there are changes in policy rules.

In practice, people are uncertain about current and future policy action, and they often have limited information about the current objectives of policy and the rules or procedures that policymakers follow. To protect against uncertainty, to reduce costs of acquiring information and to shift the costs of bearing uncertainty, society develops institutions, including money, price setting and wage setting arrangements.[3]

Whatever the reason, or reasons, for setting prices, it is a matter of common observation that some prices and money wages are fixed by contract and others are fixed, without contracts, by the actions of price setters. To argue that this fact is inconsistent

1. The person must know *all* possible states. He cannot assign some portion of the probability space to other outcomes that he cannot specify precisely. The reason is that he must know the change in the probability distributions when there is a change in the policy regime.

2. ROBERT E. LUCAS JR., *op. cit.*, 1976.

3. We discuss some of these arrangements and their relation to uncertainty in the second and third lectures.

with the Walrasian model of continuous market clearing and, therefore, must be ignored in the development of business cycle theory seems perverse. The problem lies in the hypothesis of continuous market clearing as a basis for business cycle theory. Since the hypothesis is denied by the existence of contracts and price setting behavior, the hypothesis is rejected as a foundation for business cycle theory.[1]

Fischer[2] shows that, if money wages are pre-set by multi-period contracts, policy ineffectiveness is rejected. Systematic monetary policy affects real output if the systematic policy begins to be anticipated only after contracts are written. Fischer's model implies that monetary policy does not affect output permanently; the natural rate hypothesis remains. The result is a persistent, short-term effect of money on output and long-run neutrality of money. In a subsequent paper, Brunner, Cukierman and Meltzer[3] combine one-period wage setting with a mixture of unanticipated permanent and transitory changes in money to generate persistent effects of money on output and long-run neutrality.

Barro[4] seemed to provide empirical support for the proposition that systematic monetary policy is fully anticipated, affects prices but does not affect output. His papers relied on a particular, and not very appealing rule for systematic monetary policy, however. Empirical work by Boschen and Grossman,[5] Gordon[6] and

1. The hypotheses may be (and is) useful in other contexts and can be retained in those contexts until a better hypothesis is developed.

2. STANLEY FISCHER, 'Long-Term Contracts, Rational Expectations and the Optimal Money Supply Rule', *Journal of Political Economy*, 85, February 1977, pp. 191-205.

3. KARL BRUNNER, ALEX CUKIERMAN and ALLAN H. MELTZER, 'Money and Economic Activity, Inventories and Business Cycles', *Journal of Monetary Economics*, 11, May 1983, pp. 281-319.

4. ROBERT J. BARRO, 'Unanticipated Money Growth and Unemployment in the United States', *American Economic Review*, 67, 1977, pp. 101-115; id., 'Unanticipated Money, Output and the Price Level in the United States', *Journal of Political Economy*, 86, August 1978, pp. 549-580.

5. JOHN F. BOSCHEN and HERSCHEL J. GROSSMAN, 'Tests of Equilibrium Macro-economics Using Contemporaneous Monetary Data', *Journal of Monetary Economics*, 8, 1982, pp. 309-333.

6. ROBERT J. GORDON, 'Price Inertia and Policy Ineffectiveness in the United States, 1890-1980', *Journal of Political Economy*, 90, 1982, pp. 1087-1117.

Mishkin[1] showed that, contrary to Barro, anticipated monetary policy affects output. These findings reject the policy ineffectiveness result.

As is often the case, events affected the discussion. The relatively large rise in unemployment in developed countries, and the persistence of unemployment, following the decisions of many governments to shift to a policy of disinflation in the 1980s, are difficult to reconcile with the predictions or implications of market clearing, rational expectations models. Some research turned toward models with rational expectations and less than fully flexible prices (see McCallum[2]). Some turned to models in which shocks are dominantly real and the persistence of fluctuations depends on non-monetary aspects of the economy.[3] These models treat the business cycle as a real – non-monetary – disturbance. Perceived changes in money are fully reflected in prices.

1. FREDERIC S. MISHKIN, *A Rational Expectations Approach to Macroeconometrics: Testing Policy Ineffectiveness and Efficient Markets Models*, Chicago: University of Chicago Press, 1983.

2. BENNETT T. McCALLUM, 'On "Real" and "Sticky" Price Theories of the Business Cycle', *Journal of Money, Credit and Banking*, 18, November 1986 a, pp. 397-414.

3. FINN E. KYDLAND and EDWARD C. PRESCOTT, 'Time to Build and Aggregate Fluctuations', *Econometrica*, 50, November 1982, 1345-1370; ROBERT G. KING and CHARLES J. PLOSSER, Money, Credit and Prices in a Real Business Cycle', *American Economic Review*, 74, June 1984, pp. 363-380; EDWARD C. PRESCOTT, 'Theory Ahead of Business Cycle Measurement', *Carnegie-Rochester Conference Series on Public Policy*, 25, 1986, pp. 11-44.

5. The Grand Traverse

Real business cycle theory is a triumph of ingenuity and technical virtuosity over observation. The proponents of real business cycle models return to the tradition of the Keynesian model of the 1940s by eliminating changes in money as a cause of fluctuations in output. Either money is irrelevant and does not appear in the model, or the relation between money and income results entirely from the response of the demand for money to output. Unlike their Keynesian predecessors, however, the real business cycle theorists emphasize the role of supply shocks rather than shocks to aggregate demand and treat the internal dynamics as stable, so there is no need for stabilizing fiscal policies to offset an unstable private sector. Prominent real business cycle models omit fiscal variables; indeed, they omit governments. Society consists only of a representative consumer who has no reason to trade.

Real business cycle theory is one part of what we call the grand traverse. Rational expectations models of the business cycle began with a particular way of expressing the problem of information. The representative consumer in Lucas[1] is fully informed about all policy action up to the current realization. He is unable to distinguish current monetary shocks that change the absolute price level from changes in relative prices. In the real business cycle versions of rational expectations, there are no monetary shocks. For example, in Prescott[2] all shocks are random changes in productivity. There is no money. Money could be introduced to determine the price level, as in King and Plosser,[3] without changing the non-monetary character of business cycles. For King and Plosser, money is entirely neutral. Observed correlations between money and output are analyzed as reverse causation; increases in output raise the demand for money produced by the banking system.[4] A critical assumption is that there is

1. ROBERT E. LUCAS JR., *op. cit.*, 1972.
2. EDWARD C. PRESCOTT, *op. cit.*, 1986.
3. ROBERT G. KING and CHARLES J. PLOSSER, *op. cit.*, 1984.
4. ALLAN H. MELTZER, in 'Size, Persistence and Interrelation of Nominal and Real Shocks: Some Evidence from Four Countries', *Journal of Monetary Economics*,

only a representative consumer who knows the past and current history of the monetary base, so prices fully reflect the current realization of the base. The problem of acquiring information about current and prospective policy is completely absent.[1]

The second part of the grand traverse is the shift by Keynesian economists from the neglect of monetary policy and reliance on fiscal policy, as in the 1940s and 1950s, to a reliance on activist monetary policies for economic stabilization. This shift reflects both a change in view about the potency of monetary policy and, at least in the United States, recognition that the political process places severe limits on the ability to change fiscal policy as required for prompt, discretionary counter-cyclical action. Concern about the problems of housing and construction has disappeared from major journals and from Keynesian policy discussion. Keynesians now emphasize the use of monetary policy and, most recently, many have favored adjusting money growth to achieve some target level of predicted nominal GNP growth.[2]

The grand traverse finds many of the younger economists actively engaged in research on real business cycles. It will be surprising, indeed, if their research is able to find support for short-term neutrality of money. There are three main reasons. First, experiences like the depression of the 1930s, the monetary

17, January 1986 b, pp. 161-194, investigated direct and reverse causation for four countries using a multi-state Kalman filter. He finds that reverse causation is comparatively weak relative to direct causation from money to output.

1. Many of the problems of rational expectations models arise from the laudable concern to build macroeconomics on a solid micro foundation. The problems stem from the choice of foundation with complete (or nearly complete) information and only minor adjustments to the Arrow-Debreu paradigm of Walrasian markets. This paradigm has been useful in many contexts. In our opinion, the information structure is too complete to serve as a useful basis for the analysis of money and a monetary economy. The main problems of a monetary economy arise from pervasive uncertainty about the nature and types of shocks, their duration, the range of alternatives to customary action and similar decision problems. The mismatch between existing micro and macro theories requires micro foundations that take into account uncertainty and costs of acquiring information not just a tailoring of macro theory to fit existing (or slightly modified) micro foundations.

2. ROBERT J. GORDON, 'Using Monetary Policy to Dampen the Business Cycle: A New Set of First Principles', Working Paper, n. 1210, National Bureau of Economic Research, 1983; JAMES TOBIN, 'Monetary Policy Rules, Targets and Shocks', *Journal of Money, Credit and Banking*, 15, 1983, pp. 506-518.

contraction in 1920 and wartime expansions cannot be explained entirely by supply side changes or as entirely non-monetary events. Second, real business cycle theorists deny "sticky" prices despite more than a century of observation by economists and others. One of the most persistent correlations is the positive association between real and nominal output and between changes in real and nominal output. These movements show that for most countries, nominal GNP rises and falls with real GNP. In most periods, the data show larger amplitude of fluctuations in nominal GNP growth than in real GNP growth. These patterns are difficult to reconcile with supply shocks.[1] Third, real business cycle theories contribute nothing of consequence to the theory of inflation. Since money has no real effect, there is no reason for governments to raise or lower the rate of money growth. To explain inflation or deflation, we cannot even invoke waves of maniacal behavior affecting central bankers. This would violate rationality and the government's concern for social welfare that is implicit in these models.

Evidence of "sticky" prices continues to be found, most recently in Mussa's[2] comprehensive study of changes in ex post real, bilateral exchange rates. Real exchange rates are measured by adjusting actual exchange rates for changes in actual price levels. Mussa finds that movements of nominal and real exchange rates are highly correlated and that the correlation increased under fluctuating exchange rates. The variance of changes in ex post real exchange rates rises by a factor of eight to eighty times following the change from fixed to fluctuating exchange rates. Mussa explains the increased short-term variance as the combined effect of "sticky" prices and the increased variability of nominal exchange rates under fluctuating exchange rates.

1. KARL BRUNNER, in 'The Disarray in Macroeconomics', Center for Research in Government Policy and Business, University of Rochester, 1987 a; BENNETT T. McCALLUM, *op. cit.*, 1986 a, examine critically the evidence to support real business cycle theories. See also JAMES H. STOCK and MARK W. WATSON, 'Interpreting the Evidence on Money-Income Causality', Working Paper n. 2228, National Bureau of Economic Research, April 1987.

2. MICHAEL L. MUSSA, 'Nominal Exchange Rate Regimes and the Behavior of Real Exchange Rates: Evidence and Implications', *Carnegie-Rochester Conference Series on Public Policy*, 25, 1986, pp. 117-214.

Mussa's data pose a problem for the rational expectationists' traverse to real business cycle models. Differences in the variance of real exchange rates under fixed and floating exchange rates can be explained as a response to real shocks only if the size and frequency of real shocks increased markedly in the fluctuating exchange rate period. Given Mussa's findings, this result is implausible. Further, Mussa examined countries with bilateral fluctuating rates during periods of fixed exchange rates. He found that the variance of real exchange rates rose for these countries relative to others and absolutely. Mussa concludes that the data show "fundamental inconsistency between the hypothesis of exchange rate neutrality and empirical reality".[1]

If nominal shocks and "sticky" prices cause highly correlated changes in real and nominal exchange rates, nominal shocks have real effects on domestic activity. The case for short-run monetary neutrality vanishes. This does not deny that there are real shocks or even that business cycles may be started by real shocks. Changes in money – whether they occur as initial impulses or as a response to real shocks – increase variability of output.

Evidence that short-run, non-neutral monetary changes contribute to fluctuations in output does not support recent Keynesian arguments for activist, discretionary, counter-cyclical monetary policy. Modigliani[2] and Tobin[3] argue against fixed rates of money growth, but they provide neither argument nor evidence showing that counter-cyclical monetary policy contributes more to stability than to instability. They limit their discussions to one type of rule – a constant rate of money growth – and do not show that discretionary policy is superior to a rule governing money growth. Nor do they consider the costs of variable policies including the social costs that arise if uncertainty induces the public to hold a lower stock of domestic capital.

The central issue in this discussion antedates rational expecta-

1. *Ibid.*, p. 121.
2. FRANCO MODIGLIANI, 1977, *op. cit.*; *id.*, *The Debate over Stabilization Policy*, Cambridge: Cambridge University Press for the Raffaele Mattioli Foundation, 1986.
3. JAMES TOBIN, 1980, *op. cit*; *id.*, 1983, *op. cit.*

tions, but rational expectations bring the issue to the fore by introducing adjustment to changes in policy rules. The benefits of discretion must come from superior information by policy-makers. Otherwise, discretion cannot systematically reduce variability. We return to this issue in the fourth lecture.

6. Conclusion

Our summary of developments concerning the relation of money to income traces some major shifts in professional opinion during the past four decades. As Modigliani's[1] inaugural Mattioli lectures show, many of the so-called monetarist positions, once scorned, are now widely accepted. Or, as Alan Coddington observed, Keynesian ideas "faltered sometime in the middle sixties and stumbled into the seventies".[2]

There is, again, considerable agreement about the fact that money has short-run effects on output. There is less agreement about the magnitude and durability of the short-run effect, and there is no agreement about the micro foundation that supports macro theories that imply short-run non-neutrality of money. The latter has, of course, remained true throughout the history of systematic thinking about money, prices and output. There is not a consensus, however. At present there are three main positions – called monetarist, Keynesian and rational expectations-real business cycle views – on two main issues discussed in this lecture. Table 1-1 shows the divisions.

Table 1-1. Three main positions (monetarist, Keynesian and rational expectations-real business cycle views) on two main issues discussed in the first lecture

Issues	Monetarist	Keynesian	Real
(1) monetary changes affect real income	yes	yes	no
(2) activist, discretionary policies reduce fluctuations	no	yes	no

1. Franco Modigliani, 1986, op. cit.

2. Alan Coddington, in 'Keynesian Economics: The Search for First Principles', *Journal of Economic Literature*, 14, 1976, p. 1264. Thomas Mayer, in 'The Structure of Monetarism I', in Thomas Mayer, ed., *The Structure of Monetarism*, New York: Norton, 1978, pp. 1-25, sets out a list of propositions constituting monetarism. The entire list was not accepted by most discussants of his paper, but broad agreement on several propositions is evident.

These are not the only open issues. There is little agreement on the structural model of the economy relating money to income. There are major differences about the role of government policy and its interaction with private decisions. There are differences about the roles of uncertainty and money and about the foundations of a monetary economy. And there are differences about the role of policy rules and the types of rules. These subjects are discussed in subsequent lectures.

SECOND LECTURE*
The Monetary Mechanism: Markets for Assets

1. *Two Views of Money*: i) *The Radical Keynesians*; ii) *The New Classical Macroeconomics*. – 2. *Money and Uncertainty*: i) *The Role of Money*; ii) *The Banking System*; iii) *Monetary Control*. – 3. *IS-LM and Beyond*: i)*Problems With IS-LM*; ii) *Beyond IS-LM*; iii) *Asset Market Responses*. – 4. *Further Implications of the Money-Credit Model*: i) *An Independent Credit Market Effect?*; ii) *Reverse Causation*; iii) *Interaction with the Output Market*; iv) *Interest Rate and Money Targets*.

In a Walrasian economy, transactions are made in a central market with the guidance of an auctioneer who assures that all transactions occur at market clearing prices. This arrangement removes most of the distinctive features of a monetary economy. There are no costs of acquiring information, no costs of search, and no uncertainty about the quality of goods offered in exchange. The market clears and exchanges of goods for money or money for goods occur, although no reason is given for the use of money in transactions. One-period bonds are the only non-monetary financial asset typically found, and any lending and borrowing takes the form of purchase and sale of such bonds.

The asset markets of the Walrasian economy bear little resemblance to the asset markets found in developed market economies. The latter have a much richer array of assets by type and maturity. The wider range of assets provides opportunities for wealth owners to hold portfolios that increase utility at a given wealth position. The desire to structure portfolios gives rise to intermediaries who specialize in the provision of particular services. In a world of certainty, or certain expectations, and in the absence of transaction costs, the scope for intermediary services is reduced to a minimum. In an uncertain world, the provision of intermediary services occupies the time and talent of large numbers of people, including many skilled professionals.

The study of money and other assets in a modern economy is, then, a study of asset markets in an uncertain world. The

* August 1988.

53

qualitative effects of money on output and its effect on the price level need not depend on the structure of asset markets, but the timing of responses does. Intermediation and movements of velocity alter short-run responses without necessarily affecting long-run responses. Hence a study of the relation of money to income must be concerned with the operation of asset markets.

The financing of fiscal policy also involves the asset markets. Governments issue bonds and base money to finance budget deficits and withdraw bonds and base money to finance budget surpluses. Analysis of the response to fiscal policy involves more than the "direct" effects of government on spending and output; the persistent effects of deficit finance are mainly the effects arising from the responses of asset prices to the issues of bonds and base money. These effects persist at a constant level of government spending and tax rates.

The next two lectures develop the role of the asset markets and the responses to money and debt issues in an uncertain world. The presence of uncertainty explains the use of a medium of exchange – money – the existence of intermediaries and differences between bonds and capital. The presence of uncertainty is reflected in costs of acquiring information that give rise to arrangements such as price and wage setting on markets for goods and services, including markets for labor services.

We begin by considering a different tradition, a world in which money has no effect on output; money is irrelevant for output and, in one case, for both prices and output. We then develop our analysis of a monetary economy and the reasons why a monetary economy differs from economies in which money is irrelevant. Next, we consider the role of credit markets and intermediation, contrasting the standard *IS-LM* framework, in which there is no intermediation, to the analysis we developed earlier in which credit markets and intermediation have a role in the transmission of monetary and fiscal policy to the asset and output markets. We discuss the types of shocks affecting the asset and output markets and develop some principal implications. Lecture 3 extends the analysis to incorporate fiscal policy, the reasons for price and wage inflexibility and related issues.

54

1. Two Views of Money

Monetarists and most Keynesians accept that money influences economic activity and prices. Money is neutral in long-run adjustment, when price anticipations fully reflect monetary conditions, but adjustment of anticipations is often delayed by uncertainty about the nature of shocks and their persistence. During the transition, money is not neutral.

An alternative view denies that money affects output; money is irrelevant for output. One version of irrelevance is found in the writings of the radical Keynesians and the post-Keynesians. Examples are Kaldor[1] and Robinson.[2] A second version is a feature of real business cycle theory and, therefore, part of new classical economics. We discuss the two versions in turn.

i) The Radical Keynesians

The radical Keynesians' position is open to three distinct interpretations. The first two treat the money stock as a residual magnitude in the economic process. Money is fully determined by the economy's behavior without any feedback to output. The money stock adjusts passively to the public's demand for money. The third interpretation claims that movements of money and velocity are offsetting. Changes in money give rise to opposite movements in the demand for money or velocity; the product of money and velocity is approximately constant following a change in money.

The first interpretation attributes the economy's passive response to money to a specific institutional structure under which the stock of money is demand determined. The strategy of interest rate control, exercised in the US during the 1940s, produced the pattern postulated. A tactical procedure of setting a target rate of interest for short periods would produce a similar pattern. The constraints imposed on the Italian Central Bank for a

1. NICHOLAS KALDOR, *The Scourge of Monetarism*, Oxford: Oxford University Press, 1982.
2. JOAN ROBINSON and FRANK WILKINSON, 'Ideology and Logic', in FAUSTO VICARELLI, ed., *Keynes' Relevance Today*, Philadelphia: University of Pennsylvania Press, 1985, pp. 73-98.

number of years during the 1970s offer a particular example. The central bank was obliged to hold all the securities issued by the Treasury which could not be sold on the market. The size of the deficit and the pricing of the bonds indirectly controlled the growth of the monetary base, and the deficit was determined by the political process, so the base depended on the political process and the demand for government debt. Passive accommodation of the money stock to the demand for money in this case follows from the prevalence of a specific institutional structure producing a pattern of "reverse causation".[1]

The first interpretation introduces an empirical hypothesis asserting that the requisite institutional structure predominates. The occasional occurrence of such structures is undeniable, but there is no evidence to support the hypothesis of dominant occurrence. Experience from many periods and in many countries falsifies the hypothesis. These experiences show that major changes in monetary growth were induced by persistent accelerations or decelerations of the monetary base which occurred independently of any feedback from non-monetary processes of the type usually emphasized. We mention in passing the events of 1920-1921 or 1936-1937[2] in the United States, the change of the Swiss monetary regime in 1973, and the experience of Sweden in the first years of the 1930s.[3]

The second interpretation, advanced by Kaldor, Robinson, and the Radcliffe Report, offers a more sweeping assertion. The residual character of the money stock or its passive accommodation to the economy occurs under all circumstances and with any institutional structure. The monetary system produces the money stock demanded by the economy irrespective of the behavior of the monetary authorities. Innovations within the finan-

---

1. The price level and the rate of inflation depend on the quantity of money and its rate of change, but the quantity of money depends on the demand for money under these constraints.

2. MILTON FRIEDMAN and ANNA JACOBSON SCHWARTZ, *A Monetary History of the United States, 1867-1890*, Princeton: Princeton University Press for the National Bureau of Economic Research, 1963 a.

3. LARS JONUNG, 'Knut Wicksell's Norm of Prices Stabilization and Swedish Monetary Policy in the 1930s', *Journal of Monetary Economics*, 5, 1979, pp. 459-496.

cial system allow the banks to adjust the stock of money to demand.

The emergence of new types of money has been observed in response to specific incentives in many countries and periods. This process does not operate, however, in the manner claimed. We cited some of the evidence showing that major accelerations and decelerations of the monetary base are followed by similar movements of the money stock. These experiences cannot be reconciled with a thesis of spontaneously and independently adjusting monetary innovations. Nor can the stock of base money be interpreted as an accommodation to the economic process.[1]

Both the first and the second interpretations imply a dominant reverse causation between money and income. Meltzer's[2] study of shock patterns operating in four economies in the OECD yields very little evidence in support of reverse causation. Statistical studies of the United States money supply process by Robert Rasche and James Johannes[3] provides further evidence. Rasche and Johannes developed a technique to forecast the monetary multiplier. The technique was used to forecast the base money multiplier linking the monetary base to the money stock. Forecasts were made every March and September for the subsequent six months during an eight year period. These ex ante forecasts are unbiased, and the forecast errors are serially uncorrelated. Forecasts were made independently of the projected or actual path of the monetary base.

According to the second interpretation, independent accelerations or decelerations of the monetary base should produce opposite movements in the monetary multiplier. The forecasts of the multiplier should yield serially correlated errors in any period with substantial accelerations or decelerations in the base. Since the forecasts were made for the period of rising and falling

1. With fixed exchange rates, the stock of base money is endogenous in the long-run. In the short-run, the stock is predetermined, and the change in money is endogenous.

2. ALLAN H. MELTZER, 'Size, Persistence and Interrelation of Nominal and Real Shocks: Some Evidence from Four Countries', *Journal of Monetary Economics*, 17, January 1986 b, pp. 161-194.

3. ROBERT RASCHE and JAMES JOHANNES, *Controlling the Growth of Monetary Aggregates*, Boston: Kluwer Academic Publishers, 1987.

money growth in the 1970s and 1980s, Rasche and Johannes were able to test the proposition. They found that the multiplier forecasts remain independent of the subsequent behavior of the monetary base.

The third interpretation relies on simultaneous adjustment of the demand for money and the monetary multiplier. The money market remains in equilibrium without modification of any variables transmitting impulses from the money market to the economy. Autonomous changes in the monetary base are offset either by corresponding changes in the demand for money, by offsetting changes in the banks' reserve ratio, or by some combination of the two. When costs of adjustment are relatively high, such behavior is not an irrational or improbable response to events that are perceived to be temporary. A temporary change in the base induces banks to modify their reserve position and to "immunize" their portfolio position against costly, short-run round-trips to the market. Similarly the public, facing larger transactions costs than banks, responds by holding the additional money. The failure to transmit temporary changes in reserve position to the banks' portfolio can occur even in the United States where transaction costs on the money market are low. The reserves may simply be absorbed in the Federal funds market without affecting assets with higher information and transaction costs.

The negligible response to perceived temporary events is consistent with rational behavior of banks and the public. Rational responses increase when the monetary or reserve changes are expected to persist. An economic analysis involving portfolio equilibrium cannot imply passive adjustment of reserve positions or desired money balances to permanent changes in the base or the money stock. Relative prices, and therefore real demands, adjust to the monetary changes, and output responds to money. The irrelevance proposition applies only to temporary changes.[1]

1. An implication of this analysis concerns the interpretation of statistical regressions of the demand for money. The random residual of the demand function now consists of two components: a term expressing the random character of the demand for permanent balances and a term reflecting the passive absorption of perceived transitory changes in the money stock. The larger the noise in the money stock the larger

The discussion has an implication for Poole's[1] (1970) analysis of the choice between interest rates and money as a target for monetary policy. Poole showed that a policy of setting interest rates is superior to controlling money whenever the variance of the residual in the demand for money is sufficiently large. A large variance due to the passive adjustment to transitory changes has no consequences for the output market. The *LM* curve does not shift. Poole's analysis applies only to the variance of the permanent component.

ii) *The New Classical Macroeconomics*

A variety of recent real business cycle models attempted to explain the occurrence of business cycles.[2] Some property of the production process or of the nature of market interaction is usually offered as a sufficient condition for the emergence of economic fluctuations characterizing a business cycle. The authors of the models strive for parsimonious explanations of the main features of a business cycle. Monetary forces, monetary institutions and the role of government are completely dismissed from the analysis. There are neither monetary nor fiscal shocks. Further, the models imply that economic fluctuations are not necessarily inefficient, so they offer no basis for interventionist policies. Some of the models reach conclusions about invariance of output to money similar to those of the radical Keynesians.

Some models explicitly incorporate money into the analysis,[3] but monetary forces have no real effects. The monetary base (and the nominal money stock) determine the price level, whereas the

will be the variance of the second term. Variations of the stochastic process controlling the money stock change the variance of the random residual of money demand over time. See also DAVID E. W. LAIDLER, 'The "Buffer Stock" Notion in Monetary Economics', *Economic Journal*, 1984, pp. 17-34.

1. WILLIAM POOLE, 'Optimal Choice of Monetary Policy Instruments in a Simple Stochastic Macro Model', *Quarterly Journal of Economics*, 84, 1970, pp. 197-216.

2. FINN KYDLAND and EDWARD C. PRESCOTT, 'Time to Build and Aggregate Fluctuations', *Econometrica*, 50, November 1982; EDWARD C. PRESCOTT, 'Theory Ahead of Business Cycle Measurement', *Carnegie-Rochester Conference Series on Public Policy*, 25, 1986, pp. 11-44; JOHN B. LONG JR. and CHARLES J. PLOSSER, 'Real Business Cycles', *Journal of Political Economy*, 91, 1, 1983, pp. 36-69.

3. ROBERT G. KING and CHARLES J. PLOSSER, 'Money, Credit and Prices in a Real Business Cycle', *American Economic Review*, 74, June 1984, pp. 363-380.

real volume of inside money is determined (endogenously) by the economic process. Reverse causation in the real business cycle model involves a very different process than the reverse causation emphasized by the radical Keynesians, however. For the latter, reverse causation applies to nominal magnitudes. In real business cycle models, the nominal magnitude is not subject to reverse causation. Reverse causation operates by adjusting the price level and real balances to the relative prices and output determined by real conditions.

Since the models consider only supply shocks, and nominal money is predetermined, changes in output are negatively correlated with price changes. This implies a positive correlation between output and the real money stock. A proper extension of these models to an open economy would imply that nominal shocks modify the nominal but not the real exchange rate. Variations of the latter must depend on real shocks. The irrelevance of nominal shocks combined with the observed correlation of contemporaneous changes in nominal and real exchange rates seems to support reliance on a real shock hypothesis as an explanation of economic fluctuations.[1]

The results of real business cycle analysis, obtained with substantial investment of admirable analytic skills, are remarkably meager. We learn that an imaginative array of real conditions can be sufficient to generate fluctuations in output. We obtain a theorem establishing that monetary shocks (of one fashion or another) are neither sufficient nor necessary conditions for the type of movements in output characteristic of a business cycle. The theorem is incontestable but provides no information about the relevance or irrelevance of monetary shocks and monetary institutions.

The meager content of real business cycle theories is shown also by the limited range of facts that can be explained. The observed positive co-movements between money and the price

1. MICHAEL L. MUSSA, in 'Nominal Exchange Rate Regimes and the Behavior of Real Exchange Rate: Evidence and Implications', *Carnegie-Rochester Conference Series on Public Policy*, 25, 1986, pp. 117-214, documents the correlation between nominal and expost real exchange rates. Contrary to real business cycle theories, the correlation reflects sluggish adjustment of prices.

level and between the price level and output require additional constraining assumptions. To produce a positive co-movement between the price level and the money stock, King and Plosser[1] would have to postulate a sufficiently large positive correlation between monetary base shocks and real shocks and sufficiently large variability of the monetary shocks. The same assumptions also assure co-movement of prices and output. The model provides no economic mechanism or rationale for these additional postulates. The required assumptions are arbitrary, and the model fails to clarify some of the principal facts that have been observed repeatedly.

Some real business cycle models assume the operation of an aggregate real shock. The shock is unobservable and its nature is obscure. It strains credibility to believe that the downswings of 1920-1921, 1929-1933, 1937-1938 or 1981-1982 in the United States resulted from unspecified real shocks. The European countries did not raise reserve requirement ratios or suffer the 1937-1938 downswing, so the real shock in 1937-1938 has to be confined to the United States, while the real shock of 1929-1933 seems to have varied in timing and intensity with decisions to abandon the gold standard. Britain, Sweden and the United States have very different experiences after 1931 when Britain and Sweden left the gold standard. By sheer coincidence, the negative aggregate production shock appears in Switzerland just after the round of devaluations in 1931 and lasted with a pronounced serial correlation until the devaluation of the Swiss franc in 1936.

Although the shock hypothesis of real business cycle theories cannot be tested directly, implications can be tested. Real business cycle hypotheses typically imply a joint distribution of endogenous variables; for example, consumption and output may depend on the same stochastic variables. Statements about the joint distribution can be tested. To date, the tests have yielded mainly negative results. Rejection of a specific model of the real business cycle may reflect the inadequacy of the model, not the general hypothesis, however.

1. ROBERT G. KING and CHARLES J. PLOSSER, 1984, *op. cit.*

Time series procedures have been used to investigate the general idea expressed by whole classes of hypotheses or models of the business cycle. Eichenbaum and Singleton,[1] Stultz and Wasserfallen[2] and Wasserfallen[3] find support for real business cycle theories. They find little evidence of monetary influences. Stock and Watson[4] show that the results depend on the procedures used and are not robust to a change in procedure. Meltzer[5] using a multi-state Kalman filter finds evidence in five countries for the joint operation of both monetary and real shocks.

Taken together, the accumulated empirical results are inconclusive for real business cycle theories. Moreover, the time series procedures prevent a clear interpretation of the results. The reason is that no specific hypothesis about the economic structure and the nature of the prevalent shocks is tested.

1. MARTIN S. EICHENBAUM and KENNETH J. SINGLETON, 'Post-War Business Cycles', *Macroeconomics Annual*, Cambridge, Ma.: M.I.T. Press, 1986.

2. RENÉ M. STULTZ and WALTER WASSERFALLEN, 'Macroeconomic Time Series, Business Cycles and Macroeconomic Policies', *Carnegie-Rochester Conference Series on Public Policy*, 22, 1985, pp. 9-53.

3. WALTER WASSERFALLEN, 'Makroökonomische Untersuchungen mit Rationalen Erwartungen: Empirische Analysen für die Schweiz', Habilitation Thesis Universität Bern, Switzerland: Paul Haupt, 1985.

4. JAMES H. STOCK and MARK W. WATSON, 'Interpreting the Evidence on Money-Income Causality', Working Paper n. 2228, National Bureau of Economic Research, 1987.

5. ALLAN H. MELTZER, 'Variability of Prices, Output and Money under Fixed and Fluctuating Exchange Rates: An Empirical Study of Monetary Regimes in Japan and the United States', *Bank of Japan Monetary and Economic Studies*, 3, December 1985, pp. 1-46; *id.*, 'Size, Persistence and Interrelation of Nominal and Real Shocks: Some Evidence from Four Countries', *Journal of Monetary Economics*, 17, January 1986 b, pp. 161-194.

2. Money and Uncertainty

Real business cycle theories remove a large part of the uncertainty that consumers and producers face in a market economy by excluding all uncertainty about the structure. They reduce the cost of acquiring information about money by assuming full information about money (or by omitting money from their analysis). Markets are competitive and information is not wasted, so market prices reflect the current money stock (if any) and expected future monetary growth. Under these conditions, monetary changes have no effect on real variables such as output and employment.

The choice of monetary policy or of a monetary regime is irrelevant in this case. A necessary condition for monetary shocks to exert real effects on the economy involves some imperfection in people's information about their environment. This was often implicit in monetarist analysis and occasionally expressed explicitly in statements asserting that the maintained rate of growth or trend in the money stock is fully reflected by the price level. People observe the money stock or its maintained growth rate and adjust beliefs about the rate of inflation. Departures from trend are not immediately reflected in prices, expected prices or inflation. Monetary accelerations and decelerations contain new information (innovations) not yet fully absorbed by prices, so they affect output, employment, and other real variables.

In the monetarist analysis of the 1960s, anticipations were formed by looking backward. Lucas joined the analysis of monetary innovations with the idea of rational expectations.[1] The execution of this research program required a careful, explicit specification of the nature of incomplete information. Following a suggestion made by Phelps,[2] Lucas emphasized the difference between global and local information. People know what is happening in the local markets, but acquire global information – information about money and the price level – only with a lag.

1. ROBERT E. LUCAS JR., 'Expectations and the Neutrality of Money', *Journal of Economic Theory*, 4, April 1972, pp. 103-124.
2. EDMUND S. PHELPS, 'Introduction', in EDMUND S. PHELPS, ed., *Microeconomic Foundations of Employment and Inflation Theory*, New York: Norton, 1970.

Even with full knowledge about the deterministic and stochastic structure, delay in the receipt of global information gives rise to an inference problem. Inferences are correct on average, but people confound allocative and aggregative influences on price movements at any particular time. They interpret part of the nominal effect of monetary change as an allocative effect. Nominal shocks are converted into output and employment shocks. As a result of this misperception, nominal shocks affect output and employment. The size of the effect depends on the noise in the system, specifically on the relative variances of allocative and aggregate shocks.

Lucas' paper seemed to resolve the classic problem of reconciling short-run non-neutrality with the long-run neutrality of money. Reconciliation occurs within a framework with minimal uncertainty. Anticipations are drawn from a known distribution, and realizations differ from anticipated values by a transitory error. The model remains consistent with market clearing and fully flexible prices. Prices fully adjust to all perceived ongoing shocks.

Early in the 1980s increasing doubt emerged about the relevance of the Lucas model. It was generally recognized, and conceded, that the empirical foundation of the information structure and the inference problem is very weak. Mishkin,[1] Boschen and Grossman[2] and others deepened the doubt with statistical investigations showing real effects of currently perceived nominal magnitudes.

Recognition of the failure of the Phelps-Lucas model of local-global confusion confronted macroeconomists with a choice. They could retreat to an assumption of full information, or they could recognize that the problem of incomplete information is a central problem. The new classical macroeconomists chose the first course. This choice was probably strongly influenced by their

1. FREDERIC S. MISHKIN, *A Rational Expectations Approach to Macroeconometrics: Testing Policy Ineffectiveness and Efficient Markets Models*, Chicago: University of Chicago Press, 1983.

2. JOHN F. BOSCHEN and HERSCHEL J. GROSSMAN, 'Test of Equilibrium Macroeconomics Using Contemporaneous Monetary Data', *Journal of Monetary Economics*, 8, 1982, pp. 309-333.

reluctance to abandon the assumption of full market clearing (up to the current realization of the shock) and fully flexible prices.

This choice has unfortunate consequences for the relevance of current versions of new classical macroeconomics. Insights about the role of monetary regimes and the effect of changes in monetary regimes on the relative variance of monetary shocks are abandoned. Changes in the monetary regime are immaterial. They cannot affect the economy's real processes. We also note that the volatility of exchange rates cannot be explained in terms of the new classical macroeconomics. Singleton argued effectively that we need to recognize the complexity of the information problem by admitting heterogeneous beliefs and a non-mechanical role for higher moments of the underlying distributions.[1] These features appear to explain much of the observed volatility of exchange rates.

The Walrasian foundation of the new classical program fails to recognize a fundamental condition of any relevant monetary analysis. Keynes broke with this tradition by emphasizing the role of uncertainty as a key feature of a monetary economy. We share Keynes' emphasis on the pervasive uncertainty confronting decision makers. We would add, in contrast to Keynesians, that the same uncertainty confronts policymakers.

Imperfect or incomplete information is the foundation of any relevant monetary analysis and is central to understanding a wide array of social institutions including business firms.[2] Many social institutions arise to lower information costs or to save on transaction costs. Specialized institutions, division of labor, and markets can be looked upon as arrangements to pool information. The occurrence of money as a medium of exchange arises as a solution to an information and transaction problem.[3] A

---

1. KENNETH J. SINGLETON, 'Speculation and the Volatility of Foreign Currency Exchange Rates', *Carnegie-Rochester Conference Series on Public Policy*, 26, 1987, pp. 9-56.

2. RONALD HARRY COASE, 'The Nature of the Firm', *Economica*, 1937; ARMEN A. ALCHIAN and SUSAN WOODWARD, 'Reflections on the Theory of the Firm', *Journal of Institutional and Theoretical Economics*, 143, 1, 1987, pp. 110-137.

3. KARL BRUNNER and ALLAN H. MELTZER, 'The Uses of Money: Money in Theory of an Exchange Economy', *American Economic Review*, 61, 5, 1971, pp. 784-805; ROBERT G. KING and CHARLES J. PLOSSER, 'Money as the Mechanism of Exchange', *Journal of Monetary Economics*, 17, 1, 1986, pp. 93-115.

Walrasian world has no role for money, financial intermediaries, business firms, or contractual arrangements.[1]

Price setting, i.e., the announcement of posted prices, is an integral part of the contractual behavior conditioned by information problems and transaction costs. In an uncertain world, rational agents do not immediately adjust or revise their price setting in response to every shock modifying prevalent market conditions.[2] Price setting is the product of an uncertain world where individuals and firms face transaction costs and uncertainty about the nature of shocks, their persistence, and other features of their environment.[3] In a world of price setting and transaction costs, there is a strong presumption that nominal shocks produce real effects. Money affects output, employment and other real variables during the transition from one full equilibrium to the next.

i) *The Role of Money*

Markets do not operate without costs. The execution of transactions requires an allocation of scarce resources. Acquiring information about market opportunities also uses valuable resources. In the presence of information and transaction costs, people face an optimizing problem. To solve the optimizing problem, they search for optimal arrangements for the execution of exchanges. An optimal choice of arrangements lowers uncertainty and transaction costs to the minimum attainable. Financial intermediaries and the role of money as a medium of exchange emerge from the search process.

Two basic conditions control the search for optimal market arrangements. First, uncertainty is not uniformly distributed. Transactors face a distribution of information costs defined on the characteristics of goods, their relative prices, and the charac-

---

1. The new classical approach often introduces money by means of a cash-in-advance constraint to remain consistent with the Walrasian model.

2. Rejection of fully flexible prices does not commit us either to a 'disequilibrium' analysis or to the support of an activist policy. We show below that the very conditions which create price setting behavior with comparatively inflexible but adjustable prices, viz. pervasive uncertainty, also violate the necessary and sufficient condition for a successful activist policy.

3. We develop this argument in Lecture 3.

teristics of other transactors. Some goods are associated with comparatively low information and transaction costs, while others involve high costs. Some transactors are less reliable or honest in their dealings. Second, the distributions do not shift randomly between transactions. There are similarities in the cost distributions perceived by each transactor. This information guides the selection of the transaction chains by which individuals transform their initial endowments into consumption bundles. People systematically explore opportunities to lower transaction and information costs. They do not randomly proceed with their choices of transaction arrangements.[1] Since the choice of a medium of exchange requires a degree of consensus, transactors observe other arrangements in use and learn from each other. Observation, learning, and the similarity of cost distributions encourage convergence of transaction chains. This process eventually leads to a small subset of goods or assets which are dominantly used in settling transactions. The assets used with dominant frequency in transactions are the media of exchange.

The use of a medium of exchange is a substitute for investment in information and for labor allocated to search. By using money, individuals reduce the costs of settling on exchange arrangement, and they reduce the number of transactions in which they engage to convert initial endowments into consumption baskets. The use of money increases the welfare of each transactor by reducing costs of acquiring information and transacting in an uncertain world.

Our analysis clarifies Adam Smith's remark that money facilitates exchanges and encourages specialization.[2] Recent work by King and Plosser[3] extends this analysis in a general equilibrium framework. They develop the basic information problem sufficient for the emergence and existence of a medium of exchange, money. Their analysis also clarifies the nature of the social productivity of money. The resources saved from investment to produce the information level equivalent to the use of

1. KARL BRUNNER and ALLAN H. MELTZER, 1971, *op. cit.*
2. *Ibid.*,
3. ROBERT G. KING and CHARLES J. PLOSSER, 'Money as the Mechanism of Exchange', *Journal of Monetary Economics*, 17, 1, 1986, pp. 93-115.

money is a measure of the social productivity of money – the gain to society from the use of money.

The analysis of social productivity helps to clarify puzzling implications of conventional analysis where the service of money is limited to the saving of "shoe leather" or trips to the bank. Yet, money remains in use during high inflations, when the inflation tax becomes large relative to the saving in shoe leather. Only in very large, persistent inflations, or hyperinflation, do we find the displacement of existing money.

The social productivity of money and the cost of achieving convergence to a new money explains the persistence of money in episodes of long and large inflations and the spontaneous search for new and alternative monies under large inflation and pronounced deflation. The inflation tax must be large and persistent to cover the costs of achieving consensus on a new money by private individuals. Substitution of new for old money accelerates the hyperinflation measured in the old monetary units and encourages the breakdown of the old monetary institutions, but substitution moderates the deflation.

Analysis of the private and social productivity of money provides some perspective on the issue of whether money will "wither away" in the future as a consequence of modern electronics. For centuries, technological evolution has influenced the nature of monetary institutions. Technology will continue to shape payment systems in the future. Technological evolution can reasonably be expected to modify information and transaction costs, but it is unlikely that technology will create a pattern of uniformly low costs for all goods, assets and persons. It is doubtful, therefore, that technological development will generate a pattern of universal and instantaneous clearing of mutual claims or the random use of assets as a means of settling payments. Some transaction dominating assets will most likely continue to function as money. Society will continue to benefit from the productivity of money as a medium of exchange.[1]

---

1. Credit cards, for example, reduce a seller's cost of acquiring information about the buyer and encourage the separation of payments and purchases. This increases (relatively) the use of deposits as a medium of exchange but does not eliminate the use of money.

An implication of this analysis is that the return to money differs from the return to bonds or other financial assets. More of the return to money takes the form of a service yield, a saving in the costs of acquiring information and transacting. More of the return to financial assets takes the form of an explicit payment of interest. An increase in uncertainty would, therefore, increase the real return to money and induce substitution toward money from other assets. Technological changes in the payments system and changes in costs of information also change the relative demands for money and other assets. Money and financial assets are substitutes in portfolios, but they are not perfect substitutes.

A very different type of analysis of the payments system and the use of money has attracted attention in recent years.[1] These papers construct an imagined financial system composed of mutual funds offering transaction services. Financial intermediaries accept deposits from customers. The value of the deposits fluctuates with the market value of the assets deposited. The claim against these assets, represented by the deposit, provides transaction services. The intermediaries provide an accounting system. Payments are made by shifting claims to deposits from one account to another. There is no money in this system; no small group of assets is used for transactions. Claims for any combination of wealth deposited at intermediaries are randomly used within the accounting system. Since information is costless and transactions are instantaneous, the analysis eliminates the conditions which make money socially productive. The pervasive occurrence of uncertainty, and the emergence of social institutions, including money, to cope with uncertainty is neglected.

A similar failure characterizes the attempt made by Wallace[2]

---

1. EUGENE F. FAMA, 'Banking in the Theory of Finance', *Journal of Monetary Economics*, 6, 1, 1980, pp. 39-57; ROBERT L. GREENFIELD and LELAND B. YEAGER, 'A Laissez-Faire Approach to Monetary Stability', *Journal of Money, Credit and Banking*, 15, 3, 1983, pp. 302-315; BENNETT T. MCCALLUM, 'The "New Monetary Economics"', Fiscal Issues and Unemployment', *Carnegie-Rochester Conference Series on Public Policy*, 23, 1985, pp. 13-45.

2. NEIL WALLACE, 'The Overlapping Generations Model of Fiat Money', in J. H. KAREKEN and NEIL WALLACE, eds., *Models of Monetary Economics*, Minneapolis: Federal Reserve Bank of Minneapolis, 1980.

to explain the occurrence of money in the context of an over-lapping generations model. This model is used to demonstrate that an economy without intergenerationally tradeable assets is inefficient. Efficiency can be established and welfare consequently raised by introducing opportunities for intergenerational ex-change. "Money" enters to perform this function. Any tradeable asset will do just as well; money provides no special service. The social service summarized by "general acceptability" has no meaning in the model. There is no medium of exchange and hardly any exchange in Wallace's model. "Money" is traded once in a generation. We note again that an adequate foundation of monetary analysis is replaced by a construction in which relevant uncertainty has no role. Since the model has minimal exchange, it denies the source of the service yield on money. Wallace's money functions like a Treasury bill, so he searches in later papers for institutional restrictions, regulations and arti-ficial reasons for the coexistence of money and Treasury bills in portfolios.

ii) *The Banking System*

Transaction costs, uncertainty and institutional arrangements also explain features of the banking system. The United States banks' large holdings of excess reserves in the 1930s was, in part, a response to the uncertainty generated by the doubling of re-serve requirement ratios and the uncertainty generated by the second major recession in a decade. The presence or absence of a lender of last resort has implications for the costs and uncer-tainty that banks face and the amount of reserves that banks choose to hold. Costs of information also contribute to an explana-tion of the phenomenon known as loan rationing. This section discusses some aspects of uncertainty and information costs that are relevant for the financial system.

Banks allocate their portfolios in response to the returns of-fered by various types of assets. These returns include dimensions beyond the explicit interest rate paid on the assets. Non-pecuniary returns are particularly relevant for the reserves, i.e., the base money, held by banks. Allocations to reserves in excess of re-quirements depend on the returns expected from such reserves in comparison to their costs. The costs are opportunity costs, the returns sacrificed by smaller allocations to income yielding assets. The returns associated with holding reserves in excess of requirements consist of the saving in transaction costs made possible by reserve holding.

Banks are confronted daily with net inflows and net outflows of reserves resulting from their transactions with customers and other banks. In the absence of sufficient reserves, a bank would have to adjust its portfolio to finance the net flows of reserves, thereby incurring transaction costs. Reserve holding, as a substitute for such transactions, contributes to the bank's net revenues.

Institutional arrangements affect the costs and returns and thus the allocation to reserves. In the U.S. the transaction costs most relevant for a bank's holding of reserves are for Federal funds and advances from the Federal Reserve banks. These transactions are made at comparatively low cost.[1] The existence of markets with low transaction costs lowers the return to holding reserves and reduces the average magnitude at any level of opportunity cost. In the U.K., the central bank acted for many years as "lender of first resort," supplying any reserve demands at a posted rate. The banks' conviction that they could rely on a "lender of first resort" at low cost reduced the return on reserves relative to their costs. Reserve holding in excess of requirements became negligible.

Some economists advocate "free" banking, a system in which private banks produce money and there is no central bank authorized to produce money. The role of the central bank as lender of last resort either disappears or shifts to the private banks. Private banks cannot supply unlimited quantities of base money without calling into question the solvency of the bank. To function as lender of last resort, private banks must hold reserves in gold, other commodities, or perhaps foreign exchange. A large run on the banks, a large shift in the public's demand for a relatively safe asset such as gold, can exhaust the stock of reserves.

---

1. Failure of the Federal Reserve to function as lender of last resort from 1931 to 1933 substantially increased these costs.

Uncertainty is increased. Since society must allocate a larger part of its wealth to reserves (gold), the capital stock is smaller. Increased uncertainty raises the required return to capital and lowers the stock of capital, also. Per capita income is lower. A central bank acting as lender of last resort reduces the resource costs and lowers the uncertainty of providing the function of lender of last resort.[1]

Earlier, we discussed differences in the banks' adjustment to transitory and permanent changes in reserves or base money. These adjustments depend on financial arrangements. Markets such as the Federal funds market in the U.S. reduce the cost of bearing uncertainty by lowering transaction costs. A bank that receives an increase in reserves that is presumed to be transitory can lend by selling the reserves in the Federal funds market; a bank can offset a reduction in reserves by a purchase of Federal funds. The organization of a market and the reduced cost of bearing uncertainty permit banks to hold lower reserves, lowering their costs of operation.

The adjustment of reserve positions to transitory changes by buying and selling Federal funds (or by borrowing or repaying loans at the central bank) has negligible effects on the interest rates and asset prices relevant for household and business decisions. A perceived permanent change in the monetary base initiates very different responses and has different costs. The banks' balance sheet adjustments involve all portfolio items. The responses by the banks change the money stock, affect interest rates on a variety of assets and the prices of real assets. The public responds to changing relative costs and returns between loan liabilities and real assets. The adjustment to a perceived permanent change is reinforced by changes in price expectations or adjustments of the current expected return to capital whenever permanent increases in the base are sufficiently large or persistent.

Uncertainty, costs of information and transaction costs also

1. The existence of a central bank may raise other costs, particularly costs of inflation or deflation and costs arising from variable monetary policy. A credible monetary rule that reduces these costs is discussed in Lecture 4. The lender of last resort should lend at a penalty rate.

clarify the discussion of "loan rationing." Banks face considerable uncertainty about the potential losses on particular loans. The net return on loans falls below the posted loan rate by the cost of expected losses and the costs of acquiring the information required to control the losses.

Consider the position of a loan office facing a range of potential customers. The loan office experiences a continual arrival of loan applications. Applications are widely dispersed in terms of the information and transaction costs required to reach a judgment about the characteristics of the borrower and the risk of the loan. Applications with sufficiently uncertain repayment or substantial transaction costs are rejected. Their net return is too uncertain relative to the risk-return position that the bank chooses. Applications with potentially resolvable uncertainty upon sufficient investment in information may be rejected also, if the required information cost would lower the expected net return below some relevant opportunity cost. Banks accept applications with expected net returns at least as high as the marginal benchmark set by opportunity cost.

The customers whose applications are rejected are often described as "rationed out" at the posted loan rate. The process is not very different from the behavior of a customer buying a second hand car. The relevant price includes more than the price charged for the car. The buyer pays transactions costs (visiting car lots), and incurs costs of information to learn about the state of the car. He accepts some unavoidable uncertainty about the quality of the car. His decision depends on the total effective price. Many cars are "rationed out" in the decision process to control transaction and information costs.

"Loan rationing" is occasionally singled out as a main feature of the monetary mechanism. Observations showing comparatively small changes in real rates of interest and loan rates are taken as evidence that these changes are too small to induce the relatively large portfolio changes observed during business cycles.[1]

1. BRUCE C. GREENWALD and JOSEPH E. STIGLITZ, 'Imperfect Information, Credit Markets and Unemployment', Working Paper n. 2093, National Bureau of Economic Research, 1986; BRUCE C. GREENWALD and JOSEPH E. STIGLITZ, 'Money, Imperfect Information and Economic Fluctuations', Working Paper n. 2188, National Bureau

Loan rationing or credit rationing is used to reconcile the observations on interest rates and portfolio adjustments.

Observations on real loan rates are not equivalent to changes in the effective real return to loans. Costs of default are not constant cyclically, and the expected value of repayments varies. The *net* loan rate, on which banks' decisions depend, most likely varies much more than the posted loan rate.

Frost studied bank behavior in the middle 1930s.[1] He found that a comparison of posted loan rates and the interest rate on bonds fails to explain the shift in the banks' allocation from short- to long-term securities. Frost introduced measures of transaction and information costs. He found that the difference between the posted and net loan rates increased, and the return to securities rose relative to the net loan rate. Banks invested in long-term securities and shifted portfolios away from loans in response to the (properly measured) relative price change.

The inference made by Greenwald and Stiglitz seems to us unwarranted.[2] Comparatively small changes in real interest rates offer little evidence to support the proposition that the substitution process is partly suspended. The Greenwald-Stiglitz argument appears to rely on the borrowing cost interpretation of interest rates, common in Keynesian analysis. They neglect costs of information and the role of relative prices in the asset substitution process.

iii) *Monetary Control*

Our discussion of uncertainty and costs incurred in acquiring information is applicable to central banks and the problem of monetary control. Issues arise about the credibility of monetary policy. Policymakers, no less than the public, face the problem of distinguishing between permanent and transitory changes and

---

of Economic Research, 1987; JOSEPH E. STIGLITZ and ANDREW WEISS, 'Macroeconomic Equilibrium and Credit Rationing', Working Paper n. 2164, National Bureau of Economic Research, 1987.

1. PETER J. FROST, 'Banks' Demand for Excess Reserves', UCLA Dissertation, 1966, *id.*, 'Banks' Demand for Excess Reserves', *Journal of Political Economy*, 78, 1971, pp. 805-825.

2. BRUCE C. GREENWALD and JOSEPH E. STIGLITZ, 1986, *op. cit.*

between shocks to aggregate demand and shocks to aggregate supply.

The distinction between permanent and transitory changes has implications for monetary control policy. A policy of controlling base money and allowing interest rates to adjust increases the variability of interest rates beyond the effect of other shocks, if there are errors in monetary control. Some errors are unavoidable in a world of uncertainty. In an *IS-LM* model, with a single interest rate, the variability of "the" interest rate rises under a policy of monetary control. In our analysis, if the policy of monetary control is credible, control errors are perceived as transitory deviations, so they are absorbed by changes in interest rates at the shortest end of the yield curve. Control errors produce temporary monetary shocks and variability at the short-end but not for the yield curve as a whole. The absorption of the temporary monetary shocks occurs both within the banking system and also as a temporary adjustment of the public's money balances.

The consequences differ, of course, if monetary control policies lack sufficient credibility. Control errors, particularly those exhibiting serial correlation, are interpreted partly as permanent changes. Thus, the control procedure contributes to the variability of yields on a variety of assets.

Experience in the United States from 1979 to 1982 is an example of the increase in uncertainty that can result from inappropriate control procedures and operations that lack credibility. The Federal Reserve chose an inefficient tactical procedure for the control of monetary growth – control of non-borrowed reserves. The variability of interest rates at all maturities rose following the shift to the new policy. The increased variability of interest rates contributed to a shift in the term structure of interest rates and raised the level of interest rates.[1] The evidence suggests that the social cost of bearing increased uncertainty was not negligible; interest rates on long-term maturities rose by more

---

[1]. A. MASCARO and ALLAN H. MELTZER, 'Long- and Short-Term Interest Rates in an Uncertain World', *Journal of Monetary Economics*, 12, November 1983, pp. 485-518.

than one half percentage point to compensate for the increased variability.

The use of interest rate targets to implement monetary policy imposes costs also. Policymakers, like the public, have less than full information about the future paths of inflation, output, employment and other variables of interest. They cannot reliably infer the interest rate that maintains price stability or that reduces the variability of output and prices to the minimum level inherent in nature and institutional arrangements. Their inferences about the structure of shocks are uncertain and shifting, like the inferences drawn by the public. They make both types of errors, mistaking permanent shocks for transitory changes and transitory shocks for permanent changes. These errors and misperceptions impart uncertainty to money growth and increase uncertainty about the price level and the short-run course of output.

3. IS-LM and Beyond

The *IS-LM* model, introduced in Hicks,[1] continues to be widely used in macroeconomics. It remains the preferred model for textbooks. Leading Keynesians continue to use it in their analysis.[2] The reason is not hard to find. *IS-LM* is a relatively simple model of the stock-flow interaction that is central to modern macroeconomics. Although early versions neglected prices and inflation, this deficiency was removed by introducing the Phillips curve.[3] The addition did not require any major change in the core relations representing the markets for assets and output.

This section discusses some of the main problems we find in the *IS-LM* analysis as a model of asset markets. Many of these problems reflect, in different ways, the narrow range of substitution permitted by the model. We then present an extended model with a richer menu of assets. Our discussion of both models considers a closed economy with no growth.

i) *Problems With IS-LM*

The standard *IS-LM* model consists of two equations, the equilibrium relations for the asset and output markets

$$IS: y = f(i, M/p, \ldots)$$
$$LM: M/p = \lambda(i, y, \ldots)$$

where y, i, and M/p are, respectively, output or income, the rate of interest and the stock of real balances. M is a predetermined or given, and p is either given or obtained from the Phillips

---

1. John Richard Hicks, 'Mr. Keynes and the "Classics": A Suggested Interpretation', *Econometrica*, 5, April 1937, pp. 147-159.

2. Franco Modigliani and Lucas D. Papademos, 'The Structures of Financial Markets and the Monetary Mechanism', *Controlling Monetary Aggregate, III, Conference Series*, n. 23, Federal Reserve Bank of Boston, 1980, pp. 111-155; Stanley Fischer, '1944, 1963 and 1985 Modiglianiesque Macro Models', Working Paper, n. 1797, National Bureau of Economic Research, 1986; James Tobin, 'A New Consensus on the Management of the Economy by Fiscal and Monetary Policies', *The Committee on Developing American Capitalism*, 4, 2, 1986, pp. 1-6; *id.* and Willem H. Buiter, 'Long-run Effects of Fiscal and Monetary Policy on Aggregate Demand', in Jerome Stein, ed., *Monetarism*, Amsterdam: North-Holland, 1976.

3. Lecture 1 briefly discusses the evolution of the Phillips curve.

curve.[1] Other variables, represented by the dots, may be included.

The two equations are open to different interpretations. In standard Keynesian theory, the *IS* and *LM* equations are equilibrium conditions for the output and money markets. The right side expressions describe structural demand functions and the left supplies. The left side of the output market equation follows from a characteristic view underlying Keynesian analysis; the supply quantity of output always equals the demand quantity. The equations are also used as partial reduced forms obtained from a more comprehensive system of markets with many assets and components of output. Econometric models use this procedure, but it is used also in Tobin and Buiter,[2] where a model with money, bonds and capital is reduced to *IS-LM* equations. The dots in the *IS-LM* equations represent other variables in the system, for example bonds.

Any system of $n > 2$ equations involving an interest rate and output can be reduced to two equations in the two variables. The reduction can be made in such a way that one of the two relations reflects underlying expenditure patterns and the other reflects portfolio behavior or the asset market. The equations may also reflect other components of a more complex system, e.g., the equilibrium condition for labor demand and the production function. *IS-LM* analysis derived in this manner differs substantially from the standard Keynesian framework. The aggregate demand function for output and the demand for money exhibit very different properties in the two cases. The functions in the partially reduced system contain all the exogenous or predetermined variables appearing in the equations which have been solved out. In our interpretation, the equations are structural relations, so the error terms in these equations represent shocks to the demands for money and output. On the

---

1. Let $\Delta p/p$ be the inflation rate. Then, $p_t = p_{t-1} + \Delta p$. Note that this framework does not distinguish between the maintained rate of inflation and the current rate of price change. Permanent shocks to the price level are not distinguished from maintained changes in inflation. This was the source of much confusion in the discussion of inflation and its causes.

2. JAMES TOBIN and WILLEM H. BUITER, 1976, *op. cit.*

alternative interpretation it is incorrect to interpret the random residual of the partially reduced equations as such demand shocks. It is misleading, in our judgment, to discuss the two interpretations under a single label. The two have very different implications for the monetary mechanism. We confine the term *IS-LM* to the structural use still prevalent in textbooks and journals.

We concentrate on the asset markets. Two distinct interpretations of the *LM* equation are found. The first treats money as a substitute for bonds only, or financial assets only. The second treats a broader range of substitution; money substitutes for a full range of financial and real assets, but financial and real assets are perfect substitutes in portfolios.

If money is a substitute for bonds only, the single interest rate in the *IS-LM* model is the market rate of interest on financial assets. The financial rate is the main link between money and the output market. Stock-flow interaction depends on the effect of money on the market rate and the effect of the market rate on investment or total spending.

Familiar results follow. The smaller (numerically) the interest elasticity of aggregate demand and the smaller (algebraically) the interest elasticity of the demand for money, the smaller is the responsiveness of output to monetary policy. Convergence of the interest elasticity of the demand for money to minus infinity implies that the responsiveness of output to monetary shocks converges to zero.

The sensitivity of the monetary mechanism to the system's interest elasticities contrasts with the effectiveness of fiscal policy. Fiscal policy operates directly on income by shifting the *IS* line. The analysis seemed to justify a contrast between the less certain, indirect effects of monetary policy and the more reliable, direct effects of fiscal policy found in early Keynesian discussions.

Concerns about the weak, indirect effects of monetary policy were reinforced in the early postwar period by a special interpretation of the effect of interest rates. The interest rate was interpreted as the cost payable by borrowers contemplating investment projects. Examination of expenditure categories in the national income accounts suggested that the relative significance of borrowing costs was generally trivial with the exception of a small range of investment projects. Studies such as Henderson found that businessmen did not give much attention to borrowing costs.[1] A consensus developed that the interest elasticity of aggregate demand is numerically negligible, and the *IS* line relatively steep. Consequently, stabilization policy had to rely mainly on fiscal policy, with monetary policy reduced to a passive policy of interest rate targeting to keep borrowing costs low.[2]

The consensus changed by the late 1950s. Although fiscal policy remained the preferred instrument for purposes of economic stabilization, the rationale differed. Gone was the emphasis on the low or irrelevant interest elasticity of the demand for output. The slope of the line seems to have changed. Monetary policy could significantly influence output and employment. The problem was now too much, rather than too little, effect with most of the effect concentrated on a small segment of the economy, particularly the housing sector, where borrowing and borrowing costs have a large influence on the timing of purchases. Now it was political and social considerations that limited the use of monetary policy to the passive role of maintaining an interest rate target.[3]

The second interpretation of *LM* recognizes that money substitutes over the whole spectrum of assets. *IS-LM* analysis cannot treat more than two assets, so a composite good theorem is used to compress financial and real assets into a composite asset. Two different interpretations appear in this context. One is a literal interpretation. The other restricts the range of application to circumstances in which the theorem applies.

Sargent gives a literal interpretation; bonds and real capital

---

1. HUBERT D. HENDERSON, 'The Significance of the Rate of Interest', *Oxford Economic Papers*, 1, October 1938.

2. Lecture 1 discusses the summaries of this literature by HENRY VILLARD, 'Monetary Theory', in H. S. ELLIS, ed., *A Survey of Contemporary Economics*, Philadelphia: Blakiston for the American Economic Association, 1948, pp. 314-351, and others. We note in passing a peculiarity in the Keynesian position of the early postwar period. The emphasis on low interest rates could not be justified in terms of their analysis. High interest rates would have little relevant effect on aggregate real demand, output and employment.

3. By the 1980s, the interpretation had changed again, see JAMES TOBIN 1986, *op. cit.* Borrowing costs no longer receive emphasis.

have identical rates of return.[1] This interpretation relies on the operation of a financial market to keep the real returns identical. The interpretation has several problems.

First, the relevance of the model and the operation of the monetary mechanism become totally dependent on the existence of active financial markets. Evidence does not support this conclusion. A short-run relation between money and income and a long-run relation between money and prices was observed, and continues to be found, where financial markets are primitive or non-existent.

Second, transactions costs and costs of information delay portfolio adjustments. Even where markets equalize real returns, all holders do not adjust their portfolios at the same time. Some wealthowners adjust promptly to changes in expected return or expected inflation, but others adjust slowly. Slow adjustment affects the timing or responses to policy and other changes and, therefore, affects the timing of the responses of output and prices.

Third, in an uncertain world, the perceived risk of particular assets changes, and the relative returns change. Constant risk distributions may be a useful assumption for some analytic purposes but, particularly in periods with large disturbances, the relative risk distributions change. Assuming that the risk distributions for all real and financial assets are always and everywhere identical is rejected by observations.

Fourth, the results of modern portfolio analysis do not support the literal composite good interpretation. Observable market behavior suggests that financial assets and real assets are not perfect substitutes. Risk premiums differ. In the language of the capital asset pricing models, the β coefficients measuring characteristics of individual assets are not identical, and the differences are not constant.

If the composite good theorem is interpreted as a constraint on the range of application, bonds and capital are not always perfect substitutes. The *IS-LM* analysis applies to periods with negligible changes in the returns to bonds and real assets relative to the variations (e.g., large inflation) to be explained. This in-

1. THOMAS J. SARGENT, *Macroeconomic Theory*, New York: Academic Press, 1979.

terpretation rescues the hypothesis from empirical rejection at the cost of restricting the realm of application, perhaps, to steady states.

Both interpretations of the composite good theorem exclude analysis of main aspects of financial markets and of portfolio allocation affecting the relation of money to output and prices. Also excluded are issues relevant to the analysis of monetary policy.

The *IS-LM* model has no markets for credit or loans, so claims about the significance of credit or bank loan rationing cannot be examined within the (structural) *IS-LM* framework. All shocks affecting credit markets are treated as shocks to the demand for money. An analysis that includes a separate credit market shows the two sets of shocks have different consequences. Similarly, "reverse causation" from output to loan demand and the credit market must be treated as a shift in the demand for money. Issues about intermediation and disintermediation, including their effect on the transmission of monetary and real impulses, are outside the realm of *IS-LM* analysis. Issues posed by deregulation cannot be analyzed in the *IS-LM* model. Its advocates must retreat to ad hoc constructions.

Analysis of monetary policy in the *IS-LM* framework is deficient. A single interest rate fails to represent the problem confronting central banks and may encourage the belief that monetary policy can control interest rates. In countries with developed financial markets, central banks face a spectrum of interest rates with a specific but shifting structure. The bank can control, at most, a small number of short term rates. A shifting mixture of permanent and transitory shocks and real and nominal shocks changes the relation between rates for different maturities and on real and financial assets. These changes are simply beyond understanding in an *IS-LM* framework.

ii) *Beyond IS-LM*

To extend the range of substitution, we introduce a market for bonds or a credit market. There are now three assets, base money, government debt and real capital. These assets permit wealthowners to substitute between money – a nominal asset that provides return mainly in the form of services – bonds – a nominal asset with a fixed nominal return – and real capital or claims to the ownership of real capital. By assumption the three assets are less than perfect substitutes in portfolios. Money differs from bonds and capital because of the services it provides in a world of uncertainty. Bonds and capital are subject to different risk distributions.

The public may hold assets directly or exchange securities for claims on banks and financial institutions. They can borrow from financial institutions. Banks set the services and the interest rate offered on their liabilities in response to market conditions. Each distinct liability offered by financial institutions has a separate rate set by the financial institution in response to market conditions.[1] Here, we are interested in an analysis of the role of financial markets in the money supply process, so we concentrate on the credit and money markets.[2]

Table 2-1 shows the credit and money market equilibrium conditions. The public's supply of earning assets to banks, σ, has two components. One is the desired stock of loan liabilities, and the other is the implicit supply of government securities to banks. The latter consists of the excess stock of securities not (voluntarily) absorbed in the public's portfolios at prevailing market conditions. $\sigma = L + S - \delta$, where L is the desired liability stock, S the existing stock of government securities, and δ is the public's demand for securities. The only argument requiring explanation is the negative effect of P on σ. An increase in P (with pe measuring expected nominal income on real assets, unchanged) lowers the cost of equity financing and lowers the public's supply of earning assets to banks.[3]

---

1. This assumption permits us to analyze a system with many intermediaries within the framework developed here. In previous work, summarized in KARL BRUNNER and ALLAN H. MELTZER, 'Money Supply', in BENJAMIN FRIEDMAN and FRANK H. HAHN, eds., *Handbook of Monetary Economics*, Amsterdam: North-Holland, 1990, we show that the model with base money, government debt and real capital can be expanded to include banks and other financial intermediaries without altering the structure of the model.

2. The market for real capital is deleted using the balance sheet equation.

3. The credit market equation can be reformulated as an equilibrium condition for the bond market without any intermediation. See BRUNNER and MELTZER, 1990, *op. cit.*, for the correspondence between the two procedures. The credit market equation introduces a composite goods assumption. This can be relaxed without changing the major results.

Table 2-1. The Asset Markets

The credit market

$$a(i, P, \ldots) B = \sigma (i - \pi, p, ap, P, w^h, w^n, e, S)$$
$$ + \quad - \quad + \ + \quad - \qquad +$$

The money market

$$m(i, P, \ldots) B = \lambda (i, p, P, ap, w^h, w^n, e,)$$
$$ + \ - \qquad - \ + \ + \quad - \quad + \quad + \ -$$

i = nominal rate of interest
P = price of real assets
p = price level of output
ap = the anticipated price level
B = monetary base
e = expected real return on real assets
π = expected rate of inflation
w^h = human wealth
w^n = non-human wealth
S = stock of government securities

The banks' demand for earning assets, or absorption of assets supplied by the public, is the product of the monetary base, B, and an asset multiplier, a. This multiplier depends on market conditions expressed by an interest rate, the asset price level and on other arguments, omitted here, representing institutional restrictions such as reserve requirement ratios, the discount rate and other details.[1]

The money market juxtaposes the demand for money with

---

1. The influence of the market conditions is mediated by some allocation patterns expressing the public's and the banks' behavior. The allocation of the public's money balances between currency and transaction accounts or total deposits between transaction and non-transaction accounts depends, apart from market conditions, on the banks' supply conditions of liabilities and the relative costs of using or holding currency and transaction accounts. The banks' behavior is reflected by the allocation of total assets between reserves and earning assets and the choice of interest rates and other terms on liabilities.

the money stock. The demand for money is a function of the interest rate i, the price level of output p, the anticipated price level, ap, the asset price level P, human wealth w^h, non-human wealth w^n, and the expected real return on real assets e. The terms ap and π in the σ and λ functions distinguish one-time price changes from maintained rates of change. The money stock is the product of a monetary multiplier, m, and the monetary base. The monetary multiplier depends, as does the asset multiplier, on the public's and the banks' behavior expressed by allocation ratios for currency, non-transaction accounts and reserves relative to bank deposits. The responses of the money and credit multipliers to the allocation ratios differ. Hence, changes in the composition of deposits or in the public's demand for currency change money and credit in different ways. It should be noted that the properties of the σ and λ functions differ; in particular wealth exerts little effect on σ compared to λ. This follows from offsetting effects of wealth on the components of σ.

iii) *Asset Market Responses*

The interaction on the asset markets in response to the authorities' supply of base money, B, and the stock of government securities, S, given the predetermined variables e, p, w^h and w^n, determines the interest rate i and the asset price level P. Responses of P and i to B, S, and e are shown as elasticities in Table 2-2. These elasticities are general equilibrium responses for the asset markets, holding the output market variables constant. Their components are the (partial) elasticities of the excess supplies of credit and money, defined in Table 2-2.

The general equilibrium responses of i and P to a change in the base depend on the interest elasticities and asset price elasticities of the credit and money markets. The response of the interest rate, for example, appears as the reciprocal of the average interest elasticities of excess supplies on the asset markets with weights determined by the relative asset price elasticities. It is obvious that larger interest elasticities on both asset markets (larger values of $\varepsilon(CM, i)$ and $\varepsilon(MM, i)$) increase the denominator Δ, and lower the responsiveness of interest rates to monet-

Table 2-2

Some Responses on the Asset Markets

Responses to B

$$\varepsilon(i, B|AM) = \frac{-\varepsilon(MM, P) + \varepsilon(CM, P)}{\Delta} < 0$$

$$\varepsilon(P, B|AM) = \frac{\varepsilon(MM, i) - \varepsilon(CM, i)}{\Delta} > 0$$

Responses to S

$$\varepsilon(i, S|AM) = \frac{\varepsilon(MM, P) \cdot \varepsilon(\sigma, S)}{\Delta} > 0$$

$$\varepsilon(P, S|AM) = \frac{-\varepsilon(MM, i) \cdot \varepsilon(\sigma, S)}{\Delta} > 0$$

Responses to the expected real return on real assets, e

$$\varepsilon(i, e|AM) = \frac{\varepsilon(\sigma, e) \cdot \varepsilon(MM, P) - \varepsilon(\lambda, e) \cdot \varepsilon(CM, P)}{\Delta}$$

$$\varepsilon(P, e|AM) = \frac{\varepsilon(\lambda, e) \cdot \varepsilon(CM, i) - \varepsilon(\sigma, e) \cdot \varepsilon(MM, i)}{\Delta} > 0$$

where

$$\Delta = \varepsilon(CM, i) \cdot \varepsilon(MM, P) - \varepsilon(MM, i) \cdot \varepsilon(CM, P) < 0$$

Notation:

$\varepsilon(\sigma, x)$ and $\varepsilon(\lambda, x) =$ partial elasticity of σ and λ with respect to x.

$\varepsilon(y, x|AM) =$ elasticity of y with respect to x for the general equilibrium of the asset markets, holding output and prices constant

$\varepsilon(CM, i) =$ interest elasticity of excess supply of bank credit, defined by $\varepsilon(a, i) - \varepsilon(\sigma, i) > 0$

$\varepsilon(MM, i) =$ interest elasticity of excess supply of money defined by $\varepsilon(m, i) - \varepsilon(\lambda, i) > 0$

$\varepsilon(CM, P) =$ asset price elasticity of excess supply of bank credit defined by $\varepsilon(a, P) - \varepsilon(\lambda, P) > 0$

$\varepsilon(MM, P) =$ asset price elasticity of excess supply of money defined by $\varepsilon(m, P) - \varepsilon(\lambda, P) < 0$

Responses of P and B under fixed interest rate targeting

$$\varepsilon(P, u|AM) = \frac{\varepsilon(\lambda, u)}{\varepsilon(MM, P) - \varepsilon(CM, P)} < 0$$

$$\varepsilon(B, u|AM) = \frac{-\varepsilon(\lambda, u) \cdot \varepsilon(CM, P)}{\varepsilon(MM, P) - \varepsilon(CM, P)} > 0$$

$u =$ random shock to the demand for money

---

ary policy. The lower response means that any given change in interest rates is associated with larger adjustments in portfolios. A low response of interest rates to the base does not imply, however, suspension of the substitution mechanism. The reason is that the market rate is not the only channel of substitution. Changes in the base also affect P. The responsiveness of the asset price level, P, to changes in the monetary base, $\varepsilon(P, B|AM)$, depends on the relative size of the interest elasticities on the credit and money markets. The elasticity is positive provided the interest elasticity of the credit market exceeds the corresponding elasticity of the money market; $\varepsilon(CM, i) > \varepsilon(MM, i)$. Note that the order condition matters irrespective of the magnitude of the interest elasticity of the demand for money.

Two implications of these response patterns show that the responses of interest rates differ from the responses obtained from the *IS-LM* model. We note, first, the impossibility of a general liquidity trap. In the usual case, a liquidity trap occurs if the interest elasticity of the demand for money $\varepsilon(\lambda, i)$ converges to minus infinity. The *IS-LM* framework implies that the response to all monetary impulses converges to zero in this case. This is not true in our extended analysis. The reason is that we cannot assume convergence of $\varepsilon(MM, i)$ to minus infinity without a similar convergence of $\varepsilon(CM, i)$ to plus infinity. The demand for money cannot wax supersensitive to changes in interest rates without the demand for other financial assets mirroring this pattern. This result follows from the wealth identity once we accept that money and (non-money) financial assets are closer substitutes in portfolios than money and real assets. From Table 2-2, we see that if $\varepsilon(CM, i)$ and $\varepsilon(MM, i)$ converge simultaneously to their respective limits, the response of i vanishes in the limit, but the response of P to the monetary base remains unchanged. One of the channels of transmission remains open.[1] The change in P carries the impulse, the change in the base, from the asset market to the output market.

Second, the *IS-LM* framework implies that the economy can

---

1. This conclusion bears on the claim in GREENWALD and STIGLITZ, 1986, *op. cit.* discussed above. Low variability of i can be associated with substantial responsiveness of P.

be effectively screened against random shocks to the demand for money by reliance on an interest targeting policy. This result does not extend to our analysis. Let u be a random shock to the demand for money. Table 2-2 shows that $\varepsilon(P, u|AM)$ is negative; positive shocks to the demand for money lower P and induce substitution from new production toward ownership of existing capital. Since interest rates are controlled, the monetary base increases; $\varepsilon(B, u|AM) > 0$.

Earlier, we noted that transitory changes in money mainly affect returns to short-term assets. The public and the banks absorb the transitory change. Let q be the adjustment of the demand for money in response to perceived transitory changes; q is an endogenous variable that depends on B.

$$\varepsilon(q, B|AM) = \frac{1}{\varepsilon(\lambda, q)} > 0,$$

and

$$\varepsilon(i, B|AM) = \frac{-1}{\varepsilon(CM, i)} < 0$$

If the demand for money absorbs the change in the base, the asset price level, reflecting a longer horizon, remains unchanged. The interest rate (on short-term assets) adjusts to the temporary change.

The asset market analysis provides a framework for the analysis of the money supply process. The reactions of money stock, M, and bank credit, E, to open market operations combine the responses to the base and the stock of debt from Table 2-2.

$$\frac{dM}{M} = \underset{+ \quad - \quad - \quad +}{[\varepsilon(m, i)\,\varepsilon(i) + \varepsilon(m, P)\,\varepsilon(P) + 1]} \frac{dB}{B}$$

$$\frac{dE}{E} = \underset{+ \quad - \quad + \quad +}{[\varepsilon(a, i)\,\varepsilon(i) + \varepsilon(a, P)\,\varepsilon(P) + 1]} \frac{dB}{B}$$

where

$$\varepsilon(i) = \underset{-}{\varepsilon(i, B|AM)} - \underset{+}{\varepsilon(i, S|AM)} \frac{B}{S} < 0$$

$$\varepsilon(P) = \underset{+}{\varepsilon(P, B|AM)} - \underset{+}{\varepsilon(P, S|AM)} \frac{B}{S} > 0.$$

$$\varepsilon(P, S|AM) < \varepsilon(P, B|AM).$$

An open market operation involves an exchange of base money for securities. Both M and E rise or fall in proportion to the rate of change of the base, but the proportions differ. Growth of the base raises M relative to E. The difference, at least for the U.S., is relatively small. The difference between a response to a change in the base unaccompanied by an opposite change in S and to an open market operation is relatively small also.

Observations for many countries show that stocks of credit and bank liabilities have grown relative to the money stock. The responses of M and E to the base and to open market operations imply that the observed secular differences in relative growth rates are not a result of monetary policy. The main force at work is the growth of the asset multiplier, a, relative to the growth of the money multiplier m.[1] Growth of time deposits (and other non-transaction liabilities) is a principal reason. This is shown by noting that the difference between the stocks of money and bank credit,

$$E - M = T + N - B,$$

increases with non-transaction liabilities, T, and banks' net worth, N, and declines as the base increases.

Table 2-2 shows that real shocks to the expected return to capital, e, disturb the credit and money markets also. Increases in productivity that raise the expected return to capital raise the prices of existing capital; $\varepsilon(P, e|AM) > 0$. The increase in P stimulates production of capital goods and, therefore, increases aggregate demand. The response reinforces the direct effect of the increase in e on output.

---

1. In countries with adjustable reserve requirement ratios, changes in these ratios are a policy tool. Our analysis separates policy operations from the behavior of the banks and the public. The latter are incorporated through the multipliers m and a. Adjustable reserve requirements can be treated as part of policy by an adjustment of the base and the multipliers. The adjustment of the base is achieved by incorporating the reserves liberated or absorbed by changes in reserve requirement ratios as part of the base. The adjusted ratio of reserves to deposits is then invariant with respect to changes in reserve requirement ratios. This isolates the effect of reserve requirement changes in the base and leaves the money multiplier independent of such changes. The adjustment does not completely isolate the asset multiplier from reserve requirement changes, however. See BRUNNER and MELTZER, 1990, *op. cit.*

4. Further Implications of the Money-Credit Model

Several issues about the relation of credit and money recur frequently in monetary economics. At times, credit is assigned a separate or independent role in the transmission of monetary or real changes. Or, credit may have a supplementary role, modifying or magnifying the response to money. Dependence of the money stock on output – so-called reverse causation – is a perennial issue. Discussion of these and related topics involving credit and money market interaction is the subject of this section.

i) An Independent Credit Market Effect?

Credit market responses include portfolio adjustments by the banks between loans, securities and reserve accounts and adjustments by the public, between direct ownership of securities, or real capital, money holding and borrowing from financial institutions. Intermediation and disintermediation are part of this process. Changes in the monetary base, the stock of securities, or the expected return to real capital are transmitted to the output market by changes in i and P that incorporate responses on the credit market.

Heightened uncertainty about the safety or soundness of the banking system simultaneously lowers the public's deposits, increases desired holdings of currency and government securities, and raises the banks' desired reserve ratio. Asset markets respond to these portfolio adjustments by reducing bank credit and money. The process of disintermediation, supplemented by any decline in the banks' net worth in the event of failures, lowers bank credit relative to the money stock. Asset prices fall inducing a decline in real aggregate demand and a fall in the price level. The deflation following the widespread failures of U.S. banks in the 1930s is a dramatic example of this process in operation.

Our analysis makes credit market responses an integral part of the asset market adjustment. There are no credit market effects independent of monetary effects. The issue of whether credit or money matters for output or asset prices has no meaning. This does not mean that we cannot develop an analysis with separate stocks of money and credit. Such analysis would be useless for analyzing financial systems like our own where money and credit are interrelated.

Bernanke concludes that non-monetary financial shocks operated as an independent force in the depression of the 1930s.[1] In our analysis of credit and money, the only shock from the banking system that operates on the bank credit multiplier but not the money multiplier is a shock to the banks' net worth, or the ratio of net worth to bank liabilities. A decline in N reduces bank credit. An autonomous shock to net worth would reduce bank credit and, through the money supply process, induce a decline in money. An autonomous decline in net worth is not an appealing starting place, and it does not fit the broad facts of the 1929-33 decline in the U.S.

A shock to the financial system that is not simultaneously a shock to the demand for money or the stock of money is hard to conceive. An isolated, permanent shock to σ, independent of a shock to the demand for money, requires an opposite shock to the demand for real capital to maintain the balance sheet constraint. A shock of this kind must be independent of any changes in the expected return to capital, e, since e affects the demand for money.

Suppose a shock to σ and K occurs. A shift in demand from real assets to governmental securities lowers interest rates and the prices of real assets. The two asset market responses tend to offset each other's effect on aggregate demand and output. An alternative credit market shock would simultaneously raise (or lower) the public's desired stock of liabilities (loans) to the banks and the desired stock of real assets. Interest rate and asset price both rise; again there are offsetting effects on aggregate demand and output.

Another meaning of credit shock may involve the imposition of constraints on banks' loan portfolios. Banks may be required to hold a security reserve in excess of their desired portfolio or to reduce the size of their loan portfolio. The analysis of this problem requires a disaggregation of the credit market into a loan and a securities market.[1] The constraint imposes adjustments on the balance sheets of the public and the banks. The banks acquire securities from the public. The public reduces borrowing and sells securities. The volume of bank credit, E, and the money stock are affected only to the extent that banks raise their desired reserve ratio. This response is minimal in the presence of money markets with low transaction costs. The imposition of constraints on loans (or security reserves) may induce a temporary adjustment in the economy; a temporary decline in interest rates on governement securities, as banks acquire securities in place of loans, may increase the quantity of money demanded and temporarily reduce monetary velocity.[2] The lasting effects are allocative – the creation of a larger market for the placement of government securities in bank portfolios, and possible changes in relative rates of interest.

Benjamin Friedman proposed the use of a credit aggregate as a supplement or substitute for monetary aggregates in the monetary control process.[3] He claims that credit markets contain information about aggregate economic activity not provided by the money stock. His preferred credit aggregate is more inclusive than the stock of bank credit, but the same issues arise.

The evidence Friedman presents is inconclusive on the issue of whether there is additional information in the credit aggregate. Much of the evidence suggests that credit aggregates contain information that is similar to the information in monetary aggregates. Further, Friedman's estimates come from a period in which interest rates on many bank liabilities were held below market rates by interest rate ceilings. Interest rate controls increased intermediation and disintermediation during the 1960s and 1970s

1. KARL BRUNNER, 'The Money Supply Process in Open Economies with Interdependent Security Markets: The Case of Imperfect Substitutability', in MICHELE FRATIANNI and KARL TAVERNIER, eds., *Bank Credit, Money and Inflation in Open Economies*, supplement to *Kredit und Kapital*, 1976.

2. This seems to have occurred following the imposition of credit controls in the U.S. in 1980.

3. BENJAMIN M. FRIEDMAN, 'Monetary Policy with a Credit Aggregate Target', *Carnegie-Rochester Conference Series on Public Policy*, 18, Spring, 1983, pp. 117-148.

and, therefore, changed credit relative to money. In the absence of interest rate controls, some of these effects would be absent.

We do not deny the importance of the credit market in the transmission of shocks. Credit market processes, including loan rationing, are an integral part of monetary mechanisms in our analysis but omitted in the standard *IS-LM* analysis. The transmission of monetary impulses and the joint behavior of money stock and bank credit depend on credit market responses. Main propositions of our analysis depend on the condition $\varepsilon(CM, i) >$ $\varepsilon(MM, i)$, i.e., the dominance of interest elasticities of the credit market.

Friedman's thesis seems to refer more to the occurrence of credit market shocks. Some of the shocks, considered above (p. 91), may affect aggregate demand. We noted there that a shift in the public's supply of assets to banks due to a shift from real assets to securities has an indeterminate effect on aggregate demand.

An increase or decrease in risk would affect credit absolutely and relative to money. A sudden change in the quality of borrowers would lower the net loan rate received by banks. Changes in risk rarely occur as independent events; independent shocks to the risk distribution are, at most, transitory. Permanent changes in the quality of loans reflect monetary or real shocks. The credit market responses reinforce the impulses arising from monetary or real shocks, but they are not an independent source of disturbance.

An examination of the role of the credit market against the background of a banking and debt crisis extends our argument about the interactions between money and credit. We report a passage from a recent paper[1] which addresses Bernanke's analysis of financial crises.

Bernanke reconsiders the role of banking crises in the propagation of depressions. Such crises are immediately reflected by a run on banks expressed by an increase in the ratio of currency to deposits. In the money-credit market analysis, the rise in the currency ratio lowers both the volume of bank credit and the

---

1. KARL BRUNNER and ALLAN H. MELTZER, 1990, *op. cit.*

money stock. Bank credit responds with greater sensitivity than the money stock. The reason is that the asset multiplier, linking the monetary base with bank credit, responds more sensitively to variations in the currency ratio than does the monetary multiplier (linking the base with the money stock). The effects on the asset markets are transmitted to the output market. Bernanke emphasizes correctly that these adjustments lower the degree of financial intermediation. Transaction and information costs of financial operations increase. The network of credit shrinks, and aggregate real demand for output and monetary velocity decline.

This account is incomplete. The run on banks and the resulting banking crisis would be avoided if the monetary authorities function as "lender of last resort." Their failure to do so raises the marginal productivity of the banks' reserve position, further reducing asset and monetary multipliers. Bank credit and money stock suffer a further reduction with corresponding repercussions on the output market. An unchecked run produces, with some probability, bankruptcies and closures of banks. The probability of a run rises in the absence of a lender of last resort; the total demand for reserves exceeds the outstanding stock. Interest rates rise and asset prices fall, lowering asset values. The money stock and bank credit contract further. Initially, non-bank lenders may partially substitute, at rapidly rising marginal cost, for the decline in bank credit, but the net effect will be dominated by the decline in bank credit and disintermediation.

The financial crisis, revealed by bankruptcies and closures, has further consequences. It generates a large and pervasive uncertainty. This lowers the expected net real return on real assets. The decline in expected net real returns affects both asset and output markets. The adjustment imposed on asset markets and the interaction of asset and output markets reinforce the direct effect of bankruptcies and uncertainty on the output market.

This account of banking crises shows that their consequences depend on the working of a credit market and its interrelation with a money market. The credit market plays a major role in the conversion of the initial run on banks, via bankruptcies and

94

bank closures, into a major deflationary process and, with the failure of the lender of last resort, into a possible banking crisis.

A question of interpretation remains. Are runs on banks the result of a cyclic decline or a consequence of monetary retardation? A comparison between the United Kingdom and the United States is informative. This comparison suggests that the observed differences in the two countries depend on the central bank's commitment to act as a lender of last resort and on the nature of the banking structure. An understanding by the banks and the public that the central bank accepts such a commitment moderates fears and uncertainties and avoids the subsequent banking crisis. In the United Kingdom after 1866, the central bank functioned as lender of last resort. There were no banking crises.[1] There was no central bank in the United States before 1914. The Federal Reserve failed to honor the commitment to serve as a lender of last resort in 1930-1933. Further, the repetitive occurrence of banking crises in the United States suggests that crises may be conditioned by the magnitude and virulence of the downswing.

We conclude that runs on banks and banking crises are endogenous events, conditional on the monetary propagation mechanism. The relevant conditions include the operation of a central bank, the structure of the banking system and the magnitude of the recession. Philip Cagan's observation that banking crises typically occur late in the cycle and not at the beginning of the downswing offers some support for our conjecture.[2] It follows in the circumstances that monetary policy, understood as a choice of institutions characterizing central banks and banking, shapes the likelihood and the pattern of potential banking crises.

Bernanke introduces the debt crisis as a separate and independent phenomenon, in addition to the banking crisis. He presents an impressive array of facts revealing the depth and pervasive-

1. ANNA JACOBSON SCHWARTZ, 'Financial Stability and the Federal Safety Net', in WILLIAM S. HARAF and ROSE MARIE KUSHMEIDER, eds., *Restructuring Banking and Financial Services in America*, Washington: American Enterprise Institute, 1988.

2. PHILIP D. CAGAN, *Determinants and Effects of Change in the Stock of Money*, New York: Columbia University Press for the National Bureau of Economic Research, 1965.

ness of the debt crisis during the Great Depression. The transmission of the monetary retardation initiated in 1929, amplified by the banking crises appearing in the 1930s, lowered the price level of output and, even more, the price level of real assets. This massive deflation occurred in the context of an extensive network of private debt accumulated during the 1920s. The net worth position of households and business firms fell. Given the distribution of debtor positions, the deflationary process necessarily increased the number of bankruptcies, lowering the net worth of creditors and accelerating the debt crisis fostered by falling prices (and incomes). The risk premium on many assets rose, further reducing prices on real assets. The real value of default free debts rose. (Interest rates on risk-free securities declined due to an allocational shift from real assets to such securities.) These adjustments, unleashed on the asset markets, reinforced the direct effect of monetary contraction on the aggregate real demand for output.

Our discussion makes clear that we accept Bernanke's emphasis on the role of the debt crisis as an important component of the propagation mechanism. We do not accept Bernanke's analysis of the debt crisis as a separate and independent exogenous shock. Once the monetary authorities allow the emergence of a major deflation of asset and output price levels, in a system with many holders of nominally fixed debt, a debt crisis is an induced response to the deflation. A minor debt crisis occurred in the United States early in the 1980s mainly as a result of a lower, positive rate of inflation.

Bernanke draws an important policy conclusion from the destructive effects of the debt crisis. Since he views the debt crisis as an exogenous event, he argues for selective bailouts of bankrupt firms. We find this proposal ill-advised and unnecessary. It is ill-advised because it disregards the serious moral hazard associated with such a policy and the incentives it creates in the political process. It is unnecessary, we believe, because the debt crisis, like the banking crisis, is avoidable if the monetary authority prevents severe price deflation. By preventing deflation, the monetary authority prevents the destructive effect of the money-credit decline and the wave of bankruptcies. We conclude that banking crises and debt crises can be prevented with the aid of a suitable choice of monetary arrangements.

Our emphasis on credit market processes raises a question. Could we not just as well replace the money stock with bank credit in our analysis of inflation or of monetary effects on output? We believe that organizing the argument in terms of money stock and monetary velocity has definite advantages.

The close association of the money stock and bank credit is a consequence of modern development of the financial sector. The association would be suspended by adoption of a 100 percent reserve system or other institutional changes that separate lending from money creation. The characteristics of money as a medium of exchange and the responses of output and prices to money, do not depend on the association with credit. Money, not credit, is used as a general means of payment and settling debt. Credit cards require a monetary transfer to settle debt. The stock of money exerts a decisive influence on the price level and inflation irrespective of its association with credit. Credit and credit arrangements are not irrelevant. The existence of credit markets and their operations affect the level and movement of monetary velocity.

ii) *Reverse Causation*

Reverse causation is frequently offered as an alternative explanation of the observed correlation between money and income. Influences of income or expected income on the monetary base, under interest rate contro lor a fixed exchange rate system, are undeniable. We consider, first, reverse causation when the central bank controls the monetary base.

Income affects the asset markets by changing human wealth, the expected net return on real assets and the price level of output. Income also affects the values of k and t, the ratios of currency and non-transactions deposits to transactions deposits. These ratios are components of the money multiplier. The response of the money stock to income under a policy of controlling the monetary base is given by the effect of income, y, on the money multiplier. The response, is shown as $\varepsilon(M, y|AM)$. As before, the AM in the elasticity denotes that the response is a general equilibrium response on the asset market, given the output market position.

$$\overset{+}{\varepsilon(M,y|AM)} = \varepsilon(m,i)\ [\overset{+}{\varepsilon(i,w^h|AM)}\overset{+}{\varepsilon(w^h,y)} + \overset{+}{\varepsilon(i,e|AM)}$$

$$\cdot\ \overset{+}{\varepsilon(e,y)} + \overset{+}{\varepsilon(i,p|AM)}\cdot\overset{+}{\varepsilon(p,y)}] + \overset{-}{\varepsilon(m,P)}$$

$$\cdot\ \overset{+}{\varepsilon(P,w^h|AM)}\overset{+}{\varepsilon(w^h,y)} + \overset{+}{\varepsilon(P,e|AM)}\cdot\overset{+}{\varepsilon(e,y)}$$

$$+\ \overset{-}{\varepsilon(P,p|AM)}\cdot\overset{+}{\varepsilon(p,y)}] + \overset{-}{e(m,k)}\cdot\overset{+}{\varepsilon(k,y)} + \overset{-}{\varepsilon(m,t)}\cdot\overset{+}{\varepsilon(t,y)}$$

The total response has positive and negative terms. The size of some of the terms depends on the persistence of the shock to income. A transitory shock reduces the income elasticities of human wealth, w^h, the expected net return on real capital, e, and the output price, p, to a low level. When we combine this with the low values of $\varepsilon(m,i)$ and $\varepsilon(m,P)$ in the institutional context of the U.S., we obtain a negligible level of reverse causation. A perceived permanent income shock raises the w^h, e and p responses to higher levels and may produce a sufficiently positive response to offset the negative effect from t. The case for reverse causation receives little support.

Empirical evidence also is not supportive of reverse causation. If reverse causation dominated the money stock by changing the monetary multiplier, growth of the money stock would be correlated with movements in the multiplier. This is not the case. The monetary base dominates the long-term and medium-term movements of the money stock. Possible cyclical or shorter-run influences from income to money may remain.

If reverse causation operates, it must work mainly by changing the monetary base. Reverse causation depends in this case on specific institutional arrangements. A monetary strategy of interest targeting creates a dependence of the money stock (or monetary growth) on income (or income changes).[1]

---

1. The term "reverse causation" is misleading. Under interest rate control, there is a simultaneous endogenous determination of money stock, monetary base, income and other variables. Under a policy of controlling the monetary base, in contrast, there is a simultaneous determination of money stock, income, and other variables

iii) *Interaction with the Output Market*

The transmission of monetary impulses to the output market also differs from the process described by the *IS-LM* model. We now extend our analysis to include the market for output by introducing an aggregate demand function and a (price setting) supply function. These functions are shown in Table 2-3. Total effective labor cost, w, is held constant.[1]

The response of output to the base, recognizing the stock-flow interaction, appears as a linear combination of the responses of the interest rate and the asset price level. The weights, c_1 and c_2, depend on properties of the aggregate demand function for output and the feedback from the output market to the asset market. The latter are terms such as $\varepsilon(i, y|AM)$ or $\varepsilon(P, y|AM)$ in the denominator of the output market response. The response of output to the base is

$$\varepsilon(y, B|OM - AM) = c_1\varepsilon(i, B|AM) + c_2\varepsilon(P, B|AM) > 0.$$

The elasticity does not imply that real growth is proportional to growth of the monetary base. The initial reponse of output to money differs from the final response. Adjustment of wages and prices modify the initial response to (unanticipated) changes in the base. Fiscal policy and real impulses influence output also.

Further, the size of the response to the base depends on the interpretation of the monetary impulse. A perceived transitory change in the base has little effect. Our previous discussion showed that the general substitution process does not operate in this case; the effects of changing the base are concentrated on interest rates on short-term assets. A perceived permanent change also has no effect on output if prices and wages adjust flexibly. If everyone perceives a monetary change to be permanent, its effect on output occurs only to the extent that costs of renegotiating explicit or implicit contracts delay full adjustment. This aspect will be examined in Lecture 3.

in response to the base and all other shock conditions. Under both arrangements, monetary base and money stock remain highly correlated over the middle and long-run.

1. This restriction is relaxed in Lecture 3. The responses here would be modified, as suggested by the responses in Lecture 3.

Table 2-3. Output Market Responses

Aggregate demand: $y = a(i - \pi, p, ap, P, w^h, w^n, e) + g$
$$ {-} {-} {+} {+} {+} {+} {+}$$

Aggregate supply: $p = \beta(y, K, w)$

a = real demand of private sector

g = real demand of government sector

w = total, nominal, effective labor cost per hour

Responses of output for $x = B, S, e$:

$$\varepsilon(y, x|OM - AM) = c_1\varepsilon(i, x|AM) + c_2\varepsilon(P, x|AM)$$

$$c_1 = \frac{\varepsilon(a, i)}{den}; \quad c_2 = \frac{\varepsilon(a, P)}{den}$$

$$den = 1 - \varepsilon(a, i)\,\varepsilon(i, y|AM) - \varepsilon(a, p)\varepsilon(p, y) +$$
$$-\varepsilon(a, P)\varepsilon(P, y|AM)$$

Intermediate between transitory and perceived permanent shocks are cases which arise under uncertainty. Some people perceive a change as permanent, some as transitory. Some are correct; some are wrong. These errors are unavoidable. Like the costs of adjusting contracts, errors delay the full response of all prices. Hence, they permit $\varepsilon(y, B)$ to be positive in a rational world where people use available information efficiently.

iv) *Interest Rate and Money Targets*

Introduction of the output market permits us to compare the effects on output when the central bank relies on interest rate or monetary control policies. In *IS-LM* analysis, this problem is truncated. Interest rate control prevents shocks to the demand for money from affecting output.

Suppose that there are shocks to the demand for money, μ, and shocks to the credit market, γ. Let mc and irc denote monetary and interest rate control policies.

The response of output to a money demand shock under the alternative policies is:

$$\varepsilon(y, \mu|OM - AM, mc) = \overset{-}{c_1}\varepsilon(\overset{+}{i}, \mu|AM, mc) + \overset{+}{c_2} \cdot \varepsilon(\overset{-}{P}, \mu|AM, mc) < 0$$

$$\varepsilon(y, \mu|OM - AM, irc) = \overset{+}{c_2} \cdot \varepsilon(\overset{-}{P}, \mu|AM, irc) < 0.$$

The coefficient c_2 is not identical in the two cases, but the difference is negligible. The main difference is in the asset price responses. The model implies that

$$\varepsilon(P, \mu|AM, irc) < \varepsilon(P, \mu|AM, mc),$$

so that

$$|\varepsilon(y, \mu|OM - AM, irc)| < |\varepsilon(y, \mu|OM - AM, mc)|.$$

As in the *IS-LM* model, interest rate targeting reduces the response of output to shocks affecting the demand for money; unlike *IS-LM*, part of the response remains.

The conclusion changes when we consider shocks to σ. If the asset price elasticity, $\varepsilon(MM, P)$, of the money market is not a large multiple of the interest elasticity, $\varepsilon(MM, i)$, of the same market, we obtain the opposite result

$$|\varepsilon(y, \gamma|OM - AM, mc)| < \varepsilon(y, \gamma|OM - AM, irc).$$

A demand function for money homogenous of degree one with respect to all nominal variables rules out the violation of the constraining condition. The range of variation of output generated by credit market shocks can be lowered by controlling money. Recognition of a credit market interacting with a money market substantially modifies the story derived from *IS-LM* analysis. If, as seems likely, both shocks occur, the choice depends on the size and frequency of the two types of shocks and on the magnitudes of the responses to each. This information requirement imposes severe limits on the range of policies a central bank can rationally pursue, a theme developed in Lecture 4.

The difference between our analysis and the standard *IS-LM* analysis is reinforced when we consider the consequences of productivity shocks. Productivity shocks shift the supply function and change human wealth, w^h, and the expected real return, e, on real capital both directly and indirectly in response to the supply function. We concentrate on w^h and e and examine the repercussions in the asset markets and their effects on output. We find that the information requirements for interpreting productivity shocks correctly are more severe than for credit or money shocks.

Let $y(x, z)$ [$x = w^h$, e; and $z = mc$, irc] be the response of output to a unit productivity shock operating via channels x and the policy z. To analyze the effects operating via e, we distinguish two states. A comparatively large response of asset supply σ to e and (or) a sufficiently small response of σ (relative to λ) with respect to the asset price level describes state 1. The opposite conditions characterize state 2.

Our analysis yields the following unambiguous result for w^h:

$$y(w^h, mc) > y(w^h, irc).$$

This follows from the assumption that human wealth has comparatively little net effect on the public's asset supply to banks. The responses of output to interest rates and asset price level are mutually reinforcing under a monetary control policy. An interest targeting policy removes any effect transmitted by interest rates and lowers the effect on output induced by the asset price level.

$$\text{State } 1: y(e, mc) < y(e, irc)$$
$$\text{State } 2: y(e, mc) > y(e, irc)^1$$

The effects transmitted by e differ in the two states, so policymakers must know the relative size of responses to increase stability or must make strong auxiliary assumptions about orders of magnitude of structural properties. An mc policy may be advantageous in state 1, but an irc policy seems definitely preferable in state 2.

---

1. Both sets of responses contrast with the corresponding implications of some IS-LM analysis where the shock to the production function can be neutralized with respect either to output or employment by interest targeting policy. An example is the following:

$$y = \alpha(r, y) + g$$
$$y = \beta \, F(N, K)$$
$$M/p = L(r, y)$$
$$w/p = \beta \cdot F_N (N, K)$$

where g is real government expenditure, β is the productivity shock, F(N, K) is the production function, F_N is the partial deirative with respect to N, and w is the money wage. The other symbols have the meaning already designated.

An additional problem arises for reaching conclusions about shocks to w^h and e because of temporal differences in the persistence of shocks. We have assumed, as is standard since Poole,[1] that all shocks are transitory. Permanent shocks pose an entirely different problem. They eventually modify the price level and the wage-price structure. The process of price-wage adjustment, described in Lecture 3, pushes the economy toward a new equilibrium position with a different normal output. The output-price-wage effects of productivity shocks cannot be permanently offset by monetary arrangements. An accommodating policy would unleash unstable inflationary or deflationary processes.

Finally, we note that the effects of transitory productivity shocks are unlikely to be minimized by policy action. A monetary strategy imposing contraction on the rest of the economy whenever the gods smile on agriculture contributes little to welfare.

---

1. WILLIAM POOLE, 'Optimal Choice of Monetary Policy Instruments in a Simple Stochastic Macro Model', *Quarterly Journal of Economics*, 84, 1970, pp. 197-216.

THIRD LECTURE
Fiscal Policy, Prices and Wages, Unemployment and Related Issues

1. *Fiscal Policy*: i) *Incentives and Efficiency*; ii) *Debt Finance*; iii) *Debt Finance in the Long-Run.* – 2. *Prices and Wages*: i) *Prices and Output*; ii) *Sticky Nominal Prices*; iii) *A Stylized Model.* – 3. *Unemployment.* – 4. *Impulse Patterns.* – 5. *Normal Output.*

Fiscal policy is the centerpiece of Keynesian analysis. In the *IS-LM* model, fiscal policy works "directly" by shifting the *IS* curve. The effects of debt finance in the asset market are usually neglected. In our model, with a market for credit or government debt, fiscal policy affects asset prices and interest rates. A maintained budget deficit, whether financed by debt or money, continues to affect asset prices, interest rates and aggregate demand.

Rational expectations macroeconomists assume that all prices are fully flexible. Common observations run counter to their assumption; economists have observed and discussed price setting and sluggish price adjustment for centuries. We argue that the pricing behavior commonly observed is rational in an uncertain world when costs of acquiring information and costs of recontracting are recognized.

Keynesians interpret sluggish price adjustment as evidence in support of a disequilibrium analysis. Sluggish adjustment is offered as a sufficient reason for activist financial policies intended to stabilize the economy. Costs of adjustment and costs of acquiring information are ignored.

Recognition of these costs and of the institutional structure in which unemployment occurs, leads to a different interpretation of some prevalent forms of unemployment. The different interpretation suggests different causes of currently reported rates of unemployment in Europe during the 1980s.

This lecture concerns, principally, issues that arise in the analysis of markets for output and labor. We first extend the analysis used in the previous lecture to include an output market in order to incorporate fiscal policy into the analysis. Then, we discuss fiscal policy, wage and price setting, unemployment, and some related topics.

1. *Fiscal Policy*

Real government expenditure on goods and services directly affects aggregate demand. Taxes, net of transfers, change the income from human wealth, the expected net real return on real assets, and the present value of real human and non-human wealth. Some, or all, of these variables appear in the aggregate demand and supply functions, the demand function for money and the public's supply of earning assets to banks.

Table 3-1 shows the aggregate demand and supply functions and some of the responses to fiscal policy. As before, we consider a closed economy. The aggregate demand function was introduced in Lecture 2. Variables on which taxes are levied have the symbols used previously but are now defined net of tax. Aggregate supply is a price setting function that shifts with changes in effective labor cost – labor cost including social charges adjusted for productivity and taxes.

The analysis is developed in geometric terms. Figure 3-1 shows aggregate demand, *ad*, and aggregate supply, *as*. The vertical line describes normal output which is disregarded for the present. The aggregate demand curve is the locus of all combinations of p and y that simultaneously satisfy the output and the asset market equations at given values of the other variables in *ad*. A change in these variables shifts the position of the *ad* curve in the py plane. Similarly, the aggregate supply function is the locus of p, y combinations that satisfy the price setting function. Changes in K and changes in w, other than responses to current p, shift the aggregate supply curve.

An increase in government expenditure, g, raises total spending by an amount given by the vertical shift of *ad* due to g. We denote this shift by $vs(ad)$

$$vs(ad) = \frac{-g/a}{\varepsilon(a, p|OM - AM)} > 0.^{[1]}$$

The position of the supply curve is not directly affected by changes in g. The response of p and y can be stated in geometric terms.

---

1. The notation *OM-AM* in the elasticities distinguishes total from partial elasticities. See Table 3-1 for these elasticities, the definition of a, and other terms.

Table 3-1. Output Market Responses

Aggregate demand (ad)

$$y = a(i - \pi, P, p, ap, w^n, w^h, e) + g$$
$$ - \quad + \quad - \quad + \quad + \quad + \quad +$$

a = real demand of private sector for output

g = real demand of government sector for output

aggregate supply (as)

$p = \beta(y, K, w)$ supply function

wage setting function

$w = w(p_{-1}, p, ap)$

w = effective nominal labor cost

slopes of ad and as

$$\text{slope } (ad) = \frac{y/a - \varepsilon(a, y|OM - AM)}{\varepsilon(a, p|OM - AM)} < 0$$

$$\text{slope } (as) = \frac{\varepsilon(\beta, y)}{1 - \varepsilon(\beta, w) \, [\varepsilon(w, p) + \varepsilon(w, ap)\varepsilon(ap, p)]} > 0$$

where

$$\varepsilon(a, y|OM - AM) = \varepsilon(a, y) + \varepsilon(a, i) \cdot \varepsilon(i, y|AM) + \varepsilon(a, P)$$
$$\cdot \varepsilon(P, y|AM) > 0$$

and

$$\varepsilon(a, y) = \varepsilon(a, w^h) \cdot \varepsilon(w^h, y) + \varepsilon(a, e) \cdot \varepsilon(e, y)$$

$$\varepsilon(a, p|OM - AM) = \varepsilon(a, p) + \varepsilon(a, i) \cdot \varepsilon(i, p|AM) + \varepsilon(a, P)$$
$$\cdot \varepsilon(P, p|AM) + \varepsilon(a, ap)\varepsilon(ap, p) < 0$$

$\varepsilon(a, x|OM - AM)$ indicates a response of aggregate real demand to x taking account of the interaction between output and asset markets. The elasticities $\varepsilon(a, i)$ and $\varepsilon(a, P)$ are partial elasticities.

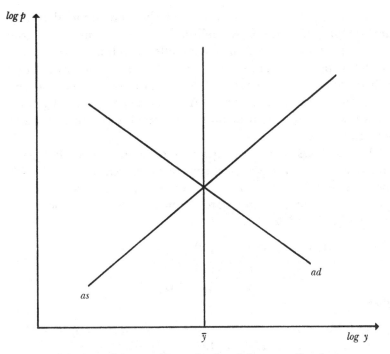

Figure 3-1. Aggregate Demand, *ad*, and Aggregate Supply, *as*

$$(3.\ 1)\quad \varepsilon(p, g|OM - AM) = \frac{vs\ (ad) \cdot slope\ (as)}{slope\ (as) - slope\ (ad)} > 0$$

$$(3.\ 2)\quad \varepsilon(y, g|OM - AM) = \frac{vs\ (ad)}{slope\ (as) - slope\ (ad)} > 0$$

A numerically larger slope (*ad*) relative to slope (*as*) reduces the price response. As slope (*as*) converges to infinity or slope (*ad*) to zero, the response of the price level converges to the vertical shift *vs*(*ad*). The response of output falls, in contrast, with a (numerical) increase of either slope. The response of output to *g* approaches zero as slope (*as*) approaches infinity.

The magnitude of the response to *g* depends on the public's beliefs about the persistence of the shock. The sensitivity of $\varepsilon(a, y|OM - AM)$ to perceived transitory shocks increases the slope (*ad*) and lowers the responses of *p* and *y*, as shown in eqs.

(3. 1) and (3. 2). The reason is that the perception that the increase in government expenditures and the consequent rise in output is temporary implies small effects on human wealth w^h and the expected net return on real assets. The responses of the relevant long-term rate and of P to y remain too small to modify aggregate demand significantly. A temporary increase of g produces a smaller reaction in both price level and output than a permanent increase.

The responses to tax changes include effects on both aggregate demand and aggregate supply. The tax parameters th and tn denote taxes on human and non-human wealth. The vertical shifts in the aggregate demand curve ad induced by changes in th and tn are:

(3. 3) $vs(ad)$ due to tx $(x = h, n)$

$$= \frac{-\varepsilon(a, tx|OM - AM)}{\varepsilon(a, p|OM - AM)} < 0$$

where

$\varepsilon(a, th|OM - AM) = \varepsilon(a, w^h) \cdot \varepsilon(w^h, th) + \varepsilon(a, i) \cdot \varepsilon(i, w^h|AM)$
$\cdot \varepsilon(w^h, th) + \varepsilon(a, P) \cdot \varepsilon(P, w^h|AM) \cdot \varepsilon(ws, th) < 0$

$\varepsilon(a, tn|OM - AM) = -[\varepsilon(a, e) + \varepsilon(a, i) \cdot \varepsilon(i, e|AM) + \varepsilon(a, P)$
$\cdot \varepsilon(P, e|AM)] + \varepsilon(e, tn) < 0$

The vertical shift in aggregate supply is

(3. 4) $vs(as) = \varepsilon(\beta, w)\varepsilon(w, tx) > 0.$

The responses of p, and y induced by tax changes are:

(3. 5) $\varepsilon(y, tx|OM - AM) = \dfrac{vs(ad) - vs(as)}{slope\ (as) - slope(ad)} < 0$

(3. 6) $\varepsilon(p, tx|OM - AM) = \dfrac{vs(ad)\ slope(as) - vs(as)\ slope(ad)}{slope(as) - slope(ad)}.$

The response of prices is ambiguous. Tax reduction raises prices if $vs(as)$ is relatively small. A large supply side effect implies that output rises and prices fall when tax rates are reduced.[1]

---

1. A common finding of so-called reduced form estimates is that tax effects exceed the effects of government spending on GNP. This result is puzzling in Keynesian

Supply side economists argue that the *IS-LM* model ignores the incentive effects of tax reduction on output. Equation (3. 5) shows that the supply effect, $vs(as)$, augments the effect of the shift in aggregate demand but does not change its direction. A relatively large supply effect would remove the ambiguity in the price level response. Prices would fall with tax reduction and rise with tax increases, as shown in eq. (3. 6). Neglect of the supply response reverses these signs; tax increases lower, and reductions raise, prices and output.

Once again, we note that the responses to permanent and transitory changes in fiscal policy differ. The responses of e, w^h and w to transitory changes are small, reducing the vertical shifts of *as* and *ad* and, thus, reducing the responses of p and y. Further, the anticipated price level, ap, does not adjust to a transitory change, so there is no response of prices, wages and nominal values to ap. The size of the permanent response of output to fiscal action exceeds the response to a transitory change as a result of the changes in e, w^h and w. Adjustment of ap moves the price level towards its equilibrium value. For taxes, the effect of price changes is ambiguous, as shown in (3. 6); it is uncertain whether the price adjustment induced by ap strengthens or weakens the response to fiscal action. For g, prompt, full adjustment of ap to the new equilibrium price level strengthens the price response and reduces the effect of g on output.

Figure 3-2 shows the interaction of aggregate demand and supply in response to a change in government spending. The same response pattern applies to any maintained change in aggregate demand. In an uncertain world, the distribution of the shock between prices and output is not constant but depends on the perceived permanence of the change.

Suppose a permanent increase in g raises aggregate demand from ad_1 to ad_2. The intersection of *as* and *ad* moves from the initial point, A, to point B. At point B, some people recognize the permanence of the change, so w adjusts to the new prices

---

analysis where taxes affect disposable income and government spending works "directly" on output. In our analysis, the result is not surprising. If g/α is small, $vs(ad)$ is small and from (3.1) and (3.2) the responses of p and y are small also.

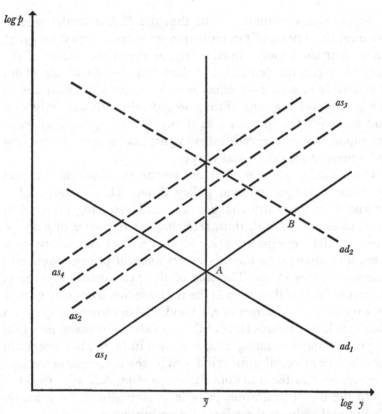

Figure 3-2. The Interaction of Aggregate Demand and Supply in
Response to a Change in Government Spending

and aggregate supply shifts to as_2. The resulting increase in p
provides information that induces others to anticipate a higher
price level, increasing w further, again shifting as. Ultimately
the process reaches a new equilibrium at the intersection of ad_2
and as_4. The position of as is determined by the full mutual
adjustment of p and w.

Aside from effects on incentives, externalities, efficiency, and
the like, fiscal policy has no permanent effect on output. Fiscal
effects are absorbed by adjustments of wages and prices. The
adjustments are one-time changes in levels, distributed over time,
not changes in maintained inflation. With relatively low trans-

action and adjustment costs, and early recognition of the persistence of the fiscal change, wages and prices adjust rapidly; effects on output are correspondingly small and short-lived. Where transaction and adjustment costs associated with revisions in fiscal policy are relatively large, information, beliefs and expectations are not revised uniformly in lock-step. A system with substantial noise delays recognition of the true nature of a permanent shock. These conditions retard wage-price adjustments, so effects on output are larger and more persistent.[1]

Our analysis of fiscal policy brings out the uncertainty that surrounds the timing and persistence of its effects. Recognition of anticipations, costs of information and adjustment removes the clearcut, direct responses to fiscal changes popularized by the *IS-LM* analysis. Recognition of the constraint imposed by normal output shifts the long-run effect of fiscal policy from output to the price level, effects on incentives and efficiency aside. Recognition of the uncertainty that surrounds the timing of responses and the magnitude and persistence of government spending programs should reduce confidence that fiscal policy is a reliable counter-cyclical tool.

i) *Incentives and Efficiency*

The long-run effects of fiscal policy on real output depend on the induced changes in normal output resulting from changes in incentives and efficiency. Frequent transitory changes in tax policy engender uncertainty about expected real, after-tax returns to investment in human and non-human wealth, reducing such investment. Permanent changes in taxes on income derived from real capital change the expected, risk adjusted, rate of net return, expressed by the ratio, pe/PK. Tax increases lower, and tax reductions raise, the net return to capital. Investment and the stock of real capital gradually respond until the rate of return

---

1. In a world of uncertainty, with frequent changes in fiscal and monetary policy action and real shocks, the public cannot readily separate one-time changes in the rate of inflation from permanent changes in the price level, induced by one-time fiscal changes, that are distributed over time. Popular discussion, and many economists, fail to distinguish the two, so it should not be surprising that markets mistake changes in level for changes in rates of change and conversely.

reaches an equilibrium with the interest rates and prevailing risk premiums associated with returns on other real assets. Changes in taxes on income derived from human capital have similar consequences; investment in skills and intensity of application responds to after-tax returns. Thus, higher taxes lower the output associated with a given physical labor input. The vertical line describing normal output moves to the left; normal output is smaller. Lower taxes encourage effort and productivity, so the normal output line in Figures 3-1 and 3-2 moves to the right.

Government spending programs have effects on efficiency and incentives also. These effects are often ignored. With the exceptions of Bailey[1] and recently Barro,[2] macroeconomists treat the government sector as a sinkhole for goods and services produced by the private sector. Attempts to replace the sinkhole introduce alternatives with limited usefulness, perhaps for analytic convenience. Either the government buys goods and services, which it redistributes to the public, or it produces goods and services with the same "technology" used by the private sector. These alternative conditions dismiss the effects on incentives, productivity and efficiency characteristically produced by nonmarket and political institutions.

A more relevant approach would disaggregate the spending accounts in the budget and treat the government sector as a production sector. "Government production" uses goods and services supplied by the private sector as inputs and converts them into an output. The following paragraphs offer some tentative suggestions along these lines. We distinguish five components of government output. The effects we discuss are independent of any burdens that arise from financing.

The first component refers to the provision of infrastructure. Many of the projects in which government invests have aspects of public goods. By providing these goods, government lowers the private sector's costs of producing a given output and the volume of private real capital. This component modifies the

1. Martin J. Bailey, *National Income and the Price Level*, New York: McGraw-Hill, 1971.
2. Robert J. Barro, *Macroeconomics*, New York: Wiley, 1984.

position of the aggregate supply curve and the position of the normal output line. Recent work by Aschauer attempts to quantify this effect.[1]

A second component, possibly related to the first, influences the expected net return on real capital. In many countries, government produces goods and services. These activities are included with private production in the national accounts. There are often systematic differences in efficiency, particularly where government enterprises are used to reduce reported unemployment rates. The efficiency loss reduces normal output. Some of the government's output may be a substitute for private real capital and some a complement. Substitutes lower private investment and the private stock of real capital. This effect on normal output may be offset by a larger volume of public investment. Complements raise private investment and the stock of private real capital; the aggregate supply curve moves to the right, and normal output rises.

A third component affects in human wealth. The nature of the educational system, a non-negligible proportion of gross national product, is a major influence. Any effect of education (or health) on human wealth shifts the aggregate supply curve and normal output.

The fourth component modifies consumption. Governments distribute privately produced goods as income transfers in kind. Such transfers affect private consumption and the allocation of resources within the consumption goods industry and between consumption and investment. Under specific circumstances labor supply may also be influenced.

Lastly, the basic functions of the state, such as execution of police powers, have a subtle but important influence. For example, the interpretation and protection of property rights has consequences for normal output. Arbitrary costs associated with various forms of regulation also shape the level of normal output. Normal output gradually declines under a regime exercising police powers in a manner imposing substantial uncertainty about

1. DAVID ALAN ASCHAUER, 'Is Public Expenditure Productive?', Working Paper, Federal Reserve Bank of Chicago, 1988.

the "rules of the game". Greater uncertainty about the course and nature of financial policies lowers long-term investment and normal output.

We doubt that the processes we have mentioned here significantly modify short or even medium-term movements in output. We submit, on the other hand, that they contribute to the longer-run evolution of aggregate supply and normal output. We believe that attention to the effects of the socio-political framework can contribute more to raise standards of living than concentration on the usual aspects of short-run "stabilization policies".[1]

ii) *Debt Finance*

Not all government expenditures are financed by taxes. The government may rely partly on newly created central bank money (i.e. the monetary base) or on borrowing on the credit market. This section and the next analyze the effects of government financial policies, particularly debt finance. We ignore effects arising from distortionary taxes.

Barro disposes of the problem of debt finance with the "Barro-Ricardo equivalence theorem".[2] Rational individuals know that current debt issues must be serviced with a future stream of taxes. The present value of these (lump sum) taxes corresponds to the value of the currently issued debt. The public's portfolio of securities on the asset side is matched by the tax liabilities on the liability side of the balance sheet. Wealth is unchanged.

Elimination of the wealth effect does not suspend all real effects of a debt financed deficit. The equivalence theorem requires that the change in the composition of the public's balance sheet never induces any substitution processes. The increase in tax liabilities must induce a matching increase in the public's demand for securities. Barro shows that a rational individual adjusts his intergenerational bequests to compensate for the change in debt.

1. Our approach to the government sector requires some changes in the national income accounts. We cannot treat all of the government activities as final goods. Some portions of g are in the nature of intermediate goods in the production of the government sector's final goods or services.

2. ROBERT J. BARRO, 'Are Government Bonds Net Wealth?', *Journal of Political Economy*, 82, 1974, pp. 1019-1117.

If he leaves more debt, he also leaves a larger inheritance and conversely.

Barro's argument fails, even in Barro's world, if we introduce more than a single household, distinguish households by income and permit government to redistribute income. The recognition of political reality, expressed by intergenerational or intragenerational income transfers, removes the invariance proposition and the equivalence theorem.[1] Additional critical arguments are addressed to Barro's invariance thesis by Brunner.[2] Barro does not explain why agents hedge their tax liabilities with securities. The incentives and mechanisms involved remain obscure. We, therefore, disregard the Barro-Ricardo equivalence theorem and recognize both wealth and substitution effects of debt finance.

Our analysis does not assign much significance to the wealth effect, however; the wealth effect of debt on aggregate demand is

$$\varepsilon(a, w^n) \, \frac{v \cdot S}{w^n},$$

where $\frac{v \cdot S}{w^n}$ is the ratio of government debt at market value to non-human wealth. The substitution effect on the other hand is summarized for the aggregate demand function by

$$(3.7) \quad \varepsilon(a, i) \cdot \varepsilon(i, S|AM) + [\varepsilon(a, P) + \varepsilon(a, w^n) \frac{PK}{w^n}]\varepsilon(P, S|AM).$$

Note that

$$\frac{vS}{w^n} < \frac{PK}{w^n}.$$

As Christ noted,[3] the effects of deficit finance are not limited to the responses of aggregate demand (or supply). An unbalanced budget changes the monetary base or government debt. The repercussions on the asset markets interact with the output market

1. ALEX CUKIERMAN and ALLAN H. MELTZER, 'A Political Theory of Government Debt and Deficits in a Neo-Ricardian Framework', Pittsburgh: Mimeo, *American Economic Review*, 79, September 1989, pp. 713-732.

2. KARL BRUNNER, 'Fiscal Policy in Macro Theory: A Survey and Evaluation', in R. W. HAFER, ed., *The Monetary versus Fiscal Policy Debate*, Totowa, N.J.: Rowman and Allanheld, January 1986, pp. 33-116.

3. CARL FINLEY CHRIST, 'A Simple Macro-Economic Model with a Government Budget Restraint', *Journal of Political Economy*, 76, January-February 1968, pp. 53-67.

to change output and the price level. The latter changes affect the budget position and induce further changes in asset stocks, output and prices.[1] Let the deficit, *def*, be defined as the difference between nominal expenditure on goods and services, *pg*,

$$(3.8) \quad def = pg + iS - t(p, y, \tau)$$

plus interest payments, *iS*, and taxes net of transfers. The nominal volume of taxes depends on the price level, *p*, output, *y*, and a tax parameter, *τ*.

Figure 3.3 incorporates the budget equation into our analysis. The *bbe* line represents the locus of points (p, y) satisfying the condition of a balanced budget, i.e. *def* = 0. The slope of *bbe* is obtained from the budget equation and can be written as

$$(3.9) \quad slope\ of\ bbe = \frac{\varepsilon(t, y)}{\frac{pg}{t} + \varepsilon(i, p|AM)\frac{iS}{t} - \varepsilon(t, p)}.$$

Under a progressive tax system both elasticities $\varepsilon(t, y)$ and $\varepsilon(t, p)$ exceed unity. Sufficiently regressive taxes would produce a positive slope for *bbe*.[2] A positively sloped *bbe* line would also result under a policy of specifying real expenditures, if taxes are based on past price levels and real income.

The *bbe* line partitions the *p, y* plane into two areas. The area under the negatively sloped line contains all combinations of (p, y) that produce a deficit for the given *g* and *τ* that fix the *bbe* line. The area above contains (p, y) combinations yielding a surplus. A positively sloped line reverses this situation.

Point *A* in Figure 3-3 describes a position of full equilibrium. Output market equilibrium, determined by the intersection of aggregate demand ad_1 and aggregate supply as_1 is at normal output. The budget is balanced. Suppose this equilibrium is disturbed by an increase in government expenditure, *g*. The aggregate demand curve shifts to ad_2 as shown previously. Short-run equilibrium moves from point *A* to point *B* along the aggre-

---

1. KARL BRUNNER and ALLAN H. MELTZER, 'An Aggregative Theory for a Closed Economy', in JEROME STEIN, ed., *Monetarism*, Amsterdam: North-Holland, 1976, pp. 69-103.
2. pg/t may be less than unity if there are relatively large interest payments.

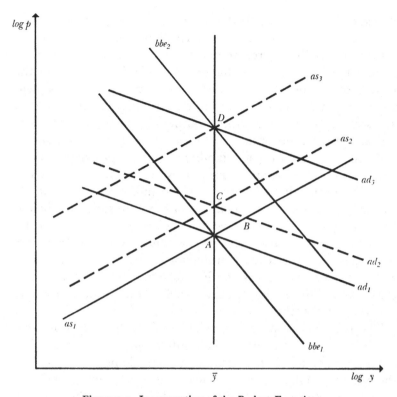

Figure 3-3. Incorporation of the Budget Equation

gate supply curve. The increase in g also shifts the bbe line from bbe_1 to bbe_2. The vertical shift in bbe is given by the expression

$$(3.\ 10) \qquad \text{vertical shift of } bbe \text{ due to } g = \frac{-1}{\dfrac{pg}{t} - \varepsilon(t,\ p)} \cdot \frac{pg}{t} > 0.$$

This shift exceeds the shift of ad, so the new short-run equilibrium at B produces a budget deficit.

Financing the budget deficit by issuing new base money or new debt raises the financial stock variables B and S. These changes impose adjustments on the asset markets which modify the position of the aggregate demand curve. The aggregate supply curve adjusts also as the public becomes aware of the price changes and anticipates further changes. The adjustment pushes aggregate supply, *as*, toward an intersection with *ad* on the normal output line. If the aggregate demand curve, *ad*, moves up more rapidly than the balanced budget line, *bbe*, in response to the growth of the nominal stocks B and S, the stock adjustment process is stable; *ad* and *as* eventually intersect at the point of intersection of *bbe* and normal output. Major fiscal action or permanent inflation ensues in the absence of these conditions.

A sufficient condition for stability is that the proportion of the deficit financed by issuing base money (or, in the case of a surplus, the proportion of base money withdrawn) is sufficiently large.[1] The reason is that changes in the base shift the *bbe* and the aggregate demand curves in opposite directions. Since increases in the base raise aggregate demand, the *ad* and *bbe* curves converge to an intersection on the normal output line at a point above A. Nominal values continue to adjust to the anticipated price level, until the supply curve reaches equilibrium. In Figure 3-3, the new equilibrium is at D.

The price increase from A to D, resulting from a permanent increase in g, has two parts. The shifts from A to B to C reflect adjustment of the output market to the change in g. This is the pure fiscal effect of fiscal policy. The adjustment from C to D reflects the effects of financing the deficit. This is the financial effect of fiscal policy.

Equations (3.11) and (3.12) formally describe the shift of the aggregate demand curve in response to B and S.

vertical shift of *ad* due to S

$$(3.11)\ \varepsilon(p, S) = -\frac{\varepsilon(a, i) \cdot \varepsilon(i, S|AM) + \varepsilon(a, P) \cdot \varepsilon(P, S|AM)}{\varepsilon(a, p) + \varepsilon(a, i) \cdot \varepsilon(i, p|AM) + \varepsilon(a, P) \cdot \varepsilon(P, p|AM)}$$

vertical shift of *ad* due to B

$$(3.12)\ \varepsilon(p, B) = -\frac{\varepsilon(a, i) \cdot \varepsilon(i, B|AM) + \varepsilon(a, P) \cdot \varepsilon(P, B|AM)}{\varepsilon(a, p) + \varepsilon(a, i) \cdot \varepsilon(i, p|AM) + \varepsilon(a, P) \cdot \varepsilon(P, p|AM)}$$

The two feedbacks from the deficit differ substantially. Since $\varepsilon(i, S|AM)$ is positive and $\varepsilon(i, B|AM)$ is negative, a change in S

1. Karl Brunner and Allan H. Meltzer, 1976, *op. cit.*

transmits two offsetting effects to prices and output, whereas a change of B induces two reinforcing effects. Base money finance, therefore, produces a larger response of aggregate demand to the financing than issuing debt.

The balanced budget line (bbe) is lowered by an increase in B but rises in response to S. The response of bbe to S is

$$(3. 13) \qquad \frac{1 + \varepsilon(i, S|AM)}{\frac{pg}{t} - \varepsilon(t, p)} \frac{iS}{t}.$$

The numerator of 3. 13 can be larger than the numerator of the corresponding aggregate demand shift, (3.11). As interest payments increase, (3.13) becomes larger. This is a source of instability. Further, the denominator of the bbe shift in (3. 13) can be smaller than the denominator of the ad shift in (3. 11); if so, the denominators contribute to instability.

We conjecture therefore that the shift in the position of bbe induced by S can exceed the shift in the position of aggregate demand. In this case, a debt financed deficit, with real expenditures and tax parameters given, fails to produce feedbacks to the output and asset markets that eventually close the budget deficit. The bbe line in Figure 3-3 shifts by more than ad, so interest payments rise and the deficit grows. Prices rise without anticipated limit unless the government reduces the budget deficit by changing fiscal policy.

iii) Debt Finance in the Long-Run

The longer run consequences of an unstable debt-deficit process have attracted considerable recent attention. The financing of relatively large United States budget deficits and the likelihood that such deficits will continue for many years, or perhaps indefinitely, raises the issue of stability. Sargent and Wallace show that when the real rate of interest is above the growth of real output, inflation rises without bound.[1] This section explores this issue in the context of the money-credit model.

---

1. Thomas J. Sargent and Neil Wallace, 'Some Unpleasant Monetarist Arithmetic', in Thomas J. Sargent, ed., *Rational Expectations and Inflation*, New York: Harper and Row, 1986, chap. 5.

Equation (3.14) introduces the financing of the deficit into eq. (3. 8). $\overset{\circ}{S}$ and $\overset{\circ}{B}$ are the changes in the stock of securities and the monetary base.

(3. 14) $\overset{\circ}{S} + \overset{\circ}{B} = pg + iS - t(p, y, \tau)$.

(3. 15) deflates each of the magnitudes by nominal income:

$$(3. 15) \quad \overset{\circ}{s} = \overline{def} + [(rr - n) + (n - \frac{\Delta y}{y}) + (\pi - \frac{\Delta p}{p})]s$$

$$- [(\pi + n) + (\frac{\Delta p}{p} - \pi) + (\frac{\Delta y}{y} - n)]b - \overset{\circ}{b}.$$

The variable $\overline{def}$ denotes the basic deficit

$$\overline{def} = \frac{g}{y} - \frac{t(p, y, \tau)}{py}.$$

The symbols rr, n and π in equation (3. 15) denote the real rate of interest, the trend rate of real growth and the expected rate of inflation. To concentrate on long-run effects, we disregard all deviations of the actual from the expected rate of inflation and of the actual from the trend rate of growth. Prices are fully adjusted under the circumstances to the monetary base, so the rate of change $\overset{\circ}{b}$ vanishes. Therefore,

$$(3. 16) \quad \overset{\circ}{s} = \overline{def} + (rr - n)s - (\pi + n)b.$$

Eq. (3. 16) shows that the long-run movement of the real debt ratio is governed by a linear differential equation. The stability of the system depends on the convergence of s to a limit and, therefore, on the sign of the derivative of the right side of (3. 16) with respect to s. The debt-deficit process is stable provided $\overline{def}_s + (rr - n) < 0$. For fixed g and τ and the range of deficits we consider, $\overline{def}_s$ is negligible. The movement of the real debt ratio depends on the sign of $(rr - n)$. With the real rate exceeding the trend growth rate, the real debt ratio s persistently rises whenever $\overline{def} + (rr - n)s > (\pi + n)b$; i.e., whenever there exists an initial deficit which is sufficiently large. With $rr < n$ trend growth is sufficient to stabilize the real debt ratio even with a maintained basic deficit.

There are two relations between the expected inflation rate π

and the real debt ratio s. Both equations are derived from equation (3.16) by setting the rate of change of the real debt ratio equal to zero.

$$(3.17) \quad \pi = \frac{\overline{def}}{b} + (rr - n)\frac{s}{b} - n$$

$$(3.18) \quad s = \frac{\overline{def} - (\pi + n)b}{n - rr}.$$

Equation (3.18) shows the equilibrium real debt ratio as a function of the inflation rate π. For $n > rr$, the equation determines a stable real debt ratio. The higher the inflation rate, the lower is the real debt ratio.[1] Equation (3.17), under the condition $rr > n$, shows the inflation rate required to maintain the real debt ratio at any given level and prevent its further increase. There is some inflation rate, sufficiently high, that stabilizes the real debt ratio, given $\overline{def}$. Achieving that inflation rate may require a policy change; with $rr > n$, the system will not produce a stable value of s, so a shift in π will be required.

Figure 3-4 represents the differential equation (3.16) describing the motion of the real debt ratio. Line 1 is based on the sum of the first two terms, $\overline{def} + (rr - n)s$. The slope of this line is independent of π, so it is a straight line in Figure 3-4. Line 2 corresponds to the third term in (3.16), $(\pi + n)b$. It has a negative intercept $-nb$ and a negative slope $-b$. The horizontal axis shows π, and the vertical axis shows the rate of change $\dot{s}$ of the real debt ratio, s

Consider the case $rr > n$. Suppose the prevailing inflation π is less than the value $\bar{\pi}$ at which the real debt ratio in eq. 3.18 is constant. The graph shows a particular $\pi < \bar{\pi}$ at the vertical line linking line 1 and line 2. The vertical distance between line 1 and the π-axis describes the positive effect of s on $\dot{s}$ expressed by the first two components of the differential equation (3.16). The vertical difference between the π-axis and line 2 describes the negative contribution of inflation to the level of s obtained from the third component of equation (3.16). The sum of the

1. In this analysis when the debt ratio is constant and base velocity, $1/b$, is constant, the real rate of interest is constant.

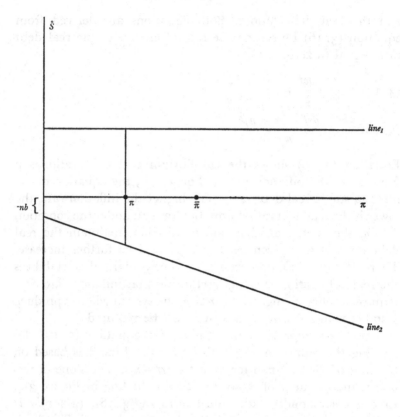

Figure 3-4. The Differential Equation Describing the Motion of
the Real Debt Ratio

positive and the negative components determines the rate of change of s. This change is positive at any level of inflation below $\bar{\pi}$. Thus the rate of increase of the real debt ratio, s, declines as π approaches $\bar{\pi}$. The increase in s associated with any $\pi < \bar{\pi}$ pushes the horizontal line 1 higher up, raising $\mathring{s}$ and accelerating s; s rises without limit as long as $rr > n$. The process can only be terminated by a policy change that lowers the basic deficit sufficiently or raises the inflation rate to at least $\bar{\pi}$.

The dynamic pattern changes when we consider the condition $rr < n$. At any level $\pi < \bar{\pi}$, the real debt ratio increases. From (3.17) we see that a larger s now lowers $\mathring{s}$; line 1 shifts down.

As the debt-deficit process unfolds, line 1 continues to shift in the direction of lower $\hat{s}$ until s reaches a value at which the vertical distances between the π-axis and lines 1 and 2 are equal. As these distances converge to equality, the real debt ratio stabilizes; the nominal stock of debt rises at a rate equal to the inflation rate plus the trend rate of real growth, $\pi + n$.

The analysis shows that the relation between rr and n determines whether a deficit is ultimately self-regulating, at least in terms of the real debt ratio and its effect on real interest rates, or whether we must rely on deliberate increases in the rate of inflation or a change in fiscal regime. This conclusion is correct but, at the same time, misleading. The reason is that we have not considered the values of s and π at which stability is achieved for $rr < n$ or the rate of inflation to which monetary policy would have to drive the economy when $rr > n$. The latter rate corresponds to $\bar{\pi}$ in Figure 3-4. Table 3-2, using values close to the steady state values in the United States or Europe, shows that the deficits experienced in the United States and Europe would, if maintained, produce a massive rise in the steady state real debt ratio. This would occur even in the context of a "stable," self-regulating process.

Table 3-2

Basic Deficit Rario and Equilibrium Real Debt Ratio Under a Stable Process

Basic Deficit Ratio ($\overline{def}$)	Equilibrium Real Debt Ratio (s) [a]
.01	0.40
.05	2.40
.10	4.90

[a] It is assumed that $\pi = 0$, $b = .05$, $rr = .02$, and $n = .04$.

The increase to 2.4 in the real debt ratio associated with a basic deficit of .05, shown in Table 3-2, suggests the longer-run problems confronting the central bank. Long before the debt ratio reaches 2.4, the real rate of interest and monetary velocity are likely to rise. The longer-run response of the financial markets, conditioned by increasing uncertainty about future inflationary finance, mobilizes political pressure on behalf of a more expansionary monetary policy. We know from long experience that central banks generally are sensitive to rising interest rates. It follows that an independent monetary course is somewhat improbable in the longer-run, under the circumstances.

Table 3-3 informs us about the long-run danger of inflation associated with a basic deficit ratio of .05 under either of the two possible states. The inflation rate is computed on the condition that the real debt ratio (s) is held constant either at .33 or .50, and base money per unit of nominal national income (b) is constant at .05. Irrespective of the stability condition $(rr - n)$, the long-run inflation threat embedded in a permanent basic deficit of 5 percent of gross national product would move us to levels of inflation not yet experienced as a maintained phenomenon in the United States or Europe.[1] Table 3-3, however, should be interpreted somewhat differently in the alternative cases. For $rr > n$, the π values show the inflation required to hold $s = .33$ (or $= .50$). Given $\overline{def}$, the π values must be set by a change in monetary policy. For $rr < n$, we obtain an equilibrium $s = .33$ (or $= .50$) for any π-values determined by equation (3.18). The inflation potential associated with a long-run deficit shown in Figure 3-4 and Table 3-3 neglects the (negative) effect of inflation on real balances; b depends negatively on π, and line 2 should be strictly concave toward the horizontal axis. The expected inflation rates reported in Table 3-3 would be correspondingly higher.

Table 3-3

Permanent Deficits and Long-Run Inflation

	Expected Inflation Rate (π)[a]			
	if $s = .33$ and		if $s = .50$ and	
Basic Deficit Ratio				
$(\overline{def})$	$rr > n$	$rr < n$	$rr > n$	$rr < n$
.01	39	10	47	7
.05	118	90	127	87
.10	218	190	227	187

[a] π = inflation rate in percent per annum, $b = .05$, $rr = .06$ or $.02$, and $n = .03$.

1. The reason for the high rates of inflation can be seen from eq. (3.18). With def=.05, nb is a tiny fraction of $\overline{def}$. A large value of π is required to keep s constant.

The argument in this section reveals potential dangers to the survival of a non-inflationary (or low inflationary) monetary regime in the presence of a substantial permanent deficit. A non-inflationary monetary regime and a permanent deficit that is above some minimum level are unlikely to coexist in the long-run. One of the two regimes must adjust to the other.

A viable non-inflationary monetary regime requires severe constraints on the fiscal regime. But we should emphasize that, with the possible exception of Italy, Israel, Argentina, Brazil and Bolivia, peacetime experience provides little evidence of large persistent deficits and high rates of inflation. The main exceptions are the hyperinflations studied by Cagan.[1] Deficits have remained small and the real debt burden manageable in most countries.

We may have entered a new age of pemanent large deficits, particularly in the United States. The behavior of the monetary authorities, so far, does not conform well to the potential threat implied by the analysis. Current experience probably generates substantial uncertainty about the future course of monetary policy. The threat of inflation remains.

1. PHILLIP D. CAGAN, 'The Monetary Dynamics of Hyperinflation', in MILTON FRIEDMAN, ed., *Studies in the Quantity Theory of Money*, Chicago: University of Chicago Press, 1956.

2. Prices and Wages

Sluggish adjustment of prices and wages is central to our analysis. As we have noted several times, in a world of uncertainty, with different types of shocks and costs of adjusting, sluggish price and wage adjustments are a rational response. This section develops these themes more fully, first, by considering the adjustment of prices, wages (or labor costs) and output, then by considering the reasons for price setting, and some consequences of price setting, more fully.

i) *Prices and Output*

The duration of monetary effects on real variables was a major issue in the Monetarist-Keynesian discussions of the 1960s. Monetarists argued that neither the money stock nor its trend, expressed by the maintained growth rate, substantially affects output and employment in the long-run. Inflation, not output, depends on the maintained rate of money growth. In our model, this proposition implies that the trend value and the trend growth of the money stock are fully reflected by the position of the aggregate supply curve. Accelerations or decelerations of money, in contrast, are not yet absorbed by the price level. There is an asymmetry in the movement of aggregate demand and supply. Adjustment of aggregate supply lags behind aggregate demand producing real effects on output and employment. The effects produced by a particular acceleration do not last, however. Aggregate supply shifts, reflecting the new trend of the money stock, and the short-run equilibrium point returns to the normal output line.

The Keynesians' version differed. Their claim was that both the money stock and its trend have permanent real effects. Early versions of the Phillips curve, when combined with *IS-LM*, implied that employment N could be solved as a function of the money stock M, the price level p, and fiscal and other predetermined variables. Equation (3. 19) is an example,

$$\frac{\Delta p}{p} = h[\bar{N} - N(M, p, x)]$$

where x refers to the remaining predetermined variables, and $\bar{N}$ is the available labor force. The magnitude $(\bar{N} - \mathcal{N})$ measures unemployment. The equation implies that unemployment can be lowered, and the lower level maintained, by raising the money stock M and maintaining monetary growth at a rate consistent with the induced higher rate of inflation. Later, the inflation augmented Phillips curve recognized that expected inflation shifts the Phillips curve but did not remove the implication that higher inflation raises output permanently. Keynesians continued to reject the long-run neutrality proposition.

Our analysis implies that maintaining output above the level of normal output requires an accelerated expansion of the money stock and an accelerated inflation. The explanation of acceleration differs, however, from the usual account based on a Phillips curve. The latter relies on a relation between the rate of inflation, the expected rate of inflation and the level of some activity measure, for example, output or unemployment. The level of output or unemployment expresses the underlying (positive or negative) position of aggregate excess demand. This interpretation is based on the idea, in Keynesian analysis, that persistent price movements must be driven by persistent market disequilibria.

We need not accept such a problematic idea. Persistent aggregate excess demand is not a necessary condition for persistent inflation; inflation persists during recessions. Our analysis explains persistent inflation by the continuous drift in the short-run equilibrium point in response to persistent, simultaneous shifts of both the aggregate demand and the aggregate supply curves. The relative speeds of adjustment of the two curves determine the magnitude of inflation and its sensitivity to eventual acceleration whenever policy attempts to hold output above the normal level of output.

Figure 3-5 shows the changing positions of equilibrium. We start from an initial position located on the normal output line.[1] An expansionary monetary policy action is undertaken to raise

---

1. This is a convenience with no effect on the argument here. Starting from a position below $\bar{y}$ would produce a benefit, the rise in output from y to $\bar{y}$. Whether or not this is a *net* benefit depends on the further consequence that the stimulus produces.

output above the normal level. Initially, output and the price level rise from point A to point B. Recognition of the permanence of the change induces a corresponding adjustment in wage contracts, pushing aggregate supply toward position C. The movement from B to C is slow if the expansionary policy action is interpreted as a transitory change and more rapid if the change is perceived to be permanent. Recognition does not occur all at once and is not uniform for all market participants. The relevant operation of transaction costs, particularly costs of negotiation, interacts with the recognition problem to delay full adjustment.

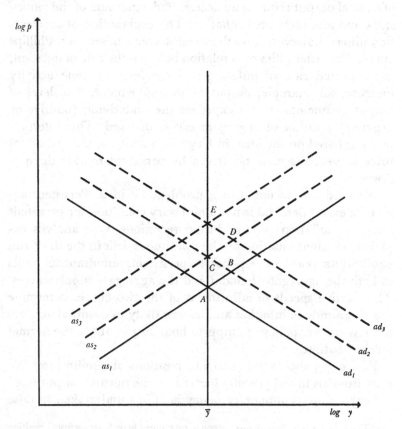

Figure 3-5. The Inflationary Process

If the authorities' commitment to raise output produces further monetary expansion, aggregate demand rises to ad_3. The short-run equilibrium moves to D, and in this new round the aggregate supply curve adjusts toward as_3, on the normal line, where the effect of the stimulus on output is offset. The monetary authority may choose to continue the policy of monetary expansion. At some point, market participants recognize that the effects on output are temporary, while the effects on prices are permanent. Wages and costs adjust more rapidly, and the aggregate supply curve moves faster; the upward shift accelerates. Changes in the nature of wage contracts contribute to the acceleration.

Our account readily explains the appearance of a relation between the rate of inflation and the level of some activity measure as in the usual Phillips curve. Motion of the equilibrium point around the normal output line may convey the idea of such a relation, even if the interaction is between prices, anticipated prices and output.[1]

Sometime in the 1970s, Keynesians accepted an accelerationist thesis, but qualified the thesis in a major way. The price-wage system is subject to pronounced inertial forces. Acceleration emerges very slowly, leaving ample room for substantial monetary manipulation to raise output and employment.

We accept the operation of inertial processes, but we reject the policy conclusion. Inertial patterns are not independent of past history and anticipated future performance. The contrary assumption, implicit in the Keynesian analysis, is untenable.

Lucas's major contribution emphasized the dependence of an economy's structure on the policy regime.[2] He argued cogently that changes in the regime, expressed by a change in the stochastic process governing monetary growth, modify the economy's response in specific ways. Changes in regime, or changes in

1. The shift in the supply curve can anticipate more price increase than occurs; transitory changes may be mistaken for permanent by some suppliers. The standard Phillips curve can have a negative slope – output falls as inflation rises in this case. Accelerating prices and falling output pose no problem for our analysis, but, as discussed below, we expect anticipations to lag in the presence of substantial transitory variance.

2. Robert E. Lucas jr., 'Expectations and the Neutrality of Money', *Journal of Economic Theory*, 4, April 1972, pp. 103-124.

stochastic processes conditioning the economy, induce revisions of perceptions about the future and relevant opportunity sets. Such revisions reflect efforts to gain from the use of information. Perceived changes affecting resources and opportunity sets modify optimal behavior patterns and change the economy's response structure. Lucas's analysis implies that inertial price-wage processes cannot be invariant with respect to changes in environmental conditions. While we can estimate current price changes as a distributed lag of past price changes, for any given sample, we should not expect the estimated inertial property to be maintained when there are major changes in underlying conditions. The assumption of an invariant inertial process is inconsistent with basic economic theory.

There remains, however, beyond invariance, the issue of the speed of adjustment to new circumstances, and thus the speed of adjustment of inertial processes. In contrast to the Keynesians, who argue that these processes respond very slowly, rational expectations analysis implies that inertial processes and other response patterns are "immediately" adjusted to new conditions. This follows from the assumptions of nearly complete stochastic information, and homogeneous decision makers with subjective probability distributions that match the true probability distributions. Both positions are unacceptable. The Keynesians fail to recognize that people learn and are not locked into their beliefs and behavior. The new classical macroeconomists introduce learning but neglect costs of acquiring information. Neglect of these costs leads them to exaggerate the speeds of learning and response in the market place and the knowledge that people have about the future in a changing and uncertain world.

New classical macroeconomists choose to remain in the Walrasian tradition; information and transaction costs have no role. There is no discussion of the development of institutions to minimize costs of acquiring information and transacting. Many phenomena remain outside their analysis, including money, financial intermediation, the business firm, the multiplicity of financial instruments, and gradual price and wage adjustments with comparatively inflexible nominal prices and wages. The irrelevance of institutional arrangements and the assumptions that markets clear and prices are fully flexible are consequences of a Walrasian market structure. Within the world described by the new classical macroeconomics, non-market clearing and inflexible prices are inconsistent with rational behavior. Rational agents exploit all mutually advantageous exchanges.

The exploitation of mutually advantageous exchanges remains true in the world of incomplete information, where there are information and transaction costs and only the weak form of rational expectations applies. Representatives of the new classical macroeconomics argue that exploitation of all mutually advantageous trades implies the occurrence of fully flexible prices.[1] The denial of such prices implies irrational behavior. Irrational behavior is unacceptable to economists, so many continue with the assumption of fully flexible prices. Generations of economists, and laymen, have recognized price setting and inflexible prices. We need not invoke irrationality to explain such phenomena. We must move beyond the Walrasian tradition, however, and recognize the relevance of information and transaction costs.

ii) *Sticky Nominal Prices*

The explanation of "sticky" nominal prices involves many of the features in our analysis of the use of money as a medium of exchange in Lecture 2. Money, price setting, and gradual price adjustment are rational responses in an uncertain world where transactions are costly and reliable information or interpretations of the future require investment of resources.

A complete analysis of "sticky" prices is lacking, but substantial progress has been made in recent years. One branch of this literature concerns the nature of the business firm and its operations, of which pricing is one important aspect.[2] Alchian and

---

1. ROBERT J. BARRO, 'Interest Rate Smoothing', Working Paper, University of Rochester, 1987.

2. RONALD H. COASE, 'The Nature of the Firm', *Economica*, 1937; ARMEN A. ALCHIAN and HAROLD DEMSETZ, 'Production, Information Costs, and Economic Organizations', *American Economic Review*, 5, 1972, pp. 777-795; OLIVER E. WILLIAMSON, *The Economic Institutions of Capitalism*, New York: The Free Press, 1985.

Demsetz emphasize that firms emerge as a response to information and transaction problems. The firm must be understood as a complex of contractual arrangements. Explicit and implicit price and wage contracts – price setting – emerge in response to specific problems facing a firm and the nature of the firm. Problems of "hold up" and moral hazard are particularly relevant. Interdependence of the resources of the contractual parties in the production process and in the firm's activities interact with possible "hold up" or moral hazard.

Resources are dependent if the value of a resource as part of a team of resources exceeds its value as a separate resource or as a member of another team. Oil producers may be dependent on a pipeline or a pipeline on a refinery. Dependence often involves situations where the cost of alternative arrangements is substantial. In such cases, the owner of the dependent resource faces potential hold up. The owner of the resources on which he depends may attempt to expropriate his quasi-rent.

The investor in the dependent resource is not fooled or misled. He understands the general problem when he invests. A contractual arrangement fixing the terms of trade and mutual obligations of interdependent resources is one solution. Even the owner of a unique resource, so important for the dependent resource, has a long-run interest in such an arrangement. Stable relationships lower uncertainty and avoid an active search for alternative marketing arrangements. Price setting, by contrast, is a rational outcome in this case.

Uncertainty about market conditions contributes to the problem faced by cooperating parties. One of the parties may find it difficult to learn whether the other party experiences a permanent change in market conditions or behaves opportunistically or attempts to expropriate the other's quasi-rent. Both parties may observe a given change but at least one party may not know whether the change is transitory or permanent. The suspicion and possibility of hold up arises in the circumstances. An agreement fixing the terms of trade removes some of the danger.

Consider the situation faced by the owner of a restaurant and his employees. They may arrange a wage that remains fixed for some time, or they may set wages at short intervals based on the demand for the restaurant's services. The latter will be associated with opportunities for hold up by either side. Further, frequent renegotiation of the terms of employment is costly in terms of time allocated to this activity and possible interruptions of service. Both parties rationally choose a contractual arrangement, based on anticipations of average or permanent demand, fixing the terms of employment for some time irrespective of intervening changes in market conditions. Persistent changes in market conditions will, in time, induce changes in the terms of trade. Again, price setting is a rational response.

Avoidance of potential hold up and moral hazard is not the only reason that we observe comparatively inflexible prices. Price setting may arise as a rational solution to the problem of organizing a market. Potential market participants can organize the market in three ways. They can set up an auction system, operating continuously or at regular intervals, select a continuous, extensive bargaining process in the manner of a bazaar, or the sellers can set posted prices.

The auction market, the choice of new classical macroeconomists, requires several conditions for its functioning. Market participants must be, more or less, uniformly informed. Each must acquire the specialized knowledge and skill to assess the qualities of the goods traded in the market.[1] Major informational asymmetries are ruled out by this assumption. Market participation must also involve a sufficiently large number of potential buyers and sellers who assemble and trade simultaneously.

Each of the conditions is more frequently violated than satisfied. They are necessary but not sufficient conditions for an auction market. People have comparative advantage in acquiring information, as in other activities. They invest in particular types of information and specialize their skills. It is irrational, and probably impossible, to become a specialist in all possible markets. This is simply a consequence of the uncertainty expressed by imperfect information and the operation of transac-

---

1. Participants can hire a professional trader to negotiate for them. An alternative is to let the better informed party set the price and rely on competition to reduce the return to specialized information to its opportunity cost.

tions costs. The simultaneous assembly of a sufficiently large number of market participants also imposes severe constraints. For many reasons, including the law of large numbers, people choose different times for their market activities. The commitment to assemble at pre-specified times for *all* marketing purposes is less preferable if not impossible. The use of an agent introduces costs of monitoring and supervision. Simultaneous assembly is replaced by arrangements whereby one market side, buyer or seller, stands ready to serve at irregular arrival times. The bazaar or a system of posted prices emerges.

The bazaar involves an investment of much time. Where the auction market requires simultaneous arrival of all participants or their agents, the bazaar depends on a trickle of arrivals. It cannot cope with large groups arriving simultaneously. It is not surprising that the bazaar is found in comparatively simple, low income economies. In these circumstances, the allocation of time to the bargaining process may be partly a consumption good. With rising opportunity costs of time, the disadvantages of the bargaining process exceed the benefits.

The working of a bazaar restricts its application. There are strict limits on the number of transactions per period. Sellers cannot serve several customers simultaneously, and to delegate bargaining to employees poses both an incentive and a moral hazard problem. Buyers pay large costs to learn about reservation prices, since information is revealed only by offers to buy and sell. These are commitments to transact. An accepted offer to purchase may be above the seller's reservation price; a refusal to sell may be based on an incorrect inference that the buyer is willing to pay more. Learning the reservation price and negotiating the market price requires a series of offers.

Sellers may recognize that the buyers face high costs of information. One, or more, may find sufficient incentive to obtain a competitive advantage by posting prices. The seller's information as a specialist is superior to the buyer's information. He shares this information by posting the price. This practice lowers information costs and removes the need to invest time in bargaining. The seller attracts buyers who value their time more than the possible saving from buying at less than the posted price. If the success of the price setters attracts imitators, the practice spreads. Once some prices are posted others, clinging to the old practice, feel the market's pressure. The posted prices provide guidelines for dealing with the other sellers.

Posted prices convey information. For example, a restaurant owner must decide on the market he wants to serve. This decision influences the kind and quality of food served, the services offered and the prices charged. By posting prices, the owner informs the buyer about his choices. Although they must sample to judge quality, the correlation between quality and price helps the buyer to decide whether to sample. A policy of frequently changing prices reduces information and places the restaurant at a competitive disadvantage.

The organization of the diamond market provides evidence on the role of information in market organizations. The wholesale diamond market is an auction market dominated by buyers and sellers who are specialists. Traders rely on their own skill in judging quality, knowledge of prices and other attributes. The retail market is very different. The sellers are mainly specialists; the buyers typically have much less information than the sellers. By posting prices, sellers exploit the correlation between quality and price to inform buyers. Buyers find it less costly to invest in information about the seller than to invest in information about the quality of diamonds, so sellers use resources to build reputation. If costs of acquiring information about the quality of diamonds were to fall to a minimal value, these arrangements would change. Diamonds might be sold in supermarkets or in retail auction markets.

In well-organized auction markets, we find people willing to pay for the right to purchase or sell at fixed nominal prices. The contracts expressing these rights, known as put and call options, give the owner the right to buy or sell at a fixed price within a fixed time period. The prices of the underlying securities and the prices of the puts and calls are determined in an auction market.

Costs of information and transactions are not uniform across goods, so no single form of market organization is likely to be found. The reason for puts and calls differs from the reason for price setting in the diamond market, just as the diamond market differs from the restaurant. The organization of the diamond market reduces the costs of bearing uncertainty about quality. The market for puts and calls permits asset owners or speculators to limit risk of wealth changes.

The examples suggest a way to model price setting formally. The seller has information that is costly for the buyer to acquire. The seller internalizes the cost of acquiring the information; it is part of his specialized knowledge, and he revises his information in the process of buying inputs. By posting a price, he exploits the correlation between price and quality. At the same time, he may offer a put – an option for the buyer to return the merchandise if the quality is not as represented or, perhaps, if the buyer finds the same merchandise at a lower price. The buyer pays for the good and for the put.

The conditions leading to price setting also apply to the labor market. The terms negotiated and the time horizon built into the agreement depend on the assessments of the parties. An assessment of the market can be interpreted in terms of a (subjective) probability distribution. The more diffuse the distribution the shorter is the time covered by the arrangement. Both parties use all information accessible to them (at some cost) to form their uncertain assessment.

Although the terms of the contract are optimal, given the different interests and assessments, realizations often deviate from the expectations expressed by the subjective probability distribution. Minor deviations matter little in the context of prevailing uncertainty. The response to major deviations depends on interpretation by the parties. All parties to the contract face a serious inference problem about the nature of unexpected changes. They have to infer from observations whether the unexpected changes are transitory or persistent.

A transitory change does not change the expected value. The event, while unexpected, occurs within the range of the parties' initial assessment. The gains and losses do not change the information on which the agreement was based. Either party may believe that a costless revision of the bargain to adjust to the passing event would be beneficial, but attempts at revision for each transitory change would raise the cost of transacting and eliminate the benefits of a longer-term agreement.

A more permanent change in conditions poses a different problem. The initial assessment of at least one party must be revised in the light of the new information. If the stakes are sufficiently high, the permanent change may justify the cost of renegotiation.

Negotiations proceed more smoothly when both parties share the reassessment of market conditions. Differences in assessment provide evidence on the extent of uncertainty. If both parties could agree on the actual shocks that occurred in the past, they could contract to compensate for unanticipated changes after they occur. Permanent changes in nominal values would not be allowed to affect real wages. Permanent changes in productivity would be paid to workers if positive and by workers if negative. That we do not observe contracts of this kind suggests that assessments differ even after the event and that reaching a common assessment of the past is costly.[1]

Parts of our discussion of price setting carry over to nominal wage setting. Observations show that real and nominal wages are inflexible – slow to adjust to changes. These observations are consistent with nominal wage and price setting. If nominal wages and prices do not fully adjust to all shocks as they occur, real wages may be sticky. Sticky real wages could also result if firms and workers use real wage contracts. Real wage contracts would be difficult to reconcile with inflexible nominal prices and wages, however. Some cost of adjusting nominal values must be present.[2]

There are two different meanings of real wages. One meaning expresses real wages in terms of the product of the firm at which the worker is employed. The second refers to the basket of goods and services that the worker can purchase. The problems of setting contract terms differ in the two cases.

Contracts that set wages in relation to productivity require a satisfactory solution to the measurement of productivity. This

1. This should not surprise historians or economists.
2. LAURENCE BALL and DAVID ROMER, 'Real Rigidities and the Non-neutrality of Money', National Bureau Working Paper n. 2476, 1987 b.

is the metering problem; both parties to the contract must agree on the measurement of productivity. Where precise measurement is difficult, as in service industries or managerial tasks, real wage contracts will be rare. Even when productivity is measured reliably as in piece-work systems, the measure does not translate directly into a wage rate. Valuation is required; often some, more or less, arbitrary system must be used to impute the price of the final product to the various inputs. Imputation and valuation bring two additional problems. One is moral hazard; the employer has some incentive to adopt a cost accounting system that benefits him. The other is the distinction between relative and absolute prices. The employer is mainly concerned with the relation of wages to product prices. The employee is concerned also, and perhaps most, about the relation of wages to the prices of consumables – the second meaning of real wages.

Real wage setting with full indexation is rare. There are few incentives to adopt such contracts. The choice of an index is a problem for both parties. Some of the problem would be removed if shocks could be identified unambiguously or if all shocks were of one kind, for example nominal, or real aggregative, or real allocative. The absence of reliable information prevents settlement on an optimal indexation formula as proposed in the literature.

Nominal wage contracting is also not ideal. In periods of moderate inflation, we observe contracts that differ in duration, in the extent of formal indexation, and in the use of clauses permitting reopening of the wage agreement during the life of the contract. We observe, also, that the types of contracts change with the rate of inflation and that employers can be induced to compensate for past inflation when (non-indexed) contracts are renewed. Thus, real considerations influence wages paid even if contracts are fixed in nominal terms.

Our emphasis on costs of acquiring information in relation to wage and price stickiness offers a perspective on recent work interpreting price setting as a "coordination failure".[1] The au-

---

1. *Id.*, 'Sticky Prices as a Coordination Failure', National Bureau Working Paper n. 2357, 1987 a.

thors argue that rigid prices arise from a failure to coordinate price changes. They introduce the idea of "price complementarity" between firms to discuss the extent that a firm adjusts its price whenever other firms adjust their prices in response to a nominal shock. A firm gains from adjusting its price as other firms adjust their prices. The degree of complementarity is not fixed; multiple equilibria may emerge in the degree of nominal price rigidity. Equilibria with less rigidity may have higher welfare.

This analysis revives old arguments about market failure at a new front. For a time, market failure was discovered whenever information and transaction costs produced departures from the Arrow-Debreu paradigm. Similarly, Ball and Romer characterize the absence of "coordinated price changes" as a market failure. It is a market failure only if we measure it against an ideal world without information and transaction costs. Failure to consider these costs and their implications neglects the central problem – why prices are not fully flexible. Further, neglect of these costs produces multiple equilibria and thus a range of indeterminacy if the degree of complementarity is not zero. Within the indeterminate range, the same conditions allow both adjustment and non-adjustment of prices to nominal shocks; the analysis offers no explanation of the different outcomes.

iii) *A Stylized Model*

A stylized model incorporates some of the ideas discussed in this section.[1] We summarize the main features of this model, in a general way.

$$f[y_t, p_t, \Delta h_t, h_{t-1}, i_t, r_t, x_t, m_t] = 0$$

$y =$ output, $p =$ price level, $h =$ stock of inventories, $i =$ nominal interest rate, $r =$ real interest rate, $x =$ exogenous real shock, and $m =$ nominal money stock. Under full information about the structure of the shocks and in the absence of transaction costs, monetary impulses cannot affect the real variables of the

1. KARL BRUNNER, ALEX CUKIERMAN and ALLAN H. MELTZER, 'Money and Economic Activity, Inventories and Business Cycles', *Journal of Monetary Economics*, 11, May 1983, pp. 281-319.

system. They are fully absorbed by the price level. Incomplete information of some sort is a necessary condition for significant monetary effects.

Rational expectations analysis introduced a specific information structure. Uncertainty is limited to misinterpretation of local and global shocks. It is now generally acknowledged that this specific information problem provides a poor basis for monetary analysis. Far more resources are invested in learning about the permanence of monetary and fiscal impulses than in separating local and global shocks.

Prices and output in our stylized model are set each period based on perceptions of underlying permanent conditions. Let x^* and m^* denote the perceived permanent component of x and m. Knowing these values, producers set output and the price level; y^* and p^* denote the producers' decisions. They are determined in accordance with the system

$$f[y_t^*, p_t^*, \Delta h_t^*, h_{t-1}, i_t^*, r_t^*, x_t^*, m_t^*].$$

The values actually emerging are x and m. With y^* and p^* adjusted to x^* and m^*, the nominal and real interest rate and the change in inventories adjust to the perceived transitory condition. This corresponds to the system

$$f[y_t^*, p_t^*, \Delta h_t, h_{t-1}, i_t, r_t, x_t, m_t].$$

The resulting change in the stock of inventories and the revision of perceived permanent values modify the initial conditions for the next period and thus move the system over time. Prices and output adjust. The nature of the information structure and the associated inference problem can produce serially correlated output movements. A comparatively large x, due to a shift in the permanent component, may be interpreted for a time as a transitory event. The lag of recognition about the true permanent position depends on the relative variances of transitory and permanent shocks. The larger the variance of transitory shocks, the greater the probability that errors will be serially correlated for some time after the shock. This will be the case even if the unconditional error in the population is serially uncorrelated.

Although prices do not fully adjust, decisions are entirely

rational. People use all available information, but they misinterpret the nature of the shock. Once they perceive that the shock is permanent, prices and output fully reflect the information.

Keynesians often treat gradual adjustment of prices and wages and inflexible prices as evidence of disequilibrium. Our analysis demonstrates the fallacy of this argument. There are different types of equilibrium positions, each dependent on the information available to participants.

Three levels of equilibrium can be distinguished in our analysis. At any moment, there is a permanent stock equilibrium characterized by the state variables x^* and m^*. This equilibrium occurs when $\Delta h = 0$. The values of all variables are adjusted to the perceived permanent shocks and the condition of unchanging inventories. The permanent stock equilibrium moves over time with x^* and m^*. A permanent equilibrium is less encompassing. The state variables in this case are x^*, m^*, and h_{t-1}. All other variables adjust to these conditions. If x^* and m^* are held fixed, the permanent equilibrium converges over time to the permanent stock equilibrium. A transitory equilibrium imposes an adjustment of the system to given values $m \neq m^*$, $x \neq x^*$, y^*, p^* and h_{t-1}. Movements of interest rates and inventory adjustment produce the transitory short-run equilibrium.

The formal analysis omits parts of our conception. There are no shocks of very short duration. These shocks were discussed in Lecture 2 as part of the transmission mechanism in the general substitution process. Such shocks could be incorporated into the model along the lines suggested earlier. They would be absorbed by a corresponding short-term interest rate or an accommodating change in the demand for money. Further, the analysis summarized by the stylized model proceeds under full information about the deterministic and stochastic structure. Even so, there is persistence. We note again that reliable information about the structure is not available. Uncertainty about the underlying structure confronts transactors with a more serious inference problem than the problem presented in the formal analysis. Agents hesitate, in the circumstances, to revise decisions with major consequences for costs and returns. They may wait until they are satisfied that the new, permanent conditions will remain.

The larger is the variance of the transitory shock, relative to the variance of the permanent shock, the slower is the adjustment to new information. Uncertainty of this kind extends the "recognition lag" for more permanent events and thus slows down the adjustment in price setting. Agents' information level is a function of the objective situation and the costs or returns associated with wrong decisions. Objective states yielding more reliable information would increase the frequency of price revisions. A similar result follows whenever the costs of wrong decisions (e.g. in large and persistent inflations) loom very large. But, in general, relatively large transitory variation lowers the frequency of price revisions on the output market. This offers monetary impulses a larger wedge to influence output and employment. The existence of this wedge offers no opportunity, however, for deliberate financial manipulation intended to control output. This theme is developed in Lecture 4.

3. Unemployment

Employment and unemployment depend on the movement of real wages and other costs of employment, so changes in unemployment are closely tied to the behavior of prices and wages. Economists traditionally distinguish three types of unemployment: frictional, cyclical and structural. These terms may appear somewhat antiquated and are not entirely fortunate. But the underlying economic processes to which these terms direct attention remain relevant.

Classification of unemployment into separate types should not be misinterpreted to mean that each type is controlled by an independent process. Frictional or, possibly better, reallocative unemployment is the unavoidable result of a continuously adjusting dynamic economy. Allocative adjustments are a necessary condition for wealth-creating economic processes. Obstructions to allocative adjustments, motivated by expectations of lower frictional unemployment, lower social wealth over time. Recognition of the social benefit of allocative adjustments does not remove the issue about how to achieve the beneficial adjustments at minimum social cost. Once more, we recognize the role of uncertainty. More reliable information for potential employers and employees would shorten the adjustment process. Heightened uncertainty retards the adjustment. A policy that remains consistent with anticipated longer-run behavior of the economy reduces the average level of reallocative unemployment.

A full analysis of reallocative unemployment lies beyond monetary analysis. Real shocks induce permanent reallocations. However, allocative shocks do not proceed at an even pace, so the level of reallocative unemployment fluctuates over time. The fluctuations modify the position of the normal output line used in our analysis.

Cyclical unemployment is, of course, a central theme of monetary analysis. Included here is unemployment associated with temporary movements in output due to a variety of shocks that shift the position of the aggregate demand and supply curves. These shocks may be permanent or transitory, real or nominal.

145

The essential point is that, if the shock does not change normal output, the effects on output, employment and unemployment do not remain. Our analysis of cyclical unemployment and its relation to policy is similar to the discussion of the adjustment of output to monetary (or fiscal) changes earlier in this lecture.[1] The temporary character of cyclical unemployment follows from the gradual accrual of information and learning which induces adjustment of the aggregate supply curve to an intersection with the aggregate demand curve on the normal output line. A large relative variance of transitory shocks produces a slower adjustment and consequently more persistence in output movements. The dependence of temporary output movements on the level of more or less reliable information implies that the responses of unemployment and other real variables to ongoing shocks vary over time in magnitude and timing. We do not expect to find any pronounced similarity of responses under a regime of shifting shock patterns.

Structural unemployment refers to a range of phenomena beyond the temporary movements around a normal output line. It reflects the position of the line. This issue is particularly relevant at present. The reason is that the pattern of European unemployment changed during the postwar period. Unemployment remained low for the first half of the postwar period compared with the United States' experience or earlier European experience. Major European countries maintained unemployment rates of 1 or 2 percent. In the 1980s, unemployment rates moved above 10 percent in many countries. Persistent unemployment at a relatively high rate has become the norm.

The interpretation of these developments and the proper remedy remains in dispute. Keynesians generally argue that monetary or fiscal expansion would substantially lower unemployment. This conclusion reflects the traditional Keynesian assumptions of slow information absorption and learning, permanent effects of nominal magnitudes on real values, and either a malleable level of normal output or a state below normal output. Without some assumptions of this kind, increased aggregate

1. See Figure 3-5, p. 130.

demand results in higher prices at the same level of output and employment.

Keynesians see European unemployment as a traditional demand deficiency problem. European unemployment drifted up throughout the 1970s with little evidence of demand deficiency. Supply side changes explain some of the drift. A wide array of labor market institutions developed. Some of these institutions, exemplified by employment protection measures and the expanding wedge between total labor cost and the wage received by employees, raised the expected real cost of employment. A reduction of real wages would have offset the effect on employment and unemployment, but real wages were sticky.[1] Unemployment rose.

The behavior of real wages, at least in part, reflects the evolution of labor market institutions and social transfers that lowered the private cost of unemployment. In contrast, the social cost of unemployment rose, and the welfare system redistributed these costs so as to maintain a low level of private costs for the unemployed. The employed maintain real wages and finance the unemployed. We suggest that in the past twenty years heightened institutional restrictions on the labor market raised the effective wage – the relevant total cost of employment per output unit – and reduced both aggregate supply and the expansion of employment. Wages, as a component of total employment cost, contribute with the non-wage component of costs to the unemployment problem, but real wages, by themselves, cannot explain European unemployment.[2]

Keynesians generally disregard or dismiss these consequences of evolving labor market institutions.[3] They adduce, beyond

1. RUDIGER SOLTWEDEL, 'Employment Problems in West Germany – The Role of Institutions, Labor Law and Government Intervention', *Carnegie-Rochester Conference Series on Public Policy*, 28, Spring 1988, pp. 153-220.

2. ANTHONIE KNOESTAR and NICO VAN DER WINDT, in 'Real wages and Taxation in Ten OECD Countries', *Oxford Bulletin of Economics and Statistics*, 49, 1, 1987, pp. 151-169, found that productivity growth dominates real wage changes in a sample of ten large economies for the main postwar years. Taxes and social contributions are important also; they explain 40 to 50 percent of real wage growth in several countries and 15 to 25 percent in others.

3. They would be pressed to explain the large underground economy in many countries.

demand deficiency, hysteresis operating in the labor market,[1] or the prevalence of efficiency wages.[2] Blanchard and Summers argue that unemployment and employment are sensitively conditioned by their respective past history. Once unemployment increases, it tends to stay high for some time. This phenomenon is consistent with the institutional changes on the labor market discussed by Soltwedel.[3]

Blanchard and Summers[4] attempt to explain evolution of the European labor market using a version of the insider-outsider hypothesis of wage-setting. The essential features of the analysis are shown in Figure 3-6. The "insiders" form the relevant pool of potential employees that influences wage setting on behalf of the workers. Wages are negotiated in the interest of the insiders. The analysis depends on the specification of this group. The simplest case identifies membership in the insider group with those currently employed by the firm. The vertical line above N_1 describes the insiders' employment level. The wage negotiated by the insiders for the period is expected to assure employment for all their members, given the expected demand for labor expressed by the firms. The expected demand curve confronting the insiders is denoted ed. The actual position of the demand curve, denoted by d, differs from ed as a result of realizations of underlying stochastic shocks. The shocks lower employment to N_2

A new insider group, N_2, forms. Wages are again set to maintain employment for all insiders in view of the expected demand for labor. Actual demand again modifies employment. It is easily seen that changes in employment move randomly over time in response to the random realizations of stochastic shocks. Consequently, the level of employment follows a random walk. Under various conditions imposed on labor force participation, unemployment would also follow a random walk.

The simple insider-outsider model is not the only representa-

1. OLIVIER BLANCHARD and LAURENCE H. SUMMERS, 'Hysteresis and European Unemployment', *NBER Macroeconomics Annual*, 1, 1986 a.

2. JOSEPH E. STIGLITZ, 'The Causes and Consequences of the Dependence of Quality on Price', *Journal of Economic Literature*, 25, 1987, pp. 1-48.

3. RUDIGER SOLTWEDEL, 1988, *op. cit.*

4. OLIVIER BLANCHARD and LAURENCE H. SUMMERS, 'Hysteresis and Unemployment', Working Paper n. 2035, National Bureau of Economic Research, 1986 b.

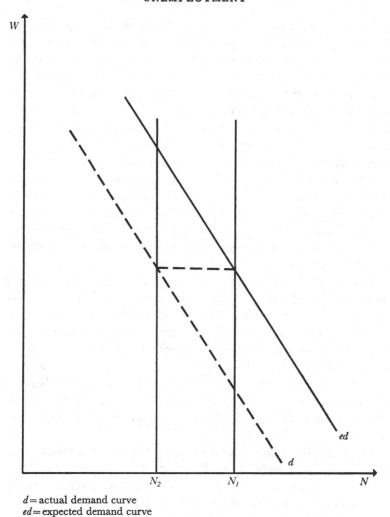

d = actual demand curve
ed = expected demand curve

Figure 3-6. The Essential Features of the Analysis of the
European Labor Market

tion of the basic idea that unionized workers must decide on a
membership rule defining the insider group. The model is sufficient to consider some general issues, however. The relevant
membership, the role of outsiders, the behavior of labor demand
and some political economy aspects require attention.

The membership rule may vary substantially. In addition to the currently employed workers, insiders may include a distributed lag (with declining weights) of currently unemployed past workers. Currently employed workers may be given weight in relation to length of service. Such differences in the definition of insiders would be reflected in the level and type of movement of both unemployment and wages. The insider-outsider model does not consider, so far, the motivation of the labor supply organization in setting the membership rule or the costs of enforcing the rule. The argument appears to have proceeded on the basis of rather arbitrary assumptions. Moreover, the pattern of real wage changes should be acknowledged as a constraint on the choice of underlying assumptions. The inconclusive cyclical movement of real wages probably rules out some versions of the basic idea.

The simple model neglects effects on the firms' behavior and on the supply of output. "Outsiders" are also assigned a passive role. There is no explanation for the difference in insider behavior in the 1960s and the 1980s. The insider-outsider model may gain power by joining the model to the institutional conjecture offered above: the insiders or their representatives use the political process to compensate the outsiders. Legislation increasing benefits for the unemployed strengthens the insiders' position. Legislation or regulation may also be required to restrict foreign competition.

The insider-outsider model combined with our political conjectures offers a testable explanation of European unemployment. The insiders' negotiations and political activities raised the expected, real, non-wage component of employment. Their negotiations prevented an offsetting adjustment of real wages. Labor demand stagnated as a result. Unemployment and the outsider group gradually expanded. Social legislation lowering the private cost of unemployment became a concern of the insider group to moderate pressures from the outsiders on the insiders' negotiation strategy. The insiders join with the outsiders to shift the costs of unemployment to others, particularly owners of capital, and non-workers.

A social equilibrium may have emerged characterized by the

condition (at the margin) that the outsiders' value of unemployment compensation, plus the value of leisure, balances the value of net benefits from employment adjusted for the disutility of work. A corresponding relation holds for the insider group. Further empirical work may show that the model explains the social stability of the status quo with large unemployment in Europe. It is noteworthy that no major political force on the European continent seems interested to change the institutional arrangements which determine this social equilibrium despite the fact that it is socially suboptimal. Why does a majority pay to support the outsiders and, thereby, increase the bargaining power of the insiders?

An alternative explanation, the efficiency wage theory[1] seems poorly designed to clarify the contemporary unemployment problem. The basic idea of the theory is that, at least over some range, higher wages raise productivity. A variety of more or less relevant reasons can be adduced: lower turnover costs, greater effort, increased loyalty, etc. Firms are assumed to be substantially uncertain about the quality of workers. To attract high quality workers, they set a "non-competitively" high wage at a level which minimizes labor costs per output unit. At this wage, there is an excess supply of labor consisting of lower quality workers.

The information structure is peculiar. Firms do not know the quality of potential employees, but they know the dependence of productivity on wages. They also seem to know that, by setting a "non-competitive" wage, they only attract high quality workers. The others ration themselves, perhaps voluntarily, into unemployment. There is no monitoring and no control mechanism to produce information about the internal labor market or to provide initial assessment and screening of potential employees. The problem of potential shirking does not exist.[2] Sufficiently high wages apparently remove all temptation to shirk or free ride.

Stiglitz's theory seems difficult to reconcile with the wide range of labor qualities which find employment and the corresponding

1. JOSEPH E. STIGLITZ, 1987, *op. cit.*
2. ARMEN A. ALCHIAN and HAROLD DEMSETZ, 'Production, Information, Costs, and Economic Organizations', *American Economic Review*, 5, 1972, pp. 777-795.

variations in wages. In his theory, the lower qualities are condemned to permanent unemployment. No one organizes a competitive firm with low wages and low productivity. In practice, firms recognize a distribution of quality classes, each with a specific efficiency wage. There is no reason why the existence of different qualities of labor should imply a permanent excess supply of labor.

Application of the efficiency wage theory to the European unemployment problem is particularly troublesome. It offers no explanation of why "excess labor" persistently increased from the late 1960s and throughout the 1970s into the 1980s. Moreover, we do not see how the theory supports a Keynesian remedy. The relevant efficiency wage must certainly be a real wage. Advocates of this theory would have to argue that rising prices, induced by financial expansion, lower real wages without raising the effective labor cost at the efficient nominal wage. Financial expansion could, then, affect employment. This is contrary to evidence on cyclical real wage changes.[1]

An equilibrium theory of unemployment, such as ours, does not imply that unemployment is at a socially optimal level or that average unemployment cannot be changed. Rejection of arguments for fiscal or monetary expansion is not a rejection of policies to reduce unemployment. The labor market restrictions that contributed to higher unemployment in the 1970s have benefits and costs – private benefits to those who gain wealth or leisure and private costs to those who are unemployed or who pay taxes to support the welfare benefits. These groups are not identical. Also, credible monetary and fiscal policies can, we believe, lower the average unemployment rate by reducing uncertainty. Our discussion of this issue continues, therefore, in Lecture 4.

---

1. M. J. Bils, 'Real Wages over the Business Cycles: Evidence from Panel Data', *Journal of Political Economy*, 93, August 1985, pp. 666-689.

4. *Impulse Patterns*

If the economic system were deterministic and a totally endogenous process, changes would reflect only the internal dynamics of the system. We reject this position. Changes in technology or changes in population may, in part, be endogenous responses to changes in the relevant environment. Many changes in population and technology are random. Technological inventions and their innovative applications in the production process are not predictable; they cannot be usefully analyzed as endogenous processes. A similar conclusion applies to policymakers' behavior. Even when political pressures, generated by economic performance, require that "something must be done," the specific measures are often poorly related to the problem and largely unpredictable in specific detail.

It seems to us advisable to proceed on the hypothesis that comparatively exogenous shocks drive the economy. The movements observed result from the interaction of a transmission or propagation process with random shocks. The nature of the shocks influences the evolution of the economy. Output, employment, real growth, price level, inflation rates and interest rates respond very differently to different shocks. Previous sections discussed some of these differences.

Four pairs of shocks may be distinguished. Any particular shock pattern is a combination of four elements, one drawn from each pair. The classification is non-exclusive with respect to the choice of one element from each pair. The pairs are:

    a. systematically dominant or an unpredictable and shifting mixture,
    b. monetary or real,
    c. aggregative or allocative,
    d. permanent or transitory,
       i. permanent shocks to the level,
      ii. transitory shocks to the level,
     iii. permanent shocks to the growth rate.

The dispute in the 1960s between the monetarists and the fiscalists centered on positions a and b. Monetarists emphasized that systematically dominant shocks occur over time, and that monetary shocks dominate the pattern. The occurrence of real shocks was not denied, but their significance was said to be either irregular or comparatively low. Monetarists claimed that dominance emerged under specific historical conditions, specifically, the institutional regime controlling money. The monetarist position did not imply irrelevance or ineffectiveness of fiscal policy or real shocks. They judged fiscal policy to be either not sufficiently variable or not sufficiently influential in comparison with monetary shocks. The variability and effects of monetary shocks were judged to be larger.

Keynesians did not accept this position. Their vision of the world was expressed by the *IS-LM* model. A steep *IS* and flat *LM* curve implied that real shocks and fiscal policy dominate the evolution of the economy. Changes in the degree of optimism or pessimism are the major source of changes in output and employment. Fiscal policy with its "direct effects" was judged to be more powerful than the "indirect" effects of monetary policy, so fiscal policy was the policy of choice to offset other real shocks. Later recognition of a potent monetary policy did not change the position on impulse patterns.

Our views have changed as evidence on shocks accumulated. We now accept a more eclectic view of impulse patterns. We acknowledge that impulse patterns involve shifting and unpredictable combinations of elements from the four pairs listed above. At times, a particular impulse dominates movements of output, as happened with the monetary decline in the 1930s or the oil shocks in the middle 1970s. The search for an unchanging distribution of systematically dominating impulses is, in our judgment, a futile exercise. The study of shock patterns remains useful, however. The studies provide useful information about the properties of alternative monetary or fiscal regimes.

Our more eclectic view does not affect the validity of a basic monetarist proposition – substantial accelerations or decelerations of the money stock modify the pace of economic activity. The nature of the impulse and its variability may change with the monetary or fiscal regime. What is true for output and employment is, to a degree, true of prices and the measured rate of price change also. We showed above that fiscal policy affects the price level. Hence, the price level and price changes depend on non-monetary impulses. The rate of price change, Δp, has two components,[1]

$$\Delta p = \pi + \varrho,$$

where π represents the persistent underlying pattern and ϱ is a more or less transitory component due to real shocks and irregular monetary and fiscal impulses. Persistent variations in rates of price change over time or between countries have been dominated in the past by differences in monetary growth rates. A dominant shock pattern still applies to the explanation of persistent inflation.

Aggregative and allocative shocks, point c, were compared in papers by John Long and Charles Plosser.[2] The first paper demonstrates that we need not necessarily invoke aggregative shocks to explain aggregate movements. The analysis establishes that an array of allocative shocks can generate fluctuations in output. A general substitution process between firms and industries across and over time transforms the allocative shocks into aggregate movements. The authors' second paper examines the relative role of aggregate and industry-specific shocks. They apply a factor analysis and decompose the output movements of a group of industries into common and specific factors. They find that common factors are, indeed, significant but not dominant. The specific factors seem to explain more of both movements and co-movements. A problem with this analysis is that aggregative impulses may appear, to some extent, as specific impulses. For example, monetary impulses may be unevenly distributed across industries. The statistical procedure could interpret the impulses as specific shocks.

An interesting statistical technique for a systematic investigation of shock patterns was introduced by Bomhoff[3] and ex-

1. KARL BRUNNER and ALLAN H. MELTZER, eds., 'The Problem of Inflation', *Carnegie-Rochester Conference Series on Public Policy*, 8, Amsterdam: North-Holland, 1978.
2. JOHN B. LONG and CHARLES J. PLOSSER, 'Real Business Cycles', *Journal of Political Economy*, 91, 1, 1983, pp. 36-69; *id.*, 'Sectoral vs. Aggregate Shocks in the Business Cycle', *American Economic Review*, 77, 2, 1987, pp. 333-336.
3. EDUARD JAN BOMHOFF, 'Predicting the Price Level in a World that Changes All the Time', *Carnegie-Rochester Conference Series on Public Policy*, 17, 1982, pp. 7-56.

tensively used by Meltzer.[1] The multi-state Kalman filter is particularly well suited for examination of the persistence of shocks, point d on the list above. The technique accommodates a comparatively complex pattern of shocks, so it can be used to explore the nature of prevailing shocks and their shifting pattern over time. Consider the following specification, used by Meltzer. Let X denote the observed value of a variable in the system. $\bar{X}$ the unobserved expected permanent component, and $\hat{X}$ the unobserved expected permanent growth rate. The interrelation between these magnitudes is defined as follows:

$$X_t = \bar{X}_t + \varepsilon_t$$
$$\bar{X}_t = \bar{X}_{t-1} + \hat{X}_t + \mu_t$$
$$\hat{X}_t = \hat{X}_{t-1} + \varrho_t.$$

The Greek symbols refer to random variables with zero expected value. The first equation states that actual output deviates randomly from expected permanent output, i.e. ε is a transitory shock to the level of the variable. The second equation presents changes in expected permanent output as the sum of a drift and a random term. The latter describes a permanent shock to the level of the variable. The drift term, in the third equation, is governed by a random walk. This means that ϱ is a permanent shock to the expected permanent growth rate. It follows that the expected permanent level appears as a random walk with a drift term randomly moving over time.

In addition to the rich specification of possible shocks, the multi-state Kalman filter also incorporates a learning process revising the relevant probability distributions on the basis of new data. Uncertainty about the structure is expressed by an array of alternative hypotheses. The probability assignment over

---

1. ALLAN H. MELTZER, 'Variability of Prices, Output and Money under Fixed and Fluctuating Exchange Rates: An Empirical Study of Monetary Regimes in Japan and the United States', *Bank of Japan Monetary and Economic Studies*, 3, December 1985, pp. 1-46; *id.*, 'Some Evidence on the Comparative Uncertainty Experienced under Different Monetary Regimes', in C. D. CAMPBELL and W. R. DOUGAN, eds., *Alternative Monetary Regimes*, Baltimore: Johns Hopkins, 1986 a, pp. 122-153; *id.*, 'Size, Persistence and Interrelation of Nominal and Real Shocks: Some Evidence from Four Countries', *Journal of Monetary Economics*, 17, January 1986 b, pp. 161-194.

this array changes with the accrual of new data. Meltzer's study of four countries tentatively concludes that permanent shocks to output and the price level dominated permanent shocks to the expected growth rate and, most particularly, transitory shocks to the output level. It also appears that the economic system was subjected to larger shocks under the gold standard, particularly for output, than under the Bretton Woods or the floating exchange rate regimes.

The evidence suggests that we should not expect stable shock patterns recurrently operating on our economy. The components of the four-way classification listed above probably shift over time. This confirms the eclectic conjecture advanced above. A shifting pattern of shocks has implications for forecasting and for policy that we consider in Lecture 4.

5. Normal Output

Our analysis of monetary and fiscal policy relies on the notion of normal output, represented by a fixed value in our analysis and a vertical line in the graphs. Normal output anchors the real system and imposes a maintained rate of inflation consistent with financial policies. The idea, if not the word, belongs to the classical tradition. Say's Law conveyed that the economy would always converge toward a "gravitational center" determined by preferences and technology. Friedman's Presidential address to the American Economic Association revived the idea;[1] he proposed that normal output could be interpreted as the solution to a Walrasian system. This suggestion implies that normal output moves independently of monetary shocks and is completely determined by real conditions – capital, labor and technology, the latter a relation between inputs and output.

The main point of the classical conception of normal output is its dependence on real conditions and independence from monetary shocks and monetary affairs. Monetary shocks produce only, more or less, temporary deviations from normal output. In the General Theory, Keynes, in contrast to the Keynesians, took a different view. He distinguished between two levels of output, actual output (or in his terms underemployment equilibrium) and maximum output. The former is the average or expected level of output that the economy achieves. The latter Keynes defined as the output level at which the elasticity of output with respect to the price level vanishes; it is the point at which further increases in the price level fail to raise output.[2]

Keynes concluded that only a fundamental institutional transformation involving state direction of investment can raise actual output to the level of maximum output. Monetary policy could

1. MILTON FRIEDMAN, 'The Role of Monetary Policy', American Economic Review, 58, March 1968, pp. 1-17.
2. KARL BRUNNER, 'The Socio-Political Vision of Keynes', in DAVID REESE, ed., The Legacy of Keynes, San Francisco: Harper and Row, 1987 c.; ALLAN H. MELTZER, 'Keynes's General Theory: A Different Perspective', Journal of Economic Literature, 19, March 1981, pp. 34-64; id., Keynes's Monetary Theory: A Different Perspective, Cambridge: Cambridge University Press, 1988.

not succeed in this task, according to Keynes, except temporarily. Keynesians, on the other hand, emphasize the important role of financial policy for moving the economy nearer to maximum output and maintaining full employment. In their vision, a proper combination of monetary and fiscal policies can always achieve full employment and maintain maximum output. This theme survives to the present.

We accept Keynes's distinction between actual and maximum output. Maximum output is a technological concept dependent on the available stocks of labor and capital and on the best available technology. In place of Keynes's expected actual output, we use normal output to refer to the expected value of output at which the economy reaches long-run equilibrium. Maximum output is an upper bound that output can reach, in principle; it is not necessarily a social optimum.

Normal output and factor productivity depend on environmental conditions apart from "technology." Productivity is significantly affected by the range of admissible organizational forms, contractual arrangements and the property rights structure.[1] Changes in this institutional environment modify firms' incentive structures and thus affect the production relation and normal output.

The significant role of institutional conditions in the determination of normal output is not limited to productivity. Our discussion of unemployment emphasized the effect of institutional arrangements, with their specific disincentives, on the rise of European unemployment during the past twenty years. These developments raised normal unemployment and lowered normal employment and normal output.

Thus, normal output depends on more than available real resources and production techniques; it depends on the institutional environment, including the characteristics of the political process and the rules of the game controlling the behavior of the government. Such rules affect the certainty, or uncertainty,

---

1. MICHAEL C. JENSEN and WILLIAM H. MECKLING, 'Rights and Production Functions: An Application to Labor-Managed Firms and Co-Determination', *Journal of Business*, 52, October 1979, pp. 469-506.

faced by producers and consumers. They condition the use made of the available resources. We, therefore, reject the characterization of normal output as a solution to the Walrasian system of equations.[1] This solution determines optimal output in the Pareto sense. Normal output, even when below Walrasian optimal output, may also be optimal relative to the constraints and incentives which produce it, but it differs from Walrasian output and is generally less than Walrasian output.

In empirical work, full employment output has been estimated in different ways. Some authors use assumptions about productivity and the unemployment rate consistent with full employment. Others draw a line connecting the business cycle peaks of gross national product. Normal output, on the other hand, was usually estimated from the trend of actual output. The trend was assumed to represent a deterministic and non-stationary growth process. Deviations from trend were assumed to result from a stationary stochastic process representing the "business cycle". In this view, monetary shocks are one of the driving forces for the deviations from trend but have no effect on the trend. Trend and deviations were assumed to be independent.

This standard scheme dominated empirical work until the early 1980s. A study by Nelson and Plosser changed the discussion.[2] These authors advanced the hypothesis of a stochastic trend. They compared two hypotheses. The trend stationary hypothesis assumes that a non-stationary time series can be represented as the sum of a deterministic trend plus a variable controlled by a stationary Arima process. The difference stationary hypothesis assumes, in contrast, that the time series under consideration is represented by an Arima process with a unit root in the autoregressive component. Tests on the United States data showed that the evidence favored the difference stationary

1. Empirical studies that condition outcomes on tastes and invariant technology most likely have the Walrasian concept in mind. It is not surprising, therefore, that these studies produce null results.

2. CHARLES R. NELSON and CHARLES J. PLOSSER, 'Trends and Random Walks in Macroeconomic Time Series', *Journal of Monetary Economics*, 10, 2, 1982, pp. 139-162.

hypothesis. Stultz and Wasserfallen replicated the test using data for several countries.[1] A typical finding of their study is a non-stationary time series consisting of the sum of a random walk and a stationary component.

A main result of the time series decomposition is the finding of a dominant contribution of the trend to observed fluctuations. Deviations from trend shrink to a small proportion of actual observations. Stationary components of output, computed from a trend stationary procedure, frequently exhibit pronounced influences from monetary shocks. Such influences are hardly discernible in the stationary component computed from difference stationary procedures. Reinforced by the traditional assumption that normal output, in this case defined by the stochastic trend, is independent of monetary actions, the conclusion of the analysis was that monetary impulses exert no real effects on the economy. Once the stationary component reduces to small proportions, monetary influences lose their potential effectiveness.

Stulz and Wasserfallen questioned a major pillar of this conclusion. They presented a model which demonstrates a (partial) dependence of the stochastic properties of the trend of output on the stochastic properties of the monetary regime. Their analysis shifted attention from monetary impulses to the characteristics of the monetary regime. The choice of a regime dominates the choice of a particular monetary course.

The conclusion about the irrelevance of monetary impulses has been challenged. McCallum shows that the discrimination between a trend stationary and a difference stationary hypothesis is very weak.[2] The test showing unit roots in autoregressive components of Arima processes cannot discriminate powerfully, against roots of .95 or even .9, but the interpretation of the result is very different and implies a much larger stationary component in the total fluctuations of output. Correspondingly, monetary

1. RENÉ M. STULTZ and WALTER WASSERFALLEN, 'Macroeconomic Time Series, Business Cycles and Macroeconomic Policies', *Carnegie-Rochester Conference Series on Public Policy*, 22, 1985, pp. 9-53.

2. BENNETT T. McCALLUM, 'On "Real" and "Sticky" Price Theories of the Business Cycle', *Journal of Money, Credit and Banking*, 18, November 1986 a, pp. 397-414.

influences have larger effects. Shapiro and Watson found that shocks to aggregate demand, productivity and labor inputs contribute to postwar fluctuations in output and that oil shocks supplemented these shocks in the 1970s.[1]

Watson and Cochrane also investigated the partition into stochastic trend and stationary cycle component.[2] Watson compared partitions based on an Arima model and an unobservable components framework with alternative assumptions about the correlations between trend innovations and stationary process innovations. His results demonstrate the fragility and non-robustness of the partitions which follow from the very nature of the problem. Comparatively short samples are used to determine an essentially long-term phenomenon. Cochrane questioned the random walk hypotheses associated with the stochastic trend. He noted that first differences computed over longer intervals exhibit variance patterns inconsistent with a random walk hypothesis. The data seem to indicate a pattern of partial mean reversal denied by a random walk hypothesis.

A recent development questions whether the trend is independent of the cycle as previous statistical work presumes. A recent paper by King, Plosser, Stock and Watson uses a further development of vector autoregression methods, in the form of co-integrated statistical models.[3] This framework partitions a multi-variate time series represented by an $n \times 1$ vector X in the following way,

$$X = a + A\tau + d(L)\varepsilon = a + X^p + X^c$$

where a is a constant vector, A an $n \times k$ matrix, τ a $k \times 1$ vector, $d(L)$ an $n \times n$ matrix of polynominals in the lag operator L and ε an $n \times 1$ vector of random terms. X^p and X^c refer to the permanent and transitory component in the partition of X. The sum $a + X^p$

1. MATTHEW D. SHAPIRO and MARK W. WATSON, 'Sources of Business Cycle Fluctuations', *Macroeconomics Annual*, 1988.
2. MARK W. WATSON, 'Univariate Detrending Methods with Stochastic Trends', *Journal of Monetary Economics*, 18, 1, 1986, pp. 49-75; JOHN H. COCHRANE, 'How Big Is the Random Walk in GNP?', Working Paper, University of Chicago, 1986.
3. ROBERT G. KING, CHARLES J. PLOSSER, JAMES H. STOCK and MARK W. WATSON, 'Stochastic Trends and Economic Fluctuations', Working Paper, University of Rochester, 1987.

$= (a + A\tau)$ represents the stochastic trend, and X^c the cyclic component. The elements of the k-dimensional vector τ consist of linear combinations of random walk variables. The innovations of these variables are in general correlated with the innovations in the cyclic component. Thus, the scheme partitions the series into a stochastic trend and cyccle and specifies potential interaction. This complex statistical procedure shows that interaction between trend and cycle is possible. Work along these lines is in its infancy. The economic models used in the tests are, at most, illustrative of the procedure. The empirical results also seem very tentative and exploratory.

Empirical analysis of normal output has expanded considerably since Nelson and Plosser initiated the discussion. Several questions have arisen.

    a. Should we recognize the trend as a stochastic phenomenon?
    b. Is the stochastic trend best represented as a random walk or as a combination of independent random walks?
    c. Is the trend independent of cyclical processes?
    d. Is the trend dependent on monetary shocks?
    e. Does normal output depend on the stochastic properties of the monetary regime?

We answer the first question affirmatively. It seems to us unreasonable to assume that normal output follows a path governed by a deterministic process while simultaneously assuming that cyclical processes are stochastic. We accept that the whole social process is stochastic. We may still summarize an economy's long-run performance with a smooth trend. Information about the average growth path and average growth rate for either the past 100 years or the past several decades is a useful summary of a main feature of the stochastic process.

We give a more tentative affirmative answer to the second question. The evidence seems to suggest that a random walk is a useful approximation to the trend. Our doubts about this conclusion arise from the nature of a random walk. A random walk proceeds without any bounds, so it cannot be reconciled with the limits imposed by our resources and potential. The dependence of output on resources and human arrangements limits the movement of output. The limits are clearly visible in the record of average real growth over time for all countries with stable political regimes. Countries with data available for many decades show few major shifts between distinct periods. Even the effects of large depressions influence the average growth path very little over the longer term. Cochrane's observation about the variance of first differences computed over longer horizons supports our contention. Cochrane's evidence of partial mean reversal seems to fit our conjecture.[1] Further, Friedman shows a significant correlation between the magnitude of the cyclical upswing and the magnitude of the preceding downswing.[2] The correlation between the magnitude of the upswing and the magnitude of the subsequent downswing is, on the other hand, comparatively small. This evidence suggests that the economy returns to a, possibly changing, trend.

We need to reconcile our tentative affirmative answer to the second question with these facts. The random walk provides a useful and simple description of output trends over a comparatively short horizon, but is less applicable for long-run behavior. Some reservation also seems appropriate in our judgment in view of the imprecision surrounding the decomposition of time series into trend and stationary components.

The facts just discussed bear on the third question. It would seem unreasonable to exclude a priori interaction between long-run and shorter-run movements. Cyclical accelerations and decelerations leave a heritage expressed by the pattern of available resources, for example, in the capital stock, that influences the subsequent evolution of output. This recognition needs to be properly understood however. The facts about long-term trends suggest that the interaction affects at most a period no longer than two or three business cycles and tends to dissipate over the very long-run. We accept, in principle, that some cyclical effects persist, although we remain skeptical about their size and about

1. JOHN H. COCHRANE, 1986, *op. cit.*
2. MILTON FRIEDMAN, 'The Monetary Studies of the National Bureau', *44th Annual Report*, New York: National Bureau of Economic Research, 1964, pp. 7-25.

the prospects for separating these effects reliably from the data on output.

The last two questions touch on matters of particular importance for these lectures. Our answer to the third question extends to the fourth. To the extent that monetary shocks contribute to cyclical processes, they also affect, indirectly, the economy's trend movement for some time. The consequences of positive and negative monetary impulses tend to cancel and any remaining effect disappears over the long term. Any medium-run effect of monetary shocks on normal output is too unreliable to offer a rational basis for activist or discretionary monetary policy. Long-run, normal output remains a function of real conditions not significantly shaped by the detailed monetary evolution.

This conclusion brings us to the last question. Our answer is already implicit in the earlier discussion of normal output. We emphasized there that normal output depends on the nature of the political regime. Major differences in the growth rates of per capita real income and the levels of output and income between countries depend on socio-economic conditions. The monetary regime is a part of these conditions. Uncertainty about short-run monetary evolution and longer-run price movements affects decisions bearing on the use and development of resources. The model developed by Stulz and Wasserfallen links the stochastic properties of the trend with the stochastic properties of the monetary regime.[1] An empirical study by Mascaro and Meltzer shows an effect of monetary uncertainty on real interest rates.[2] Bomhoff published an extensive study on the consequences of monetary uncertainty.[3] Our affirmative answer to the last question recognizes that the issue requires much more analysis and empirical work. A central aspect is the effect of uncertainty and the contribution of monetary arrangements to augment or reduce uncertainty. This is a theme of the last lecture.

---

1. RENÉ M. STULTZ and WALTER WASSERFALLEN, 1985, *op. cit.*

2. A. MASCARO and ALLAN H. MELTZER, 'Long- and Short-Term Interest Rates in an Uncertain World', *Journal of Monetary Economics*, 12, November 1983, pp. 485-518.

3. EDWARD JAN BOMHOFF, *Monetary Uncertainty*, Amsterdam: North-Holland, 1983.

FOURTH LECTURE*
Monetary Policy: Problems and Potential

1. *Three Different Visions*: i) *Keynesians*; ii) *Rational Expectations*; iii) *Monetarism*. – 2. *Rules and Discretion: Some Evidence from Forecasts*; i) *United States*: ii) *Europe and Japan*. – 3. *Rules and Discretion: Some Evidence on Alternative Regimes*: i) *The Gold Standard*; ii) *Fixed and Fluctuating Exchange Rates*. – 4. *Rules to Reduce Uncertainty*. – 5. *Conclusion*.

Did monetarism fail? Is monetarism dead? These questions were common topics for symposiums and lectures a few years ago. The popular answer was probably yes. Tobin says that is the right answer.[1] The monetarist answer was certainly not.[2] The same questions were asked earlier about Keynesianism and later about rational expectations and so-called supply side economics and received yes and no answers also.

What is failure, and what is success? For Tobin, the fact that unemployment rose after central bankers said they were controlling the money stock in the early eighties is sufficient. The fact that inflation fell, that the first effects of money were on output and that later inflation fell, as expected and predicted by the Shadow Open Market Committee and others who are called monetarists, is of no consequence. For many, the evidence of failure is the poor quality of forecasts of GNP or prices made using money. The demand for money, or velocity, shifted and, in the popular versions of the story became erratic just when central banks decided to control money. Yet, the evidence of this failure, too, is less than is commonly believed. Rasche estimated velocity equations and demand equations for money

* August 1987; revised July 1988.

1. JAMES TOBIN, 'The Monetarist Counter-Revolution Today – An Appraisal', *Economic Journal*, 91, March 1980, pp. 29-42.

2. KARL BRUNNER, 'Has Monetarism Failed?', in JAMES A. DORN and ANNA JACOBSON SCHWARZ, *The Search for Stable Money*, Chicago: University of Chicago Press, 1987 b, pp. 163-200, see also DAVID E. W. LAIDLER, *Monetarist Perspective*, Oxford: Phillip Allan, 1982, chap. 1.

using monthly, quarterly, and annual data for periods before and after 1980.[1] He found that the variance of the random walk in velocity and the variance of the demand for money equations did not increase in the later period. There is evidence of a one-time shift to a lower trend rate of growth of velocity after 1981. There is no evidence of increased variability.

Suppose, however, it were true that erratic shifts of the demand for money made forecasts of income from money unreliable after 1980. It is far from clear that an alternative theory would do better. If the forecast errors reflect shifts in portfolio allocation following financial deregulation, as many conjectured at the time, the shifts would also affect non-monetary variables. Forecasts based on Keynesian, or other models would be affected also, although the errors would be distributed over other equations. It is a testament to the lack of scientific spirit in which much of the discussion of monetarism's failure was conducted that, to the best of our knowledge, no evidence was presented that some systematic, alternative hypothesis provided more accurate forecasts.[2]

Concentration on the accuracy of quarterly or annual forecasts of velocity, money, GNP, interest rates, exchange rates or other variables assumes that this is the standard by which theories should be judged. We believe this is the wrong standard, for two reasons. The first raises an issue about the value of forecasts. The second is the issue of the standard by which we determine cognitive success and failure.

First, among the main achievements in the economics of the last twenty-five years are the theories of efficient markets and rational expectations. These theories imply that it is news, innovations, or unforeseen events that causes variables to change. Supporting this implication is evidence showing that the short-term behavior of many economic variables is described approximately by a random walk. Hence, model forecasts are not likely

---

1. ROBERT H. RASCHE, 'M1 Velocity and Money Demand Functions: Do Stable Relations Exist?', *Carnegie-Rochester Conference Series on Public Policy*, 1988.

2. That some purely pragmatic forecasts had lower forecast errors, if true for part or all of the period, has little bearing on the issue of choice between alternative hypotheses.

to do better than chance on average. Even if we accept that anticipated values have information that is useful for forecasting, it remains true that many variables of interest for policymaking are approximately random walks, at least short-term, so that much of the information which economists attempt to forecast cannot be distinguished from random changes.[1]

Suppose that the random walk is only a crude approximation, that there is reversion toward the mean. This seems plausible. Interest rates, exchange rates, monetary velocity and other economic variables range over a much smaller space than a pure random walk implies. The problem of using knowledge of reversion to improve forecast values, and thus the information problem, remains.

Second, basic differences between the groups reflect differences in perceived opportunities for policy and hypotheses about the information available to policymakers and the public. We agree with Modigliani when he insists that the distinguishing Keynesian characteristic is the claimed superiority of discretionary policy.[2] Monetarists and rational expectationists are skeptical of such claims. They favor returning to the classical position – policy means a rule; the choice of policy is a choice between rules. Rules differ on many dimensions. A rule may call for activist but predictable responses, or it may call for a fixed rate of money growth. A rule may rely on forecasts, on past data, or the rule can be independent of past, expected or predicted future values. Reliance on data from the past raises an issue about the accuracy of data, some of which are revised frequently. Reliance on forecasts raises the issue of the accuracy of forecasts and the size of

1. It is difficult to test definitively whether anticipated values affect future values. Tests introduce some hypotheses about anticipations, so the test is of the joint hypotheses and one or both hypotheses may be rejected. Generally, it will not be clear which hypothesis has been rejected. Evidence by FREDERIC S. MISHKIN, in *A Rational Expectations Approach to Macroeconometrics: Testing Policy Ineffectiveness and Efficient Markets Models*, Chicago: University of Chicago Press, 1983, ROBERT J. GORDON, in 'Price Inertia and Policy Ineffectiveness in the United States, 1890-1980', *Journal of Political Economy*, 90, 1982, pp. 1087-1117, and others provide useful evidence but do not overcome this difficulty. The best one can do is to validate the anticipations on independent data sets.

2. FRANCO MODIGLIANI, *The Debate over Stabilization Policy*, Cambridge: Cambridge University Press for the Raffaele Mattioli Foundation, 1986.

forecast errors. Both issues – the quality of published or reported data and the quality of forecasts – are part of a more general problem, the problem of information.

The quality of the information on which policy is based helps to determine whether policy augments or reduces variability and raises or lowers the risk or uncertainty that individuals and households face. Uncertainty cannot be eliminated; there are risks inherent in nature and institutional arrangements. Policy rules can reduce variability and uncertainty by placing more weight on the more reliable parts of our knowledge and less weight on data that are subject to large revisions and on relatively inaccurate forecasts. The policies advocated by Keynesians, monetarists and rational expectations theorists differ in the degree to which they rely on information. Hence, they differ in the risks and uncertainty that society bears when the alternatives are used as a basis for policy.

1. Three Different Visions[1]

Economists view the social process as a large, complex system of interacting people and institutions. Keynesians, monetarists and rational expectationists differ in their methods of analyzing social systems. Some of these differences are differences in modelling strategy, but some reflect differences in judgments about the reliability of information and the accuracy of forecasts and differences about the nature and type of uncertainty affecting the economy. This section discusses some of these differences.

i) *Keynesians*

Keynesians take as a starting point that a complex analytic framework is the most reliable way to learn about a complex economy. They presume that models with many interacting sectors improve our understanding of the ways interactions occur. They use models to simulate responses to policy. They introduce techniques like control theory from engineering to improve policy control.[2] They, often, propose policies like guideposts, guidelines, or credit controls to increase the number of policy instruments in the belief that more instruments improve control of a complex world.

In the first Mattioli Lecture, Modigliani described the Keynesian vision as the belief that "a market economy is subject to fluctuations which *need* to be corrected, *can* be corrected, and therefore *should* be corrected."[3] At one time, Keynesians

1. Parts of this section are based on KARL BRUNNER, 1987 b, *op. cit.*; THOMAS MAYER, 'The Structure of Monetarism I', in *id.*, ed., *The Structure of Monetarism*, New York: Norton 1978, pp. 1-25, provides an alternative statement of the monetarist vision.
2. J. H. KALCHBRENNER and PETER A. TINSLEY, 'On Filtering Auxiliary Information in Short-run Monetary Policy', *Carnegie-Rochester Conference Series on Public Policy*, 7, 1977, pp. 39-84.
3. Emphasis in the original. Modigliani recognizes that the imperative is a value judgment and does not defend it. With characteristic overstatement, he characterizes monetarism as belief in a fixed money growth rate, ignoring the discussion in sources such as THOMAS MAYER, 1978, *op. cit.*, and his earlier description of the central issue in FRANCO MODIGLIANI and ALBERT K. ANDO, 'Impact of Fiscal Action on Aggregative Income and the Monetarist Controversy: Theory and Evidence', in JEROME STEIN, ed., *Monetarism*, Amsterdam: North-Holland, 1976, pp. 17-42.

saw the economic system as either dynamically unstable, as in Hicks,[1] or tending to settle permanently at a position that is below full employment. The recent tendency is to treat the system as stable but slow to adjust, so policy can improve welfare by adjusting the economy toward full employment or by maintaining full employment once achieved. Recessions are usually recorded as disequilibrium positions – departures from equilibrium at full employment. Policy action can be used to restore full employment.

Large Keynesian models treat the economy's structure as deterministic. Shocks to the demand for money or to aggregate demand push the economy away from (or toward) the full employment position determined by the structure. Keynesians claim to have sufficient knowledge of the structure to be able to choose the policy mix appropriate to a given set of circumstances. Anticipations tend to be backward looking, based on past patterns, and slow to adjust to new information. Since the structure is deterministic, changes in belief, changes in policy and other changes are permitted to alter the model's structure only if the model is revised by the developers.

Keynesians have a "good will" theory of government. Governments pursue policies that are broadly in the public interest. The public interest is well-defined, free of the conflicts over income distribution, electoral success and power that could lead policymakers to pursue objectives other than full employment, stable prices, or efficient allocation.

The treatment of information and the role of government condition Keynesian policy analysis. If a model's forecast is for recession and continued inflation, additional stimulus is the usual prescription. At one time, there would have been a call for fiscal stimulus; more recently, the Keynesian response, particularly in the United States, appears to put more weight on monetary expansion or on a mix of fiscal expansion to increase output and monetary expansion to hold down, or lower, interest rates. Since many Keynesian economists accept some version of the permanent

---

1. JOHN RICHARD HICKS, *A Contribution to the Theory of the Trade Cycle*, Oxford: Clarendon Press, 1950.

income and natural rate hypotheses as the best available hypotheses, more stimulus now implies less stimulus at some unknown, future time.

Activist, discretionary policy can improve welfare only if the information about economic structure and economists' ability to forecast is sufficiently accurate. Many Keynesian policies also require that policies be reversed when circumstances change. Goodwill theories of government imply that governments will act to achieve stability independently of whether this involves stimulus or restraint. Stability is desirable, so policymakers will seek to achieve it.

Modigliani[1] follows Mayer[2] by treating the issue as a matter of distrust or dislike of government action. He neither mentions incentives nor discusses why government should be treated either as an aggregation of private welfare functions or as a supplier of a public good when choosing policies. Common observation shows that governments are more willing to reduce than to raise taxes, to increase than to lower spending. The average rate of inflation is positive, not zero, suggesting that governments are more inclined to inflate than to disinflate. Putting the issue as a matter of trust or distrust evades central questions. Does discretionary policy increase or decrease uncertainty? Do political constraints or personal incentives prevent governments from aiming at a social optimum?

ii) *Rational Expectations*

Rational expectations models also treat the government as a government of goodwill that acts as the selfless agent of the public. However, the government does not achieve this social optimum under all conditions. There are problems of inconsistency in public policies over time and a large literature showing that consistent policies are not optimal.

The information underlying the rational expectations policy position differs from the Keynesian position. Prominent among the characteristics of rational expectations models are explicit

1. FRANCO MODIGLIANI, 1986 *op. cit.*, p. 7.
2. THOMAS MAYER, 1978, *op. cit.*, p. 2.

micro foundations and explicit sources of uncertainty. The source of uncertainty differs. There may be confusion between relative and absolute price changes, as in Lucas,[1] or a stochastic process governing productivity changes, as in Prescott,[2] or some other explicit process. The main point is that information is incomplete, and the lack of information is the source of unanticipated changes.

In an influential and important paper, Lucas[3] extended and developed the implications of Marschak's[4] paper on identification. Changes in the policy regime change the structure of the model. Each different policy regime implies a different structure. Lucas draws an implication for simulations that use Keynesian policy models of alternative policy regimes; such models cannot give reliable answers about alternative policies. The estimated structure is not invariant to the change in policy regime.

If models cannot give the answers, what can? How can people adjust their subjective probabilities to match the objective probabilities of outcomes when there are actual changes in policy regime? The strong form of rational expectations assumes that people solve this problem. As we noted in Lecture one, the treatment of information in the strong form of rational expectations is either inconsistent with Lucas's demonstration that the subjective distributions of outcomes change,[5] or the information requirements are so extreme as to limit the practical relevance of the model.

The effort to build a macro theory consistent with micro theory is laudable. Rational expectationists argue, however, that theories or models that do not have appropriate micro foundations are "ad hoc" and provide no foundation for policy. To draw policy implications, they insist on a micro foundation.

1. ROBERT E. LUCAS JR., 'Expectations and the Neutrality of Money', *Journal of Economic Theory*, 4, April 1972, pp. 103-124.
2. EDWARD C. PRESCOTT, 'Theory Ahead of Business Cycle Measurement', *Carnegie-Rochester Conference Series on Public Policy*, 25, 1986, pp. 11-44.
3. ROBERT E. LUCAS JR., 'Econometric Policy Evaluation: A Critique', in *The Phillips Curve and Labor Markets, Carnegie-Rochester Conference Series on Public Policy*, 1 1976, pp. 19-46.
4. JACOB MARSCHAK, 'Economic Measurement for Policy and Prediction', in W. HOOD and T. C. KOOPMANS, eds., *Studies in Econometric Methods*, New York: John Wiley, 1953.
5. ROBERT E. LUCAS JR., 1976, *op. cit.*

This methodological position is false. Micro-foundations cannot determine the truth or falsity of policy or other implications. Further, the micro foundations chosen for rational expectations models have nearly full information and market clearing up to the current realization of the shock that generates uncertainty. Markets are characterized by price taking. With exceptions, such as Fischer[1] or Taylor,[2] the developers of these models choose to disregard, or even deny, evidence of non-market clearing. They then demonstrate a high order of technical skill and ingenuity by building into their model of nearly complete market clearing those features that generate persistence and fluctuations in output, prices, employment and other variables. Instead of accepting non-market clearing in many labor and product markets, the models develop persistence in other ways.

The intellectual quality of the work is not at issue. We reject the methodological position that claims that all policy statements must be based on models with explicit micro foundations. Such a position is not only without foundation, it is inconsistent with the behavior of (presumably) rational individuals who take policy recommendations from doctors and dentists, affecting their health or their lives, which are based on repeated observation, not a firm analytic foundation. Most human decisions are guided by experience, which is to say observation, not structural models of a system. The claim that policies cannot be improved without a structural model is untenable and to claim that economists cannot offer improvements based on evidence and systematic observation is untenable also.

Structural models with micro foundations can increase our knowledge and improve the foundations of policy rules. They are more likely to do so if their implications have been tested against alternative models. Basing policy on models that deny observations – for example that assume that all markets are characterized by price taking – has not been shown to be superior to policy rules that start from observations and lack a complete

1. STANLEY FISCHER, 'Long-term Contracts, Rational Expectations and the Optimal Money Supply Rule', *Journal of Political Economy*, 85, February 1977, pp. 191-205.
2. JOHN B. TAYLOR, 'Aggregate Dynamics and Staggered Contracts', *Journal of Political Economy*, 88, 1980, pp. 1-23.

micro structure. Scientific progress requires not one or the other activity, but both.

Typically, rational expectations models have a single representative consumer. Models of this kind have been useful for many problems. Most of the corpus of economic theory is based on the representative firm or the representative consumer. Models of the representative consumer, however, cannot distinguish between the individual and the market position. Each individual has the same cost of information and adjustment, typically zero, and therefore the same information. Once markets clear, everyone is at an optimum. The possibility that some adjust, while others with higher costs of information and adjustment do not, cannot be considered in this framework.

A main reason for the insistence that models have explicit micro foundations is that most rational expectations business cycle model are dynamic, equilibrium, market clearing models. An explicit micro foundation shows the source of uncertainty, reveals how uncertainty affects the equilibrium position and provides a foundation for the model's dynamic response to unforeseen events or surprises.

These desirable features are not the only features relevant for policy analysis. Currently available equilibrium business cycle models have two features that limit their relevance for policy. One is the information set on which the equilibrium depends. The other is the optimality of the institutional arrangements which determine the equilibrium position.

Rational expectations models would represent a major advance if they did nothing more than give explicit treatment to the information that people have and the uncertainty they face when making decisions. In contrast to the Keynesian position, which views fluctuations as disequilibrium events, the rational expectations vision recognizes that any disequilibrium position can be described as an equilibrium that is conditional on less than full information. We accept the usefulness of analyzing market positions as equilibrium positions conditional on information.

The problem is that the models do not introduce costs of acquiring information. Information is valuable, as these models recognize, but information is costly and the costs of acquiring (and interpreting) information are not zero, and they are not the same for everyone.

Another of our differences with the rational expectationists concerns the sources of uncertainty and information. For analytic convenience and tractability, the micro foundations typically introduce one type of uncertainty, one source of error. In the Marshallian tradition, the market place consists of a representative consumer and a representative producer. These assumptions, while useful for the analytic model, fail to distinguish differences in the information available to different individuals or the costs of acquiring information and differences between privately and socially optimal positions.

All individuals do not have the same information or the same costs of acquiring information.[1] Restriction of models to a single individual and a single source of uncertainty understates the uncertainty that people face when considering the distribution of outcomes.

A further difference with rational expectationists concerns the policy rule. In rational expectations models, everyone knows the policy rule and, since the policymaker seeks consistency or optimality, everyone knows that policy rules are chosen optimally. Rational expectations models dismiss major problems of policy choice and policy analysis arising from differences in private and social benefits. For example, much of the literature on credibility, following Barro and Gordon,[2] ignores the problem of achieving a social consensus to enforce the policy rule.

One of the uncertainties that people face is uncertainty about actual policy and its future course. In countries with variable policies and considerable discretion in policymaking, the public allocates substantial resources to acquiring information about current and prospective future policy and policy changes. This

1. At times, this problem is treated as a problem of bounded rationality. The language and the concept of bounded rationality mix rationality and the problem of acquiring information. Information is costly and, therefore, bounded, and the individual maximizes subject to constraints.

2. ROBERT J. BARRO and DAVID M. GORDON, 'Rules, Discretion and Reputation in a Model of Monetary Policy', *Journal of Monetary Economics*, 12, 1983, pp. 101-122.

source of uncertainty is neglected in rational expectations models. Also neglected is the uncertainty about the interpretation of policies such as tax policy or regulatory policy. Laws and regulations are often vague. Remaining in compliance is costly and uncertain.

Neglect of this broader range of uncertainty and costs of acquiring information contributes to the neglect of public choice issues in policy discussions. Differences in the properties of alternative policy rules are minimized. For example, in Sargent and Wallace's analysis,[1] systematic policies have no effect, so rules for money growth differ only, if at all, by the variance of the unanticipated changes that they generate. Models in this tradition neglect the effect of alternative rules or institutional arrangements on incentives, capital flight, resources devoted to information accrual, tax avoidance, income redistribution, opportunities for obscuring policy action and uncertainty about the economy's long-run path. Our point is not that each of these issues should be analyzed. These are examples of the uncertainties that distinguish one rule from another, distinguish the properties of one equilibrium from another and, particularly, distinguish equilibrium positions that are privately but not socially optimal from equilibrium positions that are both privately and socially optimal.

If an equilibrium position is privately optimal, there is no tendency to change the paths of output, prices and employment. The equilibrium position may not be socially optimal, however. A change in policy rules may be able to raise equilibrium output and employment by reducing risk or by removing excess burden.

An active group of rational expectations economists, associated particularly with the University of Minnesota, claim as a matter of principle that all models must rest on first principles – tastes and technology in the case of macroeconomic models. The claim is that models must rest on an invariant structure, and that taste and technology functions provide such a structure. Again, any other procedure is dismissed as ad hoc. And again, there is

1. Thomas J. Sargent and Neil Wallace, 'Rational Expectations, the Optimal Monetary Instrument and the Optimal Money Supply Rule', *Journal of Political Economy*, 83, April 1975, pp. 241-254.

no foundation for the principle that limits scientific knowledge to this class of models.

For analytic convenience, economists assume that tastes and opportunities are given and that the production function is an invariant technological relation. As we have pointed out earlier, there are no truly invariant relations unless one assumes that all policy changes and institutional restructuring are part of a single meta-structure. There is no reason to believe that economists have identified such a meta-structure.[1] Until they do, the structures we analyze are not invariant to changes in policy rules, learning, and other exogenous factors.

The National Bureau method of dating cyclical expansions and contractions shows a significant difference in the length of peacetime expansions and contractions in the United States before and after World War II (see Table 4-1). There are three distinct periods in their tabulation. The two prewar periods have approximately the same number of months of contraction as of expansion. The period after World War II differs; expansions are 30% to 40% longer on average; contractions are 50% shorter. A complete explanation of the change is lacking. Many observers assign importance to two factors, without suggesting that others may not be important also. One is the shift in production from

Table 4-1. Number of Months of Pre- and Post-war Expansions
and Contractions

Peacetime Cycles	Contractions	Expansions
1854-1919	22	24
1919-1945	20	26
1945-1982	11	34

Source: Business Conditions Digest, United States Department of Commerce, July 1987, p. 104.

1. Here is an example of societal change that significantly altered the aggregate production function. Changes in household production technology have shifted women from household production to manufacturing and services, altering the production function for marketable goods and services and for household services. One may, for convenience, assume that these are part of a meta-production function, but unless we can identify the meta-production function, output is not invariant to changes of this kind.

agriculture and manufacturing to services − a change in the relevant production function. The other is the changes in policy rules. With a larger government and increased revenues, so-called builtin stabilizers are more potent. A third possibility, often left unexplored, is the shift from the gold standard, or the interwar standard, to postwar monetary policies.

Economics does not require an assumption of absolute invariance. What is required is that the relationships under which policy rules are analyzed remain robust relative both to the changes that are contemplated and to other, unplanned changes in institutions and productivity that occur frequently. There is evidence for many such relations in economics. Examples are negatively sloped demand curves, diminishing marginal productivity, and the relation of money to income. Properly stated, these relations are found repeatedly in many different circumstances and conditions, although the parameters expressing the quantitative relation such as magnitude of response or speed of adjustment may change.

The attempt to develop dynamic policy models, conditioned only on unchanging tastes and technology, should be seen as an attempt to push out the frontiers of economics by developing empirical regularities about the dynamics of economic processes. Some regularities may be found, although the early work has produced mainly null results. The hypothesis of an invariant structure dependent only on tastes and technology, however, is a denial of the searching, striving experimenting nature of man that Hayek in particular has emphasized.[1] The insistence on policy rules is commendable. Insistence that policy analysis be restricted to relations that are invariant imposes a standard that, we believe, cannot be met. The standard denies uncertainty about the precise structure underlying the economy that, we believe, will remain.

A less ambitious, but more important, program of policy analysis stimulated by the rational expectations hypothesis starts from the analysis of time inconsistency set out by Kydland and

1. FRIEDERICK AUGUST VON HAYEK, *The Constitution of Liberty*, Chicago: University of Chicago Press, 1960.

Prescott.[1] This analysis brings out part of the problem of information facing the public and the policymaker and the value of rules or precommitment. Kydland and Prescott show that the dynamic path followed by an economy is not independent of the choice of policy rules. In their terms, discretionary policies are time inconsistent. This means that, although policy is set optimally for current and expected future conditions, with discretion actual future policy will differ from the optimal policy planned and announced for the future period. The change occurs without any new information. The reason for the change is that the public has made a commitment – e.g. to hold capital, to perform according to contract – that can be exploited by the policymaker. The public will anticipate this behavior so, in the case of inflation, on average the policymaker will achieve the expected level of output with an average rate of inflation that is higher than the optimal rate. Policy action in future periods is, therefore, not optimal from the perspective of an individual planning for the future today.

Barro and Gordon,[2] Backus and Drifill[3] and others extended the Kydland and Prescott model to produce an explanation of the positive average rate of inflation observed in many countries. Cukierman and Meltzer[4] obtain a similar result and show, also, that these results do not depend on the assumption that the policymaker and the public have the same objectives. In the Cukierman-Meltzer paper, the policymaker chooses procedures that are less accurate than other, available alternatives. The reason is that less accurate control procedures enable the policymaker to achieve personal or institutional objectives. For example, the policymaker may wish to stimulate the economy before an election. Inaccurate control procedures encourage people to believe

1. FINN KYDLAND and EDWARD C. PRESCOTT, 'Rules Rather than Discretion: The Inconsistency of Optimal Plans', *Journal of Political Economy*, 85, June 1977, pp. 473-492.

2. ROBERT J. BARRO and DAVID M. GORDON, 1983, *op. cit.*

3. DAVID BACKUS and JOHN DRIFFILL, 'Inflation and Reputation', *American Economic Review*, 75, 1985, pp. 530-538.

4. ALEX CUKIERMAN and ALLAN H. MELTZER, 'A Theory of Ambiguity, Credibility and Inflation under Discretion and Asymmetric Information', *Econometrica*, 54, September 1986, pp. 1099-1128.

that increases in money growth are not part of a systematic policy of inflation. Control procedures thus help to achieve the policymaker's objectives but do so by raising the cost of information above the minimum level. The public knows how the policymaker behaves, but it does not know the precise magnitude of the monetary change and cannot compute the change accurately until after the event. Information about the future is less accurate than could be achieved. Uncertainty is higher than the optimal level. Consequently, the public makes avoidable errors.

Much of the literature in the rational expectations tradition treats the policymaker as an agent of the public who seeks to achieve a social optimum. Since the public typically consists of a representative individual, the social objective function is the utility function of the representative household or person. Cukierman and Meltzer provide an exception in the rational expectations literature.[1] The policymaker pursues objectives that do not coincide with the public's objectives. A public choice perspective is not inconsistent with the rational expectations approach, but public choice considerations, are, generally, not part of the rational expectations vision.[2] This is a deficiency. Some efforts to remove the deficiency have started to appear.[3]

iii) *Monetarism*

Friedman introduces the problem of information and its relevance for the choice between rules and discretion.[4] He notes that policy can be stabilizing or destabilizing. A well-inten-

---

1. *Ibid.*

2. In rational expectations, real business cycle models, monetary policy affects only the price level, so we do not discuss the policy implications.

3. See, e.g., ALBERTO ALESINA, 'The End of Large Public Debts', in FRANCESCO GIAVAZZI and LUIGI SPAVENTA, eds., *High Public Debt: The Italian Experience*, Cambridge: Cambridge University Press for the Centre for Economic Policy Research, 1988 pp. 34-79, or ALBERTO ALESINA and GUIDO TABELLINI, 'A Positive Theory of Fiscal Deficits and Government Debt in a Democracy', Working Paper, National Bureau of Economic Research, 1987.

4. MILTON FRIEDMAN, 'The Effects of a Full-Employment Policy of Economic Stability: A Formal Analysis', *Economie Appliquée*, 4, July 1951, reprinted in MILTON FRIEDMAN, *Essays in Positive Economics*, Chicago: University of Chicago Press, 1953, pp. 117-132.

tioned policymaker will destabilize if he is misled by incomplete or incorrect information. For example, he may believe that the economy is about to go into recession, when it is not. Or, he may rely on a model that misstates the response to his action so that he does too much or too little.

Friedman's analysis is completely general. He uses the theorem expressing the variance of a sum

$$\sigma_z^2 = \sigma_x^2 + \sigma_y^2 + 2\text{cov}(x, y)$$

where σ^2 is a variance, x is the level of income in the absence of a policy action, y is the amount of income added (or subtracted) by policy action, and z is the level of income after the policy where[1]

$$z_t = x_t + y_t.$$

The condition for policy action to lower variability is that $\sigma_z^2 < \sigma_x^2$, which requires

$$\sigma_y^2 < -2\text{cov}(x, y) = -2\, r_{xy}\sigma_x\sigma_y$$

where r is the simple correlation between x and y.

Friedman notes that discretionary policy must do better than chance to lower variability. A chance policy has $r_{xy} = 0$, so discretionary action increases variability. The critical condition[2] for effective stabilization policy is

$$r_{xy} < -\tfrac{1}{2}\, \frac{\sigma_y}{\sigma_x}.$$

The more activist the policy, the larger the value of σ_y. The larger σ_y (relative to σ_x), the larger must be the negative co-variance and correlation between x and y if policy is to lower variability.

Brunner and Meltzer report estimates of the relevant variances and covariances using autoregressive models of money or base

---

1. MILTON FRIEDMAN, 1953, op. cit., notes that x, y and z can be deviations from trend – hence cyclical fluctuations.
2. MILTON FRIEDMAN, 1953, op. cit., p. 124.

money and the related velocities.[1] For the period 1953 to 1980 as a whole, and for the sub-periods 1953-1969 and 1969-1980, we found that the Federal Reserve's activist policies increased the variance of $\Delta lnGNP$ relative to a rule requiring constant money growth. This finding is subject to the usual caveat that a policy of constant growth would change the demand for money and the money supply function and, therefore, alter the variances of money, velocity and their growth rates. However, for the period 1969-1980, the variance of the systematic component of velocity growth would have had to double to reverse the result. For this period correlation between the systematic components in money growth and velocity growth is positive. This suggests that the Federal Reserve's activist policy increased variability, on average, in these years. The same qualitative result is found using the growth of the monetary base as a measure of money growth. A policy of constant base growth would have reduced the variance of the systematic component of GNP growth also.

A main problem for activist policy is uncertainty about information and its interpretation. There are several aspects. Economists have not produced a reliable, fully identified model relating policy variables to outcomes. There are large uncertainties about the size and timing of responses. Forecasts of the future are conditional on a number of variables, but there is uncertainty reflecting unresolved analytic differences about the elements of the set of conditioning variables. In addition, shocks to output, prices, employment and other variables are partly permanent, partly transitory. We have very little reliable information about the distributions of shocks or about how the distributions change over time. The same is true of the distributions of real and nominal shocks, of shocks to aggregate demand relative to aggregate supply, and of shocks to relative prices and output compared to absolute price and aggregate output.

Friedman's formula shows the difficult information problem posed by an activist approach. Success requires that σ_x is known. In practice, σ_x must be derived from the deterministic and sto-

1. KARL BRUNNER and ALLAN H. MELTZER, 'Strategies and Tactics for Monetary Control', *Carnegie-Rochester Conference Series on Public Policy*, 18, Spring 1983, pp. 59-103.

chastic structure of an hypothesis. To be credible and useful, the hypothesis must be tested and established as more reliable than competing hypotheses. Policymakers must know also how to produce an appropriate value for σ_y and, thus, r_{xy}.

It should not be surprising that, even with the best intentions and strong motivation to increase welfare, central bank governors can increase variability and instability. Political pressures often increase the degree of activism, before elections, after elections, to assist another country, to shift the burden temporarily from the housing industry, or the export industries, or the import industries, to finance a budget deficit at lower interest rates and for myriad other reasons. Many of these, well-known, pressures are remotely related to the public interest but closely related to independence of the central bank or the careers of the directors and staff.

The monetarist vision of the policy process emphasizes the informational and political problems that increase uncertainty.[1] Like the rational expectationists, monetarists conclude that a properly chosen rule reduces the amount of information that the public must have to plan for the future optimally. Monetarists differ from rational expectationists' and Keynesians' policy analyses by introducing public choice arguments to analyze policymaking and the policy process.

In contrast to the Keynesian, especially the early Keynesian, position, monetarists treat the economic system as stable. The system absorbs shocks and maintains stability if destabilizing policies are avoided. Major depressions and inflations are seen as the result of mistaken policies. If such policies are avoided, the system will continue to fluctuate in response to real shocks, but the shock absorbing internal dynamics bound the deviations and move the system toward equilibrium. Friedman's investigation found that real activity in a cycle upswing is more closely

1. MILTON FRIEDMAN, 1951, *op. cit.*; *id.*, *A Program for Monetary Stability*, New York: Fordham University Press, 1959; KARL BRUNNER, 'The Control of Monetary Aggregates', in *Controlling Monetary Aggregates*, III, Boston: Federal Reserve Bank of Boston, 1981, pp. 1-65; KARL BRUNNER and ALLAN H. MELTZER, 1986, *op. cit.*; and ALLAN H. MELTZER, 'Some Evidence on the Comparative Uncertainty Experienced Under Different Monetary Regimes', in C. D. CAMPBELL and W. R. DOUGAN, eds., *Alternative Monetary Regimes*, Baltimore: Johns Hopkins, 1986 a, pp. 122-153.

related to the preceding than to the succeeding downswing.[1] This suggests that disturbances to the economy reverse – that there is a tendency to return to the long-term growth path. In current parlance, there is mean reversion.

Monetarists accept the weak form of rational expectations – information is not wasted – but not the strong form. Reliable information is costly to obtain. It is sometimes suggested that these costs can be reduced by making information more readily available, by having the government collect and provide information more freely. This suggestion misses the point. Under uncertainty about the structure of the economy, the sources of shocks, and the persistence of observed changes, the main costs of information arise in interpreting data and drawing inferences about the future. An increase in money may be transitory or permanent, a change in level or in growth rate, an actual event or a statistical artifact that will be removed later, a move toward inflation or an offset to a perceived change in the demand for money, etc. The passage of time provides new information, resolving some existing doubts but creating new ones.[2] Problems of interpretation are central parts of the uncertainty that individuals face.

A frequent Keynesian criticism brings out the differences in vision. Tobin is fond of stating that it takes many Harberger (or Bailey) triangles to fill an Okun gap.[3] For him the cost of inflation is measured by the inflation tax, and the cost of disinflation is the temporary loss of output measured by the Okun gap.

The inflation tax is but one measure of the cost of a fully anticipated rate of inflation. Variable inflation imposes additional costs, particularly relevant for planning long-term saving

1. MILTON FRIEDMAN, 'The Monetary Studies of the National Bureau', *44th Annual Report*, National Bureau of Economic Research, New York, 1964, pp. 7-25.

2. The quality of money data is a much discussed topic. Critics of monetary control often point to the revisions in money stock data and to differences in definition. The same problem affects all data and is almost certainly more serious for data on saving, investment or real GNP. Problems of definition are at least as severe for fiscal policy and much more serious for concepts like real interest rates than for money.

3. See JAMES TOBIN, 1980, *op. cit.*, for one example.

and investment. Fischer discusses costs of institutional non-adaptation,[1] including non-indexed taxes, costs of uncertainty and distortions of relative prices. Cukierman in a series of papers,[2] shows that variability of relative prices is positively related to the average rate of inflation.

Tobin's comparison based on Bailey-Harberger triangles and Okun gaps is flawed. The economy loses in periods of unemployment and gains from employment above the natural rate. The Okun gap measures the loss of output during the adjustment from a higher to a lower inflation rate. This loss is not permanent. Part of the loss is transitory; normal output and lifetime earnings are not much affected by recessions.

There is also a bias inherent in Tobin's comparison. His reliance on the Bailey-Harberger triangle under the money demand curve shows that his measure of the social cost of inflation refers to a steady state with fully anticipated inflation. The comparison ignores costs of variability. The problem of inflation is not limited to a steady state with fully anticipated inflation. Due to the nature of the political process, substantial variations of inflation give rise to a diffuse uncertainty about its future course. Intermittent phases of disinflation typically emerge, but are not sustained. A policy of permanent inflation produces a series of Okun gaps. For most inflationary experiences of the last twenty years, these Okun gaps are more significant than the Bailey-Harberger triangle. The relevant present costs of an inflationary policy include not just the money demand triangles but also the discounted value of future Okun gaps. A disinflationary policy with a once and for all adjustment of inflation involves a single Okun gap.

In our view, Tobin neglects the costs arising from uncertainty – uncertainty about the levels of employment, output and prices or rates of inflation. For us, these costs are, in large part, an excess burden that can be removed by adopting more stable policies. For Tobin, Modigliani, and other Keynesians, variability

1. STANLEY FISCHER, 'Toward an Understanding of the Costs of Inflation, II', *Carnegie-Rochester Conference Series on Public Policy*, 15, 1981, pp. 5-42.

2. Summarized in ALEX CUKIERMAN, *Inflation, Stagflation, Relative Prices and Imperfect Information*, Cambridge: Cambridge University Press, 1984.

in policy arises as a consequence of actions to offset shocks. Policy variability is a cost paid to achieve any benefits resulting from discretionary policy action.

2. Rules and Discretion: Some Evidence from Forecasts[1]

The cases for rules and discretion have been stated many times. The arguments for rules are well known, for example from Friedman.[2] The arguments for discretion usually have two parts. One is a critique of Friedman's rule calling for a fixed rate of money growth. The other is a claim that information is available that can be used to stabilize the economy. Modigliani follows the traditional path. He tries to dismiss rules by criticizing Friedman's rule, and he proposes to use discretionary changes to achieve stability.[3] Modigliani's failure to mention alternative rules is a measure of the low level at which the criticism of rules usually takes place.

A key element in the case for discretion is that information is available that can be used to reduce variability and assist the economy's adjustment to unforeseen changes. This section considers one major source of information – the errors in private, government and international agency forecasts.

The thesis we present is that forecasts of main economic aggregates on which discretionary policies depend are so inaccurate on average that discretionary policies based on forecasts are unlikely to minimize variability. The thesis does not depend on any particular method of forecasting. It applies to all methods of forecasting that have been studied, including some based on judgment and some that are entirely mechanical. Nor does it depend on the choice of a particular time period. It appears to be true of all the recent time periods for which forecasts have been compared. Nor is it intended as a criticism of economists. Their forecasts, though wide of the target, may be the best available.

The record of more than twenty years of economic forecasting in the United States is summarized by the finding that, on

1. Parts of this Section and the next are from ALLAN H. MELTZER, 'Limits of Short-Run Stabilization Policy', *Economic Inquiry*, 25, January 1987 a, pp. 1-13, and *id.*, 'On Monetary Stability and Monetary Reform', *Bank of Japan Monetary and Economic Studies*, 5, September 1987 b, pp. 13-34.
2. MILTON FRIEDMAN, 1959, *op. cit.*
3. FRANCO MODIGLIANI, 1986, *op. cit.*

189

average, the most accurate forecasters cannot predict reliably at the beginning of the quarter whether the economy will be in a boom or a recession during that quarter. Although forecasting improves as the quarter passes and additional information becomes available, the statement remains true; after more than half of the current quarter has passed, forecasters cannot distinguish reliably between an above average expansion and a recession.

For several major countries, we have forecasts of annual values, in many cases for nearly twenty years. These data support a similar conclusion.[1] A policymaker who adjusts policy based on the forecast for the following year has little reason to be confident that he has changed policy in the right direction. Forecast errors are so large relative to the mean rate of change that, on average, forecasts cannot distinguish slow growth or recession from a boom. Similar conclusions hold for forecasts of inflation; forecast errors are so large relative to changes in the rate of inflation that reliance on forecasts will often mislead policymakers about the direction of change.

The size of average forecast errors poses a major problem for those who base discretionary policy on forecasts or propose rules that rely on forecasts. Our study of forecast errors using different, and possibly changing, techniques suggests that the problem is likely to remain. No single method or model seems to be superior to others. Indeed, we should not expect one method to completely dominate the others or for significant differences in forecast accuracy to persist. We would have difficulty explaining the survival of inferior models or methods in a competitive market for valuable information about the future.

One plausible explanation of the size of forecast errors is that, for the best forecasts, the average errors that remain mainly reflect unpredictable, random shocks that hit the economy. The shocks may result from real events – changes in productivity, weather, and the like – or they may result from unanticipated

---

1. MICHAEL J. ARTIS, 'How Accurate is the World Economic Outlook? A Post Mortem of IMF Forecasting', Working Paper, Manchester University, 1987, has some evidence on forecasts by IMF staff for less developed countries. Generally, these forecasts are less accurate than the forecasts we discuss.

or misperceived policy actions. Each model or method may weight the responses to a particular surprise or change in a particular time period differently, but the resulting differences – while important for explaining differences in forecasts for a particular quarter – appear to have little effect on summary measures of forecast accuracy.

A main objective of economic stabilization policy is, or should be, to reduce the uncertainty faced by consumers and producers to the minimum inherent in nature and trading arrangements. As always, there are two types of errors. Policy can be so active that uncertainty is increased. This can occur if policy actions are so unpredictable that observations of past behavior mislead the public or provide it with little information to guide current decisions. As in Friedman,[1] activist policies can increase uncertainty and variability also, if policymakers act on misjudgments – for example, mistake transitory for permanent changes, misinterpret nominal shocks as real shocks or base decisions on unreliable forecasts. On the other hand, policymakers can be too passive, as they were in the United States monetary collapse of the 1930s or in Europe and Japan when they maintained the Bretton Woods arrangement long after it had become clear that fixed exchange rates transmitted the United States' inflation to the rest of the world.

A standard conclusion in the literature on decision making is that actions should be based on all available information. Applications of this proposition to economic policy use the argument to show that a policymaker who maximizes social welfare will follow a contingent rule. The rule replicates the actions that would be chosen by a policymaker with complete discretion who acts to maximize social welfare. Assume that the policymaker seeks to stabilize the economy and reduce uncertainty. To say that the policymaker should not neglect current information is not the same as saying that he should rely on predictions or forecasts. Inaccurate forecasts can cause well-intentioned policymakers to increase variability and uncertainty, to destabilize rather than stabilize.

1. MILTON FRIEDMAN, 1951, *op. cit.*

i) *United States*

For the United States, there are a large number of public and private forecasts of quarterly and annual data. We have chosen data mainly on forecasts of real GNP and inflation, since comparative data are available for many countries, and these measures are prominent among the measures of social welfare.[1] Table 4-2 shows the size of quarterly forecast errors for various periods. Sources do not measure the error in the same way, so we have used root mean square error (RMSE) or mean absolute error (MAE) when RMSE is not available. RMSE magnifies the effect of large errors, such as those made in many countries at the time of the first oil shock. Our impression is that the two measures rarely give conflicting interpretations, although numerical values differ.

Table 4-2. Quarterly Root Mean Square Forecast Errors, United States
per cent per annum

Variable	Time Period	Range	Median or Actual	Source
real GNP growth	1980/2-1985/1	3.1-4.4	3.8	McNees (1986)[a]
	1970-73		2.1	Lombra and Moran (1983)
	1970/4-1983/4	2.8-3.6	3.0	Zarnowitz (1986)
	1970/1-1984/4	4.4-5.4	4.7	Webb (1985)
inflation	1980/2-1985/1	1.4-2.2	1.6	McNees (1986)[a]
	1970/4-1983/4	2.0-2.6	2.2	Zarnowitz (1986)
	1970/1-1984/4	1.8-2.1	1.9	Webb (1985)
nominal GNP growth	1967-82	-	5.5	Federal Reserve[b]
	1973-82		6.2	
	1970/4-1983/4	3.5-4.3	3.8	Zarnowitz (1986)

[a] 12 forecasts early in the quarter. Median values for 3 late quarter forecasts: real GNP, 2.4, inflation, 1.4.   [b] from Federal Reserve "green" books, various issues.

1. Forecasts for other data that we have reviewed include interest rates, money growth, investment, trade balance and balance of payments. Forecast errors are usually larger for these variables relative to mean values.

The mean growth rate of real GNP is 2.7% for 1970-1985 and 2.4% for 1980-1985. The rate of inflation (deflator) is 6.7% for 1970-1985 and 5.4% for 1980-1985 Nominal GNP growth is 9.5% for 1967-1982 and 9.9% for 1970-1983.

Root mean square errors are a large fraction of the reported growth rates of nominal and real GNP. Using twice the median value of the RMSE, the range within which real growth can fall during the current quarter covers the range from deep recession to a strong boom. For example, the median error for the four forecasters considered by Zarnowitz,[1] 3%, exceeds the average growth rate of real GNP, 2.4%, for the period. On average, forecasters do not distinguish between booms and recessions beginning in the same quarter. One standard error covers the range –0.6% to 5.4% and two standard errors cover the range of real growth rates –3.6% to 8.4% For nominal GNP growth, errors reported by Zarnowitz are smaller relative to nominal GNP growth for the period (9.8%). Still, the errors are large relative to the information required for stabilizing policy; two times the standard deviation covers the range 2.2% to 17.4%.

These data give no support to the idea that discretionary policy based on forecasts is likely to increase stability. The data make clear that the same conclusion follows for all quarterly forecasts considered, even if the lowest available value of the RMSE is used in place of the median, and for each of the periods considered. Large errors associated with the oil shocks may have increased forecast errors at the time but cannot explain the persistent pattern. A footnote to Table 4-2 reports the RMSE for forecasts made late in the quarter – for the current quarter – after one or two official estimates of monthly data on prices, industrial production, money, sales, jobless claims, employment and other data have been released. Forecast accuracy improves, but it remains true that the RMSE is a large fraction of the average growth rate of the period.

The errors for quarterly forecasts come from different models and methods that cover the range of techniques in common use. McNees compares judgmental forecasts compiled by the

1. Victor Zarnowitz, 'The Record and Improvability of Economic Forecasting', *Economic Forecasts*, 3, December 1986, pp. 22-30.

American Statistical Association and the National Bureau of Economic Research, large-scale econometric model forecasts sold commercially, forecasts issued by banks, the Federal government's Bureau of Economic Analysis, economic consulting firms, university research groups and the Bayesian vector autoregression model developed by Robert Litterman.[1] Webb compares seven mechanical forecasting procedures that use the autoregressive properties of economic time series to forecast interest rates, real GNP growth and inflation.[2]

At times, policymakers and their staffs have access to information that is not available to others. They have earlier access to some data of particular importance. For example, they know more about current policy than the public. Can they use this advantage to forecast more accurately than outsiders?

Lombra and Moran[3] compared quarterly forecasts by the staff of the Board of Governors for 1970-1973 to an earlier study of forecast accuracy by McNees covering six private forecasts. Lombra and Moran use mean absolute error of forecast for their comparisons. They find a small advantage in favor of the Board, 0.1% for real growth and 0.2% for inflation in quarterly forecasts for the current quarter. The advantage disappears for forecasts made four quarters ahead. Lombra and Moran also report root mean square errors for the Federal Reserve staff forecasts for the same period. The RMSE is shown in Table 4-2. For real growth, the reported error is the lowest value in Table 4-2. However, superior performance is not repeated in the nominal GNP growth forecasts available for a longer period. These are shown in the lower part of Table 4-2 where Federal Reserve forecasts errors are substantially larger than errors by other forecasters for a comparable period.

The Federal Reserve staff forecasts of nominal GNP growth for 1973-1982 appear to be biased. The mean absolute error

1. STEPHEN K. McNEES, 'The Accuracy of Forecasting Techniques', *New England Economic Review*, Federal Reserve Bank of Boston, March-April 1986, pp. 20-31.

2. ROBERT H. WEBB, 'Toward More Accurate Macroeconomic Forecasts from Vector Autoregression', *Economic Review*, Federal Reserve Bank of Richmond, July-August 1985, pp. 3-11.

3. RAYMOND E. LOMBRA and MICHAEL MORAN, 'Policy Advice and Policymaking at the Federal Reserve', *Carnegie-Rochester Conference Series on Public Policy*, 13, 1983, pp. 9-78.

for the current quarter is 5.4%, very similar to the mean error.[1] A plausible reason is that the Federal Reserve staff consistently underestimated inflation during the 1970s. This systematic error may have been the result of unwillingness to recognize internally the inflationary consequences of past policies, or the use of adaptive models that adjust slowly to the new information, or evidence of a Keynesian model structure that minimizes or denies the effect of money growth on inflation. Whatever the reason for the bias, the presence of persistent bias over a relatively long period, combined with lower accuracy than private forecasters, gives little support to arguments for discretionary policy actions intended to stabilize output and prices.

Recently, several economists have proposed using targets for expected nominal GNP growth to guide monetary policy.[2] The claimed benefit of a rule for expected nominal GNP growth is that policy offsets changes in velocity growth; money should grow faster in periods when expected velocity growth is low and conversely. In this way, monetary policy stabilizes the growth of aggregate demand.

The nominal GNP growth forecasts in Table 4-2 cast doubt on the stabilizing properties of expected nominal GNP growth targets if the targets are forecast values. The Federal Reserve's forecast error for nominal GNP growth in the current quarter is as much as 60% of the average rate of change. The smallest RMSE for private forecasts is 3.5%, more than one-third of the average growth rate for 1970-1983. These data give little reason for confidence in the stabilizing properties of this type of rule.

Quarterly data may reflect seasonal changes or transitory variations that distort the accuracy of current forecasting techniques. Also, quarterly data are not readily available for many

1. The mean absolute error four quarters ahead is 5.2% and is also very similar to the mean error. RAYMOND E. LOMBRA and NICHOLAS V. KARAMOUZIS, in 'Federal Reserve Policymaking: An Overview and Analysis of the Policy Process', *Carnegie-Rochester Conference Series on Public Policy*, 30, Spring 1989, have a more detailed discussion of Federal Reserve forecasts in the 1970s.

2. ROBERT J. GORDON, 'Using Monetary Policy to Dampen the Business Cycle: A New Set of First Principles', Working Paper, n. 1210, National Bureau of Economic Research, 1983, and JAMES TOBIN, 'Monetary Policy Rules, Targets and Shocks', *Journal of Money, Credit and Banking*, 15, 1983, pp. 506-518.

countries, but annual data are. Table 4-3 shows annual data for the United States.

Table 4-3. Annual[a] Root Mean Square Forecast Errors, United States
per cent per annum

Variable	Time Period	Range	Median or Actual	Source
real GNP growth	1980/2 1985/1	2.2-3.4	2.7	McNees (1986)[b]
	1970-73		3.5	Lombra and Moran (1983)
	1970/1 1984/4	2.0-3.2	3.0	Webb (1985)
	1973-85		2.0	IMF, Artis (1987)
	1973-85		1.7	OECD, Artis (1987)
inflation	1980/2 1985/1	2.2-3.4	2.7	McNees (1986)[b]
	1970-73		3.5	Lombra and Moran (1983)
	1970/1 1984/4	1.9-3.1	1.9	Webb (1985)
	1973-85		1.7	IMF, Artis (1987)
	1973-85		4.6	OECD, Artis (1987)

[a] Four quarter ahead forecasts are included with annual forecasts
[b] 12 forecasts early in the quarter

Several of the annual forecasts are from the same source as the quarterly forecasts, so we can observe whether the size of errors differs for quarterly and annual forecasts. No uniform pattern emerges from the comparisons available.

One notable feature of the inflation forecasts is the comparatively large errors made by the Federal Reserve for 1970-1973 and by the OECD for 1973-1985. We noted earlier that the Federal Reserve persistently underestimated inflation during the period of rising inflation. Artis shows that the OECD forecasts also underestimated inflation when inflation rose in the 1970s and overestimated inflation when the inflation rate fell in the 1980s.[1]

The RMSE in both cases is a relatively large fraction of the

1. MICHAEL J. ARTIS, 1987, op. cit., p. 46.

average rate of inflation. For 1970-1973, the deflator rose at a compound annual rate of 5.7%, so the Federal Reserve RMSE is more than 60% of the average. For 1973-1985, the average rate of inflation is 7.0%, and the RMSE is 66% of average inflation. Using two standard deviations as a measure of accuracy, the data suggest that neither the Federal Reserve nor the OECD could distinguish accurately between stable prices and double digit inflation a year in advance.[1]

Wolf[2] compared the forecasting record of fifteen private and public forecasters of the United States economy for the years 1983-1986. The average forecast error for real GNP growth for the fifteen forecasts in each of the four years has a mean of 28%. Mean errors range from 19% (1984) to 44% (1983). For inflation, as measured by the CPI, the overall mean is higher and the range is wider, The mean error for the four years is 44% of the rate of inflation, and the mean errors range from 13% (1985) to 99% (1986). The year 1986 includes a large one-time change in the price level that temporarily reduced the measured rate of change, so the 99% error may be extreme. One-time shocks occur frequently, however. Discretionary policy or rules that depend on forecasts are subject to errors of this kind. Moreover, Wolf's data, like Artis's, show large errors in predicting the rate of inflation when the rate changes. For 1983, Wolf reports an average error of 50%.

Wolf computed a measure of overall forecast accuracy for each forecaster in each year and ranked forecasters by the accuracy of their forecasts of four variables. His measure assumes that users (and society) weight errors in each variable equally, so his results may change if forecast accuracy for unemployment

1. The errors reported in MICHAEL J. ARTIS, 1987, *op. cit.*, are taken from the World Economic Outlook prepared by the IMF staff. Artis computes the errors for year ahead forecasts by comparing the forecast to the first reported results. The data for annual growth rates used in the comparisons are based on revised data published by the Federal Reserve Bank of St. Louis. The difference between the first report and the revised data affects the magnitudes but does not appear to affect the qualitative conclusions based on Tables 4-3 and 4-4. Note also that the year ahead forecasts for 1973-79 were usually made in December. For 1980-85, forecasts were made in August or September.

2. C. WOLF jr., 'Scoring the Economic Forecasters', *The Public Interest*, 88, Summer 1987, pp. 48-55.

and real growth are given larger weights than inflation or Treasury bill rates. Using his rankings, he cannot reject the hypothesis that the ranking for each forecaster in each year is independent.

The low correlation that Wolf finds between ranks suggests that differences in the quality of forecasts may arise by chance. This inference receives support from the data in Tables 4-2 and 4-3. These show that there is some suggestion of a lower bound, in the neighborhood of 1.5%, for the RMSEs shown for inflation and real growth in the United States. Further, several different forecast methods produce similar results. Similarity would arise if forecasters remove most of the systematic information in past data.

Remaining errors may not be entirely random. The managers of the various models often adjust their forecasts to reflect available information or perceptions. These adjustments do not appear to have much value on average; they do not reduce measured mean square errors for real GNP relative to the autoregressive models included in the data of Tables 4-2 and 4-3. Possibly the adjustments affect errors in particular periods without changing the root mean square error or other measures of forecast accuracy.

Evidence showing negative correlation between the forecast errors obtained using different procedures would suggest that forecast errors can be reduced by combining either procedures or forecasts. Evidence of positive correlation is consistent with the hypothesis that the errors remaining in the most accurate forecasts are mainly random deviations that are missed by different models. While we have not found a systematic study, some work suggests that forecast errors for IMF, OECD and private forecasters are positively correlated. For real GNP growth and inflation forecasts in six countries, Artis finds most correlations between errors above 0.8 and many above 0.9[1]

Litterman published an analysis of the source of his forecast error and some evidence on the relation of errors to policy actions.[2] He computed the effect of unanticipated policy changes in

1. Michael J. Artis, 1987, *op. cit.*, pp. 51-52.
2. Robert B. Litterman, 'How Monetary Policy in 1985 Affects the Outlook', *Quarterly Review*, Federal Reserve Bank of Minneapolis, Fall 1985, pp. 2-13.

1985 on his forecast for 1986 by comparing the model forecasts for 1986 made late in 1984 to the forecasts made approximately one year later. Since Litterman's autoregressive forecasting model adjusts only to past errors, changes in forecast values occur only when there are unanticipated changes – changes that were unanticipated from the past history of the series, and related series, at the time of the previous forecast. If there were no unanticipated changes in 1985, the forecast for 1986 would remain the same.

After adjusting for the relatively small changes in forecast values arising from the major revision of published historical time series, Litterman shows that most of the new information in 1985 was information about unanticipated monetary policy actions.[1] Specifically, he reports that 80% of the change in his forecast of real growth and 50% of the change in the forecast of inflation were the consequences of differences between expected and actual monetary actions in 1985. These estimates suggest that monetary policy actions account for a large part of the uncertainty and variability experienced during the sample period. Holding monetary policy constant, or otherwise making policy more predictable, would reduce this source of variability.[2]

ii) *Europe and Japan*

Since differences in policy rules and in the extent of discretionary action can affect the size of forecast errors, we consider annual forecast errors for other developed countries. The results are broadly comparable to our findings for the United States, so we limit the comparison to forecasts of real output growth.[3] Comparisons are facilitated by the availability of data on OECD and IMF forecasts for several countries and for the same time periods. These are shown in Table 4-4.

1. *Ibid.*, Table 5.
2. Litterman's quantitative estimates in ROBERT B. LITTERMAN, 1985, *op. cit.*, overstate the effect of unanticipated monetary policy action. The reason is that Litterman includes common stock prices, the value of the dollar and bond yields as well as monetary aggregates and short-term interest rates in his measure of monetary policy action. Several of these variables are affected by real shocks and by foreign nominal shocks.
3. One difference that is neglected is the difference between OECD and IMF forecasts. OECD has lower errors for growth but larger errors for inflation.

Table 4-4. Annual Forecast Errors, Europe and Japan, RMSE per cent per annum. Real Output Growth

Country	Time Period	Actual Growth[a]	Mean Absolute Actual	RMSE	Source
Germany	1969-86	2.4		1.9	Council of Econ. Experts
	1978-86	1.8		0.7	same
	1973-85	1.8	2.7	2.2	IMF, Artis (1987)
	1973-85	1.8		1.1	OECD, Artis (1987)
Holland	1953-85	3.6		3.2	Central Econ. Plan
	1975-85	1.6		2.0	same
Japan	1973-85	4.3	4.7	3.2	IMF, Artis (1987)
	1973-85	4.3		2.8	OECD, Artis (1987)
France	1973-85	2.1	2.5	1.1	IMF
	1973-85	2.1		1.5	OECD
Italy	1973-85	2.0	3.0	2.5	IMF
	1973-85	2.0		2.5	OECD
U.K.	1973-85	1.3	2.4	1.8	IMF
	1973-85	1.3		1.6	OECD

[a] From *International Economic Conditions*, Federal Reserve Bank of St. Louis, June 1987.

The IMF and OECD forecasts have very similar RMSEs for four of the six countries, and substantial differences between countries. Forecast errors by the IMF and OECD are lowest for France both absolutely and relative to the reported growth rate.[1] Forecast errors are highest for Japan, but the growth rate is highest also, so the relative forecast error for Japan is among the lowest.

The mean ratio of RMSE to actual growth is approximately 1.0 for the set of forecasts in Table 4-4. As in the United States, forecasts on average cannot distinguish booms and recessions, so they are not a useful guide for setting policies in advance of events to smooth growth. Reliance on these forecasts to direct policy would mislead policymakers at critical times. Forecast errors tend to be largest at turning points. Artis investigated the source of errors by studying the relation of forecast errors to

1. MICHAEL J. ARTIS, 1987, *op. cit.*, measures errors from the absolute value of the first reported data. These differ from the actual growth rates reported in Table 4-4. The difference is shown by a comparison of absolute growth and mean absolute actual shown for each of the five countries.

policy changes and OPEC shocks.[1] He found that the effects of the first OPEC shocks were largely unforeseen. This is not surprising. Like Litterman,[2] Artis also found that the effects of monetary restraint were often underestimated. Unanticipated fiscal policy changes proved relatively unimportant and often had the "wrong" sign.[3] Most of the errors appear to be random.

Forecast errors may depend on the choice of monetary regime. Meltzer found that forecast errors for Japan declined following the shift to fluctuating exchange rates and pre-announced targets for monetary growth.[4] The variability of annual forecast errors for Germany and Holland, based on forecasts of output by the Council of Experts and the Central Planning Bureau, also declined under the current system of pre-announced monetary growth, adjustable pegged rates within the EMS and fluctuating rates against other major currencies.[5] For Germany, forecasts are relatively accurate. The root mean square error is less than one-half the average growth rate for the period 1978-1986. It remains true, however, that policymakers who rely on forecasts to determine the time for discretionary changes will mistake booms and recessions.

Smyth studied the accuracy of OECD forecasts for seven countries – the United States, Japan, Germany, France, the United Kingdom, Italy and Canada – for the years 1968-1979.[6] He found no correlation between the errors and the year of the forecast, suggesting that forecast accuracy has not improved significantly but did not worsen after major currencies adopted the fluctuating rate system. Zarnowitz reports a similar result.[7]

Smyth reports the results of several tests. He used Theil's

1. *Ibid.*

2. Robert B. Litterman, 1985, *op. cit.*

3. Michael J. Artis, 1987, *op. cit.*, pp. 74 and 78.

4. Allan H. Meltzer, 'Variability of Prices, Output and Money under Fixed and Fluctuating Exchange Rates: An Empirical Study of Monetary Regimes in Japan and the United States', *Bank of Japan Monetary and Economic Studies*, 3, December 1985, pp. 1-46.

5. Data for seven additional German forecasters are available, but we have not computed the root mean square errors for each forecaster.

6. David J. Smyth, 'Short Run Macroeconomic Forecasting. The OECD Performance', *Journal Forecasting*, 2, 1983, pp. 37-49.

7. Victor Zarnowitz, 1986, *op. cit.*, pp. 22-30.

decomposition to show that most of the errors for output growth and inflation are random. He also compared the accuracy of forecasts to a naive model, the latter a random walk using preliminary data for the preceding year to forecast real output. He found that the OECD forecast for each country is more accurate than the random walk but, as Smyth notes, all of the improvement is in 1974-1976, following the first round of oil price increases. Information about the oil shock was available to private individuals as well as to public bodies, so the mechanical procedure probably overstates the error that people would have made. The results for other years suggest that any private information available to the OECD could not be translated into greater forecast accuracy.

Table 4-5 permits one additional set of comparisons. The table compares the mean absolute errors for year ahead forecasts by government, private and international agency groups. Mean absolute errors give less weight to large errors than RMSEs, so the reported errors are lower than in previous tables. The errors by the IMF staff are typically higher than domestic sources, with France an exception. None of the errors is less than 1.0; the best forecasters have been able to do on average is to make errors equal to 28% of the average rate of growth (Japan). For countries other than the United States and Japan, the mean absolute errors are 50% or more of the average rates of growth in Table 4-4 above.

Table 4-5. Mean Absolute Errors, Year Ahead Forecasts
Real Output Growth, 1973-1985 in percent

Country	Official[a]	Private[a]	IMF[b]
U.S.	1.4	1.0	1.4
Japan	1.2		1.8
France	1.2		1.1
Germany	1.2	1.5	1.6
Italy		1.9	2.2
U.K.		1.1	1.4

Source: Artis (1987) based on J. LLEWELLYN and H. ARAI, 'International Aspects of Forecasting Accuracy', *OECD Economic Studies*, Autumn 1984, pp. 73-117.
[a] For details, see source   [b] Artis (1987), World Economic Outlook

Private forecasters do not make larger errors in general than official agencies. Any advantage of classified information as a guide to discretionary management either does not affect the forecast or is offset by other errors. Timing cannot fully explain these data, since similar results were found using the quarterly data in Table 4-2.

Table 4-5 also compares the U.S. with Japan and the European countries. The differences appear to be relatively small in most cases. The results for the United States, and the implications for policy, apply as much to Europe and Japan as to the United States. Discretionary policies that rely on forecasts are likely to increase variability and uncertainty.

The comparisons we have made are suggestive, not conclusive. We have no direct evidence on the variability that would have resulted if a rule had been used instead of discretion or, in the case of countries that followed a rule, the variability that would have resulted under an alternative rule. Lucas' critique warns us that it is difficult to compare alternative policies.[1] Further, forecast errors often reflect more than differences in models, methods of forecasting and policies. Many forecasters use current information or intuition to adjust their forecasts. These well-known problems probably do not alter the main conclusions drawn from these comparisons.

Neither policymaking agencies nor private forecasters, using the techniques currently available, have been able to forecast, on average, whether the economy will be in a boom or recession one to four quarters ahead. Given that econometric research has been relatively unsuccessful at determining whether the lag between policy action and its effect is short or long, it is not clear whether more accurate forecasts could be used to reduce variability and uncertainty even if economists were capable of producing them. While one cannot dismiss the possibility that new research may change forecast accuracy, reliance on forecasts to change policy action does not seem useful in the current state of knowledge. Even well-intentioned efforts, based on forecasts, to dampen fluctuations can have the opposite effect of increasing fluctuations and the uncertainty borne by consumers and producers.

---

1. ROBERT E. LUCAS jr., 1976, *op. cit.*

3. Rules and Discretion: Some Evidence on Alternative Regimes[1]

The alternatives to discretionary monetary policy based on forecasts are various monetary rules committing the central bank to a predictable course of action. There are many types of rules. They differ along several dimensions. Three dimensions are particularly important. First is the decision about what is to be controlled. A rule can fix the relative price of currency, or exchange rate, in relation to other currencies or in relation to one or more commodities. Or, the rule can allow the exchange rate to fluctuate and establish an institution to control money, most often a monopoly central bank. Second, rules may minimize uncertainty about the course of policy action by adjusting to observables or setting a constant value or rate of change. Or, as in control theory, policy action may adjust to reflect the current or expected future situation. We use the term to refer to the former. Third, we must choose a criterion or standard so we can compare the operating characteristics of different rules.

We address the third issue first. The criterion we choose has two parts. The rule should achieve price stability on average or, if the optimal rate of inflation is non-zero, the rule should achieve the optimal rate. Also, the rule should minimize social cost. Again, there are two main aspects. One is the resource cost of holding reserves. The other is the cost of variability and uncertainty. A desirable rule reduces variability to the minimum inherent in nature and prevailing institutional arrangements such as trading practices, laws, political systems, etc.

The choice between fixed and fluctuating exchange rates has several aspects. Fixed exchange rates require the government to relinquish control of money and fix a relative price. Fluctuating exchange rates typically require a government monopoly to control the stock of money. Generally, economic theory supports neither price fixing nor monopoly. For these reasons alone conclusions from theoretical work about the proper exchange regime can at most be qualified and conditional. Small, open economies –

---

1. This section ignores issues that arise in the political process by which a rule would be chosen or rejected. We consider political incentives below.

like those discussed in Frenkel and Johnson[1] – are said to benefit more from fixing than from floating, but not much has been done to establish a dividing line. The small open economy model helps to explain why Holland, Belgium and Luxembourg choose to peg their exchange rate to the Deutsche Mark or why many countries in Central America peg to the dollar. The model has much less to say about the optimal choice of regime in the United Kingdom, The European Monetary System, Japan and the United States. It does not explain why Britain, the United States and Japan currently have fluctuating rates while Germany, France and Italy have adjustable, pegged rates within the bloc of countries known as the European Monetary System (EMS) and fluctuating rates outside the bloc. The model has little to say about the risk of relative price changes, or about the comparative cost of changing exchange rates instead of changing income and price levels, or about the risk of sudden policy changes.

In a comprehensive system of fixed exchange rates, some means of determining the growth of world reserves must be agreed upon. This is the n-country problem, a standard problem of price determination involving the choice of a numeraire to set, in this case, the world price level. In practice, this is a difficult problem involving comparison of the costs of holding commodities, the gains from seigniorage, the cost to the public of foregoing domestic concerns to maintain international price stability and some thorny political issues. Formal analysis of several of these issues has not produced firm conclusions. We must rely on less than fully formal analysis.

A useful starting point for discussion of exchange rate systems is Milton Friedman's "The Case for Flexible Exchange Rates".[2] Friedman considers a world in which changes in trade and payments occur continuously in response to unanticipated real and nominal changes. Adjustment to these shocks requires changes in relative prices and changes in the relative demands for assets denominated in different currencies. Friedman, and

1. JACOB A. FRENKEL and HARRY GORDON JOHNSON, eds., *The Monetary Approach to Balance of Payments Theory*, London: George Allen and Unwin, 1976.
2. MILTON FRIEDMAN, 'The Case for Flexible Exchange Rates', in *id.*, *Essays in Positive Economics*, Chicago: University of Chicago Press, 1953.

much subsequent analysis, considers four ways of adjusting, of which two are most relevant here. Countries can allow exchange rates to clear the market, or they can hold exchange rates fixed and wait until prices and money wages adjust. Where the adjustment of some relative prices and real wages is sluggish, as in most modern economies, fixed exchange rates necessarily introduce changes in relative demand and in the demand for labor and unemployment as part of the process of adjustment.

Flexible exchange rates do not avoid all changes in domestic unemployment when major trading partners experience changes in technology or change policy. But, flexible exchange rates avoid some changes in internal prices and incomes. The clearest, but not the only example, is the adjustment to an anticipated foreign inflation. The perceived costs of an inflation, anticipated as to occurrence but uncertain in magnitude and timing, became so large in the 1970s that many central bankers and governments changed their views about the relative costs of fixed and fluctuating rate systems. Flexible exchange rates can also increase stability if prices or money wages adjust slowly and there are frequent changes in relative rates of productivity growth at home and abroad.

To a considerable extent, the case in favor of fluctuating exchange rates rests on the greater stability of prices and output that can be achieved at times by allowing exchange rates to adjust prices relative to production costs and foreign prices. An added advantage, claimed for fluctuating rates, is that fewer resources are invested in holding commodity reserves or foreign exchange, so more saving is available for investment in physical capital. As far as we know, the latter argument has not been challenged; the greater resource cost of fixed rate systems is generally accepted.[1]

Against the benefits claimed for fluctuating exchange rates,

---

1. Some possible exceptions are papers that claim that price stability can be achieved using commodity money systems without holding commodities. BENNETT T. McCALLUM, in 'The "New Monetary Economics"', Fiscal Issues and Unemployment', *Carnegie-Rochester Conference Series on Public Policy*, 23, 1985, pp. 13-45, finds this argument invalid.

proponents of fixed, or fixed but adjustable rates, offer three main arguments. First is the claim that fluctuating exchange rates increase the instability of output. The main evidence of increased instability is usually the greater variability of real exchange rates. Second, fluctuating rates are said to reduce trade. The reason given is that exporters and importers face increased uncertainty about prices of traded goods, or they must pay the cost of hedging against uncertainty. Third, fluctuating exchange rates are said to cause greater variability of prices and inflation. The argument is that fluctuating exchange rates work by changing prices of foreign goods relative to prices of domestic goods and by changing product prices relative to costs of production. These changes in relative prices affect the price level and, particularly in countries with money wages indexed to the price level, they trigger price adjustment and inflation.

The claims and counterclaims are well-known by now. Advocates of fluctuating rates point out that price and output variability is caused by shocks and policies. Advocates of fixed rates respond that fluctuating exchange rates amplify the responses in two ways. First, they claim that there is destabilizing speculation under fluctuating exchange rates. Second, they argue that fluctuating rates free countries from the discipline of a fixed rate system, so countries pursue more expansive monetary policies and experience more inflation.

Support for these last conjectures is, at best, weak. There is not much evidence of a relation between the exchange rate regime and the rate of inflation. Inflation was a principal reason for ending the fixed exchange rate regime, and disinflation has been carried out in many countries under fluctuating exchange rates. Countries have learned to use crawling pegs and adjustable pegs to reconcile differences in inflation with fixed real exchange rates. If alternating periods of inflation and disinflation are a greater problem under one type of regime than under the other, much of the cost arises from variability and uncertainty. The issue is, again, one of relative uncertainty.

Mussa's comprehensive study of the variability of ex post real exchange rates shows that the short-term variability of bilateral exchange rates is higher under fluctuating rates, often substantially higher.[1] His finding is that the more rapid adjustment of nominal exchange rates, under a fluctuating rate regime, is not matched by a corresponding increase in the speed of price adjustment. Mussa notes, however, that his findings have no clear welfare implications. Nominal exchange rate changes have real effects, but these effects are the result of the slow, gradual adjustment of prices. He notes that his work does not show that fluctuating exchange rates increase the social cost of the monetary system relative to a system in which exchange rates are fixed permanently or relative to a system with discrete changes in currency parities. Exchange rate data cannot resolve the issue. The issue is whether uncertainty about variables such as output and the price level is increased or reduced, whether there are efficiency losses such as might occur if trade was more restricted under one system than another, or whether there is some evidence of an excess burden.

Studies of the effects of exchange rate variability on trade and capital movements have not produced evidence of a reliable effect. Surveys by Farrell[2] and by the IMF[3] report that the evidence is weak or inconclusive. If there is an effect of variability on trade, it has been hard to detect reliably. Farrell notes that many of the studies that have been done fail to distinguish between anticipated and unanticipated changes or between persistent and transitory changes, thereby increasing the difficulty of interpreting the empirical work.

One reason for the absence of demonstrable effects on trade may be that relevant measures of variability have not increased markedly. There is a tendency in discussions of fluctuating rates to jump from the finding of increased variability of real exchange rates to the conclusion that uncertainty has increased. An al-

1. MICHAEL L. MUSSA, 'Nominal Exchange Rate Regimes and the Behavior of Real Exchange Rates: Evidence and Implications', *Carnegie-Rochester Conference Series on Public Policy*, 25, 1986, pp. 117-214.

2. VICTORIA S. FARRELL, DEAN A. DE ROSA and ASHBY T. McCOWN, 'Effects of Exchange Rate Variability on International Trade and Other Economic Variables: A Review of the Literature', *Staff Studies*, 130, Board of Governors of the Federal Reserve System, December 1983, pp. 1-21.

3. International Monetary Fund, *Exchange Rate Variability and World Trade*, Washington, 1984.

ternative interpretation is that the variability of real exchange rates reduces the responses of prices and output to changes in the environment.

Comparisons of fixed and fluctuating exchange rates often fail to distinguish between different positions on the same transformation curve and Pareto superior positions. Evidence that real exchange rates are more variable under fluctuating rates is not evidence of excess burden; fixing the exchange rate shifts at least some of the variability elsewhere if policies remain unchanged.

Given the standard or objective of reducing uncertainty to the minimum inherent in nature and non-monetary arrangements, comparison of exchange rate systems requires a measure of uncertainty. We use computations of unanticipated variability of output and prices.[1] Since fixed exchange rate systems and commodity standards impose a burden in the form of resource costs of holding reserves, equivalence of uncertainty under fixed and fluctuating rates is sufficient to establish superiority of fluctuating rates under the specified criterion.

To advance the discussion, we require some empirical evidence on variability under different rules. Friedman has some early, relatively informal computations comparing actual policy to a rule for constant money growth.[2] Bronfenbrenner has a more detailed comparison of price variability under discretionary policy and three rules for constant money growth.[3] He recognizes that any comparison must assume that output and the demand for money or velocity do not change with the change in regime.[4] Bronfenbrenner concludes that a rule for 3% constant money growth (M_1) has less price variability than discretionary policy or other rules he considers. He notes, however, that results are not uniform across periods. Bronfenbrenner includes the periods

1. Computational methods are discussed below.
2. MILTON FRIEDMAN, 1959, *op. cit.*, pp. 95-97.
3. MARTIN BRONFENBRENNER, 'Statistical Tests of Rival Monetary Rules', *Journal of Political Economy*, 69, February 1961, pp. 1-14.
4. Martin Bronfenbrenner discusses, but does not compute, errors for a rule similar to the rule proposed by BENNETT T. McCALLUM, 'Optimal Monetary Policy in the Light of Recent Experience: The Case for Rules', Working Paper, Carnegie-Mellon University, Pittsburgh, July 1987, that adjusts the rate of money growth for deviations of real output growth from its long-run path.

1901-1914, when the United States was on a gold standard without a central bank, and the period 1915-29, years of a modified gold standard and a central bank. The judgment rule, or discretion, does better for 1901-1914, and the constant growth rule has less price variability for 1915-1929.

i) *The Gold Standard*

The right to own gold is a valuable right. The fact that many people choose to exercise the right in a non-gold standard regime provides information about their perceptions and anticipations. They may fear inflation, or confiscation of their assets, or some type of institutional change affecting property rights. Whatever the source of uncertainty, ownership of gold and other metals is perceived as privately desirable. Society bears a cost, however. The uncertainty that leads individuals to hold gold instead of productive assets lowers the capital stock and the level of income.

Under a gold standard regime, the reasons for holding gold may include the use of gold as a medium of exchange. The social cost of private or government gold holding remains. This cost is recognized generally. Proponents of the gold standard offset the cost, usually implicitly, by pointing to the benefit of price stability that the gold standard conferred in the nineteenth century.

Three issues arise. First, the price stability achieved under the nineteenth century gold standard is retrospective. Many of the costs of inflation arise from unanticipated inflation. Did wealth-owners in the nineteenth century anticipate stable prices? Second, variability and uncertainty about output and prices may be higher even if the average rate of inflation is lower. This would occur if prices or output are more difficult to forecast under the gold standard. Some who advocate the gold standard now recognize this cost.[1] Third, typically the gold standard was suspended during crises or wars, and restoration was not always at the previous exchange value. This introduces an element of uncertainty about the future price level. Schwartz discusses other

---

1. PETER BERNHOLZ, 'The Implementation and Maintenance of a Monetary Constitution', in JAMES DORN and ANNA JACOBSON SCHWARTZ, eds., *The Search for Stable Money*, Chicago: University of Chicago Press, 1987, pp. 83-118.

aspects of the gold standard and the arguments pro and con.[1] Our interest is in the comparative variability and uncertainty. Meltzer attempts to measure uncertainty under different monetary regimes.[2] The measure of uncertainty is the variance of unanticipated changes in prices and output computed from a Kalman filter developed in Bomhoff[3] and Kool.[4] Forecast errors are sub-divided into transitory errors in level, permanent errors in level (or transitory errors in the growth rate) and permanent errors in the growth rate. The latter are a measure of the stochastic component in the trend of normal output growth. Let x_t be the logarithm of the level of a particular series, $\bar{x}_t$ the permanent level and $\hat{x}_t$ the permanent, underlying rate of growth.

$$x_t = \bar{x}_t + \varepsilon_t$$

$$\bar{x}_t = \bar{x}_{t-1} + \hat{x}_t + \gamma_t$$

$$\hat{x}_t = \hat{x}_{t-1} + \varrho_t$$

so that $\qquad x_t = \hat{x}_{t-1} + \bar{x}_{t-1} + \varepsilon_t + \gamma_t + \varrho_t$

can be written as a second order equation, similar to an ARIMA model. Differences from the ARIMA model arise because the multi-state Kalman filter uses a Bayesian procedure to revise the parameters of the estimating equation each period.[5] The coefficients of the model change each period. Since the forecasts use only data for periods before the forecast, the forecasts could have been made, in principle, at the time. Forecasts and errors are for one period ahead. The estimation procedure uses information efficiently, so forecasts farther into the future can be

1. ANNA JACOBSON SCHWARTZ, 'Alternative Monetary Regimes: The Gold Standard', in C. D. CAMPBELL and W. R. DOUGAN, eds., *Alternative Monetary Regimes*, Baltimore: Johns Hopkins, 1986, pp. 44-72.

2. ALLAN H. MELTZER, 'Some Evidence on the Comparative Uncertainty Experienced under Different Monetary Regimes', in C. D. CAMPBELL and W. R. DOUGAN, eds., *Alternative Monetary Regimes*, Baltimore: Johns Hopkins, 1986 a, pp. 122-153.

3. EDUARD JAN BOMHOFF, *Monetary Uncertainty*, Amsterdam: North-Holland, 1983.

4. CLEMENS J. M. KOOL, 'Forecasts with Multi-State Kalman Filters', Appendix 1 to EDUARD JAN BOMHOFF, 1983, *op. cit.*

5. A more complete description is given in BOMHOFF, 1983, *op. cit.*, and KOOL, 1983, *op. cit.*

made by adding $(k\hat{x}_t)x_t$ to the current value, where k is the number of periods. The expected value for period $t + k$ is

$$Ex_{t+k} = x_t \left(1 + k\hat{x}_t\right).$$

This value changes each period with changes in the computed values of x_t and $\hat{x}_t$. These changes reflect the changes in the estimated transitory and permanent values of the level and growth rate.

A principal finding of Meltzer is that the level of uncertainty differs considerably under different regimes.[1] Output uncertainty is highest in the United States for the period 1931-1941, the period beginning with the breakdown of the interwar gold standard and ending with the wartime pegging of interest rates on government securities. Uncertainty about the price level is highest in the two regimes that include World Wars I and II.

Comparison of the gold standard regime with and without a central bank, 1890-1914 and 1915-1931, to experience under Bretton Woods and fluctuating exchange rates, 1951-1971 and 1972-1980, shows that the two gold standard eras produced greater uncertainty about the level and growth rate of output and prices. For real output under the gold standard, the lowest values of the variance of forecast errors for the permanent level and growth rate are 8 and 10 times larger than the highest error in the two postwar regimes. For the price level, the comparisons are less extreme but are also favorable to the postwar regimes.[2]

The finding of lower price level uncertainty in the postwar period seems anomalous. For the United States, as for many other countries, the average rate of inflation has been higher in the postwar period than under the gold standard. The resolution is straightforward. People do not expect prices to be stable; they expect prices to rise without limit. The lower variance of forecast errors in the postwar years implies that the change in prices is more predictable now than under the gold standard, even though the expected rate of inflation is higher.

1. ALLAN H. MELTZER, 1986 a, *op. cit.*
2. We compare the two postwar regimes – Bretton Woods and fluctuating exchange rates – in the next sub-section.

The conclusions from this study are based on quarterly data for a single country, the United States, from 1890 through 1980. The quarterly data prior to 1929 are interpolations by Gordon.[1] The study ignores other changes that may explain the greater variability under the gold standard, including the shift in production from agriculture to manufacturing to services, changes in the size of government that changed the importance of built-in stabilizers, and many other institutional changes.

Estimates of uncertainty using the same estimation method on annual data for seven countries are reported in Meltzer and Robinson.[2] The countries include small and large economies that differ on many dimensions, Denmark, Germany, Italy, Japan, Sweden the United Kingdom and the United States. The data analyses suggest that the principal conclusions hold for this sample. Uncertainty appears to be higher under the gold standard than under the postwar regimes.

ii) *Fixed and Fluctuating Exchange Rates*

Estimates of the comparative variability and uncertainty experienced under fixed and fluctuating exchange rates are rare. Some studies simulate alternative regimes using presumed values for the coefficients and the distributions of shocks. It is not clear how this procedure can be informative. Taylor uses a rational expectations model with contractual wages to simulate responses under fixed and fluctuating exchange rates in seven major countries.[3] He assumes that the distribution of shocks remains the same as in 1972-1984. A principal finding of his paper is that the fluctuating exchange rate system with a constant money growth rule works better than a fixed rate system, particularly for Germany and Japan.

1. ROBERT G. GORDON, 'Price Inertia and Policy Ineffectiveness in the United States, 1890-1980', *Journal of Political Economy*, 90, 1982, pp. 1087-1117.
2. ALLAN H. MELTZER and SARANNA ROBINSON, 'Stability Under the Gold Standard in Practice', in MICHAEL D. BORDO, ed., *Money, History, and International Finance: Essays in Honor of Anna J. Schwartz*, Chicago: University of Chicago Press, 1985, pp. 163-195.
3. JOHN B. TAYLOR, 'An Econometric Investigation of International Monetary Policy Rules: Fixed versus Flexible Exchange Rates', Working Paper, Stanford University, 1987.

In a series of papers, using quarterly and annual data for the Bretton Woods and fluctuating exchange rate regimes, Meltzer obtained similar results.[1] Unanticipated variability is computed by taking residuals from the Kalman filter model developed by Bomhoff.[2] The multi-state Kalman filter generates estimates of ε, γ and ϱ, (the values of transitory shocks to the level of each variable and transitory and permanent shocks to the growth rate respectively). The unanticipated variability of prices and output is computed as

$$\sqrt{V(\varepsilon) + V(\gamma) + V(\varrho)}$$

where V is the variance. For real growth and inflation, we use for the root mean square error,

$$\sqrt{V(\gamma) + V(\varrho)}.$$

Data cannot tell us what would have happened in a given period under a different monetary regime. Nor can data show whether the results would have differed if a different pattern of shocks had occurred. The measures of variability can be used, however, to reject the hypothesis that the change from fixed to fluctuating rates increased excess burdens as measured by variability.

Meltzer treats the change in Japan's monetary regime as an experiment and compares the results achieved in Japan with the results in the United States following an announced change in monetary policy procedures – the adoption in 1975 of pre-announced monetary targets with continued reliance on fluctuating exchange rates.[3]

Prior to 1971, the Japanese government controlled interest rates, allocated bank credit, subsidized credit expansion through the banking system and maintained fixed exchange rates under the Bretton Woods agreement. Suzuki discusses the main features of the Japanese system.[4] In 1975, Japan introduced a system of

1. ALLAN H. MELTZER, 1985, *op. cit.*, and 1986 b, *op. cit.*, and 1987 b, *op. cit.*
2. EDUARD JAN BOMHOFF, *Monetary Uncertainty*, Amsterdam: North-Holland, 1983.
3. ALLAN H. MELTZER, 1985, *op. cit.*, and 1987 b, *op. cit.*
4. JOSHIO SUZUKI, *Money and Banking in Contemporary Japan*, New Haven: Yale University Press, 1980; *id.*, 'Japan's Monetary Policy over the Past 10 Years', Bank of Japan Monetary and Economic Studies, 3, September 1985.

pre-announced monetary projections. The government began to deregulate interest rates and the credit market. Exchange rates fluctuated and, until the September 1985 international agreement to intervene in exchange markets, evidence suggests that generally exchange rates were freely fluctuating.[1] A comparison of the variability of output and prices under the different policy regimes in Japan shows that variability of univariate forecast errors using the Kalman filter is lower under the more liberal regime with fluctuating exchange rates and preannounced monetary projections.

The United States experience differs. The shift from fixed to fluctuating exchange rates was followed by an increase in the variability of forecast errors. The United States also announced projected rates of money growth beginning in 1975, but instead of announcing a single projection, as in Japan, the Federal Reserve announced targets for several monetary aggregates and gave ranges for each. The Federal Reserve, unlike the Bank of Japan, regularly shifts the base from which growth is measured. In practice, the Federal Reserve often fails to meet its targets, while the Bank of Japan has kept actual money growth very close to projections. When deciding how to act or react, the Federal Reserve relies much more than the Bank of Japan on short-term forecasts.

Both the United States and Japan experienced common shocks – the oil shocks, major changes in exchange rates, the Carter shock following imposition of credit controls in 1980 and other surprises. These common shocks are at least as important for Japan as for the United States. It seems reasonable, therefore, to attribute much of the *relative* improvement in forecast accuracy to the stability of Japan's policy in recent years. Table 4-6 shows the variability of forecast errors, obtained using the multi-state Kalman filter, for real output and the price deflator for the two countries under fixed and fluctuating exchange rates.[2]

1. ALLAN H. MELTZER, 1985, *op. cit.*
2. The reduction in forecast errors for Japan is not the result of a decline in the average growth rate. Estimating the coefficient of variation as the ratio of the root mean square error to the mean rate of growth gives .0077 for 1957-71 and .0065 for 1975-83. For the U.S., the comparable values are .0093 and .0170.

Table 4-6. Root Mean Square Errors of Forecasts in Japan and the
United States (in percent)

	Japan			United States		
	(1)	(2)	(3)	(1)	(2)	(3)
real output	1.9	1.1	0.7	0.8	1.2	1.2
price level	1.2	0.8	0.6	0.3	0.6	0.6

col. (1) fixed exchange rates, Japan 1957/3 – 1971/3; U.S. 1960/3 – 1971/3
col. (2) fluctuating rates, Japan 1971/4 – 1983/4; U.S. 1971/4 – 1985/2
col. (3) monetary announcements, Japan 1975/1 – 1984/3; U.S. 1975/1 – 1985/2

Japan was able to reduce variability of forecast errors for prices and output both absolutely and relative to the United States. Much of the reduction was achieved after 1975, during the period of monetary announcements and fluctuating exchange rates, shown in column 3. In the United States, the variability of forecast errors rose under fluctuating exchange rates, and there is no change in variability in the years of monetary announcements. The comparisons suggest that Japan used monetary control to give domestic consumers and producers the benefit of lower variability and less uncertainty.

In the United States, variability and uncertainty increased. For Japan, the change in policy arrangements provided an opportunity to reduce inflation and increase the credibility of economic policy. The Bank of Japan achieved rates of money growth close to projections, thereby enhancing credibility and reinforcing its commitment to lower inflation. The growth rate of money declined gradually, but persistently, and the inflation rate fell from above 20% in 1974 to about 0 to 2% in the eighties. Government spending was tightly controlled, so government spending and the budget deficit declined as a share of GNP. A period of stable growth with no recessions followed. During the decade 1976-1985, growth of real output remained between 3 and 5 percent annually.

The Federal Reserve concentrated attention mainly on domestic interest rates, free reserves and member bank borrowing under both fixed and fluctuating exchange rates. Typically the Federal Reserve ignored the announced targets for money growth, just as it had ignored its commitment to pursue policies consistent with the fixed exchange rate regime in the sixties. Shifting and ambiguous policies based on changing current conditions and forecasts of future conditions may have encouraged skepticism about the value of announcements. Although inflation declined in the eighties, the annual growth rate of output fluctuated between –2 and 6 percent. Short spurts of relatively fast growth were followed by recessions or periods of slow growth. Fiscal policy changed frequently and contributed to uncertainty.

Since forecasts are conditional on policy and outcomes depend on policy, it would not be surprising if differences in the stability of policy are a principal reason for the observed differences in the variability of output and prices and the differences in the size of forecast errors. Comparison of Japan and the United States also suggests that fluctuating exchange rates can reduce variability and uncertainty. This is more likely to happen if the country adopts a stable policy.

Additional evidence comes from a similar comparison of experience in Germany, Canada, the United Kingdom and (again) the United States using quarterly data from first quarter 1960 to third quarter 1971 for fixed exchange rates and fourth quarter 1971 to fourth quarter 1984 for fluctuating rates.[1] The principal finding is that the unanticipated variability of prices and output declined in Germany but not in the other countries, following the shift to fluctuating exchange rates. The United Kingdom particularly shows a large increase in variability and uncertainty.

Quarterly data may give excessive weight to short-term movements. We know from the econometric model forecasts reported earlier that year ahead forecasts can have smaller errors than quarterly forecasts. Also, annual data is available for many more countries that differ in size and other attributes.

For annual comparisons, we used six countries. Two countries, Germany and Denmark, are members of the European Monetary System, so they have fixed but adjustable exchange rates within the group and fluctuating rates against other major countries.

---

1. Results are not much changed if the shift to fluctuating rates is placed in first quarter 1973.

The remaining four countries have fluctuating exchange rates, but they differ in the degree to which they have intervened to affect the exchange rate or devalued their currency. All six countries were subject to similar shocks such as the oil shocks of the 1970s and the relatively large devaluation and subsequent revaluation of the dollar from 1978 to 1984. Each country has an independent fiscal policy and differs in product mix, technology change and in other ways that can affect relative variability.

Table 4-7. Root Mean Square Errors 1952-85
(annual rate in percent)

		Real Income	Growth	Price Level	Inflation
Denmark	1952-72	2.5	2.3	2.4	2.3
	1973-85	1.9	1.9	1.3	1.5
Germany	1952-72	2.3	2.1	1.8	1.7
	1973-85	1.8	1.7	0.7	0.4
Japan	1952-72	1.9	1.8	1.9	1.8
	1973-85	1.8	1.8	2.6	2.6
Sweden	1952-72	1.7	1.6	2.5	2.4
	1973-85	1.8	1.8	1.5	1.5
U.K.	1952-72	1.6	1.5	1.7	1.6
	1973-85	2.1	2.1	4.1	4.1
U.S.	1952-72	1.3	1.2	2.8	2.6
	1973-85	2.3	2.3	1.4	1.4

Table 4-7 reports the errors for uncertainty about levels and rates of change computed from annual data. Many of the errors lie in the neighborhood of 2%, not very different from the forecast errors reported for forecasting models in Table 4-3 above, but higher than the best forecasts in some countries. The errors in the earlier tables are for forecasts of growth and inflation, but most shocks are durable, so ε is generally small, and the two sets of errors are often identical at the level of accuracy reported in Table 4-7.[1]

Comparison of the fixed and fluctuating exchange rate periods

1. The errors are from univariate models, so in principle efficiency can be increased. Vector autoregressions (VAR) using unanticipated changes to money, output

provides no support for the claim that fluctuating exchange rates increased variability and uncertainty. Only one of the six countries, the United Kingdom, shows increases in uncertainty for prices, output, inflation and growth. Two countries, Denmark and Germany, show reductions in all measures, with relatively large reductions in price level (or inflation) uncertainty during the fluctuating exchange rate period. Despite the oil shocks of the 1970s, price level and inflation uncertainty declined in four of the six countries under fluctuating exchange rates.

The reduction in uncertainty for Germany is highly suggestive. Germany has pre-announced rules for money growth and exchange rates. The exchange rate rule is an adjustable peg against currencies in the European Monetary System and fluctuating rates against other currencies. To provide information about its policy and about expected inflation during the period, the central bank announces targets for central bank money, a measure very similar to the monetary base. While the targets were not always achieved, the record suggests that the government and the central bank were constrained by the targets. The Bundesbank, unlike the Federal Reserve, did not systematically exceed its money growth target. Money growth was generally within the target range.

The two rules appear to have increased stability relative to other countries and relative to the fixed exchange rate regime. The Bundesbank appears to have raised the credibility of its announced disinflationary policy by holding money growth to a pre-announced disinflationary path through the late 1970s and the 1980s. Deviations from the path, for example to support the dollar in 1978, induce a smaller flight from money if the public believes the deviations are transitory. Further, the government has not repeated its experience under Bretton Woods. It has been willing to revalue the mark rather than import inflation from other countries in the EMS.

Denmark, and the other countries in the EMS, can pursue

and prices were used in part to measure the efficiency loss from the univariate model. The reduction in forecast errors is often small. Since the VARs use data for the entire sample period to compute the error in each period, they overstate the reduction in forecast error that would be achieved in practice.

independent monetary policies, if they choose to do so. Since they bear most of the cost of such policies under the adjustable exchange rate system, they have an incentive to follow stabilizing policies. Denmark appears to have reduced variability and uncertainty relative to its experience under the Bretton Woods agreement. The data suggest that, despite the oil shocks of the 1970s and the variability of real exchange rates for the dollar, Denmark was able to reduce uncertainty by the choice of policy, in this case, membership in the EMS.

The United States is the only country showing a relatively large increase in uncertainty about output and its rate of growth. Inspection of the detail shows that much of the increase is the result of a substantial increase in the forecast error for the permanent growth rate of output. A plausible explanation of the increased uncertainty about output and its rates of growth, relative to the past and relative to other countries in the table, is the frequent change in the thrust of United States monetary and fiscal policies in the past decade. Frequent policy changes make the current and maintained rates of growth difficult to forecast, leading to frequent changes in the expected return to capital invested in the United States. These, in turn, cause changes in the demand for United States assets and in real exchange rates. This implication has not been tested.

Japan shows no reduction in output uncertainty and increased price uncertainty following the shift to fluctuating exchange rates. This differs from the results using quarterly data, but the difference is misleading. Removing one large error for prices and output changes the results. For output, the forecast error made at the time of the 1974 oil shock is more than five times the mean absolute error. For prices, the forecast error for 1975, when the Bank of Japan changed to a policy of monetary targets and disinflation, is more than four times the mean absolute error.

Table 4-8 compares the size of errors in forecasts of output for Japan and the United States in different periods by type of error. The table shows that the errors for the fixed exchange rate period are not affected by starting the period in 1950. Mean errors are not much different if 1960-72 is used instead.

For Japan, the three computed values of the mean absolute error for 1973-1985 decline, but for the United States all three increase following the adoption of fluctuating exchange rates. Omitting the year with the largest forecast error substantially reduces the mean absolute error for output (and prices) in Japan and the RMSE for Japan. Thus omitting 1974 reconciles the annual results for Japan with the results reported using quarterly data. For the United States, the largest error occurs in 1984. Omitting this year slightly reduces the mean absolute error but does not alter the direction of change or the conclusion that output uncertainty increased in the United States under fluctuating rates. Since increases are not observed for some other countries, we can reject the hypothesis that the increased output uncertainty is a consequence of the fluctuating exchange rate system.

Table 4-8. Mean Absolute Errors for Output
in Japan and the United States
annual rate in percent

	Japan			United States		
	ε	γ	ρ	ε	γ	ρ
1950-72	0.5	1.0	1.2	0.3	0.6	0.7
1960-72	0.5	1.1	1.4	0.2	0.6	0.7
1973-85	0.1	0.6	0.9	0.3	1.0	1.7
1973-85*	0.1	0.3	0.2	0.3	0.9	1.7

* omitting year with largest error, 1974 for Japan 1984 for U.S.

Two main conclusions follow from the comparisons of variability under fixed and fluctuating exchange rates. First, the choice of exchange rate regime appears to have an important quantitative influence on variability and uncertainty. Japan, Germany and Denmark were able to reduce uncertainty about output growth and inflation after the Bretton Woods system ended. Germany and Japan adopted monetary targets and made the targets credible. Denmark benefited by joining the EMS, thus importing credible policy from other countries, principally

Germany.[1] Second, fluctuating exchange rates do not assure greater stability. If countries choose to pursue highly variable policies, as in the United Kingdom and the United States, variability and uncertainty may increase under fluctuating exchange rates.

---

1. The reduced variability of output and prices resulting from a credible monetary policy may result from lower variability of money growth or from lower variability of velocity growth. The latter would occur if the public believes that deviations in money growth are transitory, so it responds much less. Experience in Switzerland and Germany in 1978 when money growth soared to support the dollar is an example.

4. Rules to Reduce Uncertainty

We have used data to compare rules with discretionary policy based on forecasts, rules that set targets for nominal GNP growth based on forecasts, rules based on past observations, and fixed and fluctuating rate rules, including the gold standard. The conclusion drawn from these comparisons is that uncertainty can be reduced most effectively by relying on rules rather than discretion, by basing rules on observations rather than forecasts and, in many countries, by choosing fluctuating exchange rates.

There is evidence that some governments have reached similar conclusions. Several countries have adopted explicit, or implicit, medium-term strategies, using pre-announced monetary targets to inform the public and fluctuating exchange rates to reduce the amplitude of shocks from abroad. Some of the countries that adopted credible, medium-term strategies have had more success in reducing price and output uncertainty than countries that continue to rely on discretionary policies based on forecasts.

This section considers alternative rules for setting the rate of money growth in a fluctuating exchange rate regime. We look at some general issues first. The discussion of monetary policy traditionally involves a conflict between rules and discretion or between activist and non-activist arrangements. We use the term "discretionary" differently than in the recent literature based on the reputation approach. The meaning used in the latter case makes the central bank's objective function identical to the social welfare function. Central banks have objectives for inflation and employment, but they have political and institutional objectives also. Political and institutional objectives cause unpredictable shifts in economic objectives.[1] The course of actual policy action is substantially less predictable than implied by recent reputational analysis.

A policy based on rules may be more stable over time and also more predictable, provided implementation of the rule does

1. KARL BRUNNER, 'The Pragmatic and Intellectual Tradition of Monetary Policy-making and the International Monetary Order', *Schriften des Vereins für Sozialpolitik*, 138, 1983; ALEX CUKIERMAN and ALLAN H. MELTZER, 1986, *op. cit.*

not require forecasts. But the rule's stability and predictability does not guarantee its usefulness in moderating economic uncertainty expressed by the variance of output and the price level. The classification based on the pair activist–non-activist cuts across the division between rules and discretion. The boundary line remains somewhat uncertain. Interpreted rigidly, it compares a constant monetary growth rule to all other proposals or possibilities for monetary policymaking.

For the purposes of our analysis of monetary policymaking, two criteria seem more useful. We distinguish policy strategies according to the information required for their successful operations and the extent to which they depend on the policymaker behaving like a benevolent dictator. The latter condition may also be formulated as the extent to which strategies impose tactical procedures that disregard the peculiar incentives and temptations of the political process. Discretionary policy and some rules rank very high in terms of required information levels and benevolence or public spirit of policymakers. We argue that such strategies are bound to fail and very likely deepen uncertainty and magnify the variance of output and the price level. Our previous discussion of forecast errors showed that all strategies, whether discretionary or based on rules, which involve forecasts in one form or another fail to provide information that is sufficiently accurate to be useful for policy. This result can be extended to rules relying only on available observations. Some rules and procedures will require information about the structure of the economy which is simply not available.

A control-theoretic approach exemplifies the problem. It is sufficient for our argument to develop the problem in fullest generality. Consider an economy represented by a vector equation

$$h(y_t, y_{t-1}, m_t, u_t) = 0$$

where y is a vector of endogenous variables; m is a monetary control variable, and u refers to a vector of exogenous random shocks. Assume that the policymakers maximize a quadratic objective function dependent on the vector y and subject to the constraints determined by the system. Maximization determines a policy rule assuring the optimal performance of the economy. The rule appears as a linear function of the most recent observation of y,

$$m_t = c(y_{t-1}, Eu_t|h, cv, k).$$

The coefficients of the rule depend on the detailed and fully specified structure of the economy expressed by (h, cv) where cv denotes the system's covariance structure, and k is a matrix of weights in the objective function.

The sensitivity of this procedure with respect to (h, cv) determines its relevance. Variations in (h, cv) change the nature of the rule. More important is the fact that we do not possess the required knowledge about (h, cv), and we are not likely to acquire such knowledge. The very nature of the economic process seems to preclude finding precise estimates of an invariant structure. The demonstration that a closed loop strategy adjusting policy actions from period to period in response to the most recent information is superior to an open loop strategy, setting the future course once and for all, is beside the point. The demonstration involves an unavailable and unattainable information level. Efforts to implement an optimal closed loop strategy in the absence of the necessary information lowers the economy's performance and raises the uncertainty that people face. Any strategy proposing to shift policy levers according to recent developments faces this unavoidable information problem. Policymakers, and would be academic advisers, are not in a position to judge reliably the consequences of such strategies.

One of the necessary conditions for strategies that seek to exploit current information for an optimal setting of policy levers thoroughly fails. Consider the second necessary condition. The assumption of reliable and detailed knowledge needs to be supplemented with the assumption that the government will always use this information in the public interest. Officials, under the goodwill or public interest hypothesis, disregard all private advantage in the execution of policy. Historical experience shows that officials respond to a variety of incentives. They seek to achieve public benefits but also act according to their own interests and interpretation. This implies that we should not expect policy to be executed in accordance with a well specified and stable social welfare function. Policymakers and public officials are also guided by their private utility functions, so they tradeoff public welfare against private considerations. Public choice theory has made us familiar with this theme which offers a much more penetrating understanding of political institutions than the public interest theory. Modigliani deals with this issue by attributing to his opponents a basic hostility to government.[1]

The necessary and sufficient conditions for successful executions of "activist" or systematic feedback policies do not exist. Rational policymaking needs to be adjusted to the actual state of knowledge and the operation of institutions, and not to an imagined ideal. Rational policy is a choice among institutional arrangements designed to lower uncertainty about the course of action to be pursued by the monetary authorities. Such arrangements are represented by rules requiring comparatively little information that offer easy opportunities for the public to monitor the authorities' performance.

Since Keynes,[2] economists who favored the goal of internal price stability have proposed rules for monetary policy under fluctuating (or adjustable) exchange rates. Friedman argues that this goal is more readily achieved if the central bank specifies the rule in terms of the money stock or its growth rate.[3] We have long argued that the path for monetary policy should be stated as a growth rate for the monetary base. The base is available daily and is much less affected by institutional changes than other measures of money.

A rule to achieve price stability[4] must specify whether the policymaker accommodates or reverses one-time changes in the price level resulting from permanent changes in productivity or other one-time changes in output. A rule that reverses permanent price changes requires the policymaker to identify all

---

1. FRANCO MODIGLIANI, 1986, *op. cit.*

2. JOHN MAYNARD KEYNES, *A Tract on Monetary Reform*, 1923, reprinted in *The Collected Writings of John Maynard Keynes*, vol. 4, London: Macmillan, 1971.

3. MILTON FRIEDMAN, 1959, *op. cit.*

4. If the optimal rate of inflation is non-zero, the rule should be stated as an optimal rate of inflation.

such changes. A rule that does not reverse price level changes allows the price level to adjust as part of the process by which the economy adjusts real values to unanticipated supply shocks. Once adjustment is complete, real values are the same under either rule. Differences arise during the adjustment, however. To reverse the price level change, the policymaker must know the proper amount by which to change money and other nominal values, so he must know structural parameters including the size of the real wealth effect, the magnitude of the productivity shock, and the price elasticity of aggregate supply. The public must have confidence that the policymaker knows these magnitudes. Such confidence would be misplaced. We simply do not know and, after several decades of empirical work in macroeconomics, we should not expect to learn these values with enough precision to improve on market adjustment of the price level to one-time shocks.

Further, there is no reason why current owners of nominally denominated assets should not share in the gains and losses resulting from changes in productivity or supply shocks. One of the main benefits of price stability is that stability of anticipated prices reduces uncertainty faced by transactors, thereby lowering the risk of long-term investment. This is, of course, the argument stressed by proponents of the classical gold standard. Another main benefit is that individuals who save for retirement (or for the distant future) and those who borrow at long-term to finance housing and other durables have less reason for concern about the form in which assets are held and less reason to fear that the real value of accumulated saving will be altered by unanticipated price changes. Stability of the price level reduces these risks.

Accommodating unanticipated price level changes does not forsake these benefits. Although the price level changes, and the anticipated price level adjusts to the changes, the rational anticipation at any point is that prices remain at their current level. There is no risk of price level drift. Under the proposed rule, the oil shocks of the 1970s would have raised the price level. The negative oil shocks of the 1980s would have reversed the direction of change, without eliminating all of the prior increases, so the actual and anticipated price levels would have increased. Productivity shocks are mainly positive shocks to the level of output that lower the price level. A bunching of positive (or negative) productivity shocks to firms, if sufficiently strong, would change the measured rate of change of output and, under the proposed rule, induce a change in money. The increased money stock would reverse the effects of supply shocks to the price level. For these reasons, and others, the price level would fluctuate, but there is no reason why the rule would produce a trend of the price level in either direction.

There are few studies of alternative monetary rules. McCallum is a recent example.[1] McCallum studied the properties of alternative rules using data for the United States from first quarter 1954 through fourth quarter 1985. All the rules are specified in terms of the monetary base, but the rules differ in the degree to which they respond to past deviations and in the information they require.

The first rule is Friedman's rule for constant money growth.[2] This rule calls for money to grow at the rate of real GNP growth minus the average growth of velocity. McCallum chose 3% as the average annual rate of real GNP growth. He set the trend growth of money to maintain price stability by letting

$$\Delta b_t = \Delta y^* - \Delta v^*$$

where Δb_t is the (constant) growth rate of the base, Δy^* is the trend growth of output, and Δv^* is the computed average rate of growth of base velocity.

This rule relies on two pieces of information that could not have been known at the time the rule was formulated. The lesser problem for the United States is the growth rate of output, since the maintained growth rate has remained within a narrow range for the past 120 years.[3] The problem would be more serious for Japan or western Europe, where decadal growth rates were

1. BENNETT T. McCALLUM, 'Optimal Monetary Policy in the Light of Recent Experience: The Case for Rules', Working Paper, Pittsburgh: Carnegie-Mellon University, July 1987.
2. MILTON FRIEDMAN, 1959, op. cit.
3. Principal exceptions are periods of major recessions particularly the 1930s depression.

considerably higher in the 1950s and 1960s than earlier or later. The greater problem for the U.S. is the assumed constant trend in velocity. Ex post estimation of this trend biases the results in favor of the constant growth rate rule.

The second rule is related to an adaptive rule proposed in several places, most recently Meltzer (1987 a). The base grows at a rate equal to the difference between the moving average growth of output and the moving average rate of growth of velocity computed to the most recent quarter for which data are available.[1] $\Delta b_t = \Delta \bar{y}_{t-1} - \Delta \bar{v}_{t-1}$, where the bar indicates a moving average. This rule requires no assumption about trends in output or velocity. If velocity and output are approximately random walks with drift and subject to unforeseen changes in the drift, this rule remains applicable. If velocity and output growth are constant, the rule converges to Friedman's rule. If the drift is constant or if mean reversal is rapid, the Friedman rule yields a smaller variance of the price level. If mean reversal is relatively slow or does not occur, the adaptive rule is superior. Friedman's rule performs best in periods of relative stability in the trend growth rates, as in the 1950s and 1960s. Differences between performance of the first and second rules in favor of the first rule are an approximate measure of the bias from assuming known, constant growth rates.[2] McCallum changed the proposed rule by replacing the moving average growth of output, $\Delta \bar{y}_{t-1}$, with the constant average growth of output for the period, Δy^*, as in rule 1.

The third rule, proposed by McCallum,[3] accepts the adjustment to the moving average of velocity but replaces the adjustment to the moving average growth rate of output with two terms.[4] One is the (constant) trend rate of growth from the

---

1. A second part of the rule, not considered by McCallum, takes account of international aspects. This is discussed below.

2. The measure of bias is approximate only. Any adaptive rule may produce some instability. This will be most likely if there are large frequent changes in the direction of change. Gradual adaptation such as the three year moving average proposed by Meltzer or the four year average used by McCallum reduces this problem.

3. BENNETT T. MCCALLUM, 1987, *op. cit.*

4. RUDIGER DORNBUSCH and STANLEY FISCHER, *Macroeconomics*, 3rd. ed., New York: McGraw-Hill, 1984.

first rule; the other is a fraction of the most recent deviation of the level of output from its trend value. These adjustments give the rule a stronger counter-cyclical response, the strength of the response depending on the fraction used for the adjustment. The rule uses more information – knowledge of the trend of output – but does not adjust for permanent changes in the growth of output. The third rule is

$$\Delta b_t = \Delta y^* - \Delta \bar{v}_t + k(y_{t-1}^* - y_{t-1}).$$

Table 4-9. Quarterly RMSE for Three Policy Rules, 1954-1985
(annual rates in percent)

Rule	RMSE
1. Constant base growth	3.9[a]
2. Adapted to moving averages	5.0
3. Adjusted for $y_t^* - y_{t-1}$ ($k = 0.25$)	2.0[b]
4. Historical simulation-deviations from trend	8.5[b]

[a] A constant base has an RMSE of 23%. Most of this large error reflects the actual inflation during the sample period.
[b] Corrected values reported in McCallum (1988). Other values are from McCallum (1987).

McCallum's simulations of quarterly values for 1954-1985 yield the values for the root mean square errors (RMSE) shown in Table 4-9. The RMSEs are measured as deviations from 3% growth.

Rule 3 which provides for changes in the trend of velocity and for deviations of output from trend has the lowest RMSE. Each of the rules lowers variability and uncertainty relative to deviations from a linear trend estimated from data for the period. An alternative comparison is to the RMSE of quarterly forecasts reported in Table 4-2. Although the periods differ, so comparisons are not exact, the best of the rules imposes variability lower than the best forecast errors for real GNP growth. The best rules are superior to the median forecast errors for long series of forecasts. To check the robustness of the results, McCallum uses vector autoregression and several structural models.[1] The results

1. BENNETT T. MCCALLUM, 'Robustness Properties of a Rule for Monetary Policy', *Carnegie-Rochester Conference Series on Public Policy*, 29, Autumn 1988.

230

are similar to those in Table 4-9. His proposed rule keeps nominal and real GNP within $1\frac{1}{2}$ to 2 percent of non-inflationary trend growth.

The comparison of the rule to forecast errors and to deviations from trend suggests that rule 3 is not likely to do worse, and would perhaps do better, than the record achieved by discretionary Federal Reserve policy based on forecasts. There are reasons for believing that the comparison understates the reduction in variability achievable with the rule.

First, each of the rules would maintain expected price stability, keep actual prices more stable and avoid inflation. Avoiding welfare losses from actual and unanticipated inflation increases the welfare gain from a rule. The weight that each person places on the gain from price stability differs but, as discussed earlier, inflation imposes an excess burden. The minimum value of the burden is equal to the inflation tax and the burden increases with uncertainty about relative prices and the (variable) rate of inflation.

Second, the computations do not allow for any welfare benefits arising from structural changes following adoption of a rule. We know that structural coefficients are not invariant to a change in regime, but we do not know, a priori, what the effect of the change in policy regime will be. If the reduced precautionary motive for holding money dominates other changes, the demand for money should fall and the capital stock increase. There is some theory and some evidence that risk premiums in interest rates and the demand for money per unit of income would decline.[1] Additional evidence is the experience of Germany, Japan and Denmark, where stability increased and uncertainty declined, following the introduction of a medium-term strategy or rule.[2]

Third, the three monetary rules aim at domestic price stability. At least since Keynes[3] economists have recognized that

1. EDUARD JAN BOMHOFF, 1983, *op. cit.*; A. MASCARO and ALLAN H. MELTZER, 'Long and Short-Term Interest Rates in an Uncertain World', *Journal of Monetary Economics*, 12, November 1983, pp. 485-518.

2. See also JOHN B. TAYLOR, 1987, *op. cit.*

3. JOHN MAYNARD KEYNES, 1923, *op. cit.*

countries acting alone must choose between internal price stability and exchange rate stability. Countries operating together can individually reduce uncertainty about domestic prices and output and collectively reduce exchange rate instability.

The rules simulated by McCallum do not take advantage of the gains from providing an international public good by increasing exchange rate stability and reducing uncertainty. This benefit can be achieved if the major countries in international trade and finance – the United States, Japan, Germany and the United Kingdom – adopt compatible rules for stability of the anticipated domestic price level. The rate of growth of the monetary base would differ with the experience of each country and would change over time. Anticipated and actual exchange rates would be subject to change with changes in relative productivity growth, rates of growth of intermediation, differences in saving rates, in expected returns, in labor-leisure choice or other real changes. Prices would continue to fluctuate, but anticipated price levels would be constant in all countries that follow the rule, so the rule eliminates this source of short-term instability in real and nominal exchange rates. The remaining changes in real exchange rates would work to facilitate the efficient allocation of resources in response to changes in tastes and technology at home and abroad.

An international rule for compatible monetary policies creates a public good. Smaller countries could choose to import enhanced price and exchange rate stability by fixing their exchange rate to a basket of the currencies of major countries or to one of those currencies. There would be no international agreement and no reason to impose the costs of a coordinating organization. Each country would choose its own course. If all countries choose independent policies, or make frequent discretionary changes, uncertainty would not be at a minimum.

There are opportunities for cheating as with any agreement. A country may choose to expand money growth to gain some temporary increase in output and employment. Cheating cannot be wholly avoided. Monitoring is improved, however, by choosing the monetary base as the policy variable and by providing prompt publication of data for the base. The base can be controlled with precision by any central bank that chooses to do so. Prompt publication of the base provides the public with information to protect their wealth against loss from inflation.

Protection of individual wealth does not avoid the social cost of variability. As discussion of the gold standard has long recognized, rules can be abandoned in periods of crisis. There are opportunities for cheating in many ways such as shaving gold coins in one case or raising the growth rate of the base in the other. A public choice perspective requires some concern for incentives which raise the cost of departing from the rule.

On several occasions we have proposed a system of incentives to enforce a monetary rule. Our specific proposal treats the problems of responsibility and accountability. An independent central bank has responsibility for monetary policy and inflation but it is not accountable directly to the public. If monetary growth produces inflation, recessions and uncertainty, the public holds elected officials accountable, not central bank governors. As Friedman and Schwartz remark,[1] central banks are adept at finding excuses for bad or unpopular results while accepting credit for good or popular results. The other side of the coin is that administrations or legislatures are blamed for the policy failures over which they have limited control.

The problem is to make the monetary authority accountable for its actions without making the monetary authority subservient to elected officials. An independent central bank has some merit. Since it is not directly under the control of political authorities it can, but does not always, protect the public from inflation. We believe that independence has some value and that the value is increased if the central bank is both independent and accountable.

Our proposal allows the central bank to choose the growth rate of money consistent with the announced monetary rule. If the central bank fails to keep the growth of the base at (or near) the announced rate, the governor (or governors) must resign. The president can accept responsibility for the deviation

1. MILTON FRIEDMAN and ANNA JACOBSON SCHWARTZ, A Monetary History of the United States, 1867-1960, Princeton: Princeton University Press for the National Bureau of Economic Research, 1963 c.

233

by reappointing the governor if he is satisfied that the deviation is appropriate.

Resignation was, at one time, a standard response for a minister of finance whose policies had led to devaluation of the currency. Our proposal would produce a similar result. Excessive money growth would devalue the currency relative to other countries following compatible rules or pursuing less inflationary policies. Failure to follow the rule would require resignation. The rule would be symmetric; too little money growth would require resignation also.

5. *Conclusion*

Most discussions of rules and discretion try to demonstrate the analytic superiority of rules or discretion. Our discussion emphasizes evidence. As is often the case, the evidence is not entirely one-sided. Simulation results of various rules show root mean square errors only slightly lower than forecast errors from conventional econometric models. Adaptive rules appear to perform at least as well as discretionary policies or policy rules based on forecasts.

Some more persuasive evidence comes from the comparison of actual policies. Germany and Japan reduced variability under fluctuating exchange rates with preannounced monetary targets absolutely, relative to their experience under fixed exchange rates, and relative to the experience of countries that faced common shocks. A main lesson for policy would seem to be that credible medium-term strategies for monetary and fiscal actions – rules or quasi-rules – can reduce uncertainty while moving toward price stability.

A main lesson for the analysis of policy would seem to be that the resources of economists have been wasted for more than a generation. Too many resources and too much effort has been allocated to developing forecasting models and procedures, generating forecasts, and discussing alternative courses of policy action. Too few resources have been allocated to policy and institutional design – to developing rules that reduce uncertainty.

Developing rules that reduce variability and uncertainty toward their minimum values is only one step toward a solution. Much more difficult, because we understand much less, is the task of developing incentives that encourage policymakers to follow rules that are advantageous to society. We have tried to join these two perspectives in our proposal, but we view our suggested incentive system as a first step, not a solution.

The classical conception of economics as a policy science viewed policy analysis as the design of rules. The shift from the design of rules to concentration on policy action is a recent development. A return to the classical conception will not leave economists like dentists, as Keynes once hoped. There is much

235

to be done to improve rules for fiscal, monetary and other policies, to improve the methods for pre-testing rules, to relate the fiscal and monetary rules and to understand the incentives that will lead governments and ultimately voters to improve policies. These issues challenge the economics profession.

DISCUSSION

EDUARD J. BOMHOFF*

1. *Importance of Uncertainty*[1]

The only comment I can pronounce in the language of our gracious hosts would be "senza dubbio è un trionfo ben meritato".
My grasp of Italian remains minute because each time I try
to read one of my favorite Italian authors in the original, the
theatre gets dark after a few pages and the music starts. He whose
knowledge of Italian is limited to opera librettos can cope with
some of the uncertainties of daily life – give me a sword/one
ultimate kiss – but will require a different language to comment
on uncertainty in the macroeconomy.

The lectures forcefully argue the case that theory as well as
applied research in macroeconomics fail to draw the consequences
from the manifold uncertainties that affect macroeconomics. Both
demand and supply of theories and empirical results explain
this neglect of uncertainty in macroeconomics. On the demand
side of the "market", the survival of astrology as an unsubsidized
activity testifies to a demand for predictions of events that may
be even harder to predict than the macroeconomy and to a
willingness not to scrutinize the techniques used in preparing
the forecasts.

In macroeconomics the forecasters have an advantage over
the astrologers: some of their important customers have an interest in downplaying the associated uncertainties. Governments
and Central Banks like to make unconditional promises to the
electorate about the ways in which they are dealing with real
or imaginary crises. Any pledge involving a variable not under
true control of the authorities – the future budget deficit, next
year's rate of inflation, the variability of the exchange rate – if
it is to be taken seriously, must be conditional upon some macro-

* Professor of Economics, Erasmus University, Rotterdam.

1. Bill Poole and Robert Rasche kindly provided the data used in their recent
work on U.S. Velocity. I am grateful to them and to my colleague Clemens Kool
for useful conversations. Marcel Vernooy very ably programmed the Kalman filter
algorithms used in these comments.

economic model. Thus, to deflect the electorate's skepticism, the politicians have a continuing incentive to claim that their theories and models are reliable and useful.

Brunner and Meltzer as well as other monetarist economists have popularized this argument for the case of a Central Bank that has to choose between some rule or pure discretion in the setting of monetary policy. No Central Banker will fly on automatic pilot only and set monetary policy for the medium term without leaving open the option of reverting to discretion. All emergency procedures require a staff that has models and forecasts in reserve. Certainly the Central Banker will claim that his people are well prepared for eventualities, and thus create an optimistic view of the robustness of his contingency planning.

Other Central Bankers will prefer to claim that a discretionary policy is always superior but requires exceptional talents (fortunately available in the incumbent office-holder) and a strong supporting staff. How large should the staff be, how should they coordinate, and what type of output should they produce? Cost-benefit analysis for Central Bankers points to a large staff (does the public really care to impose a budget constraint on the Central Bank that earns such large "profits" on its foreign exchange holdings?). The staff will be asked to produce quantitative analyses and an econometric model is the natural way to coordinate the staff outputs. To motivate the staff, and to show that Central Banking is both art and science, the reliability of the model(s) and forecasts will often tend to be exaggerated.

Thus, Central Bankers will ask their staffs to develop macroeconomic models and forecasts, and exude optimism about their accuracy. In other parts of the public sector, similar incentives operate on the demand side of the market for economic theories and econometric results. Their effect is to slight the uncertainty associated with macroeconomics.

In these comments my main theme will be why uncertainty is disregarded also on the supply side of the market for macroeconomic theories, models and forecasts. Why do economists so often claim more knowledge about the world than is warranted? Part of the critique by Brunner and Meltzer focuses on the failure to deal properly with uncertainty about different

types of exogenous shocks. On p. 153 they provide a useful typology that asks four different questions about the shocks that may hit the macroeconomy. Each of the four questions allows for two different answers:
"The pairs are:

a. systematically dominant or an unpredictable and shifting mixture,
b. monetary or real,
c. aggregative or allocative,
d. permanent or transitory,
   i.   permanent shocks to the level,
   ii. transitory shocks to the level,
   iii. permanent shocks to the growth rate."

One may add that the average size of each type of shock can vary over time. Even if only one type of uncertainty is present, economic models may implicitly (but wrongly) assume that the importance of this source of uncertainty does not change over time. If there occurs more than one type of relevant shock, and the amplitude or frequency of at least one type is not constant over time, we have the second option of pair (a).

Consider, for example, the macroeconomic demand for money. Let a demand function be identified and estimated for a particular sample period, and assume that from a certain time T onwards the residual variance of the equation is double its previous value. Financial theory assumes that higher risk implies a higher expected return, and therefore a portfolio-balance model of the demand for money and other assets should be sensitive to the amount of macroeconomic uncertainty. Empirical work in macroeconomics on the demand for money, however, rarely discusses the hypothetical event of an increase in residual uncertainty.

A related counterfactual experiment would be to ask how a given macroeconometric model would survive a sudden increase in the residual variance of all its behavioral equations by a certain factor. Suppose the world became ten times as uncertain in this specific sense, would agents alter their behavior as codified by the model? Yes, but it would require a meta-theory in Brunner and Meltzer's sense to tell us how. As the authors point out, the data to test such a theory are rarely available, and even if they are, there is no agreed statistical methodology to test the meta-theory. Brunner and Meltzer's comments about an infinite regress into meta-meta-theories apply even to this simple case, where the only change is a generalized increase in the existing pattern of uncertain shocks, without any change in the relative importance or the exact impact of each shock.

Statistical techniques are certainly available to deal with heteroskedasticity (changes in the amount of residual uncertainty), as long as the coefficients of the model do not change. Put more precisely, the estimation of the state variables in an economic system would remain feasible even if the signal-to-noise ratio changes over time as long as the coefficients of the model do remain invariant.[1] Furthermore, new estimation techniques are being applied to take certain types of conditional heteroskedasticity into account.[2] As regards forecasting, Kalman filtering provides the means to adjust forecasting schemes to changes in the signal-to-noise ratio, both for stationary and for non-stationary time-series.[3]

Thus, my first two hypothetical examples – increases in the residual variance of one or all equations in a macroeconometric model – present tough problems to the econometrician because both the states and the parameters are sensitive to the changing degree of uncertainty. Sufficiently long series of data that cover different regimes would allow us to estimate the appropriate models before and after the increase in uncertainty, but such an abundance of data is rare in macroeconomics. Even if we have "before" and "after" data, agreement about the appropriate statistical methodology to cope with learning about changing

1. We use the common delineation whereby "state" variables refer to (noisy) realizations of macroeconomic time series such as money, income, or the income velocity of money, and "behavioral parameters" are coefficients that occur in the equations that connect the state variables.

2. On an ex post basis, however, which may prove to be a major limitation.

3. Much econometrics literature on forecasting limits itself voluntarily but unnecessarily to the case of a stationary time series. A principal advantage of the Kalman filter methodology over Wiener filtering is the ability to cope with non-stationary series (and to deal with outliers in a more natural way).

uncertainty is still lacking. Thus, macroeconomics still has great difficulty dealing with the question: how does an increase in the signal-to-noise ratio affect economic behavior?[1]

The general problem of uncertainty in macroeconomics is how to model simultaneous learning about changes in time-series models for state variables and changing behavioral parameters. The "deeper" dilemmas in Brunner and Meltzer's classification do indeed involve changing behavioral parameters. Anything that changes the amount or the character of macroeconomic risk will presumably have some impact on the behavioral rules of optimizing agents. In that case, the point that there is no meta-theory that posits how agents adjust their behavior when they learn about changes in the stochastic characteristics of their environment applies with full force. However, as we have seen above, problems already arise if a changing menu of shocks leaves the behavioral parameters unchanged but has some effect on the state of the economic system.

Brunner and Meltzer choose to put most of their discussion of uncertainty in macroeconomics in that simpler context: changing patterns of unforeseen disturbances affect the state of the economy but leave the parameters (coefficients) in the decision rules unchanged. In this way, they can make many of their points about the neglect of uncertainty in an even less controversial way than if they had argued also for effects of uncertainty on changes in parameters. For each of their four dilemmas has consequences for the optimal forecasts of variables that matter for macroeconomic decisions.

For instance, the expected average rate of economic growth over the next few years depends on the dominant types of shocks that will hit the economy (another oil crisis? erratic monetary policies?); on the relative importance of monetary and exchange rate policies versus tax changes and other "real" shocks; on the importance of allocative disturbances (will exchange rate movements cause a big change in the mix of exports and imports?);

1. Perhaps a better integration of the theory of finance and macroeconomics will lead to some progress. The statistical problems associated with gradual learning about regime changes (including learning about the changing priors on possible future regime changes) remain severe.

and finally on the "shape" of all these shocks as they occur over time (temporary or permanent?).

Brunner and Meltzer ask pertinent questions about economic analysis under these types of uncertainty, for example:

– do econometric models allow for variable uncertainty?
– are policy prescriptions valid under different assumptions regarding variable uncertainty?

The authors rightly observe that many economists and policy-makers combine a cavalier neglect of changing uncertainty in many areas of macroeconomics with an extreme affirmation of its importance in domestic monetary policy. Confident predictions about the effects of lower budget deficits on exchange rates, or the impact of different tax regimes on savings, are often combined with a state of ignorance regarding the income velocity of money.

Brunner and Meltzer, by contrast, argue for more room for the effects of changing uncertainty in general, but criticize the policy views of the "velocity has been a complete mystery since 1979" school. In my comments I shall use the demand for money function as an illustration, both to discuss a possible technical solution to part of Brunner and Meltzer's critique, and to evaluate at the same time the extreme claim that the income velocity of money has become completely unpredictable.

2. The Basic Problem

When macroeconomics became a quantitative science in the early postwar period with the pioneering econometric work of Tinbergen, Klein, Goldberger and the members of the Cowles Commission, fewer statistical tools were available than today. The early modelers used ordinary least squares and derivative techniques to test the linear relations in their models. They attempted with great ingenuity to circumvent the problems of simultaneity and developed techniques to maintain statistical efficiency with heteroskedastic noise.

Success in macroeconometrics was apparently measured by the

244

explanatory power of the model or its individual equations, but the interpretation of the correlation coefficients was often unclear. Many models contained so many exogenous and endogenous variables that in principle each behavioral equation could achieve a perfect fit, given the limited number of periods for which the model was estimated. Since the reasons for excluding most variables from almost all equations were based on a priori arguments, the whole exercise – if judged by the statistical fit of the model, was nothing but a statistical representation of the modeler's a priori judgments on the macroeconomic structure.[1]

Rather than aiming at a high overall fit, researchers came to prefer more parsimonious models with high statistical significance of as many individual coefficients as possible. T-values higher than 2 became more and more important as a yardstick of success in macroeconometrics. Hypothesis testing took on its still customary form: some theoretical model was posited with implications for the signs and sometimes the magnitudes of certain coefficients connecting the variables of interest. The theory was then illustrated with data for a given historical period. In the process of estimating the model, ad hoc assumptions were added to accommodate the observed characteristics of the residuals. Accomplishment of the model was now predominantly measured by the degree of correspondence between the hypothesized and the observed coefficients.

Success in statistical forecasting remained of interest for policy-makers and forecasters, but became more and more divorced from success in econometric modeling and hypothesis testing. The influential book by Box and Jenkins[2] in practice caused the gap to deepen. Box and Jenkins popularized time-series methods, and their work stimulated statistical contests between a-theoretical time-series models and multivariate econometric structures.

1. The argument was forcefully made in contribution to the volume on econometric methodology edited by Brunner: ROBERT L. BASSMANN, 'Argument and Evidence in the Brookings S.S.R.C. Philosophy of Econometrics', chap. 3, in KARL BRUNNER, ed., *Problems and Issues in Current Econometric Practice*, Columbus, Ohio: Ohio State University Press, 1973, pp. 63-118.

2. GEORGE P. BOX and GWILYM M. JENKINS, *Time Series Analysis, Forecasting and Control*, Oakland, California: Holden-Day, 1970.

In principle, the multivariate models should have been victorious in all such comparisons, since the information set on which they were based included that of the time-series model. The frequent finding of small differences in forecasting power was interpreted as additional evidence against the usefulness of large-scale econometric models, and was one cause of their disappearance from serious scholarly work.

However, smaller theoretical models with fewer endogenous variables continued to be tested in the traditional way. The researcher stipulates a theoretical structure, constructs a data set, assumes away almost all potential trouble from measurement errors in the exogenous variables[1] as well as time-variation in the residuals and proceeds to testing the significance of his coefficients. Rarely are such models evaluated for their robustness to changes in the economy beyond the standard tests for one-time changes in some coefficients – preferably about halfway through the period of estimation – and the possible elimination of a small number of observation points if outliers are deemed to be present.

Engineers would be surprised at this minuscule allowance for modeling errors. No airplane would be certified if its navigational instruments had so little capability to deal with cumulative effects of exogenous shocks, changes in the degree of serial correlation of the observation errors, random-walk like behavior of the "constant term", persistent changes in model coefficients and other modeling errors.

Engineers have been much more successful in developing statistical techniques that are simultaneously appropriate for hypothesis testing and for forecasting. Engineers have two major advantages over economists: their data sets are much more abundant (and often can be constructed at low cost) and some of the laws of motion are known a priori with great certainty.

1. See C. A. Los, 'The Prejudices of Least Squares, Principal Components and Common Factors Schemes', *Comput. Math. Applic.*, 1988; and *id.*, 'Identification of a Linear System from Inexact Data: A Three Variable Example', *Comput. Math. Applic.*, 1988, for a powerful reminder of how essential such simplifying assumptions about errors-in-variables are in the common context of ordinary least squares.

In macroeconomics the data sets are fewer and shorter, and experimenting to construct fresh data is impossible. Thus, engineers can use a profusion of data to construct a "truth model" and discover the common types of "shocks" to which their actual models should be resistant. Often, it is feasible to make an explicit tradeoff between tracking ability for a given data set and robustness with respect to potential disturbances: a finely attuned model may do a little better than a more robust structure, but be less resistant to uncertain changes in the system or the noise.

Economists have no agreed catalog of shocks that their models should be able to survive. Also, the criterion of optimizing statistical significance leads the economist to sharpen his model specification rather than to make his model more robust. Moreover, some common engineering techniques that are used to achieve robustness, such as parallel processing of multiple models, are not suitable for testing the significance of model coefficients.[1]

Brunner and Meltzer illustrate the limitations of the coefficient-testing approach in their lectures. In my view many shortcomings are caused by the unproductive divorce between on the one hand statistical methodologies for testing coefficients in models that are unfit for forecasting, and on the other hand time-series techniques that are not useful for discriminating statistically between competing economic models.

Can the *impasse* be overcome by a renewed emphasis on forecasting ability as the testing ground for competing economic models? That is unlikely. Many comparisons of different forecasts have shown that the differences in short-term forecasting power are often minor, so that short-term tests will not be conclusive. In order to judge the qualities of an economic model one would want to judge long-term rather than short-term forecasts. However, the longer the forecast horizon, the greater the probability that unrepresentative future events have influenced

---

1. This is the main reason why the reception of the so-called multi-state Kalman filter technique by the economics profession has been lukewarm at best. Allan Meltzer's acceptance and use of the multi-state Kalman filter follows from his decision to emphasize uncertainty in macroeconomics beyond what is currently the standard for empirical work.

the forecast to such an extent that one cannot discriminate between models on the basis of only a single post-sample run. A true test of the model would involve its tracking ability in a variety of circumstances, but such an abundance of data for testing is rare in macroeconomics.[1]

Fortunately, the statistical methodology from the engineering literature can be adapted to the social sciences. We are discovering how to test hypotheses with economic content in a model that can also forecast and cope with more uncertainty than can be modelled by one-time parameter shifts or elimination of single outliers. Hopefully, the critique in Lecture 4 of current practice in much of macroeconomics will be answered by more experiments with these engineering statistical methodologies.

3. Estimation Using Kalman Filters

My comments will be within the context of a simple example: a single-equation statistical model for the income velocity of money.

$$(1) \qquad p_t + y_t - M_t = V_t = c + tr_t.a + i_t.\vartheta + u_t \qquad t = 1, .., T$$

In equation (1), p_t represents the natural logarithm of the price level in an economy, y_t the log of a measure of income appropriate to the demand for money, M_t the log of the money supply and hence V_t the log of the income velocity of money. c represents a shift term in the regression, tr_t a linear trend for the log of V, i_t the log of some relevant interest rate and u_t the residual in the regression. a and ϑ are regression coefficients to be estimated by linear least squares.

More sophisticated versions of equation (1) have been used to make the point that velocity has become highly unstable and unpredictable, at least in the United States since 1979. We can with little loss of generality focus on the simple equation (1), however.

---

1. Cross-sectional testing of hypotheses is already becoming more popular in applied macroeconomics.

Economic theory has important things to say about the shift term c and the trend term tr in the regression, especially over the longer term.[1] If the model leaves all longer-term dynamics that are not related to changes in interest rates to the constant term and the trend, there should certainly be no presumption that c is a true constant term or that the trend is always the same. Constant term and trend together have to represent permanent changes in velocity; the residuals u_t must stand for the temporary shocks to the demand for money. Such shocks may be more or less persistent, and this has to be modeled by the serial correlation coefficient of the residuals.[2]

Incorporating these (non-controversial) features of the demand for money calls for a richer stochastic structure. Time-varying stochastics offer the best chance to cope with the dynamic aspects of the demand for money listed above.[3] The natural way to embed the linear least squares equation (1) in a richer dynamic model is to change to the state-space formulation of recursive least squares. The state vector is composed of all regression coefficients plus as many current and lagged residuals as are required to represent the serial correlation in the error term.[4] The state transition matrix would be the unit matrix in the case of recursive least squares without correction for serial correlation, but can be different in order to represent dynamic features that are hard or impossible to model in the least squares context.

1. MICHAEL D. BORDO and LARS JONUNG, *The Long Run Behavior of the Velocity of Circulation, The International Evidence*, Cambridge: Cambridge University Press, 1987.

2. The list of eventualities against which the model should be prepared could be made longer: time variation in the interest (semi-) elasticity ϑ, non-linearity in the relationship, varying amounts of measurement errors in the exogenous variables causing time-varying bias in the least-squares coefficients and so on. Let's for now concentrate on the short list in the main text.

3. BORDO and JONUNG, 1987, *op. cit.* test whether empirical proxies can be found to represent some longer-term dynamics of the demand for money. They are careful not to claim that inclusion of such variables captures all permanent changes in level or growth rate of velocity.

4. Having the current residual as a state variable results in an error-free observation equation. PETER S. MAYBECK, *Stochastic Models, Estimation and Control*, vol. 1, New York: Academic Press, 1979, shows how the usual Kalman filter algorithm can be adjusted for this case.

By way of example, consider the following application of a standard state-space model to velocity:

$$(2) \qquad z_t = \overrightarrow{h_t}.\overrightarrow{x_t} + u_t$$

$$(3) \qquad \overrightarrow{x_{t+t}} = F.\overrightarrow{x_t} + G.\overrightarrow{w_t}$$

In equations (2) and (3), measurements on the scalar z are used to estimate the elements of the unobservable vector x. The vector h will represent the exogenous variables in the model. F and G are known matrices of constants with the exception of $F_{4,4}$ which is the unknown coefficient of serial correlation ϱ. Finally, the vector w is composed of the stochastic elements that are added to the state vector in each period. In our application to the income velocity of money, we require noise dynamics which is most conveniently modelled by incorporating the current output noise, u_t, in the state vector, x_t. The state-space model for velocity becomes:

$$(2a) \qquad V_t = (\begin{matrix} I & tr_t & i_t & I \end{matrix}) \begin{Bmatrix} c_t \\ o \\ \vartheta_t \\ u_t \end{Bmatrix}$$

$$(3a) \qquad \begin{Bmatrix} c_{t+t} \\ a_{t+t} \\ \vartheta_{t+t} \\ u_{t+t} \end{Bmatrix} = \begin{Bmatrix} I & I & 0 & 0 \\ 0 & I & 0 & 0 \\ 0 & 0 & I & 0 \\ 0 & 0 & 0 & \varrho \end{Bmatrix} \begin{Bmatrix} c_t \\ a_t \\ \vartheta_t \\ u_t \end{Bmatrix} + \begin{Bmatrix} I & I & 0 & 0 \\ 0 & I & 0 & 0 \\ 0 & 0 & I & 0 \\ 0 & 0 & 0 & I \end{Bmatrix} \begin{Bmatrix} 0 \\ w_{2t} \\ 0 \\ w_{4t} \end{Bmatrix}$$

In equations (2a) and (3a), the new symbols represent the serial correlation coefficient in an assumed first-order autoregressive model for the residuals, u_t, and independent white noise terms w_{2t} and w_{4t} in the vector w_t that is added during the update of the state vector. The model of equations (2a) and (3a) thus incorporates a stochastic trend and first-order serial correlation in the residuals. It could easily be extended to also cope with time-varying responses to changes in interest rates, and permanent shifts in the "constant" c.

Kalman filters are a well-known tool for forecasting state

variables in a state-space model with known parameters.[1] Simultaneous estimation of states and parameters is feasible in principle but delicate. In our specific case, there are three unknown parameters: the coefficient of serial correlation, ϱ and the required variances of w_{2t} and w_{4t}. Recursive solutions to this type of problem would be very delicate and require large runs of relatively noise-free data.[2]

Our time series for the U.S. income velocity of money consists of 72 annual observations for the period 1915-86. Visual inspection shows that the time series characteristics of the series change around the time of the establishment of the Bretton Woods exchange rate system at the end of World War II. Thus, if we wish to estimate separately for the subperiods 1915-46 and 1947-86, the number of data for each subperiod is quite limited.

I therefore compromise with the ideal of on-line estimation and investigate a technique that maintains on-line estimation of the state variables (constant term, trend, interest rate elasticity), but applies off-line estimation for the three unknown parameters (coefficient of serial correlation, variance of the innovations, variance of the changes in the stochastic trend).[3]

The algorithm uses the technique of "covariance matching" for the two unknown variance terms together with a grid search for the unknown coefficient of serial correlation.[4] It goes as follows:

1. An important exception is the state-space representation of an ordinary least squares model. In that case, one may model the unknown least squares coefficients as unknown state variables and estimate both the coefficients and the conditional forecasts of the dependent variable recursively without difficulty. This is possible because the unknown state vector is an unperturbed vector of constants.

2. LENNART LYUNG and TORSTEN SÖDERSTRÖM, *Theory and Practice of Recursive Econometrics*, Cambridge, Mass: The MIT Press, 1985, is an excellent recent reference. See also PETER S. MAYBECK, *Stochastic Models, Estimation and Control*, vol. 2, New York: Academic Press, 1982.

3. *On-line (recursive)*: the estimate of a state variable (or parameter) at period t does not require knowledge of the state variables for any periods beyond period t. *Off-line*: estimates are based on data for the complete period of estimation.

4. See PETER S. MAYBECK, 1982, *op. cit.*, chap. 10, for details about covariance matching. See J. R. M. AMEEN and P. JEFF HARRISON, 'Normal Discount Bayesian Models', in J. M. BERNARDO, M. H. DE GROOT, D. V. LINDLEY and A. F. M. SMITH eds., *Bayesian Statistics*, 2, Amsterdam: Elsevier Science Publisher B. V. North-Holland, 1985, pp. 271-298, and MIKE WEST, P. JEFF HARRISON and HELIO S. MIGON,

1) Make assumptions regarding all non-trivial elements of the process whereby the state vector is updated. In our case one would have to make assumptions about the coefficient of serial correlation, ϱ, and the variances of the two white noises, w_{2t} and w_{4t};

2) Use a backward Kalman filter to estimate the values of the state variables just before the data for the first period are processed;[1]

3) Apply the (forward) Kalman filter to the data, using the prior distribution on the states generated by the backward filter;

4) Compute the (implicitly given) values of the two variance terms from the results of the forward filter;

5) Return to step (1) if the computed variance terms differ from their assumed values by more than a specified relative amount, and use the computed variances for the next iteration.

The iterations are terminated for any given value of ϱ if there exists a close correspondence between the assumed and the computed values of the two variance terms. The same procedure is repeated for a number of different values of ϱ in order to find the degree of serial correlation that minimizes the sum of squares of the forecast errors.

4. Results for U.S. Velocity

In his stimulating recent paper, William Poole[2] reviewed the annual time series for the income velocity of money in the

'Dynamic Generalized Linear Models and Bayesian Forecasting', *Journal of the American Statistical Association*, 80, 389, 'Theory and Models', March 1985, pp. 73-83, for a very illuminating discussion of estimation in Kalman filter models and for an exposition of an important alternative to the procedure advocated here. See: C. A. Los, 'Comment on West *et al.*' *Journal of the American Statistical Association*, 1985, for comments that point to covariance matching as an attractive way to estimate parameters, but note that his specific formulas imply substantial approximation to the superior approach of Maybeck.

1. A very similar procedure has been advocated by GEORGE P. BOX and GWILYM M. JENKINS, 1970, *op. cit.*, to estimate the parameters in a univariate moving-average model for a time series. Back-forecasting is a convenient way to generate a prior distribution for the states that is not as diffuse as an uninformative prior, but at the same time non-subjective, since based on the data.

2. WILLIAM POOLE, 'Monetary Policy Lessons of Recent Inflation and Disinflation', *Journal of Economic Perspectives*, 2, 3, Summer 1988, pp. 73-100.

United States. I have used his data for M_1-velocity and the Aaa bond yield in the following illustration of the Kalman filter approach. Poole uses the natural logarithm of the Aaa bond rate and has velocity on the left-hand-side with no income variable on the right-hand-side. Thus, the coefficient on the interest rate is an estimate of the interest rate elasticity of the demand for money. Poole notes that substituting a short-term interest rate produces a much smaller elasticity (0.316 i.o. 0.669 for

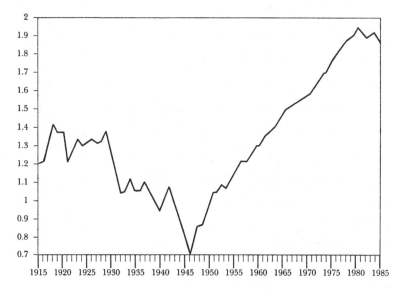

Figure 1: Log Velocity (M_1) U.S.A.

the complete sample period) and a poorer fit. He concludes that at least a large part of the perceived stochastic trend in U.S. velocity can be "covered" by the long-term interest rate. The broad pattern of the Aaa bond yield (a decline until just after World War II, a very stable upward trend until 1982 and a choppy decline in the most recent period) corresponds strongly to the secular pattern in both the long-term and the short-term interest rate. Table 1 replicates some of Poole's regressions and adds a number of alternative least squares models.

Obvious non-stationarity in velocity and the interest rates

253

Table 1: Least squares models for velocity

	ĉ	θ̂	α̂	ρ̂	adjR²	Std.err.	D.W.
			1915-1986				
I	0.2666	0.6694	–	–	0.908	0.0986	0.4542
	(0.04163)	(0.02525)					
II	0.9617	0.2636	–	0.9697	0.275	0.0557	1.4034
	(0.2077)	(0.07818)		(0.02509)			
III	0.2733	0.6005	0.002803	–	0.903	0.08582	0.5523
	(0.03627)	(0.02620)	(0.00058)				
IV	0.06557	0.2855	0.006694	0.9209	0.473	0.05499	1.3766
	(0.1533)	(0.07520)	(0.002721)	(0.04047)			
			1915-1964				
V	0.3654	0.5893	–	–	0.702	0.0994	0.4653
	(0.07373)	(0.05408)					
VI	0.6405	0.3885	–	0.8377	0.555	0.0633	1.3488
	(0.1721)	(0.1201)		(0.0788)			
VII	0.1102	0.7017	0.003826	–	0.764	0.08856	0.6440
	(0.09569)	(0.05791)	(0.001043)				
VIII	0.4344	0.4828	0.002897	0.7806	0.600	0.06346	1.3369
	(0.1924)	(0.1155)	(0.002475)	(0.08733)			

Dependent variable: log U.S. velocity
c: constant term
θ: interest rate elasticity
α: coefficient of the trend
ρ: coefficient of first order serial correlation

I, V   Poole's specification
II, VI   first-order serial correlation allowed for
III, VII   linear deterministic trend
IV, VIII   first-order serial correlation allowed for plus linear deterministic trend

makes the results heavily dependent upon the exact time period chosen for the test. Adding a standard correction for serial correlation to Poole's ordinary least squares framework perhaps alleviates but does not eliminate this problem. Permanent increases in velocity will be attributed by the computer to any explanatory variable that also exhibits long-term changes, in our case the interest rate.

Table 2 shows the results of the Kalman filter specification from the previous section. Different values for the serial corre-

Table 2: Convariance Matching and Kalman Filter Results

Period	$\hat{\rho}$	var (ω_2)	var (ω_4)	sum of squares of prediction errors
	0.75	$1.214746.10^{-5}$	$4.593686.10^{-3}$	0.147534
	0.76	$1.129992.10^{-5}$	$4.618142.10^{-3}$	0.147439
1915-1946	0.77	$1.060086.10^{-5}$	$4.643188.10^{-3}$	0.147408
	0.78	$0.999430.10^{-5}$	$4.669317.10^{-3}$	0.147440
	0.79	$0.944811.10^{-5}$	$4.697001.10^{-3}$	0.147541
	0.86	$7.241519.10^{-7}$	$5.780289.10^{-4}$	0.023847
	0.87	$7.039336.10^{-7}$	$5.750938.10^{-4}$	0.023752
1947-1986	0.88	$6.794114.10^{-7}$	$5.742437.10^{-4}$	0.023739
	0.89	$6.459305.10^{-7}$	$5.767062.10^{-4}$	0.023852
	0.90	$5.954956.10^{-7}$	$5.846679.10^{-4}$	0.024172

Kalman Filter Results of Final Iteration for $\hat{\rho}=0.77$

Year	c_t	α_t	ϑ_t
1915	1.04	0.0034	0.12
1920	0.96	0.0060	0.21
1925	1.07	0.0049	0.15
1930	1.05	0.0038	0.17
1935	1.02	−0.012	0.068
1940	0.90	−0.015	0.090
1944	0.85	−0.014	0.095
1945	0.76	−0.20	0.10
1946	0.70	−0.023	0.10

Kalman Filter Results of Final Iteration for $\hat{\rho}=0.88$

1947	0.66	0.033	0.14
1948	0.70	0.033	0.15
1950	0.78	0.034	0.15
1955	0.93	0.033	0.16
1960	1.08	0.032	0.16
1965	1.24	0.032	0.16
1970	1.36	0.027	0.14
1975	1.49	0.027	0.14
1980	1.68	0.028	0.12
1981	1.71	0.028	0.12
1982	1.68	0.025	0.12
1983	1.64	0.023	0.14
1983	1.66	0.023	0.14
1985	1.64	0.021	0.15
1986	1.56	0.018	0.17

lation coefficient were selected and for each value, the filter was iterated until the values for the two unknown variances matched the implicit values for these variances as computed from the filter results. The best results – in terms of minimizing the one-period-ahead forecast errors – were obtained for a value of ϱ equal to 0.77 for the period 1915-46 and a value of 0.88 for the post-war period.

Adding the sum of squared prediction errors for the two sub-periods results in a value of approximately 0.17 for the sum of squared forecast errors for the complete sample period.[1] This differs little from the corresponding sum of squares of the residuals in equation IV of table 1, which amounts to 0.20 for the years 1918-86. If we estimate the parameters of equation IV separately for the two sub-periods 1915-46 and 1947-86, the standard errors for 1918-46 and 1950 are respectively 0.072 and 0.027, leading to a total sum of squared errors equal to 0.16 for the full period. Thus, the Kalman filter specification leads to similar errors on the basis of the same information set, even though the coefficients on three variables (constant, trend, and interest rate) are computed recursively.

The Kalman filter procedure points to one direction in which Brunner and Meltzer's critique of current macroeconomics may be answered constructively, since it allows for a larger variety of uncertain events than an ordinary least squares model. The trend term is stochastic and changes in each period, so that not only temporary shocks to the level of velocity, but also permanent changes in its growth rate can be allowed for. An extension of the Kalman filter model would add another non-zero element in the vector that updates the state vector, so that the "constant" term of the regression does not converge to a fixed value, but becomes a random walk. Permanent learning with respect to the interest rate elasticity can be modelled in the same way.

The results confirm the conclusions of Rasche[2] that the

---

1. Prediction errors for the years 1915-17 and 1947-49 have been neglected for this calculation, in order to avoid undue influence of the initialization procedure.
2. ROBERT H. RASCHE, 'M1-Velocity and Money Demand Functions: Do Stable Relationship Exist?', *Carnegie-Rochester Series on Public Policy*, 27, Autumn 1987, pp. 9-88.

behavior of U.S. velocity did not become significantly more unpredictable after the late 1970s. Poole's conjecture that the long-term interest rate elasticity is essential to understanding velocity is confirmed as well. His estimate for the elasticity, derived from an equation without correction for serial correlation, is questioned by my results, however. A significant, but smaller elasticity reduces the difficulties of executing a credible and visible anti-inflationary monetary policy that are well discussed by Poole for the case of a very high interest rate elasticity. The Kalman filter results suggest that a middle way exists between either asking the interest rate to account for all the non-stationarity in velocity (as in Poole) or assuming that the interest rate elasticity is negligible, so that statistical modeling of the trend in velocity has to account for all secular changes. The flexibility of the Kalman filter approach has the additional major advantage that post-sample conditional forecasts are feasible without continuous re-estimation of the model parameters.

5. Conclusions

These comments have been limited to the issue of uncertainty in macroeconomic analysis. I have offered some arguments why uncertainty tends to be neglected, both on the supply side and on the demand side of the market for economic modelling. Standard econometric practice is part of the problem with its heavy emphasis on hypothesis testing within a tightly specified model that leaves little room for uncertainty beyond (correlated) noise in the observation equation. Brunner and Meltzer give a methodological critique; I try to add a technological perspective.

Recent advances in econometric technology can help us to model a richer description of uncertainty. The statistical techniques are available in the engineering literature on Kalman filtering and smoothing. A simple example shows how to estimate a model that allows for a stochastic trend to annual data for U.S. velocity. The results are preliminary, but the approach seems capable of bridging the gap between forecasting technologies that are flexible but a-theoretical and methods for hypothesis testing that are intolerant of different sources of uncertainty. Hopefully, further work in this area can provide a response to the severe, but valid critique of current macroeconometrics by Karl Brunner and Allan Meltzer.

MARIO ARCELLI*

1. Rules, Reputation of Policy Makers and Discretion

The debate "discretion" versus "rules" in economic policy has been thoroughly and exhaustively treated by Brunner and Meltzer in their fourth lecture. It has been pointed out correctly that this alternative does not coincide with the dilemma: active as against fixed rules in economic policy. There are in fact active rules – for instance, those which depend on the state of the economy in previous periods (feedback rules) – and passive, that is constant rules independent of such trends. Discretion, on the other hand, implies an activism untrammeled by rules.

Underlying the rules-discretion question is the debate on:

a) our understanding of the working and stability of economic systems;

b) the possibility of making accurate macroeconomic forecasts on the basis of available data;

c) the behavior of government authorities in relation to the type of targets pursued.

Besides the empirical evidence as to the inaccuracy of the data available to formulate short-term forecasts, Brunner and Meltzer quote Lucas'[1] criticism concerning the use of econometric models to simulate various economic policy alternatives. Thus, the inadequacies of the essential information needed for discretion and the limits of activism in economic policy are underscored.

As an issue of their convincing argument, Brunner and Meltzer reaffirm the superiority of "rules" as compared with discretionary policy, but leave open the possibility of progress in definition of these rules and in our understanding of the incentives and

* Professor of Monetary Economics, LUISS, Roma. The author wishes to thank Dr. Stefano Micossi and Gian Maria Milesi Ferretti for their valuable suggestions.

1. ROBERT E. LUCAS jr., 'Econometric Policy Evaluation: A Critique', in KARL BRUNNER and ALLAN H. MELTZER, eds., The Phillips Curve and Labor Markets, Carnegie-Rochester Conference Series on Public Policy, 1976.

penalties which influence application of economic measures by policymakers.

Re-examination of the assumption of market stability, challenged once more by recent events in the foreign exchange and stock markets, and the new theoretical approach on the credibility of announcements, or rather on the acquired reputation of economic policymakers, enable further considerations within the broad framework provided by Brunner and Meltzer's analysis.

Let us very briefly summarize the various theoretical positions. For the Keynesians, supporters of discretion in policymaking, a market economy is intrinsically unstable and thus prey to fluctuations which it is a good idea to correct, can be corrected and ought to be corrected. The objection raised against this position is that a policy of stabilization is effective if, and only if, there is adequate information on the system's economic structure and the capacity to make accurate forecasts as to changes in it. Furthermore, it has to be considered whether institutional conditions reconcile the objective function of government with the set of welfare functions of private individuals or not. In other words, whether incentives and penalties affecting policy choices are such as to make government action tend toward the "social optimum" or whether, on the reverse, discretionary policies actually increase uncertainty and instability.

Brunner and Meltzer observe that governments are more willing to lower rather than to raise taxes and, to increase rather than reduce public expenditure. It is a common observation that the inflation rate is generally positive, a clear sign of a propensity toward inflation rather than deflation on the part of governments. There is therefore the real possibility that discretionary policy measures can end up as destabilizing.

This conclusion against discretion, extremely convincing at a time of normal business cycles, becomes questionable in a context of strong market disturbances giving rise to the belief that the usual self-governing mechanisms are not working, being probably counteracted by speculation generating phenomena of dynamic instability.

In such cases, the possibility that discretionary policy measures, or measures inspired by rules which rely on the acquired credibility of the authorities, achieve positive results in restoring more orderly market conditions merits careful study.

The debate is however still open as to the causes that have led to instability, which could have been generated by previous discretionary policy interventions, by the loss of credibility by government authorities or by particularly intensive external shocks.

In contrast with the Keynesians, the monetarist position, to which the authors (if perhaps more in terms of fiscal monetarism) lend their support, stresses the importance of inaccuracies of data, lack of information and our ignorance of the functioning of economic systems. It therefore holds that good rules for economic policy, by limiting the amount of information needed by economic agents to make their choices, reduce uncertainties.

Precise policy commitments undertaken at the political level, formally backed by economic policy rules, would limit the arbitrariness of government choices inconsistent with the social optimum over the medium term. Besides reducing uncertainty, such rules would improve convergence toward equilibrium in the economic system, for monetarists essentially stable anyway.

Friedman argues that a discretionary policy is to be rejected as our knowledge of the working of the economy is so scanty that any attempt at fine tuning can only turn out to be destabilizing: the lags in the effects of monetary policy are both long and variable. Still, monetarists do not deny the possibility of being able to modify the level of unemployment in the short term, even if, according to them, with destabilizing consequences.

Finally, with the hypothesis of rational expectations (leaving aside the discussion of the questionable underpinnings of the theory) it seemed that the rules-discretion dilemma had definitively been resolved. In fact, the theoreticians of rational expectations, starting out from different premises, are even more radical than the monetarists in their conclusions, asserting the impotence of monetary policy even in the short term (at least in the extreme version of the macroeconomic model), the effects of unexpected policy excepted.

They reject an active policy as being useless. If expectations are rationally formed, any decision-making rule by the authorities will be absorbed and reflected in market expectations and will thus be neutralized by business behavior. Businessmen have the same information as the authorities, understanding of the workings of the system is sophisticated and generalized, any rule of economic policy is fully anticipated by the market and neutralized by the business community. In addition, given that economic policy seeks the optimum, everyone knows that the rules are chosen in an optimum way. Thus according to this view, Friedman is right to reject fine tuning, if for a wrong reason.

Within rational expectations theory there remains, however, the question as to whether an economic policy rule derived from the dictates of optimum control theory, that is a rule of optimum feed-back, should not be regarded as better than a simple constant rule like that proposed by the monetarists. In other words, whether the rule that determines economic policy measures systematically takes into account what is happening in the system in order to correct any deviation from an optimum path; would not better results perhaps be obtained from it rather than from a constant rule such as the simple monetarist proposition that the money supply must grow at a constant rate?

A constant rule of economic policy sets the temporal evolution of instruments at the outset and does not provide for corrections over time. Vice versa, a flexible rule decides upon measures on the basis of information acquired later, as endogenous variables change. Where it is possible to adopt a systems logic, and thus the theory of optimum control, a flexible rule should prove better than a fixed rule. How then can the superiority of a fixed rule be maintained? If one can understand rejection of discretionary policy interventions which are not firmly based on an optimizing systems logic, it would seem difficult to justify rejection of a flexible rule that aims to stabilize the system, basing itself on rational expectations.

2. *Time Inconsistency and Commitment*

Kydland and Prescott have, however, shown the inconsistency over time of such an optimum rule.[1] The time path followed by an economy is not independent of choices of rules of economic policy. In the presence of rational expectations, economic policy determined using traditional control techniques reveals itself to be suboptimal if expectation of future changes is included in the model.

Optimum control theory is in fact applicable only when the actual state and evolution of a system depend on the current situation and present and past decisions. Such an economic policy takes as granted businessmen's expectations in each period, as characteristic of the actual state. Rational expectations are not, however, immune to future economic policy plans. Being aware of the structure of the system, businessmen analyze the way economic policies will be chosen in the future and take this into account in their current expectations. For example, a change in the government coalition has an immediate effect on business-men's expectations as to future decisions in economic policy. In a context such as this, a discretionary policy that is "optimum" from period to period does not maximize social welfare, leading to an equilibrium rate of inflation, as a result of attempts to cut unemployment, higher than would be achieved by applying a monetary policy rule.

Beyond the results obtained from Kydland and Prescott's re-search, consistent with the world of rational expectations, there are important openings for analysis of the rules-discretion dilemma.

Rules are seen as commitments, if necessary contingent to a given set of exogenous circumstances. They are a kind of contract between the policy-maker and the business community which, by stabilizing expectations, assists the workings of the market.

On the contrary, a discretionary policy, to which a flexible

---

1. FINN E. KYDLAND and EDWARD C. PRESCOTT, 'Rules Rather than Discretion: The Inconsistency of Optimal Plans', *Journal of Political Economy*, 85, June 1977, pp. 473-492.

feed-back rule can be assimilated, consists in the choice at each period of the course of action believed best for a given current situation. In this case, there is no real restriction on the future course of economic policy.

Kydland and Prescott have discussed various areas of public policy in which commitments are important. The classic example is patents which encourage invention but restrict the supply of goods ex-post, holding back the diffusion of innovation.

From a purely discretionary viewpoint, it would be better to annul the validity of old patents, continuing to grant protection to new inventions.

Nevertheless, awareness of a policy of this kind by potential inventors discourages their inventiveness as they realize that their patents will soon lose any protection, with the result that they will lose their earnings. Thus, the ideal policy must be to maintain patent protection for an adequate time, ensuring validity for old patents.

Government commitment can be enshrined in law or it can be maintained by the weight of reputation. And it is precisely this latter observation which brings in the credibility of the authorities in economic policy strategy in a context of rational expectations hypothesis.

Economic policy, and particularly monetary policy, come to be seen as a strategic "game" between policy-maker and businessmen, where the institutional context, the information structure, and the objective functions (targets) of policy-maker and economic agents assume importance.

As with patent policy, the monetary authorities ought to consider the interaction between present choices (for example, to change stance in monetary policy, with a relaxation) and public expectations as to the future growth in money supply and prices. Supposing that in the short term there exists a trade-off between the rate of inflation and unemployment (which implies the existence of a Phillips curve, though augmented with expectations); there could be a propensity on the part of policy-makers to increase the level of employment (positive objective) even at the cost of setting off an unanticipated inflation (the price to be paid).

The policy-maker has an incentive to stimulate economic activity if he regards the natural level of gross domestic product as too low, setting off unanticipated inflation (there is some analogy with the case of the abolition of old patents to promote a larger supply of goods).

But businessmen guess this propensity toward inflation and expectations of high inflation are created. The sum consequence is that the authorities end up by generating high inflation without increasing employment, as the unanticipated inflation tends to be zero. (The analogy here in terms of patent policy is with the fall in the propensity to invent.)

Thus, if a discretionary economic policy designed to optimize the current situation is applied, the end result can be higher inflation without the benefits of increased employment.

The moral is that an equilibrium obtained by application of a constant rule limiting the rate of inflation is better than that can be obtained by discretionary policy.

3. Reputation of Policy-Makers

Barro and Gordon have examined the possibility of replacing a formally set out rule with an informal criterion for the behavior of the monetary authorities, sustained by their reputation.[1] In other words, the government commitment to contain the rate of inflation, rather than on an explicit rule, rests on the acquired credibility of the authorities and on the benefits to themselves of maintaining their reputation *vis-à-vis* the business sector. Poor credibility brings with it expectations of higher inflation and thus bigger costs. The policy-maker who does not respect the rule has to take into account the effect of his loss of credibility on the future inflationary expectations of businessmen and hence on future costs.

In the Barro and Gordon model, the public's inflationary expectations in fact depend on previously experienced price rises. Unlike a purely discretionary policy, here the policy-maker's decisions thus take into account the impact of his actions on the

---

1. ROBERT J. BARRO and DAVID M. GORDON, 'Rules, Discretion and Reputation in a Model of Monetary Policy', *Journal of Monetary Economics*, 12, 1983, pp. 101-122.

expected future rate of inflation. In their model, in which the policy-maker's time horizon is unlimited and the target is to minimize the currently expected level of inflation costs, Barro and Gordon establish an equilibrium of 'reputation'. A rule of economic policy can be 'kept' in equilibrium by the reputation of the policy-maker only when the incentive not to respect agreements is more than offset by the expected higher future costs generated by the loss of credibility. If costs are less than gains, the rule is not credible as businessmen know that the policy-maker is encouraged not to respect the commitment and thus will not believe him.

This shows that a 'reputation' equilibrium generates an inflation rate midway between that resulting from a purely discretionary equilibrium and that derived from a binding rule of economic (monetary) policy. The latter targets a zero inflation rate. In fact, given that the rule depends on the information available to the policy-maker, the information being symmetric, inflationary expectations equal the figure sought by policy-maker. The optimum is thus always to choose a rule which sets every time a zero inflation rate.

Reputation equilibria constitute a better result than discretionary equilibria, but are less satisfactory than an institutionally fixed rule. The possibility of assuming binding commitments permits the monetary authorities to establish exogenously and without costs the credibility of their declared economic policy. In the event that this is not, however, possible, credibility has to be won, with costs for the economy.

Apparently, the results obtained with a rule show up second best. In fact, if businessmen expect inflation to be zero in line with the rule, the monetary authorities have an incentive not to respect agreements and to create an inflationary shock. This outcome would be positive if it systematically succeeded in correcting the natural rate of unemployment. Nevertheless, this is only possible if businessmen can be systematically convinced into building mistaken expectations of low inflation. If expectations are rational, however, this cannot occur in equilibrium.

The above analysis is applicable to different fields than the Phillips curve. Unanticipated inflation, for instance, has effects equivalent to a wealth tax on financial assets such as money and public-sector debt instruments which are not index-linked to inflation.

The model which can be constructed is similar to the previous one but this time the benefits of unanticipated inflation can be seen in a higher tax take. Taxation by inflation is an instrument which acts like a lump sum tax and given its special characteristics – not least that of not being distorting as are other taxes – has certain advantages and points of preference.

A bigger stock of public-sector debt increases the benefits obtainable from taxation by inflation and gives an incentive to stimulation of unanticipated inflation. It can be deduced from this type of model that higher levels of public-sector debt will lead to a higher rate of growth of money supply, higher inflation and higher nominal interest rates. In other words, writes Barro, the forecast is that public-sector debt will in part be monetized. The same line of thought suggests that index-linking the public-sector debt to inflation, eliminating the benefits of a surprise inflation, will lead to lower rates of growth of the money supply and of inflation. In this light, the issue of inflation-proofed (real) Treasury certificates would seem particularly advisable.

4. Exploitation of Informational Advantage

The reputation equilibrium model of the Barro and Gordon type is a highly simplified reflection of reality, as Brunner and Meltzer point out. In monetary policy, it is assumed that the objective functions of the central bank and of the authorities reconcile with the social welfare function. Still it must be stressed that political and institutional objectives bring about unpredictable changes in economic targets. The course of actual economic policy is much less predictable that what is implicit in the analytical frameworks examined so far.

It can also be noted that the "penalty mechanism" foreseen by the model is arbitrarily defined and that the equilibrium rest-ing on the reputation of the authorities crucially depends on this mechanism.

For instance, longer than one period intervals before penalties engendering the loss of credibility are imposed, could determine reputation equilibria with lower inflation.

Generally speaking, these "games of strategy" with unlimited horizons have multiple reputation equilibria and do not contain mechanisms able to guarantee convergence toward the optimum path, except the credibility of announcements that anyway depend on factors like incentives and penalties to the actions of policy-makers. If the strategic horizon was finite there would certainly be infringement of rules in the last period, as this would not involve loss of credibility and the solution of the game would be found in a re-run in the opposite direction of the time path already followed.

The arbitrariness of the penalty mechanism and the excessively restrictive assumptions of preceding models have led to the development of alternative models with finite horizons and different characteristics, such as those of Tabellini, Backus and Driffill, Barro and Rogoff.[1] In the Backus and Driffill model there is a non-cooperative game between government authorities and fragmented rational businessmen. These latter are uncertain of the objective function of the policy-maker and thus of his strategy. They do not know whether the authorities aim to fight inflation or, rather, wish to pursue a target of output and employment growth.

Here businessmen obtain information on the policy-maker's preferences, examine his behavior, and modify their response via a learning process. The authorities can exploit the businessmen's lack of information to create for themselves an anti-inflationary credibility, even when in actual fact they are aiming

---

1. GUIDO TABELLINI, 'Accomodative Monetary Policy and Central Bank Reputation', Los Angeles: University of California, mimeo, 1983; DAVID BACKUS and JEROME DRIFFILL, 'Inflation and Reputation', *American Economic Review*, 75, 1985, pp. 530-538; ROBERT G. BARRO, 'Reputation in a Model of Monetary Policy with Incomplete Information, *Journal of Monetary Economics*, 17, 1986, pp. 101-127; KENNETH ROGOFF, 'Reputation Contraints on Monetary Policy', NBER, working paper, 1986.

to expand output: by doing this they can lower inflationary expectations to obtain subsequent greater advantage from a surprise inflation.

Similarly, Cukierman and Meltzer, to quote from the Brunner and Meltzer fourth Lecture, consider the case in which the policy-maker chooses less accurate operational and control procedures than other alternatives available.[1]

The reason is that less accurate control procedures enable the policy-maker to attain personal or institutional goals. For example, the policy-maker may wish to stimulate an economy in the run-up to an election. Difficult to control procedures encourage the public to believe that the increase in the rate of growth of the money supply is not part of a systematically inflationary policy. The public knows how the authorities behave, but does not know the precise size of the change in the money supply, except a posteriori. The control procedures facilitate attainment of the policy-maker's goals, raising the cost of information.

Barro and Rogoff, if each in different ways, expand on the results of Backus and Driffill, where sequential equilibria had been established, to arrive at extremely interesting conclusions for the interpretation of real events.[2] For instance, the policy-maker who consistently chooses zero target inflation for a certain period of time does not necessarily obtain to lower businessmen's inflationary expectations because on the one hand the probability that he is creating an artificial credibility declines with time and on the other hand, the probability that he is actually aiming at false credibility increases, with the purpose to harvest the benefits of an unanticipated inflation. Slight changes in public expectations can have major consequences on the path to equilibrium.

The existence of asymmetry in information available to authorities and public makes identification of reputation and optimum rule equilibria all the more indeterminate. In the event of

1. ALEX CUKIERMAN and ALLAN H. MELTZER, 'A Theory of Ambiguity, Credibility and Inflation under Discretion and Asymmetric Information', *Econometrica*, 54, September 1986, pp. 1099-1128.
2. ROBERT G. BARRO, 1986, *op. cit.*, KENNETH ROGOFF, 1986, *op. cit.*; DAVID BACKUS and JEROME DRIFFILL, 1985, *op. cit.*

exogenous shocks, unforeseeable when the rate of growth of money supply was being fixed, the assessment of impact by the monetary authorities, with much more information at their disposal, can be different from that by the public. Businessmen cannot establish how much the impact on prices is due to the shock and how much to the discretionary behavior of the monetary authorities. They cannot base any judgment on announcements by the authorities if an incentive exists for the central bank to provide distorted information in order to exploit the advanteges of the inflation-unemployment trade-off.

Canzoneri infers that, in such cases, to resolve the problem of credibility it is necessary to set certain restrictions on the policy-maker, though still leaving him sufficient scope to pursue stabilizing policies.[1]

The existence of strong destabilizing impulses giving rise to market instability, information asymmetry and rapid structural changes make formulation of contingent optimum rules highly problematic. In such situations, the trade-off between more discretion required for stabilization and more rules needed for credibility renders the identification of an optimum strategy difficult. In addition, empirical experience has often disproved the assumption of a trade-off between inflation and unemployment, so that the advantages of unanticipated inflation could at times show up as disadvantages.

Finally, although economic theory has improved its ways of determining expectations, increasingly using any information that is available, and has formulated coherent behavioral models, results are often out of line with forecasts. Economic agents' responses to announcements and to changes in the international situation provoke exceptional volatility in economic variables compared with past experience. Both international coordination of economic policy and the adoption by major countries of compatible rules for stability of the anticipated domestic price level are lacking.

Interdependence between economies and the scale of exogenous shocks are such as to make it difficult for any one country's

1. MATTHEW B. CANZONERI, 'Monetary Policy and the Role of Private Information', *American Economic Review*, 12, 1985, pp. 1056-1070.

authorities to build up credibility showing regular behavior able effectively to influence businessmen's behavior. Often statements by government members and by experts or even gossip affect expectations in a disorderly way, sometimes cancelling out the relief of fundamental economic variables. Events on the foreign exchange and equity markets, where sudden sharp fluctuations in values are common and can sometimes be traced back to mere expression of experts' opinion, are symptomatic and carry us to the realm of paradox.

Economic policy problems have increased above all in countries where circulation and processing of economic information are greatest.

In current circumstances, a medium-term strategy is certainly still necessary, but degrees of discretion to recover stability improve rather than diminish the reputation of the authorities – and thus the effectiveness of their policy.

RAINER S. MASERA*

1. Introduction

It is a privilege and an honor to offer my comments on the splendid lectures of Professors Brunner and Meltzer. They took us on a unique tour of micro and macroeconomics, the evaluation of monetary and fiscal policies, and the presentation of their approach to economic analysis in the light of cogent critical assessment of other schools of thought.

That monetarism is still alive and well must be a foregone conclusion for all of us who have had the good fortune to attend the 1987 Raffaele Mattioli Lectures. I venture to say that to a large extent this is precisely because over the past twenty-five years Brunner and Meltzer have succeeded in developing a broad, integrated monetary approach going well beyond the somewhat simplistic early presentations based on narrow analyses of money demand and supply functions.

Indeed, we are all monetarists now, in the sense that all (or nearly all) would agree that while (with floating exchange rates) the real stock of money is primarily determined by the conditions of demand, the nominal stock is (or, under appropriate institutional settings, can be) under the control of the monetary authorities. But monetarists too have come to agree that money must be viewed as one stock in an overall portfolio composed of financial as well as real assets. The integration of portfolio choices and the accumulation of financial and real assets, and hence a focus on the interactions between stocks and flows, is now a trait shared by neo-Keynesian, monetarist and new classical economists. The shifts in *expected* holding-period yields on the whole range of assets are key elements of the process leading to stock-flow equilibrium.

In this broader framework of analysis, credit markets, markets for financial assets other than money, and in particular markets for government debt cannot be neglected. In addition to the budget constraint facing the private sector, explicit consideration

* Director General Istituto Mobiliare Italiano, Roma.

273

must be given to the budget constraint of the government sector, which becomes a key relationship simultaneously linking stocks with flows and private with government decision-makers in the economy.

To these developments in economic analysis, which have taken us well beyond the *IS-LM* framework, Brunner and Meltzer have made outstanding contributions. In this respect, I would suggest that – beyond the very important differences between the various schools of thought, so brilliantly traced by Brunner and Meltzer – there are also fundamental points in common. These depend heavily on seminal work by Brunner and Meltzer.

I shall therefore begin by stressing some of the key elements in Brunner and Meltzer's analysis, that I feel warrant special attention.

First, as I have mentioned, there is the explicit integration of money, credit, and assets in a general model, with crucial importance attached to the dynamic implications of the government budget constraint. This leads to explicit recognition of the interdependence between monetary and fiscal policy, when the latter is characterized by structural imbalances. I shall return to this point presently.

Central to Brunner and Meltzer's analysis is the information-theoretic content attached to monetary balances. Money's primary role is that of reducing information and transactions costs. Recognition of this point leads to Brunner and Meltzer's fundamental attack on the extreme rational expectations approach.

After having underscored the significant contribution that acceptance of a rational expectations scheme in its weak form can make to our understanding of the workings of economic systems, Brunner and Meltzer proceed to a brilliant and cogent explanation of the basic inconsistencies of this school in its more radical versions.

Once the dust of micro-theoretic foundations has settled, the importance of Brunner and Meltzer's analysis will be fully understood. My "Hicksian heritage" made me – I believe – especially receptive to their arguments: I certainly regard Brunner and Meltzer's explanations of why price setting is highly rational, while bazaars and auctioneers can indeed be irrational, as a crucial contribution to the reassessment of the new classical school.

In this vein, I would also like to express my full agreement with their analysis of the role and possible functions of the government sector. I find, indeed, that the integration of public-choice considerations with their analytical apparatus, which explicitly allows for the importance of institutional settings, can greatly enrich our analysis of the working of our admittedly "mixed" economies.

Finally, Brunner and Meltzer's analysis of the combination of exogenous impulses, propagation mechanisms and endogenous developments is especially fruitful, when compared to the alternative view that economic systems can be depicted as totally endogenous processes.

It is clear that I could develop my comments by concentrating and elaborating upon one of these key areas of agreement with and praise of Brunner and Meltzer's work. And on many counts this would indeed be the most appropriate choice. But, as we know, a commentator – a commentator, moreover, who belongs more to the world of policymakers than to that of acedemics – must inescapably face an assignment problem. As I have been reminded, my task today is primarily to find areas of less than full agreement, or in any event to raise additional questions not already addressed and explained by the authors.

In this vein I shall therefore refer now to two issues that I would like to debate with Professors Brunner and Meltzer.

The first concerns certain implications of their analysis of the debt finance problem in the long run and its implications for monetary rules. The second refers to the role and use of macro-econometric models.

2. Debt finance in the long run and some implications for monetary rules

As Brunner and Meltzer point out, the longer-run consequences of an unstable debt-deficit process have recently attracted a great deal of attention. Special interest in the issue can be found in

Italy, as a consequence of our very large government deficits and high debt/income ratio.

2. 1. Brunner and Meltzer begin their analysis of this issue by focusing, in the context of their money-credit model, on the following linear differential equation:

(1) $\qquad \dot{s} = \overline{def} + (rr - n)s - (\pi + n)m$

which is obtained by deflating the budget constraint by nominal income.[1]

In deriving (1) Brunner and Meltzer make two important, related assumptions that must be noted: namely, that prices fully adjust to the monetary base and that the base/income ratio is constant.

What emerges from eq. (1) is that the stability condition depends, in general, on the relationship between rr and n. If the rate of interest on the government debt is lower than the rate of growth, the real debt tends to converge to a finite value, even in the presence of a primary deficit. On the other hand, when the real interest rate exceeds the trend growth rate, the real debt ratio tends to rise persistently; this implies an unstable situation.

Brunner and Meltzer emphasize, however, that a special case can always be found where $\dot{s} = 0$, i.e. where the real debt ratio is maintained at any given level. This point had been already recognized, but only to show that even if the transversality condition is satisfied and a primary deficit exists, an equilibrium can exist.[2]

---

1. The variable $\overline{def}$ denotes the basic deficit; s and m are respectively the stock of interest-bearing securities and the monetary base (all variables deflated by nominal income). The symbols rr, n and π denote the real rate of interest on government debt, the real rate of growth and the rate of inflation. Since the analysis is focused on long-run effects, deviations of the actual from the trend rate of growth are disregarded.

2. On this see RAINER S. MASERA, 'Four Arguments for Fiscal Recovery in Italy', in MICHAEL J. BOSKIN, JOHN S. FLEMMING and STEFANO GORINI, eds., Private Saving and Public Debt, London: Blackwell, 1987, and A. CIVIDINI, GIAMPAOLO GALLI and RAINER S. MASERA, 'Vincolo di bilancio e sostenibilità del debito: analisi e prospettive', in Debito Pubblico e politica economica in Italia, Collana Giorgio Rota, Ricerca n. 1, 1987.

Brunner and Meltzer seem, however, to overstate their case. In fact they show, also by a graphical approach, that even if $rr > n$, an appropriately high inflation rate can always be selected to stabilize the real debt ratio, given $\overline{def}$.

To recall, let us depict equation (1) in the plane $\dot{s}$, π: we suppose that $\overline{def} > 0$, $(rr - n)s > 0$. Both terms are independent of π and can be therefore represented as a line [1] parallel to the horizontal axis. The final term in the equation $(\pi + n)m$ can be depicted as a negatively sloped line [2] in the same plane. Since the rate of change of s is composed of a *constant* positive component and a negative component with absolute value increasing linearly in π, it appears that by selecting an appropriately high π – i.e. an appropriately high rate of growth of the nominal stock of the monetary base – the real debt ratio can always be stabilized (as in Figure 1, where for $\pi = \pi^*$, $OA = OC$).

Brunner and Meltzer themselves are not fully at ease with this conclusion, which they term "correct, but at the same time misleading".

I would go further and argue that the conclusion is not even correct, since it carries the assumption of a given money/income ratio over to the analysis of varying rates of inflation. It is only this assumption, which has neither micro nor macro foundations, that allows the conclusion that permanent unsustainable real deficits can be cured by a high, and yet finite, rate of inflation. The paradox is also made evident by the observation that money, which is assumed to be neutral in the long run, would in this formulation appear to be capable of solving a "real" imbalance.

To clarify this issue, which hinges on the inflation tax, let us note to start with that the quantity theory underlines the role of money in inflation, and the opportunity cost incurred in holding real balances during inflation. Precisely because real money balances are regarded to have no close substitute, the effect of anticipated inflation is to reduce the demand for money, but not actually to eliminate it. As Brunner and Meltzer themselves indicate, "only in very large, persistent inflations, or hyperinflations, do we find the displacement of existing money". It is precisely the social productivity of money – as measured by saving of resources that would otherwise be used to produce

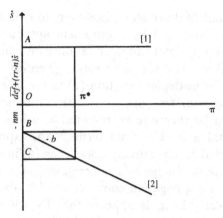

Figure 1. The dynamics of the debt-to-income ratio under
constant velocity and variable inflation

the level of information equivalent to the use of money – that
explains the persistence of money even in periods of high and
very high inflation.

Yet this by no means implies that we can ignore the opportunity cost of holding money (equal to $i = r + \pi^e$); rather, for a
given real rate of interest, we have to treat it in analogy with a
tax on a commodity: the inflation tax on money. It is therefore
definitely inappropriate – on both micro and macro grounds –
to adopt a constant-velocity assumption in terms of any meaningful monetarist demand-for-money approach, except when we
can also assume that prices are expected to be stable. In this
respect, it may be recalled that the major difference that used
to distinguish Keynesian and quantity theories was that the
former, but not the latter, was satisfied with the assumption of
unit elasticity of price expectations.

Let us therefore, like Brunner and Meltzer, assume fully anticipated inflation and disregard both deviations of the actual
rate of growth from the trend rate and changes in the real rate
of interest. The latter can thus be treated as a constant parameter and ignored in the money demand equation.

We can thus contrast the naive formulation of the quantity
approach:

(2) $$B/yp = \bar{m}$$

278

with the simplest version that allows for the ratio of real balances to income to adjust to the alternative opportunity cost of holding money:

(3) $$B/yp = m = Ae^{-k\pi}$$

By recalling familiar concepts, it is now easy to evaluate the total yield from the inflation tax in the two cases.

Let us start with the latter, where we have:

$$T = \pi \cdot m = \pi Ae^{-k\pi} \qquad k > 0, A > 0$$
$$T(0) = 0$$
$$\lim_{\pi \to \infty} T = 0$$

In order to determine max T we set:

$$\frac{dT}{d\pi} = Ae^{-k\pi} + \pi Ae^{-\pi k} (-k) = 0$$

$$1 - k\pi = 0$$

$$\pi = 1/k$$

hence $T \max = 1/k \ Ae^{-k.1/k} = \dfrac{A}{ke}$

In general, we have:

$$dT/d\pi = 0 = \frac{d}{d\pi} (\pi \cdot m) = m + \frac{dm}{d\pi} \cdot \pi = m (1 + \eta)$$

i.e. the yield of the inflation tax is maximized when the elasticity of m with respect to π is equal to -1, i.e. at the point where the percentage fall in the tax base offsets the percentage increase in the tax rate.

If we consider, instead, the fixed-velocity case we can write:

$$T = \pi \bar{m}$$
$$T(0) = 0$$
$$\lim_{\pi \to \infty} T = \infty$$

In this second case, $\eta = 0$, and the total tax revenue can therefore be raised monotonically with π. However, as has been pointed out, this variant of the quantity theory is devoid of empirical and analytical content, since no explanation can be provided for the assumed constancy of m, in the presence of π assuming different positive values.

These concepts are expounded graphically in Figure 2, where I have drawn in the plane (π, m) the derivation of the inflation tax revenue as a proportion of national income (the rectangle I) and the collection cost (the approximate Bailey-Harberger triangle W, which is a measure of the waste of resources, i.e. the welfare loss). The general case, represented by a downward-sloping demand curve, is shown by line [1]. The special case in which the demand is rigid (which corresponds to the "naive" quantity assumption) is represented by line [2].

In the bottom part of Figure 2, which depicts the plane (T, π) – where, to recall, T is the revenue from the inflation tax on money as a proportion of national income – we can see that in general the total revenue is a bell-shaped function that approaches zero asymptotically. Maximum yield is obtained at a finite level of inflation, where, as we know, the elasticity of m with respect to π is equal to one. In the special case in which $m = \bar{m}$, T will tend to rise linearly with π ($T = \bar{m}\pi$).

It is now easy to apply these considerations to the issue of debt finance in the long run under inflationary conditions.

For this we go back to the budget constraint, which we again deflate by nominal income, but without imposing a constant base/income ratio. Instead, we allow the ratio of money to income to adjust to the opportunity cost of holding money according to equation (3).

Equation (1) thus becomes:

$$(1) \quad \dot{s} = \overline{def} + (rr - n)s - m\dot{B} = \overline{def} + (rr - n)s - (\pi + n)\, Ae^{-k\pi}$$

where $\dot{B}$ denotes the rate of growth of B, and the price level is defined on the assumption that the system is always on the saddle path ($\dot{B} = \pi + n$).[1]

It is easy, to start with, to graph the changes that this makes in Brunner and Meltzer's analysis. The bottom part of Figure 1

1. See Appendix, eqs. (6), (7) and (8).

is drastically altered, as indicated in Figure 3. In particular, the downward sloping line [2] is replaced by the bell-shaped lines [3], which have a negative intercept $(\frac{-nA}{Y})$ and approach asymptotically the π axis.

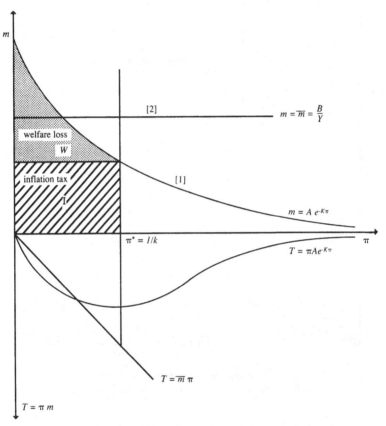

Figure 2. The inflation tax: constant velocity $(m = \bar{m})$ and variable money-to-income ratio $(m = Ae^{-k\pi})$

It is therefore no longer possible to rely on a sufficiently high inflation rate to maintain the real debt ratio at any given level and prevent its further increase. In particular, as indicated by line [3b], for given values of the basic deficit, with $rr > n$, the parameters of the demand-for-money function may well be

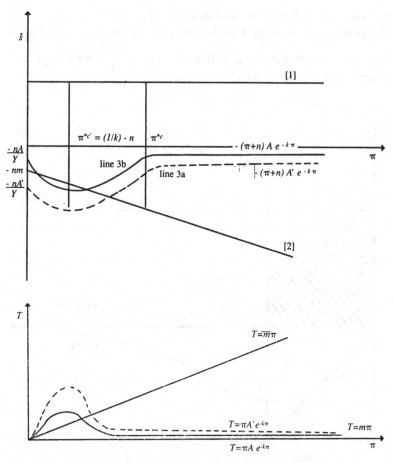

Figure 3. The dynamics of the debt-to-income ratio and
the inflation tax under constant and variable velocity.

such as to prevent the stabilization of the debt-to-income ratio.

More generally, and more importantly, it can actually be shown that even when an equilibrium position exists π^{*c}, as shown by line [3a], this is an unstable equilibrium[1]

It is now clear that Brunner and Meltzer's conclusion – that it is always possible to select an appropriately high rate of mon-

1. See Appendix.

etary expansion, and thus a high but constant rate of inflation, in order to close a real gap in the budget – cannot be accepted. This is so quite apart from any complication arising from likely adverse shifts in the required real rate of interest on government debt, or as a result of discontinuities in portfolios when the debt/income ratio moves to high values.[1]

2.2. To elucidate further these points it can be useful to refer explicitly to the so-called Hicksian income correction.[2] The correct integration of stocks of real and financial assets and flows of income and expenditure requires explicit consideration of the definition of real wealth in the economy and of the public sector budget constraint. Planned savings equals desired accumulation of wealth, which is the difference between end-of-period and beginning-of-period real stocks. The difference is accounted for by two components, net capital gains and the flow of new savings – i.e. that part of the flow of disposable income of the private sector that is allocated to the accumulation of real wealth. In principle, this aggregate approach can be regarded as the result of summation over all assets. Portfolio choice and savings would then represent simultaneous and integrated decisions, with perfect fungibility between net capital gains on existing assets and net new acquisitions.[3]

It is easy to show that the definition of the disposable income of the private sector that is consistent with this scheme is different from the traditional one, since a link has been established between stocks of wealth and flows of income. If we consider government bonds as real wealth, assume that the price of claims on

1. On this see, among others, GIAMPAOLO GALLI 'Tasso reale, crescita e sostenibilità del debito pubblico', Banca d'Italia, *Contributi all'analisi economica*, 1, 1985, and LUIGI SPAVENTA, 'The Growth of Public Debt: Sustainability, Fiscal Rules, and Monetary Rules', IMF *Staff Papers*, 2, June 1987.

2. JOHN RICHARD HICKS, *Value and Capital*, Oxford: Clarendon Press, 1946.

3. For a detailed analysis of these points see JOHN RICHARD HICKS, *op. cit.*, S. J. TURNOVSKY, *Macroeconomic Analysis and Stabilization Policy*, Cambridge: Cambridge University Press, 1977, RAINER S. MASERA, *Disavanzo pubblico e vincolo di bilancio*, Milan: Edizioni di Comunità, 1979, and JAMES TOBIN, *Asset Accumulation and Economic Activity*, Chicago: The University of Chicago Press, 1980. Needless to say, I find this approach entirely consistent with the broader framework of Brunner and Meltzer's money-credit model.

productive capital in terms of currently produced output cannot vary, and consider the Hicksian corrected disposable income (YD^H), we have:

$$(4) \quad YD^H = Y - T + (i - \pi) S - \pi B \qquad (T = \text{"explicit" taxes on income})$$

It is apparent from equation (4) that the effective degree of "fiscal pressure" cannot be subsumed by the ratio of T to Y, because of the inflation tax on government debt holdings, which, in general, can be taken to encompass the difference between the monetary erosion on the initial stock of debt and on the flow of new debt and the flow of interest payments.

As has been suggested by Buiter, Ricardo's equivalence case and the above equation defining disposable income can be taken as special cases of a general model of direct crowding out.[1] In such a model public expenditure can be considered as income in kind and therefore as a substitute for private expenditure. Correspondingly, if public deficits are taken to imply future taxes, government bonds can no longer be thought of as a *full* component of private sector wealth.

The consumption function and the corresponding definitions of wealth and disposable income thus become:

$$(5) \quad C = C(YD^H/P, v, C^P)$$

$$(6) \quad v = B/P + a\,S/P + K/P$$

$$(7) \quad YD^H = Y - T + (i - \pi)\, aS - \pi B + \beta C^P - (1 - a)\, \Delta s$$

where C^P is public consumption, $1 - a$ denotes the fraction of the interest-bearing debt that is counterbalanced by the present value of the future taxes acknowledged as necessary to pay off the debt, β denotes the proportion of current public spending considered as disposable income in kind, and K is the stock of physical capital at current prices.

In the ultra-rational model of equivalence, *à la* Barro, $a = 0$,

1. WILLEM H. BUITER, 'Crowding out and the Effectiveness of Fiscal Policy', *Journal of Public Economics*, 7, 3, 1977, pp. 309-328.

$\beta = 1$ and C^p should not figure at all in eq. (5).[1] In this case we have total direct crowding out.

If, as Brunner and Meltzer suggest – and I concur with their analysis – considerations of money and real uncertainty mean that interest-bearing debt represents net wealth, we have $0 < \alpha \leqslant 1$. At the limit $\alpha = 1$, $\beta = 0$.

In this model, as soon as we introduce yield-elastic relative demands for components of wealth, we can easily ascertain that the maximum yield of the inflation tax as a ratio to income is given. In conclusion, therefore, I wish to reiterate that there is no easy way out of structural budgetary imbalances. A monetary solution, which would be equivalent to the attempt to raising the inflation tax, can prove more difficult to achieve than real adjustment on explicit revenue and spending parameters. This is because the economy can and does adjust endogenously to the levying of the tax, which puts an effective constraint on its maximum yield.[2]

1. ROBERT J. BARRO, 'Are Governement Bonds Net Wealth?', *Journal of Political Economy*, 82, 1974, pp. 1015-1117.

2. Another illuminating way of looking at the issue is the following. Let us start with the assumption that the government sector and the central bank are formally separate. Any variation of the monetary base must therefore be the counterpart to the purchase of government securities by the bank. Let us indeed assume that this is the only source of monetary base creation, and that the interest revenues of the bank are handed back to the government sector. In this case, which reproduces some features of the current U.S. institutional setting, the budget restraint can be written as follows:

(1) $$\overset{\circ}{S} = DEF + iS - iS_{CB}$$

where S_{CB} denotes government securities held by the central bank. We observe that, if it denotes the rate of interest on interest-bearing debt, the average effective rate of interest on total government debt held by the private sector is given by the ratio of interest payments (net of retrocessions) to total debt:

(2) $$i_s = \frac{iS - iS_{BC}}{S} = i\,(1 - B/S)$$

It is only in the special case where we can assume that money and bonds can be maintained in a given proportion to each other for a *given* real rate of interest on bonds, and irrespective of the actual inflation rate, that equation (2) simplifies to

$$i_s = i\,(1 - \delta) \qquad \delta = B/S \qquad 0 \leqslant \delta \leqslant 1$$

But, writing (1) in proportion to income, we have

$$\overset{\circ}{s} - [(rr + \pi)\,(1 - \delta) - n]s = \text{def}.$$

If I may be allowed a short digression referring explicitly to the Italian situation, this is the policy conclusion I would stress, and I think that in general terms Brunner and Meltzer would not disagree. Budgetary adjustment, mainly on expenditures, but perhaps also on the revenue side, is now urgent. It cannot be avoided by monetary relaxation.

This does not imply that I would concur with the view that the real rate of interest on total debt will have to continue to be higher – or indeed substantially higher – than the real rate of growth of the economy, as we have experienced in the recent past.

Adjustment, however, should not be sought by forcing up the rate of inflation domestically. Rather, I believe, it will come both internationally and domestically as the traditional relationship of approximate balance between the two will be re-established. The recent turmoil in world stock exchanges may well accelerate this process, unless uncoordinated – or indeed incompatible – economic policies do not set off a recession.

To clarify these points, I believe it is relevant to look at the issue in a long-term perspective.

2.3. In some recent theoretical literature the rate of interest is constrained, a priori, to be higher than the rate of growth. In neo-classical models of growth this restriction may be justified on the ground that otherwise (i.e. with an interest rate lower than the growth rate) the system would be in the inefficient region relative to the golden rule, unless the rate of depreciation of the capital stock is sufficiently high to make up for the difference. A regime of *laissez-faire* in which agents have finite horizons may lead to such a situation; it is, however, easy to imagine a public intervention to discourage investment and produce a rise in the sustainable steady-state level of consumption.

The data reported in Figures 4, 5, and 6 for the United States, the United Kingdom and Italy indicate, however, that most

With these special assumptions it would be clear that the stability condition

$$(rr + \pi) (1 - \delta) - n < 0$$

could always be satisfied by selecting an approprimately high value of δ, even if $rr > n$.

of the time the rate of interest on the debt has been lower than the rate of growth. In the United States in the period 1890-1985 the average growth of nominal GNP was slightly below 6 per cent while the nominal interest rate on long-term public bonds was 4. 84 per cent; dividing the flow of interest paid by the Federal Government (including that paid to the Federal Reserve) by the overall debt (again including debt held by the Fed), one obtains an average cost of the debt of 3.75 per cent (Fig. 4). Similar conclusions are reached by Darby[1] using the yields on the United States Treasury bills elaborated by Ibbotson and Sinquefield[2] for the period 1926-1981. There are exceptions,

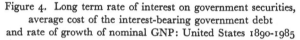

Figure 4. Long term rate of interest on government securities, average cost of the interest-bearing government debt and rate of growth of nominal GNP: United States 1890-1985

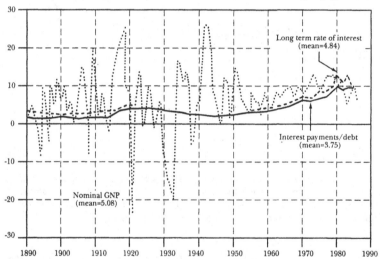

Source: United States Department of Commerce, 'Historical Statistics of the United States', USGPO; 'Economic Report of the President', February 1986; Budget of the United States Government – Fiscal Year 1987.

Note: The item "interest payment/debt" includes interest received in the numerator and the debt held by the Central Bank in the denominator. It measures the average cost of the whole mix of interest yielding liabilities of the government.

1. MICHAEL R. DARBY, *Some Pleasant Monetarist Arithmetic*, NBER, W.P. 1295, 1984.
2. ROGER C. IBBOTSON and R. A. SINQUEFIELD, *Stock, Bonds, Bills and Inflation: the Past and the Future*, Charlottesville, Va.: The Financial Analysts Research Foundation, 1982.

though, the most relevant including the beginning of the 1920s and the years of the Great Depression. For the present analysis the most important exception is that of the 1980s, with the rate of interest rising to values that are unprecedented and well above the rate of growth.

Figure 5. Long term rate of interest on government securities, average cost of the interest-bearing debt and rate of growth of nominal GNP: United Kingdom 1856-1985.

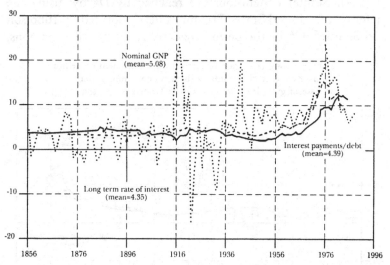

Source: C. B. FEINSTEIN, *National Income Expenditure (1855-1965)*, Oxford: CUIP, 1972; B. R. MITCHELL, *Abstratct of British Historical Statistics*, Oxford: Cambridge University Press, 1962; B. R. MITCHELL and H. G. JONES, *Second Abstract of British Historical Statistics*, Oxford: Cambridge University Press, 1971.

For the United Kingdom the evidence is similar, albeit less clearcut. Between 1856 and 1985 the average growth of nominal GNP (5. 08) exceeds the long-term rate of interest and the average cost of interest-yielding debt by about 70 basis points (Figure 5). But this average result is heavily affected by the observations covering the two wars and the first half of the 1950s. Both before the First World War and after it until the mid-1930s the rate of interest considerably exceeded the nominal rate of growth. As in the United States, the 1980s are a notable exception to the pattern prevailing since the Second World War: nominal interest rates are very high by historical standards and exceed the rate of growth of nominal GDP.

Figure 6 reports data which have recently been produced for Italy covering the period between 1915 and 1941. The pattern for this period is similar to that of the United Kingdom, with the rate of interest exceeding the nominal growth rate between

Figure 6. Long term rate of interest on government securities, average cost of the interest-bearing debt and rate of growth of nominal GNP: Italy 1915-1941

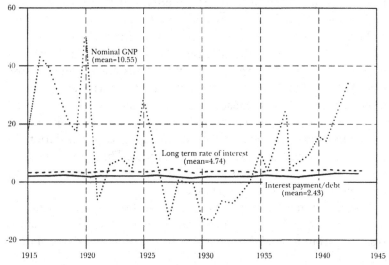

Source: A. CONFALONIERI and E. GATTI, *La politica del debito pubblico in Italia*, Milano-Bari: Cariplo-Laterza, 1986.

1926 and 1934. The year 1982 is again a notable exception to the post-war pattern.

Note that in these three countries the movements of the GNP series far outweigh those of interest rates. The latter appear virtually constant, in spite of wide variations in nominal GNP. Only in the 1970s did they start to rise, first in line with inflation and then faster.

To conclude, most of the time in the three countries the nominal rate of interest falls short of the nominal rate of growth. The opposite has nonetheless also been true for fairly lengthy periods, which have generally been times of recession or depression. In the light of this historical perspective, the unprecedented rise in interest rates of the 1980s warrants special attention and would require specific investigation.

I come now to some brief comments on rules vs. discretion in policy setting – an issue which has just been so well treated by Professor Arcelli. Perhaps because I am less skeptical than Brunner and Meltzer on the possibility of a non-mechanical use of econometric models as a tool for forming views about possible future economic developments – a point to which I shall come in a minute – I would be less drastic than they seem to be on the merits of strict adherence to fixed rules.

Let it be clear that the difference – if there is a difference – is essentially one of emphasis. I am, for instance, among those who believe that the adherence to a predetermined path of monetary-base growth consistent with gradual disinflation played a crucial role – together with the undertaking of maintaining an EMS exchange rate link – in bringing down inflation in Italy from over 20 to 5 per cent in the 1980s. This required corresponding institutional adaptations, notably the "divorce" between the Central Bank and the Treasury.

The adherence to monetary and credit targets was not mechanical, though. In many instances evidence of portfolio shifts resulting from financial innovation, integration and deregulation on the one hand and changes in preferences and expectations on the other suggested the acceptance of temporary short-run deviations from set paths.

I would thus be less drastic than Brunner and Meltzer in asking for a minister's or governor's resignation if he fails to adhere strictly to his announced targets. Without much overemphasizing the point, I cannot help recalling, for example, that the superimposition of the simplest monetarist rule (a predetermined rate of growth of the money base) on a price-elastic money demand function and a budget constraint can lead in general to an *unstable* equilibrium, as can be easily shown adopting the very approach developed by Brunner and Meltzer to deal with inflationary finance (see Appendix 1).

On the other hand, on "public choice" grounds I believe it would be appropriate to set a medium-term strategy for fiscal outcomes, as Professor Brunner himself has argued in general terms in earlier papers[1] and as I advocated with specific reference to the Italian situation.[2]

3. Econometric models and economic forecasts

Finally, I would like to make some remarks on the specific issues of the use of econometric models, their forecasting accuracy, and policy-making. In arguing that discretionary policies are not feasible due to errors in predictions, Brunner and Meltzer provide evidence of economic forecasts' inaccuracy. Accordingly, they state (in Lecture 4, pp. 191 ff.) that "to say that the policy-maker should not neglect current information is not the same as saying that he should rely on predictions or forecasts. Inaccurate forecasts can cause policymakers to destabilize rather than stabilize . . . The range within which real growth rate can fall during the current quarter covers the range from deep recession to a strong boom . . . On average, forecasters do not distinguish between booms and recessions beginning in the same quarter".

The existence of stochastic elements in economic variables and the difficulty of economic forecasting are hardly at debate. Paul Samuelson himself dwelled on the degree of forecasting accuracy in order to warn the policy-maker whether he should be risking a destabilizing course of action.[3] But he pointed out that the nature of the difficulty encompasses the very process of observation of economic variables, and it is indeed against

1. See for instance KARL BRUNNER, 'Inflation, Money and the Role of Fiscal Arrangements: An Analytic Framework for the Inflation Problem', in MARIO MONTI, ed., The 'New Inflation' and Monetary Policy, London: Macmillan, 1976; and the specific comments made on his paper by Mario Monti in the same volume.

2. RAINER S. MASERA, 'Moneta, credito e prezzi: considerazioni sull'esperienza italiana', in Quale politica monetaria, Roma: Centro Ricerche Economiche Applicate, 1974.

3. PAUL A. SAMUELSON, 'The Art and Science of Macromodels over 50 years', in G. FROMM and LAWRENCE R. KLEIN, eds., The Brookings Model, Amsterdam: North-Holland, 1975.

this acknowledgement that forecasts should be assessed: "It is as if there is a Heisenberg Indeterminacy principle dogging us, which will limit the asymptotic accuracy of forecasting we shall be able to attain". In other words, we cannot reduce an existing error level of 1 per cent in forecasting real GNP if real GNP cannot be observed with less than 1 per cent error.

An interesting comparison, then, is between the error of model forecasts and the degree of data revision by statistical agencies. The econometric model builders can hardly be expected to do better in forecasting than those agencies do in observation.[1] From this perspective, Brunner and Meltzer may not be wholly fair to the record of economic forecasters.

Another issue that Brunner and Meltzer fail to bring to the fore concerns the evidence that forecast errors exhibit a diminishing trend through time. In this respect Zarnowitz reaches conclusions that Brunner and Meltzer do not report but do not challenge either.[2] Indeed, in assessing the performance of forecasters through time, Zarnowitz shows that correlations between predicted and actual changes in key macrovariables are all significantly positive and suggests some improvement in recent years. This can be shown both by a reduction of average forecast absolute errors in more recent periods and by a reduction in the relative error between model-based and mechanically extrapolative forecasts. By this criterion, annual forecasts of GNP growth may actually have improved since the 1950s.[3]

Possibly the discrepancy between Brunner and Meltzer's conclusions and Zarnowitz's is to be attributed to the use of different error measures. The former argue on the basis of Root Mean Square Error (RMSE), whereas the latter uses Average Absolute Errors. On the use of RMSE as a "standard deviation" one might point out that RMSE is a "descriptive measure and some-

---

1. LAWRENCE R. KLEIN, *Econometric Models as Guides for Decision Making*, New York: Free Press, 1981.
2. VICTOR ZARNOWITZ, 'On the Accuracy and Properties of Recent Macroeconomic Forecasts', *American Economic Review*, 68, 2, May 1978; *id.*, 'The Record and Improvability of Economic Forecasting', *Economic Forecasts*, 3, December 1986, pp. 22-30.
3. *Id.*, 1986, *op. cit.*, p. 24.

what arbitrary".[1] If we wish to construct a confidence interval of forecasts around an average GNP growth rate, it would indeed be best – I suggest – to resort to stochastic simulation. In fact, once a certain RMSE, say 3 per cent, has been computed, it is somehow uninformative to add and substract it from an average GNP growth rate, without specifying the underlying stochastic structure of the problem. A standard deviation vanishes asymptotically with the square root of the sample size. But in this case what is the sample? The number of periods ahead or the number of econometric models or something else?

Yet Brunner and Meltzer are certainly right in stressing the deterioration of forecasts as the horizon extends. McNees[2] concludes that the 4- to 8-quarter forecasts of such variables as real GNP are generally worse than 1-quarter forecasts. In general, forecasts *not* based on formal econometric models appear to be at least as accurate as econometric forecasts. But, especially when there have been significant shocks (e.g. oil shocks), forecasts based on judgmental or autoregressive schemes have proved inferior.[3]

To the extent that Brunner and Meltzer argue mostly on the basis of quarterly forecast errors, one may observe that "it is generally the case that smoother variables will be simulated with a much smaller percentage error than will be the case for volatile ones".[4] This is so, for instance, in the case of annual vs. quarterly variables. In this respect, forecast error of GNP annual growth seems to be contained in the neighborhood of 1 per cent in recent experience (see the following Table 1 taken from Zarnowitz).[5]

For instance, the model at the Bank of Italy is built on a quarterly basis, to allow for relatively frequent updating, among other things, but it is much more commonly used to forecast *annual averages* rather than detailed quarter-to-quarter changes.

1. LAWRENCE R. KLEIN, *Lectures in Econometrics*, Amsterdam: North Holland, 1983.
2. STEPHEN K. McNEES, 'An Evaluation of Economic Forecasts', *New England Economic Review*, Nov.-Dec. 1975.
3. LAWRENCE R. KLEIN, 1981, *op. cit.*
4. *Id.*, 1983, *op. cit.*
5. VICTOR ZARNOWITZ, 1986, *op. cit.*

Table 1. Summary measures of error for annual forecasts of percentage changes in aggregate income, output, and the price level, 1953-1984

Period and years covered (1)	Line (2)	LIV[a] (3)	SPP[b] (4)	NYP[c] (5)	ERP[d] (6)	ANB[e] (7)	MIM (8)	WHM (9)	Mean (10)	XP (11)	Relative error (10):(11) (12)
				Growth Rate of Gross National Product (GNP)							
1	1953-76(24)	1.6	1.2						1.4	2.3	0.6
2	1956-63(8)	1.7	1.4	1.7					1.6	1.9	0.8
3	1963-76(14)	1.1	0.9		0.9		1.3	0.8	1.0	1.8	0.6
4	1969-76(8)	1.0	0.6		0.8	1.0	1.0	0.9	0.9	2.0	0.5
5	1977-84(8)				1.8	1.5	2.0	1.6	1.7	2.8	0.6
				Growth Rate of GNP in 1972 Dollars (RGNP)							
6	1959-67(9)	1.3					1.0		1.2	1.7	0.7
7	1962-76(15)				1.1		1.4		1.2	2.6	0.5
8	1969-76(8)				1.2	1.0	1.6	0.9	1.2	3.6	0.3
9	1977-84(8)				1.2	1.0	1.0	1.0	1.0	3.2	0.3
				Rate of Inflation in the GNP Implicit Price Index (IPD)							
10	1959-67(9)	0.6					0.7		0.6	0.3	2.0
11	1962-76(15)				1.0		1.0		1.0	1.3	0.8
12	1969-76(8)				1.4	1.3	1.4	1.4	1.4	2.0	0.7
13	1977-84(8)				0.9	1.0	1.2	1.2	1.1	1.3	0.8

[a] Based on surveys conducted by Joseph A. Livingston, syndicated columnist. Published in the *Philadelphia Bulletin* and *American Banker*; in recent years, in the *Philadelphia Inquirer*. Of the semiannual surveys, only the end-of-year ones are used here; questionnaire typically mailed in November, results published in December. Coverage: 44-62 persons.

[b] Mean of end-of-year forecasts from the following sources: (1) *Fortune* magazine ('Business Roundup'): (2) Harris Bank; (3) IBM Economic Research Department; (4) National Securities and Research Corporation; (5) NICB now Conference Board 'Economic Forum'; (6) R. W. Paterson, University of Missouri; (7) Prudential Insurance Company of America; (8) UCLA Business Forecasting Project. The earliest of these predictions were made in October, the latest in January. Most of these forecasts are quarterly.

[c] Group mean forecasts from the New York Forecasters Club. Of the semiannual forecasts, only the end-of-year ones are included. Coverage: 31-39 individual respondents. Dates: 1956-1958, October: 1959-1963, December. Collected through 1963 and analyzed in the NBER studies referred to in note b.

[d] Annual forecasts by the Council of Economic Advisers (CEA) as stated in the *Economic Report of the President* published as a rule in January. Often midpoints in the relatively narrow range, in a few cases interpolated and checked with the source for approximate accuracy.

[e] Source: Quarterly releases by the American Statistical Association (ASA) and the National Bureau of Economic Research (NBER), published by ASA in *AmStat News* and by NBER in *Explorations in Economic Research* and, more recently, NBER *Reporter*. Median Forecasts from the November surveys only are used. Coverage varied between 25 and 84, but mostly 30-50. See NBER studies quoted in note b; also, Zarnowitz.

Source: ZARNOWITZ, 1986, *op. cit.*

I would like to conclude by stressing what is perhaps a commonplace – namely, that models are tools to help policy-makers form their judgments, *not* a mechanical substitute for judgment. Resources devoted to developing models, generating forecasts, and discussing alternative scenarios and possible courses of action are not I believe ill-employed, because they are part of the intellectual development of our profession. As we read in Goethe's Faust

> While Man's desires and aspirations stir
> He cannot choose but err.

Through their constant use, refinement and development, thanks in part to their very mistakes, econometric models can improve our understanding of macrosystems, imposing logical and consistency constraints on economists and policy-makers alike. Structural models with adequate microfoundations and analysis of how expectations are formed and revised can – I believe – help improve the formulations of policy-making. Forecasting is not and should not be their primary purpose; still, subject to the perennial risk of fallibility, I, for one, would venture to say that even today they can help us to make more intelligent guesses about the course of future economic developments.

Appendix*

To recall, when the opportunity cost of holding money is allowed for and we assume that the money supply function is described by adherence to a constant growth rate rule, the debt/income differential equation is

$$\mathring{s} = (rr - n)s + \overline{def} - (\pi + n)Ae^{-k\pi} \qquad (1)$$

This is an ordinary linear differential equation of the first order, with non constant coefficients, since π cannot in general be regarded as a constant.

To show this latter point we write

$$B = Ayp e^{-\pi k} \qquad A > 0, \qquad \pi = \mathring{P}/P \qquad (2)$$

$$m = \frac{B}{yp} = Ae^{-\pi k} \qquad (3)$$

Differentiating equation (3) we obtain

$$\mathring{m} = \frac{\mathring{B}py - B\mathring{p}y - Bp\mathring{y}}{(yp)^2} = -k\mathring{\pi} Ae^{-k\pi} \qquad (4)$$

If we now assume that $\mathring{B}/B = \hat{B}$, $\mathring{y}/y = n$ we can write (4) as follows:

$$m(\hat{B} - n - \mathring{\pi}) = -k\mathring{\pi} Ae^{-k\pi} \qquad (5)$$

Upon substitution of (3) into (5) we have:

$$\mathring{\pi} = \frac{(n - \hat{B})}{k} + \frac{\pi}{k} \qquad (6)$$

The integral of (6) is

$$\pi(t) = ae^{\frac{1}{k}t} + (\hat{B} - n) \qquad (7)$$

$$\pi(0) = a + (\hat{B} - n) \rightarrow a = \pi(0) - (\hat{B} - n) \qquad (8)$$

The differential equation (6) has an unstable equilibrium position for $\bar{\pi} = \hat{B} - n$. And this is consistent with the traditional findings of the literature, according to which models of money

---

* This Appendix has been written in collaboration with A. Cividini.

and growth that assume perfect foresight are dynamically unstable.[1]

Substituting (8) into (7) we obtain the general expression of the differential equation describing the inflation rate.

$$\pi(t) = (\pi(0) - (\hat{B} - n))e^{\frac{1}{k}t} + (\hat{B} - n) \qquad (7)'$$

Taking into account equation (7)' we can thus proceed to solve equation (1) for s:

$$s(t) = e^{(rr-n)t}\left\{ K + \int (\overline{def} - (\pi(t) + n)Ae^{-k\pi(t)})e^{-(rr-n)t}dt \right\} \qquad (9)$$

where K is the constant in integrating.

In the special case where $\pi(0) = \hat{B} - n$ equation (9) simplifies as follows:

$$s(t) = e^{(rr-n)t}\left\{ K + \int (\overline{def} - \hat{B}Ae^{-k(\hat{B}-n)})e^{-(rr-n)t}dt \right\} \qquad (10)$$

$$= Ke^{(rr-n)t} + \frac{\overline{def} - \hat{B}Ae^{-k(\hat{B}-n)}}{-(rr-n)}$$

According to our assumptions, the second term is a constant; the equilibrium therefore hinges on the sign of $(rr - n)$.

---

1. For a review of these points and a possible way out, see THOMAS J. SARGENT and NEIL WALLACE, 'The Stability of Models of Money and Growth with Perfect Foresight', *Econometrica*, 6, 1973.

MARIO MONTI*

With their contribution, Professors Karl Brunner and Allan Meltzer have given us an outstanding interpretation of the original spirit and purpose of the Mattioli Lectures – bringing the development of economic analysis to bear on issues of relevance to current policies.

Not much remains to be said, after the thorough comments provided by Mario Arcelli, Eduard Bomhoff and Rainer Masera. I would like, however, to make a few points. In presenting them, I shall begin – and conclude – with two personal notes.

1. Brunner and Meltzer's Analytical Framework: From 1974 to 1987 – and Beyond

In 1974 I first had the privilege of being the discussant of a paper prepared by Karl Brunner[1] for a conference which was also organized in Milan by the two institutions which brought us here today.

At a time when the inflation problem seemed to many economists "intractable" and was considered by most to be related almost exclusively to the first oil shock, which had occurred only a few months earlier, the framework developed by Brunner on that occasion led him to conclude, quite provocatively for the time, that:

> The central association and causal relation between monetary growth and price movements remains indisputably at work. The new element in the inflation problem must be recognised in the role of the budget process and the effect of political processes on persistent and even expanding deficits. The effect on the financial stocks ... is moreover reinforced by the consequences on normal output. Increasing absorption of output and labour by the government sector lowers the private sector's capital intensity and available labour supply. Fiscal

* Professor of Economics and Rector, Università Commerciale Luigi Bocconi, Milano.

1. KARL BRUNNER, 'Inflation, Money and the Role of Fiscal Arrangements: an Analytic Framework for the Inflation Problem', in MARIO MONTI, ed., *The "New Inflation" and Monetary Policy*, London: Macmillan, 1976.

policy thus lowers in the long run the private sector's normal output. The social cost of erratic inflation conditioned by the prevailing financial evolutions produced by government policies is amplified by the long-run effects of the underlying fiscal patterns on the level of normal output (pp. 80-81).

The nature of this framework induced me to define it "fiscal monetarism" in my comment. Since much of the content of Brunner and Meltzer's Mattioli Lectures represents an outgrowth of theoretical seeds that were discernible in their initial framework, as presented by Brunner in 1974, it is natural for me to look back at the remarks made in discussing that paper.

At the analytical level, three remarks are worth recalling, concerning respectively the labor market, the credit market and the output market.

Wage adjustment and stability of the private sector. Underlying the 1974 paper was a conjecture about an inherently stable and shock-absorbing private sector and a destabilizing government sector. While this conjecture was still to be considered a postulate, Brunner emphasized in this connection the role of the wage-adjustment equation, which was seen as determining "a process producing and disseminating information over the economic system" (p. 36). This aspect, however, was not explicitly incorporated in the 1974 paper and the author stated his intention to develop it on another occasion. My remark was that similar developments would contribute significantly to generating testable hypotheses about the crucial issue of whether the private sector is inherently stable, as postulated by the author (p. 85).

It is not evident whether Brunner and Meltzer, in their Mattioli Lectures or elsewhere in their work, have adequately pursued this particular approach – centered on the labor market – to the issue of the stability of the private sector. A comment by them on this aspect would be helpful.

Disaggregation in the credit market. In Brunner's 1974 model no disaggregation was to be found within the banks' absorption of earning assets and within the public's asset supply. I noted that, as in previous works by Brunner and Meltzer, no distinction was made between the bank loan market and the market for securities. "It would be interesting, and perhaps vital for a realistic monetary analysis, to trace the absorption of government securities in the banks' portfolio and their substitution effects with respect to bank financing to the private sector, through loans or investments in corporate bonds. Twists in the interest rate structure as between the banks' lending rates and the bond market rates, ceilings on loan expansion, compulsory bank investments in bonds are among the features frequently encountered in economies characterized by relatively large government budgets and inflationary trends. Unless a reader is thoroughly convinced of the 'aggregative irrelevance of these allocative aspects', he would wish the Brunner model threw some light on them, since it is specified to explain precisely the environment in which their occurrence is likely" (pp. 86-87).

In their Mattioli Lectures, Brunner and Meltzer have gone a long way towards developing these aspects. In fact, already in 1976 Brunner followed up this suggestion to some extent:[1]

Another meaning of credit shock may involve the imposition of constraints on banks' loan portfolios. Banks may be required to hold a security reserve in excess of their desired portfolio or to reduce the size of their loan portfolio. The analysis of this problem requires a disaggregation of the credit market into a loan and a securities market ... (Lecture 2, pp. 91-92).

Can these exercises be really incorporated in the formulation of their present model?

Role of government, with special regard to the output market. The analytical treatment of the government sector in Brunner's 1974 model lent itself to several comments. In particular:

– The government absorbed output, labor services and credit to produce essentially economic instability and inflation. It produced no goods or services, as shown by the fact that there was

1. KARL BRUNNER, 'The Money Supply Process in Open Economies with Interdependent Security Markets: The Case of Imperfect Substitutability', in MICHELE FRATIANNI and KARL TAVERNIER, eds., *Bank Credit, Money and Inflation in Open Economies*, supplement to *Kredit und Kapital*, 1976.

no government component on the supply side of the equilibrium condition for the output market (p. 88);

– This analytical strategy had several implications: (a) the result that an expansion in the budget, even a balanced one, reduced "normal output" derived directly, though implicitly, from the assumption that any absorption of resources by the government served no productive purpose; (b) the formulation of expenditure programs in nominal terms, recommended by Brunner, obviously had no drawbacks, simply because inflation would reduce the real volume of inputs in a productive process which yielded no output anyway; (c) disregard for the manner in which resources were used by the government might lend theoretical legitimacy to a relaxation of economic and legal controls over its activity, an implication that would certainly have been rejected by Brunner; (d) it was irrelevant, even in the long run, whether a given budget deficit was generated by government dissaving through a current account deficit or was determined by capital account expenditures; (e) references made by Brunner to "productivity considerations" in government activities were, strictly speaking, inconsistent with the framework used (pp. 88-89);

– It could be concluded that:

Traditional monetarism ignores the fiscal role of government. Keynesian economics and Brunner's "fiscal monetarism" emphasize it. Keynesian economists concentrate on the effects of the budget on the demand side of the output market. Brunner recognizes these effects and stresses the financial effects of the budget through the asset markets. Both approaches neglect the influence of the budget through the supply side of the output market.

I suggested that the inflation problem could not be adequately explored unless a framework were developed to take account of what the government does, in terms of production of goods and services, and how productively it does it. How much it spends and taxes and how it finances its deficit are important information, but only a part of the picture (p. 89).

In reading Brunner and Meltzer's Mattioli Lectures, I was particularly interested in finding out whether and how they had modified their framework in these respects concerning government and supply.

Initially, one is inclined to think that they have not. The authors make it clear that "the position of the supply curve is not directly affected by changes in *g*" (real demand of government sector for output) (p. 107). They also stress that "in *Keynesian analysis*, (my italics), . . . government spending works 'directly' on output" (pp. 110-111, footnote 1).

As their analysis proceeds, however, they turn to the central issue raised above and provide a major breakthrough in the desired direction. They observe that, with few exceptions, "macro-economists treat the government sector as a sinkhole for goods and services produced by the private sector. Either the government buys goods and services from the private sector, which it redistributes to the public, or it produces goods and services with the same 'technology' used by the private sector. These alternative conditions dismiss the effects on incentives, productivity and efficiency [. . .]. A more relevant approach would disaggregate the spending accounts in the budget and treat the government sector as a production sector. 'Government production' uses goods and services supplied by the private sector as inputs and converts them into an output" (p. 114).

They go on offering "some tentative suggestions along these lines". To do so, they distinguish five conponents of government output (provision of infrastructure, production of goods and services with different degrees of efficiency, provision of education, income transfers, protection of property rights). They briefly discuss the effects of each component on the position of the aggregate supply curve and on normal output. Such effects are "independent of any burdens that arise from financing" government spending (p. 114).

The authors also offer a concluding appraisal and a technical corollary. Their concluding appraisal is the following: "We doubt that the processes we have mentioned here significantly modify short or even medium-term movements in output. We submit, on the other hand, that they contribute to the longer-run evolution of aggregate supply and normal output. We believe that attention to this socio-political framework can contribute more to raise standards of living than concentration on the usual aspects of short-run 'stabilization policies'" (p. 116).

As a technical corollary, they note that their "approach to the government sector requires some changes in the national income accounts. We cannot treat all of the government activities as final goods. Some portions of g are in the nature of intermediate goods in the production of the government sector's final goods or services" (p. 116, footnote 1).

It would be very interesting if the authors could provide us with further insights on what changes and extensions to their present framework they regard as necessary in order to fully implement this promising line of research.

2. The Role of Supply and "Supply-side Economics"

Besides the role of government in determining supply – which was discussed above – the role of supply itself within the macroeconomic mechanism is given considerable attention in Brunner and Meltzer's analysis. Yet, supply does not emerge in its bold incarnation as a school of thought on economic policy – the so-called "Supply-side Economics" – as the authors lead us through contemporary macroeconomic debates. The four schools they consider are Keynesianism, Monetarism, the Rational Expectations approach, the Real Business Cycle approach.

Yet, Supply-side Economics has recently enjoyed a phase of popularity, especially in the United States. It also has been active in criticizing monetarist policy proposition, a criticism which we do not find responded to, or reciprocated, in Brunner and Meltzer's lectures.

I would like to ask them three questions in this context: (a) Why did they feel it unnecessary to dwell on the Supply-side school?; (b) What is their view on the analytical basis of that school?; and (c) May the changes in regulations, usually advocated by supply-siders, be considered in line with their own fundamental views?

3. International Policy Coordination

Brunner and Meltzer have expressed in their lectures a position on international policy coordination which is less critical than those expressed by other prominent monetarists. Unlike, for example, Milton Friedman,[1] Brunner and Meltzer do not rule out policy coordination, but stress that it can make sense only if some rules are specified and adhered to (and, hopefully, announced to the market).

In this context, the authors have deeply criticized the "Louvre Agreement" of February 1987 on target zones for exchange rates. I would like to raise three questions on this issue:

a. Are Brunner and Meltzer against a non-announced policy-coordination rule on exchange rates because it is not announced, or because it concerns exchange rates, or for both reasons?

b. Would they favor, under present circumstances, an announced target-zone coordination policy?

c. Related to the issue of exchange-rate instability is the proposal – enjoying some academic support, most recently by Rudiger Dornbusch – of a dual exchange-rate system (one rate for current-account transactions, one for capital-account transactions), as a device to make free capital mobility consistent with exchange rates which would not destabilize current balances. What is Brunner and Meltzer's view on this subject?

4. Institutional Arrangements to Reduce Uncertainty

A theme underlying Brunner and Meltzer's lectures is the need for institutional arrangements to reduce uncertainty. Concerning this theme, I would like to submit three remarks, perhaps motivated in part by policy debates currently going on in Europe.

Financial regulation and uncertainty. To assess the implications of monetary and financial policies in terms of the uncertainties they generate, the authors consider: (a) the behavior of central banks in conducting monetary policies within a given institutional framework, and (b) how the institutional framework guiding monetary and fiscal policies should be changed, so as to make

---

1. See, e.g., his article 'The Virtue of Exchange Rate Volatility', *Wall Street Journal*, June 24, 1987.

it less advantageous for the authorities to behave in such a way as to generate uncertainty and inflation.

What they do not consider is the role of the monetary authorities and governments in designing, through regulations, the structure of the asset markets. This role can be viewed, I submit, as an important component of the process of building an institutional arrangement conducive to budget discipline and monetary certainty. This is a component for which more remains to be done in Europe (and in countries like France and Italy in particular) than in the United States. The elimination of direct controls in the domestic credit markets, as well as the removal of restrictions on international capital flows, is regarded – and advocated – by many of us in Europe not only as a policy aimed at increasing the allocative efficiency of financial markets, but also as a strategy that would increase the discipline on domestic fiscal and monetary policies, thus reducing the authorities' ability to conduct them in ways that generate inflationary trends and uncertainty.[1]

I submit that Brunner and Meltzer, if they were to work more specifically in the context of some European countries characterized by a relatively high degree of financial repression, would stress very much the role of changes in financial regulation in creating institutional arrangements to reduce uncertainty.

The political economy of giving up discretion. Concerning the institutional rules (as distinct from the market structures) conditioning fiscal and monetary decisions, the evolution in Brunner and Meltzer's thinking is highly interesting.

I must confess, however, that I still see to some extent the problem that I mentioned in commenting on Brunner's 1974 paper, i.e. "about the consistency between Brunner's analysis of the incentive structure confronting policy-makers and his recommendation that discretionary fiscal policy be traded-off against

---

1. This view has been presented, for example, in MARIO MONTI, 'Integration of Financial Markets in Europe', in HERBERT GIERSCH, ed., *Free Trade in the World Economy: Towards an Opening of Markets*, Tübingen: J. C. B. Mohr, 1987; and FRANCO BRUNI, ALESSANDRO PENATI and ANGELO PORTA, 'Financial Regulation, Implicit Taxes and Fiscal Adjustement in Italy', in MARIO MONTI, ed., *Fiscal Policy, Economic Adjustment and Financial Markets*, Washington, D.C. and Milano: International Monetary Fund and Centro di Economia Monetaria e Finanziaria, 1989.

a system of automatically operating fiscal arrangements. If really fiscal policy is destabilising because policy-makers and legislators do not refrain from a *day by day* use of their discretionary powers which produces inflation for the economy and political rewards for themselves, how can they be expected to give up those powers *once and for all?*" (p. 85).

On this issue, which of course points to a problem for any type of constitutional approach to changes in economic policy-making, Brunner and Meltzer may want to provide further insights. The only element of reflection I have to offer is that there are occasions on which – because of episodes of "crisis" (e.g. in the external accounts) or because of a specific procedural step (e.g. the annual discussion on the budget) – the weight of preoccupations concerning inflation or the budget deficit in the public's perception, and thus of concern to politicians at that particular time, is greater than it is during the day by day activity by parliament and government on spending matters. There is some scope, therefore, for exploiting the opportunities arising from these asymmetries over time, to use such occasions in order to make binding commitments that may hold for a subsequent period.[1]

Nominalism, indexation and uncertainty. One important interpretation of institutional arrangements to reduce uncertainty is based on strict adherence to the nominalistic principle. It is a fact that one of the least inflationary countries, the Federal Republic of Germany, is very rigid in sticking to that principle, with the implication that the concept of indexation is fully rejected, in all markets and forms.

On the other hand, many economists have long argued that if governments issue indexed bonds there would be a number of advantages, including that of reducing uncertainty and possibly the government's propensity to inflate. In Italy, as recalled by Mario Arcelli in his remarks, this debate has been particularly

---

1. For an example of institutional arrangements along these lines, see GUIDO TABELLINI, 'Monetary and Fiscal Policy Coordination with a High Public Debt', in FRANCESCO GIAVAZZI and LUIGI SPAVENTA, eds., *High Public Debt: the Italian Experience*, Cambridge: Cambridge University Press, 1988, p. 120.

lively.[1] Would Brunner and Meltzer care to comment on the issue of index bonds and how it would fit in their framework of institutional policy?

5. Agreements and Disagreements on Monetarism

I would like to end my remarks with a personal note. It relates to a question I posed ten years ago in this Aula Magna to Franco Modigliani, in the debate following his inaugural Mattioli Lecture. The question concerned a paper by Thomas Mayer, also referred to by Brunner and Meltzer in their lectures.[2]

In his presidential address to the American Economic Association, Modigliani[3] had argued that in the previous years there had been many convergences of views between the neo-Keynesian and the monetarist school, and that the only outstanding fundamental divergence was on the role of stabilization policies. On the other hand, an economist with monetarist sympathies like Thomas Mayer had reached the conclusion that basically "every single proposition of monetarism is one which a Keynesian could accept while rejecting others, and still maintain his adherence to basic Keynesian theory. In particular, the policy propositions are readily detachable from the theoretical propositions of monetarism, and can be accepted without qualms by a Keynesian".

Thus for Modigliani there was a *divergence* between monetarists and neo-Keynesians regarding the role of stabilization policy, whereas for some monetarists there was a *convergence* between them and the neo-Keynesians on this same issue. I therefore asked for Modigliani's comments on Mayer's statement and for his opinion on whether it would be fair to say that the rival

1. For a discussion of the issue, with particular reference to Italian debt management policy, see MARIO MONTI, 'Indexation of Government Debt and its Alternatives', in B. P. HERBER, ed., *Public Finance and Public Debt*, Detroit: Wayne State University Press, 1986.

2. THOMAS MAYER, 'The Structure of Monetarism', in THOMAS MAYER, ed., *The Structure of Monetarism*, New York: Norton, 1978.

3. FRANCO MODIGLIANI, 'The Monetarist Controversy, or Should we Forsake Stabilization Policies?', *American Economic Review*, 67, 2, March 1977, pp. 1-19.

schools could agree that there was a growing agreement between them but disagreed as to the points on which they agreed.[1]

Modigliani answered that the difference with Thomas Mayer arose primarily from a difference in the definition of the essence of monetarism.[2] To him the essential monetarist was Friedman, and the distinctive component of his view was that governments could not be trusted with discretionary powers. On the other hand, the essence of the Keynesian position, in his view, was that they did not regard the system as sufficiently stable, if left alone, and held that discretionary policy, or at any rate more complex stabilization rules, could be used by the government to improve the situation. Most other differences were to be regarded as "quantitative" rather than qualitative.

As an echo from one Mattioli Lecture to the other, I wish to ask Brunner and Meltzer for their comments on the characterization made by Modigliani.

Finally, I have to express again my great admiration to Karl Brunner and Allan Meltzer for delivering these very important lectures and for the way in which they have been able to combine passion and equilibrium, analytical sophistication and policy relevance.

---

1. 'Discussion' in FRANCO MODIGLIANI, *The Debate over Stabilization Policy*, Raffaele Mattioli Foundation, Cambridge: Cambridge University Press, 1986, pp. 183-184.
2. FRANCO MODIGLIANI, *op. cit.*, pp. 207-208.

RICCARDO ROVELLI*

The degree of uncertainty in our knowledge of the stochastic structure of economic systems implies that activist Keynesian policies should not be pursued. I agreed with this non-activist position of the lecturers. However I suspect that a rule such as a fixed target rate of money growth performs inadequately as well.

I support my claim by presenting evidence from an empirical study of the Italian monetary system.[1]

First of all, the equilibrium relationship between money and prices is not simple to detect: time series of money and prices are either integrated of a different order or, if of the same order, they are not cointegrated in a bivariate model.

Moreover both the demand for money and the demand for loans are found to be unstable in a Kalman filter estimation despite a careful specification selection; this phenomenon is reflected in the instability of elasticity with respect to the interest rate. I accept Karl Brunner's argument that the opportunity cost for loans is not observable and does not coincide with the loan rate. However, from an operational point of view it does not help to know that a function is stable with respect to an unobservable variable.

The lack of data concerning the determinants of the key elements of the transmission mechanism prevents policymakers from predicting the consequences of a monetary rule; hence the desirability of fixed targets is severely lessened.

Another relevant aspect concerns the behavior of Italian monetary authorities. Monetary base does not appear to be exogenous with respect to bank deposits according to a causality test performed on the permanent components of bank deposits and monetary base held by banks. Thus monetary policy cannot be described a soperating in terms of monetary base control.

* Professor of Economics, Università degli Studi di Cagliari.

1. VALENTINA CORRADI, MARZIO GALEOTTI, RICCARDO ROVELLI, 'Il sistema bancario e il meccanismo di trasmissione', in FRANCESCO CESARINI, MICHELE GRILLO, MARCO ONADO, MARIO MONTI, eds., Banca e Mercato, Bologna: Il Mulino, 1988.

GIANLUIGI MENGARELLI*

I would first question the empirical validity of some extreme implications of rational expectations, namely the ineffectiveness of monetary policy rules. Credit availability is crucial in constraining economic activity when money is tight, and availability of real resources is a necessary condition for "easy money" rules to be unable to raise production.

I would then ask the lecturers' opinion on two issues. The first one concerns the monetarist proposition according to which a constant rate of growth of money supply stabilizes money velocity. After the observed fluctuation of money velocity in the 1980s shouldn't we give more importance to elements unrelated to the actions of monetary authorities?

My second question concerns the role of monetary policy in the business cycle: should it be calibrated in order to dampen recessions as well as expansions, or should it continually sustain the latter?

* Professor of International Economics, Università degli Studi di Venezia.

COMMENTS
by Karl Brunner and Allan H. Meltzer

We are grateful to the discussants of our lectures for giving us the benefit of their many comments and questions. The lectures cover a large number of issues. The comments and questions bear on a small part of the material. We are encouraged by the broad agreement that we appear to share with the discussants about many issues in macroeconomics.

Eduard Bomhoff

Nowhere is this agreement clearer than in the comments by Eduard Bomhoff who shares our view about one of the main themes – importance of uncertainty. Bomhoff's past work on uncertainty, and his pioneering efforts to introduce and develop procedures for treating uncertainty, have influenced us, as the lectures make clear. We welcome his efforts, exemplified by his comments, to explore alternative statistical procedures in this area.

Mario Arcelli

Mario Arcelli accepts the general principle that uncertainty reduces the scope for discretionary activism that is consistent with welfare enhancing economic policy. He believes this argument is applicable mainly to small shocks, such as those that occur in a typical, postwar business cycle. For large shocks, Arcelli favors a more activist policy, although he recognizes not only that the issue is open but that the large shock may be the result of either previous discretionary policy or loss of confidence in the government actions.

In our view, the size of the shock is not relevant for the choice of an activist policy. Suppose a large productivity shock lowers output throughout the society. The loss of output cannot be recovered by distributing money or by increasing aggregate demand. An unanticipated distribution of money, however, mixes the signals received by households and businesses. They cannot separate reliably that part of the price increase induced by the productivity decline from the general increase in prices induced by monetary expansion. Uncertainties – and errors – increase. If instead the government continues to follow a policy rule, such as the adaptive rule we propose in the lectures, the public has

317

more reliable information and uncertainty is lower. The public incurs lower cost of learning that the price increase is a one-time price change induced by the productivity shock.

Policy should be based on what we know reliably. Knowledge that there has been a large shock is not sufficient. To make a welfare improving policy change, we must have information about the duration of the shock, the magnitude of its effects, and the required quantitative change in the variables that the policymaker uses to offset the effects of the shock. Reliable information of this type is rarely available. Economists have not been able to develop procedures to forecast with sufficient accuracy, estimate structural parameters with sufficient reliability, or identify lags in response with sufficient precision.

Rainer S. Masera

In our analysis of the long-run consequences of a sustained budget deficit, we hold velocity constant. We show two solutions, depending on the relation of the real rate of interest to real growth. Either the economy reaches an equilibrium ratio of debt to output, or the rate of inflation must be adjusted to hold the debt ratio constant. A main implication of the analysis is that, under prevailing conditions, the equilibrium rate of inflation implied by a deficit equal to 5% of GNP (or more) is so high that, despite the differences in the rates of inflation for the two solutions, both rates of inflation are far above the level experienced in developed economies.

Rainer Masera points out that we should not keep velocity constant. Velocity should increase with the anticipated rate of inflation. He shows that, when the real rate of interest (rr) is above the real growth rate (n), there may be no inflation rate that stabilizes the debt ratio. Also, there may be no equilibrium debt ratio when $rr < n$, if velocity depends on the rate of inflation. We agree with his conclusion and his criticism. Constant velocity is inappropriate in an analysis of inflation.

Masera's result strengthens the conclusion that we reach. A substantial permanent deficit may be inconsistent with a non-inflationary monetary regime. It remains true, however, that a moderate budget deficit, if sustained, generates rates of inflation much greater than the rates observed in countries with persistent budget deficits.

The puzzle we noted remains. Governments have run persistent deficits without generating rates of inflation approaching those implied by either our analysis or Masera's extension. While we noted that there are exceptions, for example in Latin America, peacetime experience does not show either a strong association between persistent deficits and high or rising rates of inflation or the high rates of inflation implied by our numerical calculation. In fact, countries with persistent deficits have reduced their rates of inflation, in recent years, while continuing to run deficits.

Masera suggests also that countries may have real rates of interest below the growth rate of output. If true, this would reduce the rate of inflation consistent with any maintained deficit. His comparison of a relatively riskless rate of interest on government bonds to the risky stream of real output is not entirely appropriate. A proper comparison would use the returns on an asset with risk properties similar to output.

Mario Monti

Mario Monti asks us to extend our discussion to include supply-side economics, to consider proposals for policy coordination and financial deregulation, and to comment on Franco Modigliani's much revised view of the differences between monetarists and Keynesians. Monti also raises a number of issues that ask for analyses beyond the level of our lectures or this response.

As Monti notes, our text does not consider supply-side economics as a distinct hypothesis. The reason is that, when stripped of some exaggerated claims, supply-side economics is basic to economics. Every elementary course in economics, we expect, discusses the effects of relative prices on incentives and resource allocation. For many years, our work at the macro level has distinguished between aggregative and allocative effects of economic policies. Our discussion of taxes and the budget in these lectures emphasizes differences in the allocative effects of different components of government spending. We refer to the textbook by Martin Bailey, where this distinction was developed fruit-fully, and at length, years ago. The same types of analyses would apply to regulation; the principal effects of different regulations are allocative, but the cumulative effect of complex regulation, high taxes and a large government sector increases uncertainty and excess burden, as we have noted here and elsewhere.

What Monti calls the "supply-side school" must be credited with emphasizing these allocative effects and the long-term conse-quences of a large government sector. They have not provided a distinct hypothesis, and are not a separate "school". Further, we find a puzzling inconsistency. Many of those who have force-fully presented supply-side arguments have restricted their con-cern to taxes and neglected the allocative effects of spending. Some work suggests the emphasis on taxes may be misplaced; the allocative effects of government spending policies may be more important than the allocative effects of taxes.[1]

Monti asks us to comment on issues related to so-called policy coordination. Coordination is a large subject, which does not have even a common definition. Many proponents of coordination favor activist, discretionary policies. They write and talk as if economists could predict the future paths of interest rates and exchange rates for many countries or could choose policies to coordinate these movements. There are many variants of this approach. Some propose to adjust the fiscal and monetary policies of many countries to achieve coordinated results. An alternative meaning of coordination is that countries follow compatible poli-cy rules. Other alternatives are advanced also.

Our proposal for monetary policy is a pre-announced, adaptive rule that is common to all major countries and does not rely on forecasting. As is well-known, countries can achieve price sta-bility and reduce exchange rate instability simultaneously only if they pursue policies that are mutually compatible. Our rule would keep policies compatible. It provides a system of coordi-

---

1. See JOHN PIGGOTT and JOHN WHALLEY, 'A Summary of some Findings from a General Equilibrium Tax Model of the United Kingdom', in KARL BRUNNER and ALLAN H. MELTZER, eds., *Carnegie-Rochester Conference Series on Public Policy*, 14, Spring 1981, pp. 153-201.

nated policies – specifically, monetary policies consistent with price stability, as defined in the proposal, and fiscal policies in each country consistent with the maintenance of the country's monetary policy. Coordination of this kind does not require greater knowledge of economic structure and of the nature of shocks than economists or government officials can demonstrate that they possess. Our position on issues of this kind is discussed in our lectures as well as in our previous work.

Our response to proposals for "target zones" follows from our analysis. Economists do not know, and cannot predict, the correct price of any asset. Our models tell us, at most, that prices reflect available information plus noise. They do not tell us what the numerical values of equilibrium prices will be. How, then, can we use economic theory to choose a "target zone" for any asset price, including exchange rates?

We believe that the answer is that we cannot. Even after the fact, economists cannot explain why asset prices in all countries were much lower on October 20, 1987 than a week earlier. Nor can we separate reliably real and nominal shocks or compute the persistence of each type of shock to asset prices even after the event. Yet, information of this kind must be the basis for knowing where to set target zones for exchange rates or interest rates and when to change the zones.

An announced target zone improves opportunities for wealth-maximizing speculators who believe that a permanent change, or a mistaken policy, has made the current exchange rate inconsistent with the domestic policy goals of participating countries. An unannounced target exchange rate regime cannot persist. The reason is that costs of information in exchange markets are not so high that market participants will fail to discover the boundaries of the zone.

As we emphasize in our lectures, the aim of policy should be to reduce excess burdens and lower variability to the minimum inherent in nature and market arrangements. Exchange rate changes, or their absence, should not be policy goals. Exchange rates are relative prices and, as is well known, adjustment of relative prices is the means by which economies achieve efficiency. We argue that policymakers contribute most to stability by pursuing pre-announced policy rules that reduce uncertainty.

Monti's last query asks us to compare our view of monetarism to Franco Modigliani's statements in a previous Mattioli lecture series. In his response to a question, Modigliani equated monetarism with Milton Friedman's proposed rule calling for a constant rate of money growth. This is a peculiar definition and, as we note in our lectures, a change from Modigliani's earlier statements. Having recognized and conceded many of the issues in the monetarist-fiscalist debate, Modigliani[1] tried to redefine what the debate was about.

The choice between rules and discretion was surely an issue, but it is untrue that all the participants on the monetarist side supported Friedman's rule. There were other issues and other policy rules.

Recent work shows that some type of rule is likely to add more to welfare than complete discretion; the latter, an unpredictable policy, hardly qualifies as a policy. Systematic actions are predictable actions, or rules. The issue, then, is what kind of rule is likely to reduce variability to the minimum inherent in nature and trading arrangements. Lecture 4 discusses this issue at length.

Riccardo Rovelli and Gianluigi Mengarelli

Professors Mengarelli and Rovelli commented from the floor on some of the issues raised by the lectures. We believe that, in our response to Professor Monti and our discussion in Lecture 4, we have discussed a rule calling for a fixed rate of money growth and our reasons for preferring a rule that uses current information in a systemic, non-discretionary way. Our rule would adjust current money growth to the three-year moving average rates of growth of output and velocity, so it would respond in a mildly counter-cyclical fashion to recessions and booms.

On one issue, we disagree with Professor Rovelli. A systematic relation between past money growth and inflation has been noted and commented on for centuries. We have not seen the work to which he refers, so we cannot comment further on any problems in the methods or procedures.

---

1. FRANCO MODIGLIANI, 'The Monetary Controversy or, Should We Foresake Stabilization Policies?', *American Economic Review*, 67, March 1977, pp. 1-19.

Once again, we want to express appreciation to our discussants and commentators for their constructive comments and questions. Their interest, and the interest of the many participants at the lectures, greatly increased our pleasure in presenting the lectures and participating in the discussion.

BIOGRAPHIES

of Karl Brunner and Allan H. Meltzer

KARL BRUNNER

1. *A Professional Biography**

Karl Brunner was born in Zurich on February 16th, 1916. He entered the University of Zurich in 1934. After studying history for one year, he decided that economics could better satisfy his desire to understand man considered in the context of human society. He believed in individual opportunities to shape one's own life. Hence he did not choose economics because of concerns for social problems.

It was not until 1937, when he registered for one year at the London School of Economics, that he encountered modern economic analysis. Upon resuming his studies at the University of Zurich in 1938 he laid out by himself his own course of learning. He wrote his doctoral dissertation on the Anglo-Saxon theory of international trade, which was published in 1945.[1]

He joined the Economics Department of the Swiss National Bank in 1945. After one year he left his post in order to become a lecturer at the University of St. Gällen and research associate at the Swiss Institute of Foreign Trade.[2] Due to his dissatisfaction with the quality of research at the department and his fights to improve on it he had to leave in 1948.

While working for the Swiss Watch Chamber of Commerce and for the Economic Commission for Europe,[3] Brunner applied to the Rockfeller Foundation which was offering fellowships for European scholars. The Rockfeller Fellowship Research Grant allowed Karl Brunner to go to the United States for two years. After spending one semester at Harvard University in fall 1949,

---

* Written by Giovanna Nicodano, Associate Professor, Università degli Studi di Torino. The author acknowledges special reference to KARL BRUNNER, 'My Quest for Economic Knowledge', in MICHAEL SZENBERG, ed., *Eminent Economists. Their Life Philosophies*, Cambridge: Cambridge University Press, 1992, pp. 84-97, and to interviews recorded in June and September 1988.

1. *Studies in the Theory of International Trade*, Zurich: Verlag Schulters A.G., 1945.
2. MARK BLAUG, ed., *Who's Who in Economics*, Cambridge, Mass.: The M.I.T. Press, 1983.
3. 'The Economic Effect of the Marshall Plan', in *The Annual Report of the Economic Commission for Europe*, 1948.

he obtained permission to spend the following eighteen months at the Cowles Commission for Research in Economics. It is easy to uncover the influence of his years in Chicago in his subsequent research. His research clearly displays attention both to the methodological aspects of economic analysis and to the empirical content of theories. At the Commission, he enjoyed a good working relation with Carl Christ,[1] with whom he read Paul Samuelson's *Foundations of Economic Analysis'*.[2] With Harry Markowitz[3] he worked through von Neumann and Morgenstern's *Theory of Games*.[4] He also attended regular seminars which emphasized application of mathematics to economic analysis and econometrics. In 1950 came his first publication in an American journal.[5] The journal in question was, significantly, *Econometrica*, which had originated out of a joint venture between the founding fathers of the Econometric Society – Irving Fisher, Ragnar Frisch and Charles F. Roos – and Alfred Cowles.[6] The Cowles Commission and *Econometrica* can be contrasted with the Economics Department at the University of Chicago and the *Journal of Politiccal Economy*,[7] in which

1. Carl Finley Christ had received his Ph.D. from the University of Chicago in 1950. He later became Associate Professor at the University of Chicago (1955-1961). His principal contributions, ranging from econometrics to macroeconomic theory, include the econometric evaluation of U.S. macroeconomic policy since World War II and the analysis of effects on macroeconomic equilibrium of the government budget constraint. See MARK BLAUG and PAUL STURGES, eds., *Who's Who in Economics*, Brighton, Sussex: Wheatsheaf Books, 1983.

2. PAUL A. SAMUELSON, *Fondations of Economic Analysis*, Cambridge, Mass.: Harvard University Press, 1947; 2nd edition, 1982.

3. Harry Max Markowitz completed his Ph. D. at the University of Chicago in 1954. He was later research associate at the Rand Corporation, Professor of Finance at UCLA, Wharton School and Rutgers University. His principal area of interest is economics of uncertainty and information. See MARK BLAUG, ed., *Who's Who in Economics*, Brighton, Sussex: Wheatsheaf Books, 1986.

4. JOHN VON NEUMANN and OSKAR MORGENSTERN, *Theory of Games and Economic Behaviour*, Princeton: Princeton University Press, 1944; 3rd ed., 1953.

5. 'Stock and Flow Analysis in Economics', *Econometrica*, 18, 3, July 1950, pp. 247-251.

6. CARL F. CHRIST, 'History of the Cowles Commission 1932-1952', in *Theory and Measurement: A Twenty-Year Research Report*, Chicago: Cowles Commission for Research in Economics, 1952.

7. "... a distinct place exists for a journal of political economy which, while welcoming the discussion of theory, may be devoted largely to a study of practical problems of economics, finance and statistics", in J. LAURENCE LAUGHLIN, 'The

Brunner published several papers. They represented two often contrasting tendencies: striving towards analytical rigor and emphasis on empirical relevance. When the contrast between the two could not be resolved, the second tendency prevailed. Karl Brunner justified his choice on two grounds. Analytical tools do not appear to be enough developed to cope with problems posed by uncertainty in incomplete markets. Moreover the emphasis on "first principles" by most theorists is misplaced. There are no "rock bottoms, neither of certainty nor of invariance".[1]

Particularly intriguing to the young scholar was the contrast between the seminars at the Cowles Commission and the discussions at the department of Economics of the University of Chicago. Here a group around Aaron Director,[2] Milton Friedman[3] and Frank Knight[4] advanced the relevance of economics as an empirical science beyond the formal exercises and statistical apparatus of econometrics. The beginning of Brunner's inquiry into the nature of the cognitive process dates back to this period.

Armen Alchian[5] interviewed him for a position as assistant professor at the University of California, Los Angeles (UCLA). Brunner accepted the offer from UCLA. With Alchian he further discussed the purpose and the nature of the cognitive process in economics. He read Hans Reichenbach's *Experience and Pre-*

Study of Political Economy in the United States', *The Journal of Political Economy*, vol. I, 1892-1893, p. 19.

1. 'My Quest for Economic Knowledge,' *op. cit.*

2. Aaron Director was professor of economics at the Law School of the University of Chicago from 1946 to 1972. His principal areas of research have been monetary theory and monopoly and competition. See JAQUES CATTELL PRESS, ed., *American Men and Women of Science. Economics*, New York: R. R. Browker Co., 1974.

3. Milton Friedman has been professor of economics at the University of Chicago since 1948 and senior research fellow at the Hoover Institution since 1983. His best known contributions relate to consumption and monetary theory. He received the Nobel Prize in 1976. See MARK BLAUG, ed., *Great Economists since Keynes*, Brighton, Sussex: Wheatsheaf Books, 1985.

4. Frank Hyneman Knight taught at the University of Chicago from 1927 till 1955. His main contributions belong to profit theory and capital theory. He also wrote essays in social philosophy and methodological issues in relation to economics. See MARK BLAUG, ed., 1985, *op. cit.*

5. Armen Alchian was economist with the Rand Corporation in Santa Monica (1947-1964). He was also professor of economics (1958-1985) and then professor emeritus (from 1985) at UCLA. Among his writings are essays on information theory and the competitive mechanism.

diction',[1] which opened a phase of study in logic and philosophy of science. Among the outcomes of this research is his 1969 essay,[2] in which he argues that no use made by economists of the term "assumption" permits one to infer the confirmation of a theory from the confirmation of its underlying assumptions.

"The innumerable and long discussions on wide-ranging subjects shaped my thinking over the years and sharpened my sense about the nature of the issues. For almost 30 years we had worked well together. It should not be surprising that our views merged to a large extent into a similar pattern."[3] This is how Karl Brunner recalls his association with Allan Meltzer, which began at UCLA where Meltzer was a graduate student from 1955 to 1957. Beginning in 1962, they worked together on various aspects of monetary theory and monetary policy. A milestone in their collaboration is their analysis of Federal Reserve policymaking.[4] This study influenced Brunner's subsequent views about behavior of central banks, and revived impressions developed during his short stay at the Swiss National Bank.

He became Associate Professor in 1953 and Professor in 1961. He visited the University of Wisconsin, Michigan State and Northwestern University between 1965 and 1966. Brunner liked the department at UCLA, and had established good relations with Armen Alchian, Harold Demsetz[5] and Jack Hirshleifer.[6]

---

1. HANS REICHENBACH, *Experience and Prediction*, Chicago: The University of Chicago Press, 1938. In his preface the philosopher writes: "It is this combination of the results of my investigations on probability with the ideas of an empiricist and logistic conception of knowledge which I here present as my contribution to the discussion of Logistic empiricism".

2. '"Assumptions" and the Cognitive Quality of Theories', *Synthese*, 20, 4, December 1969, pp. 501-525.

3. 'My Quest', *op. cit.*, p. 9.

4. *An Analysis of Federal Reserve Monetary Policymaking* with ALLAN H. MELTZER, House Committee on Banking and Currency, Washington: Government Printing Office, 1964.

5. Harold Demsetz has been Associate Professor of Economics at UCLA from 1960 to 1963, Professor at the University of Chicago until 1970 and Professor of Economics at UCLA from 1971 on. He worked in the fields of industrial organization and public policy towards monopoly and competition. See MARK BLAUG, ed., 1986, *op. cit.*

6. Jack Hirshleifer's research centered on the economics of uncertainty and information. He has been part of the faculty at UCLA since 1960, after appointments at Rand Corporation and the School of Business at the University of Chicago. See MARK BLAUG, ed., 1986, *op. cit.*

However, he left the department in 1966 and joined the faculty at Ohio State University, where he was appointed Everett D. Reese Professor.

While at Ohio State University he initiated the *Journal of Money, Credit and Banking* in 1969, of which he was editor until 1974. For the next nine years he was the editor of the *Journal of Monetary Economics*, which he founded in 1975. The new journal was devoted to the publication of papers concerned with the role of institutional arrangements, the welfare aspects of structural policies, the consequences of changes in the banking structure and the operation of credit markets. The editor also promoted the developing and application of rational expectation to monetary economics. What prompted its founding was the awareness that his views were not promoted by well established institutions, such as the National Bureau of Economic Research and the Brookings Institution. He believed that "since good words do not talk for themselves somebody has to talk for them". He decided to encourage certain directions of research through conferences and publications, although he did not often publish in the journals he edited. He was also member of the editorial board of *Policy Review*, *Cato Journal* and *Strategic Review*.

Meanwhile he began his association with the Graduate School of Business Administration at the University of Rochester. He entered as Professor of Economics in 1971 and has been Fred H. Gowen Professor of Economics since 1979. He also directed the Center for Research in Government Policy and Business.

From 1968 on he developed relations with European universities and scholars. He was permanent guest professor at the University of Konstanz until 1973, where he directed since 1970 the annual international conferences on "Monetary Theory and Monetary Policy". He was professor at the University of Bern from 1974 till 1985. In the meantime he received two Honorary Doctor Degrees, from the Catholic University of Louvain in 1976 and from the University of St. Gallen – where he had begun amid obstacles his academic career – in 1982.

In 1974 he initiated the Annual Interlaken Seminar on Analysis and Ideology. Its purpose is best explained by Brunner's own words: "Purist advocates of a traditional view (of economic

331

analysis) . . . condemn any extension of economic analysis to social issues as an escape into 'ideology'. Others argue the need for an 'interdisciplinary approach' involving sociology, social psychology, or anthropology as necessary strands in a useful understanding of social, institutional, and human problems of contemporary societies . . . The successful development of a coherent analytic framework in the context of economic analysis – contrasting with shifting ad hoc constructions in social or behavioral psychology and empirical sociology, and contrasting also with the essentially programmatic and nonanalytic outlines and speculations in theoretical sociology and the pronounced analytic flaws or metaphysical intrusions in Marxian thought – suggests the . . . extension of economic analysis to the full sweep of social phenomena".[1]

Karl Brunner's conviction that intellectual life remains embedded in a social and political context and that intellectual pursuits are tied to institutional arrangements which condition its character, motivated the scholar to develop together with Allan Meltzer the Carnegie Rochester Conference on Public Policy. The volumes of the proceedings constitute a *summa* of scholarly debate on policy methodology and measures designed to cope with domestic and international economic problems. Another initiative of theirs, the Shadow Open Market Committee, was instead founded in order to articulate publicly their concerns about the drift in monetary, fiscal and international economic policy.

Karl Brunner's last major work was the preparation and presentation, together with Allan Meltzer, of the lectures published in this volume. He died in Rochester on May 9th, 1989.

Beside philosophy of science, two strands of ideas have attracted Karl Brunner's attention: monetary economics and the debate over the nature of political institutions.

He turned to the study of monetary theory after reconsidering his early Keynesian conviction and his consequent emphasis on real causes of the business cycle. He was convinced that the literature did not offer more than fragments of a theory explain-

1. KARL BRUNNER, ed., *Economics and Social Institutions: Insights from the Conferences on Analysis and Ideology*, Boston: Martinus Nijhoff Publishing, 1981, pp. vii-viii.

ing the behavior of the money stock. Hence he started his research on money supply[1] aiming at a theory which could be used to understand different institutional arrangements. This evolved into the construction of a model of the transmission mechanism. The theoretical framework was already outlined by 1963.[2] Its purpose was to explain the usually neglected role of credit and, more generally, of asset markets in the monetary process. Three conditions needed to be met in order to show that money matters for income determination. It was necessary[3] to show that (i) macrotheories formulated as demand and supply functions for assets provide relations that are more stable than theories based on flows; (ii) adequately specified demand and supply functions for money are more useful tools for predicting income than other relations; (iii) there exists an appropriate definition of money. This research agenda was respected. Subsequent work[4] formulates and estimates alternative specifications for money demand and supply.

Results constitute the empirical foundation of Brunner and Meltzer's well-known 1972 paper.[5] Their generalization of the "Keynesian cross" is based on substitutability among assets and on an explicit treatment of credit markets. It also includes the financial activities of a budget-constrained government. After imposing the assumption of a sluggish adjustment of prices and income, they are able to draw conclusions on the effects of monetary and fiscal policy and highlight the adjustment process.

Brunner and Meltzer later built on this framework to get the following monetarist propositions:[6] the private sector is stable;

1. 'A Schema for the Supply Theory of Money', *International Economic Review*, 2, 1, January 1961, pp. 79-109.

2. 'The Place of Financial Intermediaries in the Transmission of Monetary Policy', with ALLAN H. MELTZER, *Papers and Proceedings, American Economic Review*, 53, 2, May 1963, pp. 372-382.

3. 'Predicting Velocity: Implications for Theory and Policy', with ALLAN H. MELTZER, *Journal of Finance*, 18, 2, May 1963, pp. 319-354.

4. 'Some Further Investigations of Demand and Supply Functions for Money', with ALLAN H. MELTZER, *Journal of Finance*, 19, 2, May 1964, pp. 240-283.

5. 'Money, Debt and Economic Activity', with ALLAN H. MELTZER, *Journal of Political Economy*, 80, 5, September-October 1972, pp. 951-977.

6. 'An Aggregative Theory for a Closed Economy', with ALLAN H. MELTZER, in JEROME STEIN, ed., *Monetarism*, Amsterdam: North-Holland, 1976, pp. 69-103.

adjustment to monetary shocks involves substitution among all assets and production; the long-run position of the economy depends on stocks. Brunner and Meltzer's own monetarist *manifesto* is shaped over at least five years of meditation. The objects of their reflections are monetary theory in general,[1] Milton Friedman's monetary theory,[2] and the *IS-LM* framework in particular.[3] They share monetarists' views that monetary shocks are the dominant force shaping prices, that the private sector is stable and that there is no long-run inflation-unemployment tradeoff. Within the debate among monetarist economists, however, Brunner and Meltzer emphasize credit and securities markets, hence public debt and the money supply process, hence fiscal arrangements and asset prices.

Other studies concentrated instead on the structural aspects of central banks' operations. The debate concerned the identification of a reliable measure of monetary policy. The "indicator problem" addresses the relative merits of a number of variables often used to detect the current direction of monetary policy and its future effects. The choice of an indicator or a target cannot be bypassed, according to Brunner, by resorting to a multiplicity of indicators and targets. Both classificatory and comparative statements presuppose in fact a uni-dimensional scale. The ideal indicator[4] is a function of policy variables and of structural parameters. However, consideration of the imprecise knowledge of the latter leads to the money stock – defined as currency plus demand deposits – as the best approximation to the true indicator.

The issue of actual controllability is addressed later,[5] and two

1. 'A Survey of Selected Issues in Monetary Theory', *Schweizerische Zeitschrift für Volkswirtschaft und Statistik*, 107, 1, March 1971, pp. 1-146.

2. 'Friedman's Monetary Theory', with ALLAN H. MELTZER, *Journal of Political Economy*, 80, 5, September-October 1972, pp. 837-851.

3. 'Issues of Post-Keynesian Monetary Analysis', *Kredit und Kapital*, 1, 1976.

4. 'The Meaning of Monetary Indicators', with ALLAN H. MELTZER, in GEORGE HORWICH, ed., *Monetary Process and Policy: A Symposium*, Homewood: Richard D. Irwin, 1967.

5. 'The Control of Monetary Aggregates', *Controlling Monetary Aggregates*, III, Federal Reserve Bank of Boston, 1981.

procedures are outlined which should enable policymakers to tame monetary aggregates. The case against activist policy is also made: the latter appears to be optimal only if there exist full information and respect for public interest, but both are missing.

The scholar's interest in the nature and the role of monetary policymaking was ignited both by his work on the theoretical foundations of the money supply mechanism and by "casual empiricism". During the preparation of the above mentioned study for the Committee on Banking and Currency he discovered the Federal Reserve behavior contrasted with common propositions of economics. Brunner's inquiry in monetary policy has taken many directions. His evaluation of policies implemented by monetary authorities began in 1961 and has evolved lately in the frequent comment on policy actions by the Shadow Open Market Committee. Research has been extensively devoted to the interaction of monetary and fiscal arrangements and their role in perpetuating inflation during the 1970s. Financial inflation is caused by a monetary acceleration and affects nominal interest rates. Wicksellian inflation is instead ignited by a positive shock to the real return on investment, whereas a continuous increase in the government sector's real absorption leads to Keynesian inflation[1].

The contrast between the monetarist and Keynesian diagnoses of the causes of inflation can thus be resolved.[2] In the 1960s Keynesians had stressed that sustained fiscal policies could generate persistent inflation. Monetarism maintains that the dominant cause of inflation is monetary expansion. The analytic framework of the transmission mechanism shows that fiscal policies exert a long-run effect on the economy because fiscal arrangements are the long-run determinants of financial stock variables. Although the Keynesian conclusion is preserved, the mechanism is essentially monetarist.

1. Implications concerning inflationary processes of their 1972 model are studies in 'Credit Market, Interest Rate and Three Types of Inflation', *Kredit und Kapital*, 1973-74.
2. 'Inflation, Money and the Role of Fiscal Arrangements: An Analytic Framework for the Inflation Problem', in MARIO MONTI, ed., *The "New Inflation" and Monetary Policy*, London: Macmillan, 1976, pp. 25-61.

Policymaking bears major responsibility in the years of the Great Depression. The theory of the liquidity trap is in fact falsified both analytically and by empirical evidence.[1] The Federal Reserve, guided by that wrong theory, constantly misinterpreted events and took actions that worsened the situation.[2]

The scholar's interest in political institutions, sociology and history spans his whole life. History had been his first choice when he entered university. "Institutional arrangements which minimize the dependence of our fate on chance occurrence of superior wisdom, love, consideration, and rational intelligence among the operators of the administrative apparatus" are advocated in 1970.[3] According to Karl Brunner, the destruction of traditional orientations offered in philosophy and religion has created a search for new values and commitments. This concern has been misused to disregard the contribution of properly executed learning in the choice of intelligent actions. Values and valuations do not yield rational decision. Institutions emerge as a solution to irrational decision-making.

Two different policy conceptions can be juxtaposed:[4] the institutional policy, based on a set of general rules monitored and enforced by government; and an open-ended action oriented policy. After an examination of the tradeoffs characterizing social choices and information problems, the institutionalist solution is depicted as the rational cooperative solution to a prisoner's dilemma.

Lately, a theory connecting a conception of man and a related vision of justice to a typology of institutions has been shaped.[5] The conception of human beings as maximizing agents conditioned only by biological needs leads to a view of a government

1. 'Liquidity Traps for Money, Bank Credit and Interest Rates', with ALLAN H. MELTZER, *Journal of Political Economy*, 76, 1, January-February 1968, pp. 1-37.

2. KARL BRUNNER, 'Understanding the Great Depression', in KARL BRUNNER ed., *The Great Depression Revisited*, Boston: Martinus Nijhoff Publishing, 1981

3. 'Knowledge, Values and the Choice of Economic Organization', *Kyklos*, 23 3, 1970, pp. 558-580, p. 579

4. 'The Limits of Economic Policy', *Schweizerische Zeitschrift für Volkswirtschaft und Statistik*, 121, 3, September 1985, pp. 213-236.

5. 'The Perception of Man and the Conception of "Society". Two Approaches to Understanding Society', *Economic Inquiry*, 25, July 1987, pp. 367-388.

oriented to *laissez-faire*. On the contrary, the sociological model considers humans as passive agents of society; it hence encourages and justifies the shaping of society by the state and its agencies.

Keynes' early writings and The *General Theory* are investigated in order to understand his system of values.[1] After a taxonomy of the sociopolitical spectrum in the first part of the century, Keynes is depicted as close to the social democrats. Although he rejected state socialism, he shared some views with the socialists and the corporativists. Brunner criticizes Keynes, diagnosis of market flaws: "A religion addressed to the 'politics of society' yields a human catastrophe. Our century extended the historical record already available from the Inquisitors, the American Colonial experience (in moderate form), and other examples with a terrifying proportion. The irreligiousness of capitalism, deplored by Keynes, forms thus an important virtue of the system".

---

1. 'The Socio-Political Vision of Keynes', in DAVID REESE, ed., *The Legacy of Keynes*, San Francisco: Harper and Row, 1987.

2. Bibliography

Books and Monographies

Studies in the Theory of International Trade, Zürich: Verlag Schulters A.G., 1945.

An Analysis of Federal Reserve Monetary Policymaking with Allan H. MELTZER, House Committe on Banking and Currency, Washington: Government Printing Office, 1964. The sections of this report have been published separately as well as under the titles *Analysis of the Federal Reserve Approach to Policymaking*, February 1964; *The Federal Reserve's Attachment to Free Reserves*, May 1964; and *An Alternative Approach to the Monetary Mechanism*, August 1964.

Targets and Indicators of Monetary Policy, San Francisco: Chandler, 1969.

Proceedings of the First Konstanzer Seminar on Monetary Theory and Monetary Policy, Karl BRUNNER, ed., Berlin: Duncker & Humblot, 1972.

Problems and Issues in Current Econometric Practice, Karl BRUNNER, ed., Columbus, Ohio: The Ohio State University Press, 1973.

Geldtheorie, Karl BRUNNER, Hans G. MONISSEN, Manfred J. M. NEUMANN, eds., Köln: Kiepenheuer und Witsch, 1974.

Credit Allocation, Where Do We Go From Here?, Karl BRUNNER, ed., Institute for Contemporary Studies, 1975.

The Carnegie-Rochester Conference Series on Public Policy, Karl BRUNNER and Allan H. MELTZER, eds., Amsterdam: North-Holland, 1976.

The First World and the Third World, Karl BRUNNER, ed., Rochester, NY: University of Rochester Policy Center Publications, 1978.

Economics and Social Institutions: Insights from the Conferences on Analysis and Ideology, Karl BRUNNER, ed., Boston: Martinus Nijhoff, 1981.

The Great Depression Revisited, Karl BRUNNER, ed., Boston: Martinus Nijhoff, 1981.

Theory, Policy, Institutions: Papers from the Carnegie-Rochester Conferences on Public Policy, Karl BRUNNER and Allan H. MELZER, eds., Anniversary Volume, Amsterdam: North-Holland, 1983.

Monetary Economics, with Allan H. MELTZER, Oxford: Basil Blackwell, 1989.

Articles

'The Mechanism of International Equilibrium', *Swiss Journal of Economics and Statistics*, 1947.

338

'The Economic Effect of the Marshall Plan', in *The Annual Report of the Economic Commission for Europe*, 1948.

'Stock and Flow Analysis in Economics', *Econometrica*, vol. 18, n. 3, July 1950, pp. 247-251.

'Gravitationszentrum und dynamischer Ablauf', *Kyklos*, vol. 4, n. 1, 1950, pp. 24-59.

'A Generalization of the Multiplier Concept', *The German Econometric Journal*, 1951.

'Inconsistency and Indeterminacy in Classical Economics', *Econometrica*, vol. 19, n. 2, April 1951, pp. 152-173.

'A Survey of Econometric Research', *Swiss Journal of Economics and Statistics*, 1955.

'Ein Ausblick auf die Okonometrische Forschungsarbeit', *Schweizerische Zeitschrift für Volkwirtschaft und Statistik*, vol. 91, n. 2, June 1955.

'On the Construction of Theories in Economics', paper presented by invitation at the Annual Meeting of the Swiss Society of the Natural Sciences, and published in *Acte de la Société Helvétique des Sciences Naturelles*, 1958.

'A Case Study of U.S. Monetary Policy: Reserve Requirements and the Inflationary Gold Flows of the Middle 30s', *Schweizerische Zeitschrift für Volkswirtschaft und Statistik*, vol. 94, n. 2, June 1958, pp. 160-201.

'An Evaluation of Alternative Monetary Theories', Proceedings of the Thirty-Fifth Annual Conference of the Western Economic Association, 1959.

'Financial Intermediaries, Velocity and the Effectiveness of Monetary Policy', Proceedings of the Thirty-Sixth Annual Conference of the Western Economic Association, 1960, pp. 40-45.

'A Schema for the Supply Theory of Money', *International Economic Review*, vol. 2, n. 1, January 1961, pp. 79-109.

'Some Major Problems in Monetary Theory', *Papers and Proceedings, American Economic Review*, vol. 51, n. 2, May 1961, pp. 47-56.

'The Report of the Commission on Money and Credit', *Journal of Political Economy*, vol. 69, n. 6, December 1961, pp. 605-620.

'The Importance of Rules in the Competitive Market for Ideas', *Schweizerische Zeitschrift für Volkswirtschaft und Statistik*, 1962.

'The Place of Financial Intermediaries in the Transmission of Monetary Policy', with Allan H. MELTZER, *Papers and Proceedings, American Economic Review*, vol. 53, n. 2, May 1963, pp. 372-382.

'Predicting Velocity: Implications for Theory and Policy', with Allan H. MELTZER, *Journal of Finance*, vol. 18, n. 2, May 1963, pp. 319-354.

'The Discrepancy Between Fiscal Reserve Policy and Federal Reserve Statements', Opening Statement at Hearings of the Subcommittee on Domestic Finance of the Committee on Banking and Currency, 88th Congress, House of Representatives, vol. 2, February-March 1964.

'Comments on Federal Reserve Policy', with Allan H. MELTZER, *Banking Journal of the American Bankers' Association*, April 1964.

'Some Further Investigations of Demand and Supply Functions for Money', with Allan H. MELTZER, *Journal of Finance*, vol. 19, n. 2, May 1964, pp. 240-283.

'Institutions, Policy and Monetary Analysis', *Journal of Political Economy*, vol. 73, n. 2, April 1965, pp. 197-218.

'Reply', with Allan H. MELTZER, to 'Should Federal Reserve Float be Abolished and its Check Activities Curtailed?' by Irving Auerbach, *Journal of Finance*, vol. 22, n. 3, September 1965, pp. 496-498.

'The Triple Revolution: A New Metaphysics', *New Individualist Review*, vol. 4, n. 3, Spring 1966.

'A Credit Market Theory of the Money Supply and an Explanation of Two Puzzles in U.S. Monetary Policy', with Allan H. MELTZER, *Rivista Internazionale di Scienze Economiche e Commerciali*, vol. 13, n. 5, May 1966, reprinted in Tullio BAGIOTTI, ed., *Essays in Honor of Marco Fanno*, Padova: Cedam, vol. 2, pp. 151-176.

'The U.S. Economy in the Cross Currents Between Monetary and Fiscal Policy: A Reconsideration of the "New Economics"', *Bulletin of Business Research*, Columbus, Ohio: The Ohio State University, vol. 42, n. 2, February 1967.

'The Controversy Between "Quantity-Theory" and "Keynesian-Theory": A Case Study of the Importance of Appropriate Rules for the Market in Ideas and Beliefs', *Schweizerische Zeitschrift für Volkswirtschaft und Statistik*, vol. 103, n. 2, June 1967, pp. 173-190.

'The Meaning of Monetary Indicators', with Allan H. MELTZER, in George HORWICH, ed., *Monetary Process and Policy*: A Symposium, Homewood: Richard D. Irwin, 1967.

'Rejoinder to Chase and Hendershott', with Allan H. MELTZER, in George HORWICH, ed., *Monetary Process and Policy: A Symposium*, Homewood: Richard D. Irwin, 1967.

'Comment', with Allan H. MELTZER, on 'Interpretation of "Predicting Velocity"' by Daniel BRILL, in George HORWICH, ed., *Monetary Process and Policy: A Symposium*, Homewood: Richard D. Irwin, 1967.

'Economies of Scale in Cash Balances Reconsidered', with Allan H. MELTZER, *Quarterly Journal of Economics*, vol. 81, n. 3, August 1967, pp. 422-436.

'Money Supply Theory and British Monetary Experience', with Robert CROUCH, in Rudolf HENN, ed., *Essays in Honor of Wilhelm Kridle*, Verlag Anton Hain, 1967.

'Liquidity Traps for Money, Bank Credit and Interest Rates', with Allan H. MELTZER, *Journal of Political Economy*, vol. 76, n. 1, January-February 1968, pp. 1-37.

'What Did We Learn from the Monetary Experience of the United States in the Great Depression?', with Allan H. MELTZER, *Canadian Journal of Economics*, vol. 1, n. 2, May 1968, pp. 334-348.

'The Role of Money and Monetary Policy', *Federal Reserve Bank of St. Louis Review*, vol. 50, n. 7, July 1968, pp. 8-24.

'Comment: the Contribution of Macro and Micro Studies to Policy-Making', on 'Cross-Section Analysis and Bank Dynamics' by Donald HESTER and James PIERCE, *Journal of Political Economy*, vol. 76, n. 4, part. II, July-August 1968, pp. 777-785.

'Comment on the Long-Run and Short-Run Demand for Money', with Allan H. MELTZER, *Journal of Political Economy*, vol. 76, n. 6, November-December 1968, pp. 1234-1240.

'On Lauchlin Currie's Contribution to Monetary Theory', in Lauchlin CURRIE, *The Supply and Control of Money in the United States*, 2nd edition, New York: Russell & Russell, 1968.

'The Monetary Fiscal Dilemma', *Bulletin of Business Research*, Columbus, Ohio: The Ohio State University Press, vol. 46, n. 6, June 1969.

'The Policy Discussions by Stein and Worswick, A Comment', *Journal of Money, Credit, and Banking*, vol. 1, n. 3, August 1969, pp. 496-502.

'The Drift Into Permanent Inflation', *Wharton Quarterly*, Philadelphia: University of Pennsylvania, Fall 1969.

'"Assumptions" and the Cognitive Quality of Theories', *Synthese*, vol. 20, n. 4, December 1969, pp. 501-525.

'The Nature of the Policy Problem', with Allan H. MELTZER, in Karl BRUNNER, ed., *Targets and Indicators of Monetary Policy*, San Francisco: Chandler, 1969.

'Some Reflections on the State of Econometric Practice', in Edwin FREHNER, ed., *Vielfalt der Wirtschaftspolitik. Festgabe für Richard Büchner*, Zürich: Schulthess, 1969.

'Eine Neuformulierung der Quantitaetstheorie des Geldes. Die Theorie der relativen Preise, des Geldes, des Outputs und der Beschäftigung.', (The Relative Price Theory of Output and Employment), *Kredit und Kapital*, vol. 3, n. 1, 1970.

'The "Monetarist Revolution" in Monetary Theory', *Weltwirtschaftliches Archiv*, vol. 105, n. 1, 1970, pp. 1-30.

'Knowledge, Values and the Choice of Economic Organization', *Kyklos*, vol. 23, n. 3, 1970, pp. 558-580.

'A Survey of Selected Issues in Monetary Theory', *Schweizerische Zeitschrift für Volkswirtschaft und Statistik*, vol. 107, n. 1, March 1971, pp. 1-146.

'"Yale" and Money', *Journal of Finance*, vol. 26, n. 1, March 1971, pp. 165-174.

'The Monetarist View of Keynesian Ideas', *Lloyds Bank Review*, n. 102, October 1971, pp. 35-49.

'The Uses of Money: Money in the Theory of an Exchange Economy', with Allan H. MELTZER, *American Economic Review*, vol. 61, n. 5, December 1971, pp. 784-805.

'Ineffectual Policy of Misconceived Theory', in Herbert GIERSCH, ed., *Demand Management Globalsteuerung*, Kiel, 1972.

'The Ambiguous Rationality of Economic Policy', *Journal of Money, Credit and Banking*, vol. 4, n. 1, February 1972, pp. 3-12.

'A Monetarist Framework for Aggregative Analysis', with Allan H. MELTZER, Proceedings of the First Konstanzer Seminar on Monetary Theory and Monetary Policy, Supplement to *Kredit und Kapital*, Berlin, Spring 1972, pp. 31-88.

'The Case of Automobile Prices', Opening Statement at the Hearings of the Price Commission, September 1972.

'Money, Debt and Economic Activity', with Allan H. MELTZER, *Journal of Political Economy*, vol. 80, n. 5, September-October 1972, pp. 951-977.

'Relative Prices and Tax Policies: Some Preliminary Implications and Results', with Allan H. MELTZER, In Ernesto D'ALBERGO, ed., *Scritti in memoria di Antonio de Viti de Marco*, Bari: Cacucci, 1972.

'Friedman's Monetary Theory', with Allan H. MELTZER, *Journal of Political Economy*, vol. 80, n. 5, September-October 1972, pp. 837-851; also published in Robert J. GORDON, ed., *Milton Friedman's Monetary Framework: a Debate with his Critics*, Chicago & London: The University of Chicago Press, 1974, pp. 63-76.

'Mr. Hicks and the "Monetarists"', with Allan H. MELTZER, *Economica*, vol. 40, n. 157, February 1973, pp. 44-59.

'Fiscal and Monetary Policies in Moderate Inflation: Case Studies of Three Countries', with Michele FRATIANNI, Jerry JORDAN, Allan H. MELTZER and Manfred J. M. NEUMANN, *Journal of Money, Credit, and Banking*, vol. 5, n. 1, February 1973, pp. 313-353.

Review of *Econometric Models of Cyclical Behavior*, by Bert G. HICKMAN, *Journal of Economic Literature*, vol. 11, n. 3, September 1973, p. 96.

'Commentary' on 'The State of the Monetarist Debate' by Leonhall C. ANDERSEN, *Review*, Federal Reserve Bank of St. Louis, vol. 55, n. 9, September 1973, pp. 9-14.

'U.S. Monetary Stability and International Monetary Stability', *The Banker*, vol. 123, n. 574, December 1973, pp. 1445-1451.

'Money Supply Process and Monetary Policy in an Open Economy, in Alexander SWOBODA, ed., *International Trade and Money*, London, 1973, pp. 127-166.

'A Diagrammatic Exposition of the Money Supply Process' *Schweizerische Zeitschrift für Volkswirtschaft und Statistik*, vol. 109, n. 4, December 1973, pp. 481-533.

'Credit Market, Interest Rate and Three Types of Inflation', *Kredit und Kapital*, 1973-74.

'Position Papers', prepared for the Shadow Open Market Committee Meetings, 1974-1988.

'Two Alternative Theories of the Money Supply Process: Money Market Theory vs. The Credit Market Theory', in Karl BRUNNER, Manfred J. M. NEUMANN and Hans-Georg MONISSEN, eds., *op. cit.*

'Monetary Management, Domestic Inflation, and Imported Inflation', in Robert Z. ALIBER, ed., *National Monetary Policies and the International Financial System*, Chicago & London: University of Chicago Press, 1974, pp. 179-208.

'Friedman's Monetary Theory', in Robert J. GORDON, ed., *Milton Friedman's Monetary Framework*, University of Chicago Press, 1974.

'Monetary Growth and Monetary Policy', *Banca Nazionale del Lavoro Quarterly Review*, vol. 111, December 1974, pp. 271-293.

'Monetary Policy and Monetary Control in 1975', Statement Prepared for Senate Banking Comittee, April 1975.

'Comment' on 'The Demand for and Supply of Inflation' by Robert J. GORDON, *Journal of Law and Economics*, vol 18, n. 3, December 1975, pp. 837-857.

'The Phillips Curve and the Labor Markets', with Allan H. MELTZER, the Carnegie-Rochester Series, Supplement to *Journal of Monetary Economics*, vol. 2, January 1976.

'Monetary and Fiscal Policy in Open Interdependent Economies with Fixed Exchange Rates', with Allan H. MELTZER, in Emil-Maria CLAASSEN and Pascal SALIN, eds., *Recent Issues in International Monetary Economics*, Amsterdam: North-Holland, 1976.

'An Aggregative Theory for a Closed Economy', with Allan H. MELTZER, in Jerome STEIN, ed., *Monetarism*, Amsterdam: North-Holland, 1976, pp. 69-103.

'Monetarism: The Principal Issues, Areas of Agreement and the Work Remaining', with Allan H. MELTZER, in Jerome STEIN, ed., *Monetarism*, Amsterdam: North-Holland, 1976, pp. 150-182.

'The Money Supply Process in Open Economies with Interdependent Security Markets: The Case of Imperfect Substitutability', in Michele FRATIANNI and Karl TAVERNIER, eds., *Bank Credit, Money and Inflation in Open Economies*, Supplement to *Kredit und Kapital*, Berlin: Dunker & Humblot, 1976, pp. 19-75.

'Monetary and Fiscal Policy in Open Interdependent Economies with Fixed Exchange Rates', Emil-Maria CLAASSEN and Pascal SALIN, eds., *Recent Issues in International Monetary Economics*, Amsterdam: North-Holland, 1976.

'A Fisherian Framework for the Analysis of International Monetary Problems', in Michael PARKIN and George ZIS, eds., *Inflation in the World Economy*, Manchester: University of Manchester Press, Toronto and Buffalo: University of Toronto Press, 1976, pp. 1-38.

'Inflation, Money and the Role of Fiscal Arrangements: An Analytic Framework for the Inflation Problem', in Mario MONTI, ed., *The "New Inflation" and Monetary Policy*, London: Macmillan, 1976, pp. 25-61.

'Government, the Private Sector and "Crowding Out"', *The Banker*, vol. 126, n. 605, July 1976, pp. 765-769.

'Issues of Post-Keynesian Monetary Analysis', *Kredit und Kapital*, vol. 1, 1976.

'The 1976 Nobel Prize in Economics', *Science*, vol. 194, n. 4265, 5 November 1976, pp. 594-596.

'The New International Order: A Chapter in a Protracted Economic Conflict', *Orbis*, vol. 20, n. 1, 1976, pp. 103-121.

'Statement on Monetary Policy', testimony prepared for the House Committee on Banking and Currency, 4 February 1977.

'The Perception of Man and the Conception of Government', with William H. MECKLING, *Journal of Money, Credit, and Banking*, vol. 9, n. 1, part 1, February 1977, pp. 70-85.

'The Explanation of Inflation: Some International Evidence', with Allan H. MELTZER, *Papers and Proceedings, American Economic Review*, vol. 67, n. 1, February 1977, pp. 148-154. Simultaneously published in *Transaction Society*, vol. 14, March-April 1977, pp. 35-40.

'Politica monetaria, sviluppo economico e costo sociale', *Rivista di Politica Economica*, vol. 67, n. 11, November 1977, pp. 1115-1133.

'Milton Friedman in Our Time', Statement prepared for the Luncheon honoring the Nobel Laureate for 1976, Annual Meeting of the American Economic Association, December 29, 1977.

'Probleme der Post-Keynesianischen Geldtheorie', *Die Monetarismus-Kontroverse*, Supplement to *Kredit und Kapital*, Heft 4, 1978. Also published in Thomas MAGER *et al.*, eds., *The Structure of Monetarism*, New York & London: Norton, 1978.

'The First World, the Third World, and the Survival of Free Societies', in Karl BRUNNER, ed., *The First World and the Third World*, Rochester, NY: University of Rochester Policy Center Publications, 1978.

'Reflections on the Political Economy of Government: The Persistent Growth of Government', *Schweizerische Zeitschrift für Volkswirtschaft und Statistik*, vol. 114, n. 3, 1978, pp. 649-680.

345

'The Commitment to Permanent Inflation', *Alternative Policies to Combat Inflation*, Center for the Study of American Business, Washington University, Working Paper, n. 40, St. Louis, January 1979. Also published in *Society*, vol. 16, n. 5, 1979, p. 4.

'Statement on Monetary Policy', prepared for the Committee on Housing, Banking and Urban Affairs, February 22, 1979.

'A Monetarist Assessment of Recent Policy and the Outlook', *Data Resources U.S. Review*, March 1979.

'Reflections on the State of International Monetary Policy', *Banca Nazionale del Lavoro Quarterly Review*, vol. 32, n. 131, December 1979 pp. 361-375.

'Theories of Inflation and the Explanation of Intractable Inflation', in Arthur WOLL, ed., *Inflation*, London: John Martin Publishing Ltd., 1980. Originally published by Verlag Franz Vahlen, Munich, 1979.

'Geldpolitik', in W. ALBERS *et al.*, eds., *Handwörterbuch der Wirtschaftswissenschaft*, Tübingen: J. C. B. Mohr, 1979.

'The Choice and Implementation of Monetary Policy', Statement prepared for a Session of the House Subcommittee on Domestic Monetary Policy and the House Subcommittee on International Trade, Investment and Monetary Policy, December 4, 1979.

'The Four Disciplines and the Two Encouragements: President Carter's Economic Recovery Plan', *Challenge*, vol. 23, n. 2, May-June 1980, pp. 49-51.

'Stagflation, Persistent Unemployment and the Permanence of Economic Shocks', with Alex CUKIERMAN and Allan H. MELTZER, *Journal of Monetary Economics*, vol. 6, n. 4, October 1980, pp. 467-492.

'A Fascination with Economics', *Banca Nazionale del Lavoro Quarterly Review*, vol. 33, n. 135, December 1980, pp. 403-426.

'Time Deposits in the Brunner-Meltzer Model of Asset Markets', with Allan H. MELTZER, *Journal of Monetary Economics*, vol. 7, n. 1, January 1981, pp. 129-139.

'The Control of Monetary Aggregates', in *Controlling Monetary Aggregates, III*, Boston: Federal Reserve Bank of Boston, 1981, pp. 1-65.

'The Case Against Monetary Activism', *Lloyds Bank Review*, n. 139, January 1981, pp. 20-39.

Statement Prepared for the Joint Economic Committee, U.S. Congress, Washington D.C., February 25, 1981.

'Understanding the Great Depression', in Karl Brunner, ed., *The Great Depression Revisited*, Boston: Martinus Nijhoff, 1981.

'The Problem with What They Do and Why They Do it: A Comment on the Paper prepared by Lawrence R. Klein, E. Philip Howrey, Michael D. McCarthy and George R. Schink', in Jan Kmenta and James Ramsey, eds., *Large-Scale Macro-Econometric Models: Theory and Practice*, Amsterdam: North-Holland 1981, pp. 129-138.

'The Art of Central Banking', *Geld, Banken und Versicherungen*, Band 1, University of Karlsruhe, 1981.

'Economic Development, Cancun and the Western Democracies', *The World Economy*, vol. 5, n. 1, March 1982, pp. 61-84.

'Will the Fed Ever See Its "Shadow"?', *Altair Away*, Fall 1982.

'Is "Supply-Side Economics" Enough?', *The Cato Journal*, vol. 2, n. 3, Winter 1982, pp. 843-849.

'The Perception of Man and Justice and the Conception of Political Institutions, in Fritz Machlup, Gerhard Fels and Hubertus Mueller-Groeling, eds., *Reflections on a Troubled World Economy: Essays in Honor of Herbert Giersch*, London: Macmillan for the Trade Policy Research Center, New York: St. Martin's, 1983.

'International Debt, Insolvency and Illiquidity', *The Journal of Economic Affairs*, vol. 3, n. 3, April 1983, pp. 160-166.

'Money and Economic Activity, Inventories and Business Cycles', with Alex Cukierman and Allan H. Meltzer, *Journal of Monetary Economics*, vol. 11, n. 3, May 1983, pp. 281-329.

'Strategies and Tactics for Monetary Control', with Allan H. Meltzer, *Carnegie-Rochester Conference Series on Public Policy*, vol. 18, Spring 1983, pp. 59-103.

'The Pragmatic and Intellectual Tradition of Monetary Policy-Making and the International Monetary Order', *Schriften des Vereins für Sozialpolitik*, vol. 138, 1983.

'Mr. Magoo and the State of Economic Policy', *Cross Currents*, n. 12, 1983.

'Resolving the Debt Problem: Some Policy Considerations', *The Cato Journal*, vol. 4, n. 1, Spring-Summer 1984, pp. 97-103.

'Conversation with a Monetarist', in Arjo Klamer, ed., *Conversations with Economists*, Totowa, NJ; Rowman & Allanheld, 1984.

'Monetary Policy and Monetary Order', *Aussenwirtschaft* (The Swiss Review of International Economic Relations), vol. 39, n. 3, September 1984, pp. 187-206. Reprinted in Karl BRUNNER *et al.*, eds., *Monetary Policy and Monetary Regimes*: *A Symposium Dedicated to Robert E. Weintraub*, Rochester, NY: University of Rochester, Center for Research in Governmental Policy and Business, 1985, pp. 4-21.

'The Poverty of Nations', *Business Economics*, vol. 20, n. 1, January 1985, pp. 5-11. Aso published in the *Cato Journal*, vol. 5, n. 1, 1985, pp. 37-49.

'Ideology and Analysis in Macroeconomics: Some Comments', in Peter KOSLOWSKI, ed., *Economics and Philosophy*, Tübingen: J. C. B. Mohr, 1985.

'The Limits of Economic Policy', *Schweizerische Zeitschrift für Volkswirtschaft und Statistik*, vol. 121, n. 3, September 1985, pp. 213-236.

'Fiscal Policy in Macro Theory: A Survey and Evaluation', in R. W. HAFER, ed., *The Monetary Versus Fiscal-Policy Debate: Lessons from Two Decades*, Totowa, NJ: Rowman & Allanheld, January 1986, pp. 33-116.

'Monetarism Isn't Dead', *Fortune*, vol. 113, n. 12, June 9, 1986.

'Deficits, Interest Rates and Monetary Policy', *The Cato Journal*, vol. 5, n. 3, Winter 1986, 709-726.

'High Powered Money and the Monetary Base', in John EATWELL, Murray MILGATE and Peter NEWMAN, eds., *The New Palgrave: A Dictionary of Economic Theory and Doctrine*, London: Macmillan, vol. 2, 1987, pp. 654-655.

'Has Monetarism Failed?', *The Cato Journal*, vol. 3, n. 1, Spring 1983, pp. 23-62. Also published in James DORN and Anna J. SCHWARTZ, eds., *The Search for a Stable Money: Essays on Monetary Reform*, Chicago: University of Chicago Press, 1987, pp. 163-199.

'Money Supply', in John EATWELL, Murray MILGATE and Peter NEWMAN, eds., *The New Palgrave: A Dictionary of Economic Theory and Doctrine*, London: Macmillan, vol. 3, 1987, pp. 827-829.

'The Socio-Political Vision of Keynes', in David REESE, ed., *The Legacy of Keynes*, San Francisco: Harper and Row, 1987, pp. 23-56.

'Armen A. Alchian', *Journal of Institutional and Theoretical Economics, Zeitschrift für die gesamte Staatswissenschaft*, vol. 143, n. 1, March 1987, pp. 229-231.

'The Perception of Man and the Conception of "Society". Two Approaches to Understanding Society', *Economic Inquiry*, vol. 25, July 1987, pp. 367-388.

'Economic Inequality and the Quest for Social Justice', *The Cato Journal*, vol. 7, n. 1, Spring-Summer 1987, pp. 153-158.

'Money and Credit in the Monetary Transmission Process', with Allan H. MELTZER, *Papers and Proceedings, American Economic Review*, vol. 78, n. 2, May 1988, pp. 446-451.

'The Disarray in Macroeconomics', in Forrest CAPIE and Geoffrey WOOD, eds., *Monetary Economics in the 1980s*, London: Macmillan Press in Association with Centre for Banking and International Finance, The City University, 1989, pp. 197-233.

'Socio-Economic and Constitutional Implications of Alternative Perceptions of Man', *The Cato Journal*, 1989.

'The Role of Money and Monetary Policy', *Review*, Federal Reserve Bank of St. Louis, vol. 71, n. 5, 1989, pp. 4-22.

'Money Supply', with Allan H. MELTZER, in Benjamin FRIEDMAN and Frank HAHN, eds., *Handbook of Monetary Economics*, Amsterdam: North-Holland, 1990, pp. 357-398.

'My Quest for Economic Knowledge', in Michael SZENBERG, ed., *Eminent Economists. Their Life Philosophies*, Cambridge: Cambridge University Press, 1992, pp. 84-97.

ALLAN H. MELTZER

I. *A Professional Biography**

Allan Meltzer was born in Boston on February 6th, 1928. At the age of 16 he left Boston for Duke University, where he received his Bachelor of Arts in Economics in 1948. He chose to study economics as a discipline that could be used to improve welfare. In 1953 he went to graduate school, after having worked in a number of businesses for five years. At the time, the Ph.D. program in Economics at the University of California in Los Angeles (UCLA) was small and relatively new. Nevertheless he chose it because he had lived in Los Angeles since 1950. At UCLA he met Karl Brunner. In his own words: "Brunner has been my teacher, collaborator and lifelong friend. We have worked together and talked about so many things that it is not so surprising that we often think alike. What is surprising is that we often think differently. The benefits of collaboration come in no small measure from ability to use what we agree upon to resolve many of our disagreements. We have also learned to use, and rely on, each other's comparative advantages to gain from the exchange."[1]

In Allan Meltzer's account of those years, Brunner – then in his second year as an assistant professor – was a dedicated teacher. Allan learnt through conversations with him over coffee how to analyze issues first and apply value judgements later. He attended his night seminars, which Brunner had organized in order to help students work through Samuelson's *Foundations of Economics Analysis*.[2] It was Brunner who both urged him to begin systematic study of mathematics and advised him on his dissertation.

His thesis, written on the determinants of the stock of money

---

* Written by Giovanna Nicodano, Associate Professor, Università degli Studi di Torino. The author acknowledges special reference to ALLAN MELTZER, 'My Life Philosophy', *The American Economist*, 34, 1, 1990, pp. 22-32, and to an interview recorded in September 1988.

1. ALLAN H. MELTZER, 'My Life Philosophy', *op. cit.*
2. PAUL SAMUELSON, *op. cit.*

351

during wartime and postwar inflation in France,[1] was his first research experience. He enjoyed both the analysis and the empirical investigation. The field of research – money and inflation – has ever since remained in the foreground. He began to write it in France: after receiving his Master of Arts Degree from UCLA in 1955, he had applied for and received a Fulbright scholarship and a grant from the Social Science Research Council.

Upon returning home he accepted an offer as lecturer at the Wharton School. However, he did not find the environment stimulating. Working at night he rushed to finish the empirical part of his dissertation.

He then became assistant professor at the Carnegie Institute of Technology, and later University Professor and John M. Olin Professor of Political Economy and Public Policy. In 1961 he became associate professor, then professor in 1964 and University Professor and Maurice Falk Professor six years later. In 1980, he became University Professor and John M. Olin Professor of Political Economy. Over the years he also accepted various administrative responsibilities. At Carnegie he appreciated the small and enthusiastic research environment.

He was also visiting professor at the University of Chicago (1964-1965) and at Harvard (1967-1968). He visited the Hoover Institution during 1977. Since 1968 he has established relationships with scholars outside the United States. He spent the spring semester at the Yugoslav Institute for Economic Research in 1968. Eight years later he visited the Fundaçao Getulio Vargas in Rio de Janeiro. He moreover enjoys visiting and honorary positions at the City University in London and at the Bank of Japan. Since 1989 he has been a (part-time) Visiting Scholar at the American Enterprise Institute for Public Policy Research.

Allan Meltzer never changed his original belief that economics is a policy science, not a branch of applied mathematics, and that research does influence practice. Therefore, together with Karl Brunner, he has organized groups such as the Shadow Open Market Committee since 1974 and the Shadow European

---

1. It was later published as 'The Behavior of the French Money Supply, 1938-54', *Journal of Political Economy*, 68, 3, June 1959, pp. 275-296.

Economic Policy Committee. Their members are economists from banks, business and academic institutions who gather in order to issue policy statements about current events. The Carnegie-Rochester Conference on Public Policy, initiated in 1976, was instead designed to draw academic attention to policy issues.

In 1988 he was a member of President Reagan's Economic Policy Advisory Board.

Four interrelated areas emerge most clearly in Allan Meltzer's research. The first concerns the effect of regulation on welfare, and the behavior of regulatory authorities. His interest in this issue developed through various experiences. While writing his doctoral dissertation he found out that in early postwar France prices were controlled and wages were indexed to prices. Yet the government would remove items from the price index or make large imports of items that rose in price in order to contain the increase in the price index and hence in nominal wages. To him this was another piece of evidence – to be added to his own experience during the Wallace campaign[1] – against a goodwill theory of government.

In 1960 Senator Paul Douglas, then Chairman of the Joint Economic Committee, invited the young economist to lead a study of the dealer market for government securities.[2] The interest awakened by this study brought Meltzer his first assignment in government. First as Treasury assistant, then as Treasury consultant, he wrote a research study on the taxation of interest on municipal bonds.[3] By confronting the environment at the Treasury and at the Congressional Joint Economic Committee, he realized that the former was much more restricted. Political constraints influenced the choice not only of policies, but of topics for discussion as well.

1. Henry Agard Wallace ran for presidency of the U.S.A. in 1948. He had been Secretary of Agriculture in President Franklin Roosevelt's Cabinet (1933-1940), Vice President of The U.S. (1941-1945) and Secretary of Commerce (1945-1946). See *Who Was Who in America*, vol. IV, 1961-1968, Chicago: Marquis, 1968.

2. *A Study of the Dealer Market for U.S. Government Securities*, with G. VON DER LINDE, Joint Economic Committee, U.S. Congress, 1960.

3. *Federal Tax Treatment of State and Local Securities*, with DAVID OTT, Washington: The Brookings Institution, 1963.

The study on the dealer market showed signs that the Federal Reserve methods of conducting policy caused some problems. Congressman Wright Patman invited Allan Meltzer, who was joined by Karl Brunner, to study Federal Reserve policymaking.[1] The result of their analysis was that the Federal Reserve relied on improper control procedures. And no effort was made, moreover, to improve on them. The economist's skepticism about performance of government agencies and discretionary policies increased. Reading Hayek's *Constitution of Liberty*[2] and Popper's *The Open Society and Its Enemies*[3] confirmed his appreciation of institutions and rules that restrict arbitrary actions of government.

He argues[4] that costs of regulation may outweigh benefits. This occurs when the overlapping of new controls with old ones renders a market even less competitive than before antimonopoly rules were imposed.

This same outlook motivates his proposal[5] for replacing the then existing controls on the banking industry with a set of new rules. As far as banking is concerned, the case against controls over private enterprises is reinforced by the natural monopoly of the input "monetary base" enjoyed by the policy-makers.

In a comment to an essay by Musgrave, Allan Meltzer warns against stop-and-go policies implemented in the United States during the sixties. His disagreement with advocates of discretionary policy concerns theories which are used to causally order events rather than goals. His interpretation of historical evidence reveals that inflation always results from sustained

1. *An Analysis of Federal Reserve Monetary Policymaking*, with KARL BRUNNER, House Committee on Banking and Currency, Washington: Government Printing Office, 1964.

2. FRIEDRICH A. VON HAYEK, *The Constitution of Liberty*, Chicago: The University of Chicago Press, 1960.

3. KARL R. POPPER, *The Open Society and Its Enemies*, Princeton: Princeton University Press, 1965.

4. 'On Efficiency and Regulation of the Securities Industry', in HENRY MANNE, ed., *Economic Policy and Regulation of Corporate Security*, Washington, D.C.: American Enterprise Institute, 1969, pp. 217-238.

5. 'Major Issues in the Regulation of Financial Institutions', *Journal of Political Economy*, 75, 4. Part II, Supplement, August 1967, pp. 482-500.

6. 'Comment' on 'Blend of Fiscal and Monetary Policies' by RICHARD MUSGRAVE, in *Fiscal Policy and Business Capital Formation*, Washington: American Enterprise Institute, 1967, pp. 187-193.

monetary expansion despite governments' attempts to shift responsibility for inflation to the private sector. The optimality – from a welfare point of view – of institutional arrangements is advocated in subsequent work.[1] It is argued that, if government has an informational advantage and there are periodic elections, the cost of a discretionary policy is positive. It is however also pointed out that an optimal state contingent policy rule would not be immune from implementability problems. The latter can partially be solved in practice by keeping the contingent rule as simple as possible, and by basing it on past outcomes alone. Thus rules cannot insure against mistakes because new future events are not accounted for. Rules do insure, however, against repetition of mistaken procedures and against misuse of available information. More research in economics ought to be devoted, according to the economist, to the study of how rules and institutions emerge, of the outcome of alternative arrangements and of the information set they are conditioned upon.

Adaptive policy rules which do not depend on forecasts are advocated in his Presidential Address to the Western Economic Association.[2] Forecasting inaccuracy across different methods and models is such that a boom cannot be distinguished from a recession a quarter ahead. In such conditions, discretionary policy is likely to increase uncertainty, thereby reducing output and living standards. A specific policy rule is also proposed, namely setting the annual growth of the monetary base equal to a moving average of past output growth minus a moving average of base velocity growth. Countries adopting this rule would form a "cartel of financial stability". More stable domestic prices would lead to increased stability of nominal and real exchange rates. Central banks should also precommit to act as lenders of last resort in order to prevent banking and debt crises.[3]

---

1. 'A Positive Theory of Discretionary Policy, the Cost of Democratic Government and the Benefits of a Constitution', with ALEX CUKIERMAN, *Economic Inquiry*, 24, 3, July 1986, pp. 367-388.

2. 'Limits of Short-Run Stabilization Policy: Presidential Address to the Western Economic Association', *Economic Inquiry*, 25, 1, January 1987, pp. 1-14.

3. 'Money and Credit in the Monetary Transmission Process', with KARL BRUNNER, *Papers and Proceedings, American Economic Review*, 78, 2, May 1988, pp. 446-451.

Monetary arrangements do not render policy measures ineffective – as maintained by new classical economists – as long as central banks enjoy monopoly of some private information. Monetary authorities do protect their monopoly – and thereby policy effectiveness – through inaccurate policy-making.[1] Inaccuracy allows the central bank to confuse the public's inferences about which policy is being enacted. Common knowledge of rules notwithstanding, effective policy surprises are possible.

A question concerning the consideration of public preferences by government had already attracted the economist's attention.[2] It was then maintained that changes in relative prices express the public's preferences and, if economic freedom matters, those preferences ought not be overriden by controls. The choice appeared to be one between society's objectives as expressed by the market place rather than by government agencies.

His definition of market responses has enlarged with the progress of economic research. It now encompasses "allocational mechanisms other than explicit prices" whenever "uncertainty about major aspects of the relevant product or service has a large role".[3] The underlying idea is that a market will always implement the best feasible outcome. Organizations characterized by standardized operating procedures will always outperform discretionary intervention.

This issue has evolved into Meltzer's second main field of research, which concerns how agents' preferences interact with voting mechanisms in the determination of government policies. Most of his essays concern fiscal redistribution of income. According to the scholar, economics is about the level of income and its functional distribution following Marshallian principles. Politics – a voting rule – determines the amount of redistribution. Once redistribution begins to affect incentives to work and invest, the level of aggregate income is modified. Policies which do not

1. 'A Theory of Ambiguity, Credibility, and Inflation Under Discretion and Asymmetric Information', with ALEX CUKIERMAN, *Econometrica*, 54, 5, September 1986, pp. 1099-1128.
2. 'Comment' on 'Blend of Fiscal and Monetary Policies' by RICHARD MUSGRAVE, in *Fiscal Policy and Business Capital Formation*, Washington: American Enterprise Institute, 1967, pp. 187-193.
3. 'Money and Credit in the Monetary Transmission Process', *op. cit.*, p. 450.

damage the saving rate through redistributions allow society to achieve a higher level of income. Allan Meltzer interprets the history of the last 200 years, and that of the last 50 years in particular, as showing that incentives and growth increase living standards for many people more effectively than temporary gains induced by redistribution.

Redistribution explains the size of the institution "government", defined as the share of government spending in total output. It is obtained as the equilibrium outcome of choices by rational voters.[1] The public's choices include the amount of desired income redistribution. The growth of the size of government in recent years is explained by the decision of voters to redistribute income by means of health care, security benefits and other transfers.

Redistribution is the central issue in a later essay, too.[2] The authors try to explain why some welfare policy proposals such as the negative income tax which are favored by many economists and some policy advisers are not enacted. The answer is found in every voter's desire to preserve other voters' incentives to work, which is not taken into account in specialists' evaluation. A proposal which does not ensure preservation of these incentives will not be implemented.

The economist's best known area of interest is monetary economics. It is also the area where his interest in economics as a policy science merges with extensive use of econometric techniques. After writing his dissertation and an empirical paper on trade credit,[3] Meltzer began to study the demand for money. Three issues were first scrutinized through econometric analysis.[4] First, the arguments of the demand for money. Second, the sta-

---

1. 'A Rational Theory of the Size of Government', with SCOTT RICHARD, *Journal of Political Economy*, 89, 5, October 1981, pp. 914-927.

2. 'A Positive Theory of In-Kind Transfers and the Negative Income Tax', with SCOTT RICHARD, Carnegie Papers on Political Economy, *Public Choice* 47, 1, 1985, pp. 231-265.

3. 'Mercantile Credit, Monetary Policy and Size of Firm', *Review of Economics and Statistics*, 42, 4, November 1960, pp. 429-437.

4. 'The Demand for Money: the Evidence from the Time Series', *Journal of Political Economy*, 71, 3, June 1963, pp. 219-246.

bility of that function. Third, the definition of money which ought to be used in monetary analyses. The answers to these questions were to become a building block in the construction of the model of the transmission mechanism, which was developed jointly with Karl Brunner: non-human wealth and interest rates were found to be the key explanatory variables, where the latter exert a marked impact on monetary velocity; in the first six decades of the twentieth century parameters of the money demand function had not changed significantly; finally, the sum of currency and demand deposits appeared as the most useful definition of money.

His inquiry into money demand continued with a paper aimed at reconciling the implications of the quantity and wealth-based theories with the Baumol-Tobin choice theoretic approach.[1] In particular, the authors showed that a unit elasticity of money demand with respect to transactions could be the approximate outcome of a modified Baumol-Tobin model.

Later,[2] they argue that asynchronization of receipts and payments cannot offer alone a good reason for holding money. What is needed in order to explain the private and social productivity of money, and hence the search for and the acceptance of an asset to be used as money, is the uneven distribution of information. It follows that the theory of exchange must be extended to include the cost of acquiring information.

Various researches proceeded in parallel. The study of the transmission mechanism, outlined in part in Karl Brunner's biography, first concentrated on asset markets, then gradually evolved in a closer scrutiny of the real sector. Allan Meltzer's survey of theories relating intermediation and growth,[3] and a study of the correlation between mortgages and investment in housing, which was aimed at questioning the relevance of credit availability,[4]

1. 'Economies of Scale in Cash Balances Reconsidered', with KARL BRUNNER, *Quarterly Journal of Economics*, 81, 3, August 1967, pp. 422-436.

2. 'The Uses of Money: Money in the Theory of an Exchange Economy', with KARL BRUNNER, *American Economic Review*, 61, 5, December 1971, pp. 784-805.

3. 'Money, Intermediation, and Growth', *Journal of Economic Literature*, 7, 1, March 1969, pp. 27-56.

4. 'Credit Availability and Economic Decisions: Some Evidence from the Mort-

witness his interest in "the other side" of the transmission mechanism.

It is however in the eighties that the formalization of a phenomenon conjectured in an earlier paper is offered.[1] The phenomenon in question is the sluggish adjustment of prices, and hence of employment and output, due to information costs. Sequences of persistent equilibrium unemployment are consistent with market rationality. They are generated by agents' uncertainty about the persistence of shocks.

In a subsequent essay[2] the authors show how incomplete information leads to a short-run output-inflation tradeoff. The realization of monetary shocks cannot be exactly anticipated by the public even if all agents know and optimally use their knowledge about the structure generating them. Their misperception causes short-run disequilibrium absorbed by inventory adjustment. And this adjustment translates perceived monetary shocks into serially correlated output movements.

Three empirical papers follow. The first[3] presents evidence relative to the late seventies showing that increased variability of interest rates raises the demand for money and lowers that for real capital. The second[4] analyzes the persistence, comparative size and interaction of real and monetary impulses in four countries during the Bretton Woods and post Bretton Woods monetary regimes. The same technique had been used before[5] to

gage and Housing Markets', *Journal of Finance*, 29, 3, June 1974, pp. 763-778.

1. 'Stagflation, Persistent Unemployment and Permanence of Economic Shocks', with KARL BRUNNER and ALEX CUKIERMAN, *Journal of Monetary Economics*, 6, 4, October 1980, pp. 467-492.

2. 'Money and Economic Activity, Inventories and Business Cycles', with KARL BRUNNER and ALEX CUKIERMAN, *Journal of Monetary Economics*, 11, 3, May 1983, pp. 281-329.

3. 'Long-and-Short-Term Interest Rates in a Risky World', with A. MASCARO, *Journal of Monetary Economics*, 12, 4, November 1983, pp. 485-518.

4. 'Size, Persistence and Interrelation of Nominal and Real Shocks: Some Evidence from Four Countries', *Journal of Monetary Economics*, 17, 1, January-February 1986, pp. 161-194.

5. 'Variability of Prices, Output and Money Under Fixed and Fluctuating Exchange Rates: An Empirical Study of Monetary Regimes in Japan and the United States', *Bank of Japan Monetary and Economic Studies*, 3, 3, December 1985, pp. 1-46.

examine the interrelation between shocks to the U.S. and to Japan under fixed and fluctuating exchange rates.

A scholar's identity emerges most clearly by juxtaposing his own views with opinions of different scholars. The importance of Allan Meltzer's measurement of the distance between himself, new classical economists and real business cycle theorists – presented in this volume in the first lecture – is overwhelmed by his recurring studies of Keynesians' views. Contrary to Keynesian interpretations, Allan Meltzer believes average equilibrium unemployment and excess supply rather than sticky nominal wages to be central in Keynes's work. And he reminds us that the former phenomena are consistent with real wage rigidity as well. As far as monetary theory is concerned, he rules out Keynes's emphasis on the liquidity trap. According to his reading of the *General Theory*,[1] monetary policy can always reduce interest rates temporarily. However, it is only through a reduction of the volatility of investment, and hence through a fall in the required risk premium, that a permanent fall in the interest rate can be achieved.[2] Allan Meltzer's study on Keynes extends to the *Treatise on Money*,[3] and to all major works, articles, comments and letters between 1920 and 1946. Consistent both with his own conception of economics and with Keynes's active participation in policy debates, Meltzer accompanies his appraisal of the Cambridge economist's monetary theory with a discussion of Keynes's approach to society, thoughts on monetary reform and the international monetary system. Keynes did trust policymakers' intentions and effectiveness. At the same time, though, he implicitly stressed the relevance of contingent rules such as the Bretton Woods system to reduce uncertainty. Stop and go policies, i.e. discretion, would not achieve this goal.[4]

1. JOHN MAYNARD KEYNES, *The General Theory of Employment, Interest, and Money*, 1936, reprinted in *Collected Writings*, London: Macmillan for the Royal Economic Society, 1973.
2. 'Keynes's General Theory: A Different Perspective', *Journal of Economic Literature*, 19, 1, March 1981, pp. 34-64.
3. JOHN MAYNARD KEYNES, *A Treatise on Money*, 1930, reprinted in *Collected Writings*, London: Macmillan for the Royal Economic Society, 1971-1973.
4. *Keynes's Monetary Theory: A Different Interpretation*, Cambridge: Cambridge University Press, 1988.

A Monetarist's reading of Keynes thus leads to questioning the legitimacy of the label "Keynesian" to policy measures such as consumption stimulus and fiscal redistribution. This is one part of Meltzer's challenge to James Tobin[1] – a Keynesian who also considers economics as a policy science.[2]

1. James Tobin is Sterling Professor of Economics at Yale University since 1957. His contributions deal with monetary, financial and growth theory, besides econometric applications. He received the Nobel Prize in 1981. See MARK BLAUG, ed., *Who's Who in Economics*, Cambridge, Mass.: The M.I.T. Press, 1983.

2. 'Tobin on Macroeconomic Policy: A Review Essay', *Journal of Monetary Economics*, 23, 1, January 1989, pp. 159-173.

2. Bibliography

Books and Monographies

A Study of the Dealer Market for U.S. Government Securities, with G. Von Der Linde, Joint Economic Committee, U.S. Congress, 1960.

Federal Tax Treatment of State and Local Securities, with David Ott, Washington: The Brookings Institution, 1963.

An Analysis of Federal Reserve Monetary Policymaking, with Karl Brunner, Hause Committee on Banking and Currency Committee, Washington: Government Printing Office, 1964. The sections of this report have been published separately as well as under the titles *Analysis of the Federal Reserve Approach to Policymaking*, February 1964; *The Federal Reserve's Attachment to Free Reserves*, May 1964; and *An Alternative Approach to the Monetary Mechanism*, August 1964.

The Wadsworth Series in Finance, with John Frederick Weston, Belmont, California: Wadsworth, 1966-68 (various dates).

The Carnegie-Rochester Conference Series on Public Policy, Karl Brunner and Allan H. Meltzer, eds., Amsterdam: North-Holland, 1976-.

The Carnegie Papers on Political Economy, Allan H. Meltzer, Peter Ordershook and Thomas Romer, eds., The Hague: Martinus Nijhoff, 1981-1986.

Ensaios Em Economia Politica (Essays in Political Economy), 'Controlling Money', 'The Decline of the Liberal Economy' and 'Keynes's General Theory: A Different Perspective', A. M. Silveira, ed., Rio de Janeiro; Edicoes Multiplic, February 1982, published in Portuguese.

International Lending and the IMF - A Conference in Memory of Wilson Schmidt, Allan H. Meltzer, ed., Washington D.C.: The Heritage Lectures 21, Heritage Foundation, 1983.

Theory, Policy, Institutions: Papers from the Carnegie-Rochester Conferences on Public Policy, Karl Brunner and Allan H. Meltzer, eds., Anniversary Volume, Amsterdam: North-Holland, 1983.

Onzekere Wereldeconomie, Rotterdamse Monetaire Studies, 14, 1984.

Monetarism and Contemporary Monetary Policy in the U.S., Committee of International Programs, Meiji University, Tokyo, 1985, published in Japanese.

Keynes's Monetary Theory: A Different Interpretation, Cambridge: Cambridge University Press, 1988.

362

Economic Report of the President 1989, with Beryl W. SPRINKEL and Thomas G. MOORE, Washington: Government Printing Office, 1989.

Monetary Economics, with Karl BRUNNER, Oxford: Basil Blackwell, 1989.

Political Economy, with Alex CUKIERMAN and Scott RICHARD, Oxford: Oxford University Press, 1991.

Articles

'A Comment on Market Structure and Stabilization Policy', *Review of Economics and Statistics*, November, 1958.

'The Behavior of the French Money Supply, 1938-54', *Journal of Political Economy*, vol. 68, n. 3, June 1959, pp. 275-296.

'Mercantile Credit, Monetary Policy and Size of Firm', *Review of Economics and Statistics*, vol. 42, n. 4, November 1960, pp. 429-437.

'Portfolio Selection: A Heuristic Approach', with Geoffrey P. CLARKSON, *Journal of Finance*, vol. 15, n. 4, December 1960, pp. 465-480.

'The Place of Financial Intermediaries in the Transmission of Monetary Policy', with Karl BRUNNER, in *Papers and Proceedings, American Economic Review*, vol. 53, n. 2, May 1963, pp. 372-382.

'Predicting Velocity: Implications for Theory and Policy', with Karl BRUNNER, *Journal of Finance*, vol. 18, n. 2, May 1963, 319-354.

'The Demand for Money: the Evidence from the Time Series', *Journal of Political Economy*, vol. 71, n. 3, June 1963, pp. 219-246.

'Yet Another Look at the Low Level Liquidity Trap', *Econometrica*, vol. 31, n. 3, July 1963, pp. 545-549.

'The Demand for Money: A Cross-Section Study of Business Firms', *Quarterly Journal of Economics*, vol. 77, n. 3, August 1963, pp. 405-422.

'Monetary Policy and the Trade Credit Practices of Business Firms', *Commission on Money and Credit*, vol. x, Prentice-Hall, 1963.

'A Weekly New Issue Yield Curve for Municipal Bonds', *National Banking Review*, December 1963.

'Monetary Policy for 1963', Hearings before the Joint Economic Committee on the President's Economic Report, Washington: Joint Economic Committee, 1963.

'Comments on Federal Reserve Policy', with Karl BRUNNER, *Banking Journal of the American Bankers' Association*, April 1964.

'Some Further Investigations of Demand and Supply Functions for Money', with Karl BRUNNER, *Journal of Finance*, vol. 19, n. 2, May 1964, pp. 240-283.

'Comment' on 'Financial Markets in Business Cycles: a Simulation Study' by Frank DE LEEUW and on 'Longer Waves in Financial Relations: Financial Factors in the More Severe Depressions' by Hyman MINSKY, *Papers and Proceedings, American Economic Review*, vol. 54, n. 3, May 1964, pp. 340-343.

'Public and Private Financial Intermediaries', *Review of Economics and Statistics*, vol. 46, n. 3, August 1964, pp. 269-278.

'A Little More Evidence from the Time Series', *Journal of Political Economy*, vol. 72, n. 5, October 1964, pp. 504-508.

'Some Suggested Changes in Monetary Arrangements', Hearings before the Banking and Currency Committee, U.S. Congress, Washington, D.C., 1964.

'Rejoinder to Professor West', *National Banking Review*, vol. 4, December 1964, Government Printing Office, pp. 261-262.

'Reply' to G. S. MADDALA, Robert C. VOGEL and Eduard WHALEN's Comments on 'The Demand for Money: a Cross-Section Study of Business Firms' by Allan H. MELTZER, *Quarterly Journal of Economics*, vol. 79, n. 1, February 1965, pp. 162-165.

'What Should We Teach in a Money and Banking Course: Discussion', *Journal of Finance*, May 1965.

'Improvements in the Balance of Payments. A Response to Monetary Policy or to *Ad Hoc* Fiscal Policies', *Journal of Business*, vol. 38, n. 3, July 1965, pp. 267-276.

'Reply', with Karl BRUNNER, to 'Should Federal Reserve Float be Abolished and its Check Activities Curtailed?' by Irving AUERBACH, *Journal of Finance*, vol. 22, n. 3, September 1965, pp. 496-498.

'Monetary Theory and Monetary History', *Schweizerische Zeitschrift für Volkswirtschaft und Statistik*, vol. 404, December 1965, pp. 404-422.

'The Money Managers and the Boom', *Challenge*, March-April 1966.

'A Credit Market Theory of the Money Supply and an Explanation of Two Puzzles in U.S. Monetary Policy', with Karl BRUNNER, *Rivista Internazionale di Scienze Economiche e Commerciali*, vol. 13, n. 5, May 1966, pp. 405-432; reprinted in Tullio BAGIOTTI, ed., *Essays in Honor of Marco Fanno*, Padova: Cedam, vol. 2, 1966, pp. 151-176.

'The Regulation of Bank Credits Abroad: Another Failure for the Balance of Payments Program', in George SCHULTZ, ed., *Guidelines, Informal Controls and the Market Place*, Chicago: University of Chicago Press, 1966.

'On Human Wealth and the Demand for Money', *Journal of Political Economy*, vol. 75, n. 1, February 1967, pp. 96-97.

'Irving Fisher and the Quantity Theory of Money', *Orbis Economicus*, in Honor of Patinkin's *Money, Interest and Prices*, vol. 10, n. 9, March 1967.

'Money Supply Revisited: A Review Article', *Journal of Political Economy*, vol. 75, n. 2, April 1967, pp. 169-182.

'The Meaning of Monetary Indicators', with Karl BRUNNER, in George HORWICH, ed., *Monetary Process and Policy: A Symposium*, Homewood: Richard D. Irwin, 1967.

'Rejoinder to Chase and Hendershott', with Karl BRUNNER, in George HORWICH, ed., *Monetary Process and Policy: A Symposium*. Homewood: Richard D. Irwin, 1967.

'Comment', with Karl BRUNNER, on 'Interpretation of "Predicting Velocity"' by Daniel BRILL, in George HORWICH, ed., *Monetary Process and Policy: A Symposium*, Homewood: Richard D. Irwin, 1967.

'Comment' on 'Some Implications of Money Supply Analysis' by David I. FAND, and on 'Keynes and the Keynesians: A Suggested Interpretation' by Axel LEIJONHUFVUD, *Papers and Proceedings, American Economic Review*, vol. 57, n. 2, May 1967, pp. 426-427.

'Is Secular Inflation Likely in the U.S.?', in *Monetary Problems of the Early 1960s: Review and Appraisal*, Proceedings of the Third Annual Conference on Economic Affairs, Atlanta: Georgia State College, May 1967, pp. 29-42.

'Major Issues in the Regulation of Financial Institutions', *Journal of Political Economy*, vol. 75, n. 4, Part. II, Supplement, August 1967, pp. 482-500.

'Economies of Scale in Cash Balances Reconsidered', with Karl BRUNNER, *Quarterly Journal of Economics*, vol. 81, n. 3, August 1967, pp. 422-436.

'Comment' on 'Blend of Fiscal and Monetary Policies' by Richard MUSGRAVE, in *Fiscal Policy and Business Capital Formation*, Washington: American Enterprise Institute, 1967, pp. 187-193.

365

'Liquidity Traps for Money, Bank Credit and Interest Rates', with Karl BRUNNER, *Journal of Political Economy*, vol. 76, n. 1, January-February 1968, pp. 1-37.

'What Did We Learn from the Monetary Experience of the United States in the Great Depression?', with Karl BRUNNER, *Canadian Journal of Economics*, vol. 1, n. 2, May 1968, pp. 334-348.

'Predicting the Effects of Monetary Policy', *Business Economics*, Spring 1968, pp. 7-13.

'Comment on the Long-Run and Short-Run Demand for Money', with Karl BRUNNER, *Journal of Political Economy*, vol. 76, n. 6, November-December 1968, pp. 1234-1240.

'On Efficiency and Regulation of the Securities Industry', in Henry MANNE, ed., *Economic Policy and the Regulation of Corporate Security*, Washington, D.C.: American Enterprise Institute, 1969, pp. 217-238.

'Money, Intermediation, and Growth', *Journal of Economic Literature*, vol. 7, n. 1, March 1969, pp. 27-56.

'Controlling Money', *Review*, Federal Reserve Bank of St. Louis, May 1969, pp. 16-24.

'The Nature of the Policy Problem', with Karl BRUNNER, in Karl BRUNNER, ed., *Targets and Indicators of Monetary Policy*, San Francisco: Chandler, 1969.

'The Appropriate Indicators of Monetary Policy', in *Savings and Residential Financing*, Conference Proceedings, U.S. Savings and Loan League, 1969.

'The Role of Money in National Economic Policy', in *Controlling Monetary Aggregates*, Federal Reserve Bank of Boston, June 1969, pp. 25-30.

'Tactics and Targets: Discussion', in *Controlling Monetary Aggregates*, Federal Reserve Bank of Boston, June 1969, pp. 96-103.

'A Comment on Hester's Paper', *Journal of Money, Credit and Banking*, vol. 1, n. 3, August 1969, pp. 618-624.

'Public Policies as Causes of Fluctuations', *Journal of Money, Credit and Banking*, vol. 2, n. 1, February 1970, pp. 45-55.

'Selecting Creative Ph.D. Candidates for Admission', with Judith GERTLER, *Journal of Experimental Education*, vol. 38, n. 3, Spring 1970, pp. 15-18.

'Is There An Optimal Money Supply? A Discussion', *Journal of Finance*, vol. 25, n. 2, May 1970, pp. 450-453.

'Restoring A Healthy Economic Environment', *Proceedings of the American Insurance Association*, May 1970; reprinted in *Kredit und Kapital*, n. 2, 1971.

'Regulation Q – The Money Markets and Housing', in *Housing and Monetary Policy*, Federal Reserve Bank of Boston, Conference Series n. 4, 1971.

'The Uses of Money: Money in the Theory of an Exchange Economy', with Karl BRUNNER, *American Economic Review*, vol. 61, n. 5, December, 1971, pp. 784-805.

'A Monetarist Framework for Aggregative Analysis', with Karl BRUNNER, Proceedings of the First Konstanzer Conference on Monetary Theory and Policy, Supplement to *Kredit und Kapital*, Spring 1972, pp. 31-88.

'Aggregative Consequences of Removing Restrictions', *Journal of Bank Research*, vol. 3, n. 2, Summer 1972, pp. 72-83.

'Automobile Pricing', Hearing before the Price Commission, Washington, D.C., 13 September 1972.

'Friedman's Monetary Theory', with Karl BRUNNER, *Journal of Political Economy*, vol. 80, n. 5, September-October 1972, pp. 837-851; also published in Robert J. GORDON, ed., 'Milton Friedman's Monetary Framework: a Debate with his Critics', Chicago & London: The University of Chicago Press, 1974, pp. 63-76.

'Money, Debt and Economic Activity', with Karl BRUNNER, *Journal of Political Economy*, vol. 80, n. 5, September-October 1972, pp. 951-977.

'What the Commission Didn't Recommend', *Journal of Money, Credit and Banking*, vol. 4, November 1972, pp. 1005-1009.

'Relative Prices and Tax Policies: Some Preliminary Implications and Results', with Karl BRUNNER, in Ernesto D'ALBERGO, ed., *Scritti in memoria di Antonio de Viti de Marco*, Bari: Cacucci, 1972.

'Price and Wage Controls', Proceedings of Subcommittee on Antitrust and Monopoly of the Committee on the Judiciary, United States Senate 92nd Congress, January 1973, pp. 88-90.

'Fiscal and Monetary Policies in Moderate Inflation: Case Studies of Three Countries', with Karl BRUNNER, Michele FRATIANNI, Jerry JORDAN and Manfred J. M. NEUMANN, *Journal of Money, Credit and Banking*, February 1973.

'The Markets for Housing and Housing Services', with Francisco ARCELUS, *Journal of Money, Credit and Banking*, vol. 5, n. 1, part 1, February 1973, pp. 78-89.

'Mr. Hicks and the "Monetarists"', with Karl BRUNNER, *Economica*, vol. 40, n. 157, February 1973, pp. 44-59.

'The Dollar as an International Money', *Banca Nazionale del Lavoro Quarterly Review*, Rome, vol. 26, n. 104, March 1973, pp. 21-28.

'A Reply to Craig Swan', with Francisco ARCELUS, *Journal of Money, Credit and Banking*, vol. 5, n. 4, November 1973, pp. 973-978.

'Discussion' on 'Policy Implications of a Flow-of-Funds Model' by James S. DUESENBERRY and Barry BOSWORTH, and on 'Short Term Financial Models at the Federal Reserve Board' by James L. PIERCE and Thomas T. THOMSON, *Journal of Finance*, vol. 29, n. 2, May 1974, pp. 360-364.

'Credit Availability and Economic Decisions: Some Evidence from the Mortgage and Housing Markets', *Journal of Finance*, vol. 29, n. 3, June 1974, pp. 763-778.

'A Plan for Subduing Inflation', *Fortune*, vol. 90, n. 3, September 1974, pp. 112-115.

'The Conduct of Monetary Policy', *Monetary Policy Oversight*, Hearings before the Senate Committee on Banking, Housing and Urban Affairs, Washington, D.C.: Government Printing Office, February 1975.

'Ending Inflation' in David MEISELMAN and Arthur LAFFER, eds., *The Phenomenon of World Wide Inflation*, Proceedings of Conference on War, Revolution and Peace, Washington and Palo Alto: American Enterprise Institute and Hoover Institution, May 1975.

'Inflation, Energy and the World Economy, Prospects for International Cooperation', in Penelope HARTLAND-THUNBERG, ed., *Selected Papers on Inflation, Recession, Energy and the International Financial Structure*, Washington, D.C.: Center for Strategic and International Studies, Georgetown University, May 1975, pp. 53-66.

'Current Policy and the Future Capital Stock', Senate Budget Committee, Subcommittee Seminar, Washington, D.C.: Government Printing Office, September 10, 1975.

'Housing and Financial Policy', *Challenge*, vol. 18, n. 5, November-December 1975, pp. 61-64.

368

'Financial Institutions and the Nation's Economy, Discussion Principles', House of Representatives, Hearings before the Subcommittee on Financial Institutions Supervision, Regulation, and Insurance, of the Committee on Banking, Currency and Housing, Washington, D.C.: Government Printing Office, December 2, 1975.

'The Effect of Aggregate Economic Variables on Congressional Elections', with Francisco ARCELUS, *American Political Science Review*, vol. 69, n. 4, December 1975, pp. 1232-1239.

'Aggregate Economic Variables and Votes for Congress: A Rejoinder', with Francisco ARCELUS, *American Political Science Review*, vol. 69, n. 4, December 1975, pp. 1266-1269.

'The Effects of Economic Policies on Votes for the Presidency: Some Evidence from Recent Elections', with Marc VELLRATH, *Journal of Law and Economics*, vol. 18, n. 3, December 1975, pp. 781-798.

'The Phillips Curve and the Labor Markets', with Karl BRUNNER, The Carnegie-Rochester Series, Supplement to *Journal of Monetary Economics*, vol. 2, January 1976, pp. 118.

'The Monetary Approach to Inflation and the Balance of Payments: Theoretical and Empirical Contributions at the Leuven Conference', *Kredit und Kapital*, May 1976, pp. 579-617.

'Monetary and Fiscal Policy in Open, Interdependent Economies with Fixed Exchange Rates', with Karl BRUNNER, in Emil-Maria CLAASSEN and Pascal SALIN, eds., *Recent Issues in International Monetary Economics*, Amsterdam: North-Holland, 1976, pp. 328-359.

'An Aggregative Theory for a Closed Economy', with Karl BRUNNER, in Jerome STEIN, ed., *Monetarism*, Amsterdam: North-Holland, 1976, pp. 69-103.

'Monetarism: The Principal Issues, Areas of Agreement and the Work Remaining', with Karl BRUNNER, in Jerome STEIN, ed., *Monetarism*, Amsterdam: North-Holland, 1976, pp. 150-182.

'Ending Inflation: The Next Steps', Statement on Monetary Policy, Committee on Banking, Currency and Housing, U.S. House of Representatives, Washington, D.C.: Government Printing Office, June 24, 1976.

'Why Government Grows', International Institute for Economic Research (UCLA) Original Paper, n. 4, August 1976.

'Monetary and Other Explanations of the Start of the Great Depression', *Journal of Monetary Economics*, vol. 2, n. 4, November 1976, pp. 455-471.

'Statement on Monetary Policy', Fourth Meeting on the Conduct of Monetary Policy, Hearings before the Committee on Banking, Housing and Urban Affairs, U.S. Senate, Washington, D.C.: Government Printing Office, November 15, 1976, pp. 69-75 and 102-120.

'The Decline of the Liberal Economy', *Vie et Sciences Economiques*, vol. 72, January 1977, pp, 1-77.

'Anticipated Inflation and Unanticipated Price Change: A Test of the Price-Specie Flow Theory and the Phillips Curve', *Journal of Money, Credit and Banking*, vol. 9, n. 1, part II, February 1977, pp. 182-205.

'A decadencia da economia liberal', (The Decline of the Liberal Economy), *Revista Brasileira de Economia*, Rio de Janeiro, Fundacão Getulio Vargas, vol. 31, n. 1, January-March 1977, pp. 205-220.

'The Explanation of Inflation: Some International Evidence', with Karl BRUNNER, *Papers and Proceedings, American Economic Review*, vol. 67, n. 1, February 1977, pp. 148-154. Simultaneously published in *Transaction-Society*, vol. 14, March-April 1977, pp. 35-40.

'Too Much Government?', in R. BLATTBERG, ed., *The Economy in Transition*, New York: New York University Press, 1977.

'It Takes Long-Range Planning to Lick Inflation', *Fortune*, vol. 96, n. 6, December 1977, pp. 96-106.

'Monetarist, Keynesian and Quantity Theories', *Kredit und Kapital*, vol. 10, n. 2, 1977, pp. 149-182. Reprinted in Thomas MAYER, ed., *The Structure of Monetarism*, New York: W. W. Norton, 1978, pp. 145-175.

'Inflation and Price Changes: Some Preliminary Estimates and Tests of Alternative Theories', with Pieter KORTEWEG, Carnegie-Rochester Conference Series on Public Policy, Supplement to *Journal of Monetary Economics*, vol. 8, January 1978, pp. 325-353.

'The Effects of EFT on the Instruments of Monetary Policy', *Journal of Contemporary Business*, vol. 7, n. 2, Spring 1978, pp. 101-125.

'The Conduct of Monetary Policy Under Current Monetary Arrangements, *Journal of Monetary Economics*, vol. 4, n. 2, April 1978, pp. 371-388.

'Why Government Grows (and Grows) in a Democracy', with Scott RICHARD, *The Public Interest*, n. 52, Summer 1978, pp. 111-118.

'Principios que Orientam a Políticá Monetària Brasileira', (Principles Guiding Brazilian Monetary Policy), *Debate Economico*, vol. 1, n. 3, September 1978.

'The Effects of Financial Innovation on the Instruments of Monetary Policy', *Economies et Societies*, Cahiers de L'Ismea, vol. 12, n. 10-11-12, October 1978, pp. 1889-1916.

'The Spending Limitation Approach', in P. TRULOCK, ed., *Balancing the Budget*, Washington: Heritage Foundation, 1979, pp. 7-13.

'The Problem of Stagflation', in *Stagflation Hearings Before the Special Study on Economic Change of the Joint Economic Committee*, Congress of the United States, Washington, D.C.: Government Printing Office, 1979, pp. 136-142.

'Europe Enters the Eighties', with Shadow European Economic Policy Committee, *Banca Nazionale del Lavoro Quarterly Review*, vol. 32, n. 129, June 1979, pp. 117-132.

'Economic Policy after the 1979 Oil Shock', Hearings before the Committee on Banking, Housing and Urban Affairs, United States Senate, Washington, D.C.: Government Printing Office, 1979.

'Perspekteren in Sicherung der Unternehmungsautonomie', Proceedings of the International Management Symposium, Bern: Verlag Paul Haupt, 1979, pp. 115-122.

'Federal Reserve Policy and Federal Reserve Policy Actions', Hearings before the Committee on Banking, Housing and Urban Affairs, United States Senate, Washington, D.C.: Government Printing Office, 1979.

'The Case for Gradualism in Policies to Reduce Inflation', *Stabilization Policies: Lessons from the '70s and Implications for the '80s*, Conference Proceedings, Center for the Study of American Business, Working Paper n. 53, April 1980.

'Discussion' on 'A Consistent Characterization of a Near-Century of Price Behavior' by Robert J. GORDON, *Papers and Proceedings, American Economic Review*, vol. 70, n. 2, May 1980, pp. 258-259.

'Stagflation, Persistent Unemployment and Permanence of Economic Shocks', with Karl BRUNNER and Alex CUKIERMAN, *Journal of Monetary Economics*, vol. 6, n. 4, October 1980, pp. 467-492.

'Central Bank Policy: Some First Principles', in Centre for Banking and International Finance, *Annual Monetary Review*, n. 2, December 1980, pp. 27-33.

'Appropriate Monetary Policy Guidelines for 1980 and Beyond', in Michael J. HAMBURGER, ed., *Issues in Financial and Monetary Policy*, New York: New York University, 1980, pp. 13-14.

'Monetarism and the Crises in Economics', *The Public Interest*, Special Issue, 1980, pp. 35-45; also published in Daniel BELL and Irving KRISTOL, eds., *The Crises in Economic Theory*, New York: Basic Books, 1981, pp. 35-45.

'Time Deposits in the Brunner-Meltzer Model of Asset Markets', with Karl BRUNNER, *Journal of Monetary Economics*, vol. 7, n. 1, January 1981, pp. 129-140.

'Comment on "Monetarist Interpretation of the Great Depression"', in Karl BRUNNER, ed., *The Great Depression Revisited*, Boston: Martinus Nijhoff, 1981, Chapter 6.

'Keynes's General Theory: A Different Perspective', *Journal of Economic Literature*, vol. 19, n. 1, March 1981, pp. 34-64.

'Principios que Orientam a Política Monetària Brasileira', *Edicoes Multiplic*, April 1981, pp. 73-82.

'A Rational Theory of the Size of Government', with Scott RICHARD, *Journal of Political Economy*, vol. 89, n. 5, October 1981, pp. 914-927.

'Epistle to the Gold Commission', Report to the Congress of the Commission on the Role of Gold in the Domestic and International Monetary Systems, vol. 2, March 1982, pp. 459-460.

'The Thrift Industry in the Reagan Era', in *Managing Interest Rate Risk in the Thrift Industry*, Proceedings of the Seventh Annual Conference, San Francisco: Federal Home Loan Bank of San Francisco, 1982, pp. 5-14.

'Comment on Papers by Henderson and Waldo and by McKinnon' in Jacob S. DREYER, Gottfried HABELER and T. WILLET, eds., *The International Monetary Systems*, Washington, D.C.: American Enterprise Institute, 1982, pp. 364-371.

'Comment on National Financial Policies in the Interdependent World', in Jacob S. DREYER, Gottfried HABELER and T. WILLETT, eds., *The International Monetary Systems*, American Enterprise Institute, Washington, 1982, pp. 513-519.

'Discussion' of E. Kane 'External Pressures and Operations of the Federal Reserve', in Raymond LOMBRA and Willard E. WITTE, eds., *Political Economy and International Domestic Monetary Relations*, Iowa City, University of Iowa Press, 1982.

'Comment' on 'Federal Reserve Control of the Money Stock', by Ralph C. Bryant, *Journal of Money, Credit and Banking*, vol. 14, n. 4, part II, November 1982, pp. 632-640.

'Comment on 'Flexible Exchange Rates, Prices and the Role of News: Lessons from the 1970s', by Jacob A. Frenkel, in Roy A. Batchelor and Geoffrey E. Wood, eds., *Exchange Rate Policy*, London: Macmillan, 1982, pp. 94-98.

'Comment' on 'Exchange Rates, Interest Rates and the Mobility of Capital', by Andrew Britton and Peter Spencer, in Roy A. Batchelor and Geoffrey E. Wood, eds., *Exchange Rates Policy*, London: Macmillan, 1982, pp. 226-231.

'Rational Expectations, Risk, Uncertainty and Market Responses', in Paul A. Wachtel, ed., *Crises in the Economic and Financial Structure*, Lexington, Mass.: Lexington Books, Heath and Co, 1982, pp. 3-22.

'Towards a Stable Monetary Policy', Debate between Allan Meltzer and Alan Reynolds, Heritage Foundation, Monograph, 1982.

'Interpreting Keynes', *Journal of Economic Literature*, vol. 21, n. 1, March 1983, pp. 66-78.

'Money and Economic Activity, Inventories and Business Cycles', with Karl Brunner and Alex Cukierman, *Journal of Monetary Economics*, vol. 11, n. 3, May 1983, pp. 281-329.

'Monetary Reform in an Uncertain Environment', *Cato Journal*, vol. 3, n. 1, Spring 1983, pp. 93-112.

'Strategies and Tactics for Monetary Control', with Karl Brunner, *Carnegie-Rochester Conference Series on Public Policy*, vol. 18, Spring 1983, pp. 59-103.

'Deficits and Inflation', *Toward a Reconstruction of Federal Budgeting*, The Conference Board, 1983, pp. 46-51.

'Five Reasons for Opposing the IMF Quota Increase', in M. Holbert and Allan H. Meltzer, eds., *Constructive Approaches to the Foreign Debt Dilemma*, Washington D.C.: Taxpayers' Foundation, 1983.

'Industrial Policy', in *Industrial Policy, Economic Growth and the Competitiveness of U.S. Industry*, Hearings before the Joint Economic Committee, 98th Congress, Washington, D.C.: Government Printing Office, October 1983, pp. 83-92.

'Long-and-Short-Term Interest Rates in a Risky World', with A. Mascaro, *Journal of Monetary Economics*, vol. 12, n. 4, November 1983, pp. 485-518.

373

'A Way to Defuse the World Debt Bomb', *Fortune*, vol. 108, n. 11, November 1983, pp. 137-141.

'Present and Future in an Uncertain World', in *Legislation for Alternative Targets for Monetary Policy*, Hearings before Subcommittee on Domestic Monetary Policy Committee on Banking, Finance and Urban Affairs, 98th Congress, Washington, D.C.: Government Printing Office, 1983, pp. 347-369.

'On Keynes and Monetarism', in David WORSWICK and James TREVITHICK, eds., *Keynes in the Modern World: Proceedings of the Keynes Centenary Conference*, Cambridge: Cambridge University Press, 1983, pp. 49-77.

'Present and Future in an Uncertain World', *The Interest Rate Dilemma*, ITT Key Issues Lecture Series, NY KCG Productions, 1983.

'Tests of a Rational Theory of the Size of Government', with Scott F. RICHARD, *Public Choice*, vol. 41, n. 3, 1983, pp. 403-418.

'Discussion of Financial Innovation and Financial Instability, by Hyman Minsky', in *Financial Innovations*, Federal Reserve Bank of St. Louis, Boston; Lancaster: Kluwer Nijhoff, 1984.

'Keynes's Labour Market: A Reply', *Journal of Post Keynesian Economics*, vol. 6, n. 4, Summer 1984, pp. 532-539.

'The International Debt Problem', *Cato Journal*, vol. 4, n. 1, Spring-Summer 1984, pp. 63-69.

'The Cure for Monetary Madness', *Policy Review*, vol. 27, Winter 1984, pp. 72-74.

'Deficits and Inflation', in Albert SOMMERS, ed., *Reconstructing the Federal Budget: A Trillion Dollar Quandry*, New York: Praeger, 1984, pp. 117-129.

'The Fight Against Inflation: A Comment', in Brian GRIFFITHS and Geoffrey E. WOOD, eds., *Monetarism in the United Kingdom*, London: Macmillan, 1984, pp. 61-66.

'The Case for a Monetary Rule', in Thomas M. HAVRILESKY, ed., *Modern Concepts in Macroeconomics*, Harlan Davidson Inc. 1985.

'Overview', in *Price Stability and Public Policy*, Federal Reserve Bank of Kansas City, 1985, pp. 209-222.

'Policies for Growth with Low Inflation and Increased Efficiency', in *Monetary Policy and the Changing Financial Environment*. Proceedings of Seminar Commemorating the 35th Anniversary of the Bank of Korea, June 1985, pp. 1-22.

374

'Comment' on 'Economic Stabilization and Liberalization in Korea 1980-84', by Yung Chul PARK, *Monetary Policy and the Changing Financial Environment*. Proceedings of Seminar Commemorating the 35th Anniversary of the Bank of Korea, June 1985, pp. 141-147.

'Financial Failures and Financial Policies', Report of the Technical Committee, New York: Global Action Institute, September 1985, pp. 57-71.

'A Positive Theory of In-Kind Transfers and the Negative Income Tax', with Scott RICHARD, Carnegie Papers on Political Economy, *Public Choice* vol. 47, n. 1, 1985, pp. 231-265.

'How to Cut the Trade Deficit', *Fortune*, November 25, 1985, pp. 111-112.

'Variability of Prices, Output and Money Under Fixed and Fluctuating Exchange Rates: An Empirical Study of Monetary Regimes in Japan and the United States', *Bank of Japan Monetary and Economic Studies*, vol. 3, n. 3, December 1985, pp. 1-46.

'Size, Persistence and Interrelation of Nominal and Real Shocks: Some Evidence from Four Countries', *Journal of Monetary Economics*, vol. 17, n. 1, January-February 1986, pp. 161-194.

'Comment on Real and Pseudo-Financial Crises', in Forrest CAPIE and Geoffrey WOOD, eds., *Financial Crises and the World Banking System*, London: Macmillan, 1986, pp. 32-37.

'Financial Failures and Financial Policies', in George KAUFMAN and Roger KORMENDI, eds., *Deregulating Financial Services – Public Policy in Flux*, Cambridge, Mass: Ballinger, 1986, pp. 79-96.

'The Credibility of Monetary Announcements', with Alex CUKIERMAN, in Manfred J. M. NEUMANN, ed., *Monetary Policy and Uncertainty*, Baden-Baden: Nomos Verlagsgesellschaft, 1986, pp. 39-67.

'Kotei-Hendo Kawase Sobaseika ni okeru Bukka, Sanshitsuryo oyobi Tsukaryo no Hendo: Nichibei no Tsukaseido ni Kansuru Jissho Kenkyu', *Bank of Japan Monetary and Economic Studies*, vol. 5, n. 2, April 1986, Japanese Edition. Also published as 'Variability of Prices, Output and Money under Fixed and Fluctuating Exchange Rates: An Empirical Study of Monetary Regimes in Japan and the United States', *Bank of Japan Monetary and Economic Studies*, vol. 5, n. 2, December 1986, English Edition.

'A Positive Theory of Discretionary Policy, the Cost of Democratic Government and the Benefits of a Constitution', with Alex CUKIERMAN, *Economic Inquiry*, vol. 24, n. 3, July 1986, pp. 367-388.

'Comment' on 'Money, Credit and Interest Rates in the Business Cycle', in Robert J. Gordon, ed., *The American Business Cycle: Continuity and Change*, Chicago and London: University of Chicago Press & NBER, 1986, pp. 441-450.

'A Theory of Ambiguity, Credibility, and Inflation Under Discretion and Asymmetric Information', with Alex Cukierman, *Econometrica*, vol. 54, n. 5, September 1986, pp. 1099-1128.

'Some Evidence on the Comparative Uncertainty Experienced Under Different Monetary Regimes', in C. D. Campbell and W. R. Dougan, eds., *Alternative Monetary Regimes*, Baltimore: Johns Hopkins University Press, 1986, pp. 122-153.

'Lessons from the Experience of Japan and the United States Under Fixed and Fluctuating Exchange Rates', *Bank of Japan Monetary and Economic Studies*, vol. 4, n. 2, October 1986, pp. 129-145.

'Commentary' on 'Increasing Indebtedness and Financial Stability in the United States', in *Debt, Financial Stability, and Public Policy*, Proceedings of Symposium. Federal Reserve Bank of Kansas City, 1986, pp. 55-61.

'Monetary and Exchange Rate Regimes: A Comparison of Japan and the United States', *Cato Journal*, vol. 6, n. 2, Fall 1986, pp. 667-683.

'Limits of Short-Run Stabilization Policy: Presidential Address to the Western Economic Association', *Economic Inquiry*, vol. 25, n. 1, January 1987, pp. 1-13.

'International Debt Problems', *Contemporary Policy Issues*, vol. 5, n. 1, January 1987, pp. 100-105.

'Monetary Reform in an Uncertain Environment', in James A. Dorn and Anna J. Schwartz, eds., *The Search for Stable Money: Essays on Monetary Reform*, Chicago: University of Chicago Press, 1987, pp. 201-220.

'Trade and Debt', Testimony before U.S. Senate Committee on Housing, Banking and Urban Affairs, Washington, D.C.: Government Printing Office, February 18, 1987.

'And We've Gone Into Hock to the Rest of the World', *Washington Post*, April 5, 1987, pp. C1-4.

'Who Should Bail Out the Banks?', in Martin Geisel and Svetozar Pejovich, eds., *What are All Those Deficits About?*, Studies in Political Economy, vol. 2, Texas A&M University, 1987, pp. 35-52.

'Debt for Equity Swaps', The Euromoney-Mexico Debt to Equity Conversion and Investment Conference, *Euromoney Conference Reports*, May 1987.

'On Monetary Stability and Monetary Reform', *Bank of Japan Monetary and Economic Studies*, vol. 5, n. 2, September 1987, pp. 13-34.

'Notes on the Problem of International Debt', in Zannis RES and Sima MOTAMEN, eds., *International Debt and Central Banking in the 1980s*, London: Macmillan, 1987, pp. 21-29.

'On Monetary Stability and Monetary Reform', in Y. SUZUKI and M. OKABE, eds., *Toward a World of Economic Stability*, University of Tokyo Press, 1988.

'Economic Priorities for the Next President', *Policy Review*, vol. 44, Spring 1988, pp. 18-19.

'Money and Credit in the Monetary Transmission Process', with Karl BRUNNER, *Papers and Proceedings, American Economic Review*, vol. 78, n. 2, May 1988, pp. 446-451.

'Economic Policies and Actions in the Reagan Administration', *Journal of Post-Keynesian Economics*, vol. 10, n. 4, Summer 1988, pp. 528-540.

'Overview', in Robert W. KAMPHUIS JR., Roger C. KORMENDI and J. W. Henry WATSON, eds., *Black Monday and the Future of Financial Markets*, Homewood, Fl.: Dow Jones-Irwin, 1988, pp. 1-33.

'The Policy Proposals in the AEI Studies', in William S. HARAF and Rose Marie KUSHMEIDER, eds., *Restructuring Banking and Financial Services in America*, Washington, D.C.; American Enterprise Institute for Public Policy Research, 1988, pp. 440-447.

'De Stabiliteit van de Wereldeconomie', *Rotterdamse Montaire Studies*, n. 33, Erasmus Universiteit, 1988.

'Reaganomics im Urteil der Wirtschaftswissenschaft', in *Steuersystem und Wirtschaftswachstum*, Frankfurter Institut, 1988, pp. 27-33.

'Economic Policies and Actions in the Reagan Administration', *Financial Markets and Portfolio Management*, January 1989.

'The Great Deficit Debate', *National Review*, January 27, 1989.

'Tobin on Macroeconomic Policy: A Review Essay', *Journal of Monetary Economics*, vol. 23, n. 1, January 1989, pp. 159-173.

'Some Lessons on Monetary Management', *Kredit und Kapital*, vol. 22, n. 1, 1989, pp. 43-65.

'A Political Theory of Government Debt and Deficits in a Neo-Ricardian Framework', with Alex CUKIERMAN, *American Economic Review*, vol. 79, n. 4, 1989, pp. 713-732.

'Stability under the Gold Standard in Practice', with Saranna ROBINSON, in Michael D. BORDO, ed., *Money, History, and International Finance: Essays in Honor of Anna J. Schawrtz*, Chicago: University of Chicago Press, 1989, pp. 163-195.

'Efficiency and Stability in World Finance', *Bank of Japan Monetary and Economic Studies*, vol. 7, n. 2, 1989, pp. 1-14.

'Keynes on Monetary Reform and International Economic Order', in F. CAPIE and G. WOOD, eds., *Monetary Economics in the 1980s*, Macmillan, 1989.

'International Monetary Coordination', with J. P. FAND, *The AEI Economist*, July 1989.

'On Monetary Stability and Monetary Reform', in J. DORN and W. NISKANEN, eds., *Dollars, Deficits and Trade*, Cato Institute, 1989, pp. 63-85.

'Eliminating Monetary Disturbances', *Cato Journal*, vol. 9, n. 2, 1989, pp. 423-428.

'Money Supply', in Benjamin FRIEDMAN and Frank HAHN, eds., *Handbook of Monetary Economics*, Amsterdam: North-Holland, 1990, pp. 357-395.

'Karl Brunner, 1916-1989', *Economic Inquiry*, vol. 28, n. 1, 1990, R7-R8.

'My Life Philosophy', *The American Economist*, vol. 34, n. 1, 1990, pp. 22-32.

'Comment on What Washington Means by Policy Reform', in J. WILLIAMSON, ed., *Latin American Adjustment – How Much Has Happened?*, Washington, D.C.: Institute for International Economics, 1990.

'Diritti di voto e redistribuzione: Implicazioni per le democrazie', (Voting Rights and Redistribution: Implications for Liberal, Democratic Governments), *Biblioteca della Libertà*, 109, April 1990, pp. 27-47.

'Japanese Competition is No Threat', *Water*, Spring 1990, pp. 24-25.

'Trade Policy: What Next?', *American Enterprise*, May-June 1990, pp. 88-91.

'What Should Be Done About Exchange Rates?', *Wirtschaftspolitische Blatter*, vol. 37, n. 4, 1990.

'Recent Exchange Market Interventions', *Hearings before the Committee on Banking, Finance and Urban Affairs, U.S. House of Representatives*, August 14, 1990, Washington, D.C.: Government Printing Office, 1990.

'Kontrolle Reicht Nicht' (Deposit Insurance System Was Culprit in S&L Mexx), *Wirtschaftswoche*, November 23, 1990, pp. 106-113.

'Productivity Perplex: A Review of "Productivity in American Leadership" by W. J. Baumol, S. A. Blackman and E. N. Wolff', *Public Interest*, 101, Fall 1990, pp. 139-145.

'Some Empirical Findings on Differences between EMS and Non-EMS Regimes: Implications for Currency Blocs', *Cato Journal*, vol. 10, n. 2, 1990.

'Commentary: The Financial System and Economic Performance', *Journal of Financial Services Research*, 4, 1990, pp. 301-305.

'The Fed at Seventy Five', in M. BELONGIA, ed., *Monetary Policy on the 75th Anniversary of the Federal Reserve System*, Boston: Kluwer Academic Publishers, 1991, pp. 3-65.

'Folgenschwerer Irrtum', *Wirtschaftswoche*, 17, April 19, 1991.

'Keynes war kein Keynesianer', *Neue Zurcher Zeitung*, April 28, 1991, pp. 41-42.

'The Growth of Government Revisited', in S. G. PENDSE, ed., *Perspectives on an Economic Future-Forms, Reforms, and Evaluations*, New York: Greenwood Press, 1991, 131-143.

'U.S. Policy in the Bretton Woods Era', *Review*, Federal Reserve Bank of St. Louis, vol. 73, n. 3, 1991, pp. 54-83.

INDEX

INDEX

RAFFAELE MATTIOLI LECTURES

SCIENTIFIC COMMITTEE: Sergio Steve, Chairman; Carlo Filippini, Mario Monti, Adalberto Predetti, Sergio Siglienti, Franco Venturi; Enrico Resti, Secretary.

ORGANIZATION: Banca Commerciale Italiana-Università Commerciale Luigi Bocconi · Milano.

ADMINISTRATION: Banca Commerciale Italiana · Milano.

PUBLISHER: Cambridge University Press · Cambridge.

RAFFAELE MATTIOLI FOUNDATION
Fondazione Raffaele Mattioli
per la Storia del Pensiero Economico

Published

RICHARD F. KAHN, *The Making of Keynes' General Theory* (First edition: May 1984; Japanese edition, Tokyo: Iwanami Shoten, Publishers, April 1987).

FRANCO MODIGLIANI, *The Debate over Stabilization Policy* (First edition: July 1986).

CHARLES P. KINDLEBERGER, *Economic Laws and Economic History* (First edition: December 1989; Italian edition, Bari: Laterza, 1990; Spanish edition, Barcelona: Editorial Crítica, December 1990).

ALAN PEACOCK, *Public Choice Analysis in Historical Perspective* (First edition: March 1992).

SHIGETO TSURU, *Institutional Economics Revisited* (First edition: January 1993).

KARL BRUNNER - ALLAN H. MELTZER, *Money and the Economy. Issues in Monetary Analysis* (First edition: June 1993).

To be published

PAUL P. STREETEN, *Thinking About Development*.

HERBERT A. SIMON, *An Empirically Based Microeconomics*.

ERIK F. LUNDBERG, *The Development of Swedish and Keynesian Macroeconomic Theory and its Impact on Economic Policy*.

NICHOLAS KALDOR, *Causes of Growth and Stagnation in the World Economy*.

RICHARD STONE, *Some British Empiricists in the Social Sciences*.

ERRATA CORRIGE

Page 84. For line 3 read:

$$a(i, P, \ldots) \; B = \sigma \; (i - \pi, \; p, \; ap, \; P, \; w^h, \; w^n, \; e, \; S)$$
$$\underset{+}{} \; \underset{+}{} \qquad \underset{-}{} \qquad \underset{+}{} \; \underset{+}{} \; \underset{-}{} \qquad \underset{+}{}$$

Page 100. For line 10 read:

$$den = 1 - \varepsilon(a, \; i) \; \varepsilon(i, \; y | AM) - \varepsilon(a, \; p)\varepsilon(p, y)$$

Page 110. For line 19 read:

$$\cdot \; \varepsilon(w^h, \; th) + \varepsilon(a, \; P) \cdot \varepsilon(P, \; w^h | AM) \cdot \varepsilon(w^h, \; th) < 0$$

DESIGN, MONOTYPE COMPOSITION AND PRINTING
BY STAMPERIA VALDONEGA, VERONA
JUNE MCMXCIII

Printed in the United States
By Bookmasters